PRIME-TIME TELEVISION
THROUGH THE LENS OF FAITH

WATCHING
What We
WATCH

WALTER T. DAVIS JR. • TERESA BLYTHE

GARY DREIBELBIS • MARK SCALESE, S.J.

ELIZABETH WINANS WINSLEA • DONALD L. ASHBURN

Watching What We Watch

"Watching What We Watch"

Prime-Time Television
through the Lens of Faith

Walter T. Davis Jr. • Teresa Blythe
Gary Dreibelbis • Mark Scalese, SJ
Elizabeth Winans Winslea • Donald L. Ashburn

Geneva Press
Louisville, Kentucky

Scripture quotations, unless otherwise indicated, are from the New Revised Standard Version of the Bible, copyright © 1989 by the Division of Christian Education of the National Council of the Churches of Christ in the U.S.A., and are used by permission.

Book design by Sharon Adams

Cover design by Design Point

First edition
Published by Geneva Press
Louisville, Kentucky

This book is printed on acid-free paper that meets the American National Standards Institute Z39.48 standard.☉

PRINTED IN THE UNITED STATES OF AMERICA

01 02 03 04 05 06 07 08 09 10 – 10 9 8 7 6 5 4 3 2 1

Cataloging-in-Publication Data for this book is available from the Library of Congress.

ISBN 0-664-50193-1

Contents

Acknowledgments

The authors and contributors wish to express appreciation to several generations of students at San Francisco Theological Seminary (SFTS) and the Graduate Theological Union (GTU) who helped shape our perspective for watching television through the lens of faith. In addition, we wish to thank those people and institutions that contributed directly to the writing of this book and the production of a related video. The Louisville Institute, under the leadership of Dr. James W. Lewis, provided a generous grant that covered expenses related to writing the book, producing the video, and testing our method of television analysis in congregations, national workshops, and professional meetings across the country. Through the academic dean Ronald White and the chief financial officer Scott Schaefer, San Francisco Theological Seminary provided institutional support for this project.

Dr. James Noel and Jason Santalucia of SFTS advised us at various points; Patricia Perry edited the entire manuscript for style and substance; our editors at Geneva Press, G. Nick Street and David Dobson, provided early encouragement and helped shape the structure of the book as well as the details of each chapter; Stuart Johnson offered invaluable advice on graphics and created a website for the project (www.lensoffaith.org); Frangene Andrews of Golden Gate Productions shepherded the video production process.

We tested and refined our method through interactions not only with our students at SFTS and the GTU, but also with a dozen adult education classes in congregations in the San Francisco Bay area, with media literacy advocates at a national workshop, and with colleagues at the annual meetings of several professional associations. The input from this diverse group of people encouraged and challenged us as we made this project even more of a community effort.

We also express appreciation to the Cartoon Bank for permission to use a cartoon by Frank Cotham from *The New Yorker* collection (p. xi) and McFarland & Company, Inc., Publishers, for permission to use the chart "Law programs 1950–1992 as a percentage of crime shows" (p. 109).

About the Co-Authors and Contributors

Walter T. Davis Jr. is Professor Emeritus of Sociology of Religion and former Director of the Advanced Pastoral Studies Program at San Francisco Theological Seminary (SFTS). He received an A.B. from Davidson College, an M.Div. from Union Theological Seminary in New York City, and a Ph.D. in social ethics from Boston University. He is author of *Shattered Dream: America's Search for its Soul*, published in 1994 by Trinity Press International. Dr. Davis is one of the three general editors for this project and the author of the Introduction, the section on violence in the Interlude, chapters 6 and 11, Appendices A and B, and portions of the Conclusion and Appendix C.

Teresa Blythe (tblythe@jps.net) is a freelance writer, spiritual director, and media literacy advocate with an extensive background in broadcast news. In the early 1990s on KNST radio in Tucson, she hosted *The Teresa Blythe Show* which was voted "Best Talk Show" by *The Tucson Weekly*. She received a B.A. in political science from the University of Alabama Huntsville and both an M.Div. and a Diploma in the art of spiritual direction from San Francisco Theological Seminary. One of the three general editors, Ms. Blythe is the author of chapters 1, 3, 5, 9, and 10 and portions of Appendix C.

Gary Dreibelbis is Professor of Speech Communications and Television at Solano College and Adjunct Professor of Communications at San Francisco Theological Seminary. He has also taught in the Communication departments at Bradley University and Northern Illinois University. Dr. Dreibelbis holds an Ed.D. and an M.A. from Northern Illinois University and a B.A. from Wheaton College. He has published articles in such journals as *Feedback*, *Communication Quarterly*, and *Educational and Industrial Television*. Dr. Dreibelbis is one of the general editors and the author of the Part I overview section on situation comedies, chapters 12, 13, 14, and portions of the Conclusion and Appendix C.

Mark Scalese, SJ, is a Roman Catholic priest and an MFA student in Film and Media Arts at Temple University. He has taught video production at Gonzaga College High School in Washington, D.C. Fr. Scalese has an M.A. in theology from the University of Notre Dame and an

M.Div. from the Jesuit School of Theology at Berkeley. He is the author of the Parts II and III overview sections on dramas and fact-based programming, as well as of chapter 7.

Elizabeth Winans Winslea is a Presbyterian campus minister at Portland State University. She is developing university courses that promote empowered reading of television. She received a B.A. in English from the College of Wooster, an M.A. in women's studies from Ohio State University, and an M.Div. from Colgate Rochester Divinity School. Ms. Winslea is the author of chapters 4 and 8.

Donald L. Ashburn is Associate Pastor of the First Presbyterian Church of Oakland, California. He was press secretary and media adviser for a 1992 U.S. congressional campaign and has worked in the press office of the Latin American Council of Churches in Quito, Equador. Mr. Ashburn received a B.A. in history and an M.A. in sociology from the University of California, San Diego, as well as an M.Div. from San Francisco Theological Seminary. He is the author of chapter 2 and contributed to chapters 1 and 12.

Kimberly Ayers (kimberly@upthink.com) is a story producer for *National Geographic Today,* a daily national news program on the National Geographic channel. She has worked professionally in the broadcast news industry and in corporate multimedia production for twenty-three years. Ms. Ayers received her B.A. in mass communications from the University of Delaware and worked as a reporter, writer, and producer at network affiliates in Rochester, New York; Pittsburgh; and San Francisco. She edited the introductory paragraphs to most chapters, wrote the Interlude section about sex on prime time, and contributed to chapter 11.

Lonnie Voth is Director of Educational Media at San Francisco Theological Seminary. He holds a B.A. from Whitworth College and an M.Div. from San Francisco Theological Seminary. He has produced many videos on Central American religious, political, and social issues and is currently producing a documentary on David Nadel and the Ashkenaz Music and Dance Community Center in Berkeley, as well as a documentary on Heinrich Richert and the immigration of Mennonites from Russia to Kansas in 1874. Mr. Voth provided technical assistance, did the still video "grabs" that appear in the text, and served as video consultant to the project.

The website for this project is **www.lensoffaith.org**

A related twenty-eight-minute video showing the authors analyzing a commercial by Adbusters is available for purchase from Lonnie Voth (lvoth@sfts.edu), The Center for Electronic Media, San Francisco Theological Seminary, 2 Kensington Road, San Anselmo, California 94960.

Introduction

American Popular Religion

"Perhaps we should provide for the separation of state and entertainment."

We live in a *mental* environment as well as a physical environment. Our mental ecosystem is created by stories. Television has eclipsed the family, the church, and the school as the dominant storyteller in American culture. The primary function of television is to entertain. Howard Beale (the actor Peter Finch), the newscaster in the film *Network,* said it best: "We're in the boredom-killing business!" Nothing sinks a program faster than an audience response of "Boring!" Under the guise of entertainment, television teaches the hidden curriculum of our society. As a result, television "has made entertainment itself the natural format for the representation of all experience."[1]

Frank Cotham, the *New Yorker* humorist who sketched the cartoon on page xi, is just catching up with what has become a common view among scholars: Entertainment is our popular religion and television is its oracle.[2] Because the media have a monopoly on storytelling in American society, George Gerbner, former dean of the Annenberg School of Communications at the University of Pennsylvania, believes they function as "a virtual private Ministry of Culture and Established Church rolled into one."[3]

A religion consists of four elements: a worldview composed of a web of mutually reinforcing beliefs and values; a moral code; periodic public rituals; and a community of believers who practice these rituals. Television provides all four. As our national storyteller, television shows us what the world is like and what our place in it is. Artists, actors, and anchors have replaced religious leaders and public officials as the predominant creators of meaning in American society.

Television presents our society's repertoire of stories—social, economic, political, religious, artistic—that function as blueprints for living. Even a thirty-second television commercial portrays a minidrama of sin and salvation: depicting evil, its source, who or what can save us, the happiness that follows deliverance, and what we must do to be saved.

We mold our personal identity from the stories we embrace and live into. Television's stories tell us what the good life is and how to attain it; what is right and wrong, true and false, beautiful and ugly; who is in and who is out; what roles are prescribed for women and men, whites and people of color, rich and poor, gay and straight, Americans and people of other nationalities. By identifying with fictional television characters, we confront our own desires and anxieties and fantasize about how we might navigate in a confusing world of troublesome personal and social issues.

The English word "religion" comes from the Latin *religare,* which means to bind together. A religion is by nature social, binding diverse peoples into a collective body sharing similar beliefs and values. Television is religious because it creates a virtual community of those who share the same worldview and the same unquestioned goals, which are ritually reinforced by celebrations: the Olympics and the Super Bowl, nightly newscasts, favorite programs, and, above all, commercials. National tragedies like the bombing in Oklahoma City or the killings at Columbine High School in Colorado knit us together in compassion and mutual support. Even those who do not watch television cannot escape the mental environment it creates, because conversations around the water cooler on the job or in the locker room at school presuppose an acquaintance with television's fare.

When confronted with the notion that television operates as the functional equivalent of religion in modern societies, students frequently raise two issues. The first is: Does television support or undermine Christian, Jewish, and other religious views of life? Mark Silk identifies certain "simple and uncomplicated themes of a general character" that appear repeatedly in the news.[4] These themes include praise for good works, especially service to the poor; the virtue of tolerance and the vice of intolerance; condemnation of hypocrisy; warnings against false prophesy; and the merits of an inclusive, pluralistic community. In spite of this, the dominant message of commercial television—salvation by consumerism—undermines traditional religious beliefs and values.

The second issue is often expressed as an objection: Television programs are not religious because they are not serious enough. Religion deals with ultimate concerns, the great heights and depths of existence; television rarely rises above the ordinary and the trivial. This common perception of television is inaccurate. Some programs examine the full range of human hopes and fears at profound levels, given the constraints imposed by commercial interruptions every twelve minutes. Even if we grant that television only rarely rises above the uninspiring concerns of everyday living, however, many viewers claim to find as many "highs" on television—for example, the ecstatic moments of the NBA finals or the NFL Super Bowl or the season finales of *Ally McBeal*, *NYPD Blue*, and *Homicide: Life on the Street*—as they do in services of worship.

Religions are just as concerned about ordinary events as they are about the heights and the depths of human experience, and many people have "peak experiences" only once or twice during their lives. Some people never develop their faith beyond a quid pro quo bargain with God. As the Yoruba of Nigeria are wont to say, popular religion is first and foremost about *omo* (children—i.e., virility and fertility), *owo* (money and success), and *alafia* (peace and happiness). If one god does not deliver, maybe another one will. The fact that television preaches an illusory gospel and does not deliver on many of its promises in no way nullifies it as a religious force.

The Structure of the Book

The book is organized by program genre into four parts (sitcoms, dramas, news and sports, and advertising-ownership issues), which reflect the viewing experience of most people. The introductions to each part provide a historical overview of programs in that genre. The chapters in each part illustrate the use of our "reading" method by applying it to a specific episode of a current or recent popular show.

In the remaining portion of this Introduction, we outline two methods for "reading" television: lens and field of view analysis.

Method 1: Lens Analysis*

In academic circles, television analysis and criticism are done most often by teachers of sociology, communications, cultural studies (England), and

---

*For a more extended discussion of lens analysis, see Appendix A.

popular culture (the United States). Each discipline approaches the subject from its own perspective, but uses other perspectives as well. We have identified five major schools of interpretation that overlap and complement one another. Each school concentrates on different aspects of television "texts." We have named these aspects narrative, structure, signs, power, and function, and we think of them as different filters or lenses of a video camera.

Each lens contains certain unique optical properties, refracting the light in such a way that some things are brought into view while others are obscured. Each lens gives viewers a different set of questions with which to watch what we watch. Some chapters examine a show through the sequential use of each lens. Other chapters illustrate the interpenetrating character of the lenses by using a simultaneous combination of them.

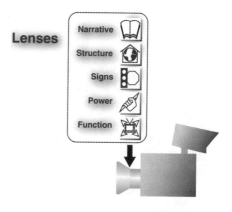

As producer of consensus narratives, television is the site for the continual rehearsing, testing, and even occasional revision of the central myths and values of popular culture.[5] By systematically using one lens and then another until we have scrutinized a narrative with all five, we can deconstruct and then reconstruct various levels of meaning in the "texts" themselves and also within the culture of the audiences that view the "texts."

1. **The Narrative Lens** is represented by an icon depicting a play script. Literary criticism concentrates on three elements of narrative: setting, character, and plot. Almost everything on television, even the thirty-second commercial, comes in story form. Since the 1980s, the pace and complexity of televised narratives have increased.[6] Whereas earlier programs had a central plot and perhaps one subplot, now the flow of the central plot in a situation comedy or drama is constantly intercut with two or three subplots that unfold simultaneously.

Here are some of the questions explored by literary criticism: How is the central plot related to the subplots? From whose point of view is the story told? What is the setting, and how does it influence plot and character? Who are the protagonists and the antagonists? What are their motivations? Are the characters well developed, or are they stereotypical figures designed to represent particular points of view? How does the episode's major dilemma, enigma, or problem relate to the recurring themes of the series and of the genre? What is the cause-effect chain?

What is the dominant or preferred reading of the narrative? What subordinate readings are possible? How does the narrative accommodate interruption for commercials?

2. **The Structural Lens** is represented by a globe in the outline of a house, conveying the idea that we all inhabit constructed views of the world, which frame the way we look at life. This lens examines the types, structures, and codes of narratives. One way of describing the purpose of this book is to say that we try to uncover the "language" of television, which most people vaguely understand intuitively but which is largely invisible to them. By uncovering the rules and applications of this language, we can (1) reflect on how meanings are created by television and (2) assess the truth and value of those meanings. This lens helps us explore the structure of beliefs, values, desires, and emotions in particular programs. For example, chapter 1 examines the techniques used in *Seinfeld* to express a vapid and cynical humor in the lives of young white people in New York City in the 1990s. Other chapters explore how gender, race, class, family life, and sexuality are structured by the "language" of television.

Much structuralist writing is rather inaccessible to the average student or religious leader. Happily, John Dominic Crossan's work is both accessible and adaptable to the task of "reading" television. Crossan, a New Testament scholar, starts with the concept of myth and then classifies stories into five types, situated along a continuum, as follows:

Myth	Apologue	Action	Satire	Parable

He explains how each type functions for the reader or viewer: "Myth establishes world. Apologue defends world. Action investigates world. Satire attacks world. Parable subverts world."[7] The settings, the characters, and the plots of each type of story are structured differently, and each type has a different effect on the audience.

Crossan and other structuralists employ these terms in a precise manner that is contrary to their popular usage. Most of us think of a myth as a fable, a fictitious story about superhuman beings, heroes, and villains. For structuralists, a myth is a story that tells us what the world is like and how the world works. A myth builds a social world and asks us to consider living in it. A parable does just the opposite. In popular usage, a parable is a nice little story with an object lesson or a moral teaching. Not according to Crossan: For him, parables are revolutionary. In his study of the parables of Jesus, Crossan demonstrates how parables undercut expectations and upset accepted norms. Thus, parable subverts what myth tries to establish, undermining the credibility of a social world and asking us to consider abandoning it.

Between these two polar opposites lie other types of stories that take their character from their proximity to either myth or parable. Apologues (from the Greek word *apologia*, "a verbal or written defense") are close cousins to myths because they defend a worldview against its critics, showing why it is believable. Satire is a close cousin to parable because it ridicules and raises questions about the credibility and justice of established systems. In the middle, taking a more neutral position, are action stories. They describe and investigate what happens—the adventures that are permitted—in a particular socially constructed mental environment.

Although most programs do not fit neatly into a single category—for example, *NYPD Blue* sometimes mixes myth, action, and satire in a single episode—these categories provide clues to the central message, often called the dominant or preferred reading, of a particular program. Moreover, they provide a framework for comparing audience responses to different programs of the same genre and for understanding mutations that occur through time in a single genre. For example, *M*A*S*H*, a satire on war that appealed to those who were disillusioned with the war in Vietnam, first aired September 17, 1972, on CBS at 8:30 P.M. During the same time slot, ABC ran *The FBI*, an action story with a heavy apologia (defense) for the American way of life, and NBC ran the second half of *The Wonderful World of Disney*, an unabashed myth. The audience was offered a choice of programming that spanned the spectrum from satire on misplaced patriotism to uncritical support for an idealized United States. In the 1990s, the airing of a satire (*The Simpsons*) on Fox and a myth (*Touched by an Angel*) on CBS during the same time slot offered viewers a choice between a comedy that ridicules traditional views of American family life and a drama that portrays traditional religious perspectives in American society. The classification below is based on the dominant reading of each program.

Of course, a program series can change categories over time, often beginning as myth and evolving into apologue or as satire blending into parable.

Myth (Builds world)	Apologue (Defends world)	Action (Describes world)	Satire (Criticizes world)	Parable (Undermines world)
Star Trek	Father Knows Best	Buffy the Vampire Slayer	The Simpsons	Harvest of Shame
Wide World of Disney	Touched by an Angel	48 Hours	Grosse Point	Anti-tobacco commercials
Monday Night Football	Newscasts	Walker, Texas Ranger	PJs	Married, with Children
The Waltons	West Wing	ER	Spin City	St. Elsewhere

3. The Lens of Signs and Codes is represented by an icon of a traffic light and a stop sign. Cultures are complex systems of signs. Some signs, for example, the English alphabet or the flashing red traffic light, derive their meaning by convention. One must know the culture to interpret the sign. Other signs, like the yellow caution signs with the black figure of a child on them, posted at school crossings, carry a likeness of that to which they point. In recent years, perhaps because of increasing diversity in American society, signs in public places make use of visual likeness. For instance, signs on restroom doors depict the figure of a woman in a skirt or a man in trousers. Signs on interstate highways announce service stations with a drawing of a gasoline pump, motels with that of a bed, and restaurants with that of a knife and fork. On a deeper level, there are iconic signs, like the electronic hearth (television set) in *The Simpsons*, which convey a metaphoric meaning that extends far beyond their literal message.

A sign is something we see, hear, touch, smell, or taste. All experience, then, consists of multiple signs. Each shot and scene of a television program has a verbal script, a sound script, and a sight script. Lighting and camera angles, music and sound effects, visual setting, physical appearance of characters, movements of people and things, and dialogue between characters all contain interconnecting signs. These signs are governed by codes that are rules or culturally based conventions giving rise to different meanings in different contexts. For example, viewers intuitively understand the network newscasters' dress code, which changes from site to site. When reporting from the CBS studio headquarters in New York City, Dan Rather wears a business suit. When reporting from the scene of a natural disaster, he wears a trench coat without a necktie. If he wore a business suit while surveying the damage of a hurricane on the Carolina coast, the message received by viewers would be slightly confusing because of the broken dress code.

Each area of life—fashion, food, sports, the arts, the marketplace, school, government, family life, recreation—is governed by its own codes. Codes are sets of rules that govern the meaning of signs in particular contexts. Like the rules of a board game, codes establish the parameters of meaning. They are context specific. The same sign—for instance, a person with head bowed and eyes closed—communicates one message in a worship service and a very different message at an NBA basketball game, because the codes that apply to these two contexts are different. When the group of Washington lawyers who call themselves "Hoggettes" appear on *Monday Night Football* wearing dresses and pig snouts, these signs operate in the code of sports fanatics. In that context, they epitomize the ideal football fan. Were they to wear the same dress at work, they would be held in contempt of court because the code of courtroom decorum condemns foolishness.

We mentioned above that some signs are icons that communicate rich metaphoric meaning. In this book, we follow the definition of icons provided by Jack Nachbar and Kevin Lause. They point out that in popular culture icons evoke emotional and intellectual meanings that extend far beyond their physical appearance. For them, icons are signs that express "deep-seated, significant messages of faith, bind believers together in a community or belief, and impart magical powers to those who venerate the icon. . . . A sign is just a signal; an icon is also a talisman."[8] In *The Simpsons*, Bart's skateboard is an icon. It "is not simply a thin plank with four wheels attached which enables him to avoid having to walk home from school; Bart's skateboard is a magical steed which lifts him out of his schoolroom cell, enables him to express his individuality and his absolute contempt for civic order and authority (to ignore sidewalks, pedestrians, signs, streets, buildings, cars) and to bind him together with all those who feel the same way he does about the repressive forces of modern society."[9] The television set in *The Simpsons* is an icon because it serves as an electronic hearth to bring a cozy harmony to a dysfunctional family with serious communication problems. This icon provides a mythical twist—"we are all one happy family"—to what is otherwise an unrelenting satire. In chapter 7, we discuss the iconic meaning of stethoscopes around the necks of nurses and doctors on *ER*, which identify these people as wise, authoritative healers who can save the life of a loved one or even our lives. In chapter 12, we discuss the iconic power of the "gotcha" gestures of NFL linebackers when they sack the quarterback, which are so powerful that the NFL has banned the throat-cutting gesture as too provocative.

By carefully examining the major signs in each shot or scene and then exploring the codes that govern their usage in different contexts, we can understand how the television text builds messages and constructs nuanced, multiple meanings for diverse audiences. This is especially useful when applied to the issues that the fourth lens raises.

4. **The Lens of Ideology and Power** is represented by an icon of a fist grasping a lightening bolt. At the highest level, this lens focuses on the manufacturing of culture for profit by a few corporations that control vast amounts of capital. This perspective is particularly helpful in charting the deterioration of televised news during the past two decades. In addition, we use this lens to examine the relationships among characters in television narratives. Who has power over whom, for what purposes, and with what consequences? How are race, class, gender, sexual orientation, age structured on various shows? How are

scarce resources allocated in the narrative? How is conflict resolved? Who wins and loses? Do perpetrators of violence suffer negative consequences? What group of people is over-represented? What group is under-represented? The National Association for the Advancement of Colored People (NAACP) and La Raza have protested the lack of African-American and Latino lead actors on prime-time television. As a result, in the past year ABC, CBS, and NBC have indicated their intention to broaden their representation of people of color. ABC now ties executive salary raises to progress in hiring more racial and ethnic minorities.

5. Our icon for **The Lens of Function** is a television set with arrows pointed in all directions, representing the variety of roles that television plays in the lives of individuals and society. This lens includes an examination of why people watch what they watch and how what they watch affects them, as well as the effects of television on groups of people and on culture in general. Our understanding of television as American popular religion is based on a functional definition of religion. Functional studies cover a vast range. At the macrolevel, media scholars like Neil Postman (in *Amusing Ourselves to Death: Public Discourse in the Age of Show Business*: see Resources) explore television as a medium and its effects on cultural and political life. At the microlevel, lawyers (like those who defended Jonathan Schmitz after he killed a man who appeared on the *Jenny Jones* talk show) examine the degree to which a ten- or fifteen-minute segment of one program can cause their client to commit murder.

For decades, the television industry and many First Amendment watchdogs have dismissed studies purporting to show a cause-effect relation between violence depicted on television and violence in real life. Nevertheless, the use of rating codes (G, PG, R) and the ban on television tobacco and alcohol commercials are based on the assumption that what we watch influences how we act. Corporations must have some evidence for this as well, or they would not spend $25 billion each year on television advertising.

One of the most dramatic cause-effect studies was conducted in 1998 by Anne Becker, an anthropologist and psychiatrist at the Harvard University Eating Disorders Center. Becker examined the effect of watching television on the body image of teenage girls in Fiji. Before television was introduced to the island in 1995, big was beautiful, and dieting was almost unheard of. After thirty-eight months of watching *Beverly Hills 90210* and *Melrose Place*, 74 percent of the young women in this study felt "too big or too fat" at least some of the time, and 62 percent said they had dieted in the past month.[10]

Method 2: Fields of View

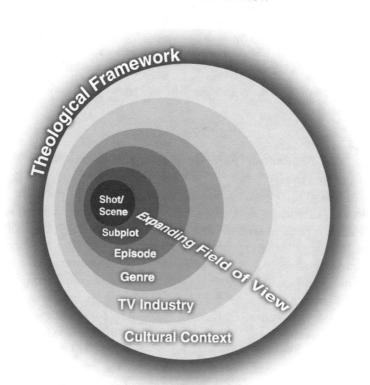

Before settling on the term "fields of view," we debated several other names for our second method: frame analysis, focal length, arena analysis, and the like. Each term captures an element of this method, which explores each level of the production-consumption process by which value (meaning) is added to the cultural product.[11] Frame or arena analysis implies that each level can be isolated, framed, and examined in its own right, somewhat like taking apart Chinese boxes within boxes. The optical term "focal length" also points to the same process of focusing attention successively on close-up, then on medium shots, and finally on long shots. We finally settled on the term "fields of view," with the emphasis on the enlarging spheres involved in the production process. Using this method, we start with an examination of the smallest unit of production, the single shot and scene. Then we move up the scale to plot, episode and series, genre, and network and industry, until we reach the broad frame of American culture in its global context.

We noted earlier that the five lenses described above are not discrete, self-contained methods for "reading" television. Rather, they overlap, interpenetrate, and complement one another. The same holds for field-of-view analysis, which applies the five *lenses* to the various *levels* of television production. In exploring fields of view, a cultural product is examined "from top to bottom," starting at the bottom. That is, a frame is placed around each arena of the production-consumption process so that those aspects unique to each field of view can be explored in depth.

Examining a television product in different fields of view supplements and expands lens analysis. Although some repetition is inevitable when moving from one method to the other, certain perspectives are missed without the use of fields of view. For example, we make extensive use of Field 5, network and industry analysis, in chapter 11, "Televised News: If It Bleeds, It Leads," and in chapter 14, "The Business behind the Box." In the latter chapter, we also examine Field 6, the global cultural impact of American television, noting that television is a major U.S. export and that mindless but sexy, action-packed *Baywatch* was the most popular program in the world in 2000.

In Field 1, shot and scene, we examine the words that are spoken (verbal script), other sounds like music, doors closing, and sirens (sound script), and the images that are seen (sight script) of each shot and scene. We dissect these scripts for their signs, codes, and messages. In Field 2, we explore how the plot and subplots contribute to the overall themes of the episode and what appeal the various subplots have for different audiences. The series is studied in light of the episode in Field 3 and the genre in terms of the series in Field 4. In Field 5, we probe the intended audience, the sponsors, the producers, and other aspects of the television industry. Finally, Field 6 provides the occasion to examine the two-way relationship of television to American society, as well as the global reach of American television culture at the beginning of the new millennium.

Theological Interpretation

Theology does not provide a separate lens or frame for "reading" television. Theological interpretation emerges from deep and broad reflection on the results achieved by using all of the approaches discussed above.

As applied to popular culture, theology is an inductive art, not a deductive science. Understanding emerges from a saturated immersion in various levels of meaning. Theological sensitivity, however, does involve asking certain questions that are not usually asked by other methods of analysis: How does this show depict the human condition? What view of good and evil is implied? What change is desired in this show? Who changes? How? In response to what? With what consequences? Who helps others change? When and where does transcendence (an experience of grace, wonder, mystery, getting outside ourselves) occur? Is character development subtle, depicting ambiguity and depth? Is there an encounter with mystery and grace? What vision of life does the show recommend? What desires and passions does the show incite? What is the common good and the nature of community depicted here? In what ways is this slice of American popular religion similar to or different from a Christian view of life?

Each program genre explores its own repertoire of issues, giving rise to different theological questions. We situate contemporary programs in the history of the genre and then examine the genre repertoire from a theological perspective. For example, in the section on violence in the Interlude, we trace the antecedents of the cop show genre in the Western, the whodunit mystery, and the hard-boiled detective show. This genre presents popular definitions of good and evil in the context of the criminal justice system, where justice is usually a code word for revenge. We examine these programs by using a worksheet for cop shows, which draws on John Calvin's three uses of the law and on theological concepts of sin, punishment, repentance, forgiveness, reparation, and restoration. We also note how cop shows rarely deal with systemic evil in the structures of society and therefore tend to blame the victims. In chapter 6, our study of a particular show, *Law & Order*, describes the techniques that television uses to communicate both the typical messages of the cop show genre and the particular messages unique to this program.

The following graphic seeks to capture visually the relation between (1) lens and fields of view analysis and (2) theological interpretation.

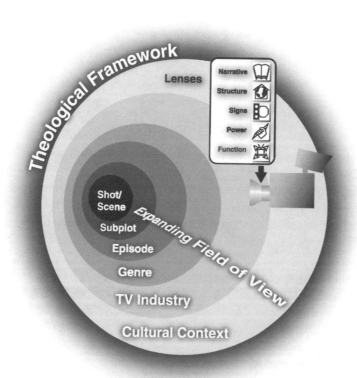

PART I

Are Situation Comedies
Really a Laughing Matter?

If we accept the premise that television is our civil religion, then situation comedies (sitcoms) constitute a major denomination of that religion. Sitcoms have been television's most reliable genre for over half a century, accounting for more top-rated shows than any other type. Although other once-popular program genres such as variety shows and Westerns are either dead or on life support, sitcoms continue to thrive in the early twenty-first century, accounting for over one-half of the prime-time program lineup.

In the introduction to his book *Honey, I'm Home! Sitcoms: Selling the American Dream*, Gerald Jones makes several observations about the importance of the sitcom to American popular culture. Jones believes that sitcoms promulgate many ideals of American society: "The promises of bureaucratic democracy, managerial capitalism, secular humanism, and mass consumption are miniaturized, tested and found true in the funny travails of TV families. The sitcom is the miracle play of consumer society."[1] Jones believes the sitcom is a teacher, and tells of times that, when growing up, he looked to sitcoms for cues about how adults acted in the workplace and how the world outside his home functioned.

For Jones, the sitcom provides a "foggy mirror with a rosy glow," showing fictional American families that can serve as models of family dynamics (such as the Huxtables and the Cleavers) or as models to laugh at and avoid (such as the Bundys or the Conners). Family sitcoms may be the flash points for political debate, as we see later in this chapter.

Even the production of and trends in sitcoms are uniquely American. The genre is a corporate product assembled in much the same way as an automobile and made in the same reliable pattern year after year, with only a few surface changes. Dependable plot formulas resurface and receive fresh coats of paint, reflecting the cultural trends of the times.

Sitcoms are like fun house mirrors—we see reflections of ourselves and society, but humor distorts those reflections. We are the people we see in the mirror, but through altered Hollywood and Madison Avenue filters. Through these mirrors, we can examine America's culture from the postwar years into the early twenty-first century. No other program genre can provide such glimpses of the way we were and wanted to be. These glimpses fall into discernible periods in the sitcom's history.

The Early Years: Diversity and Money Aren't Funny

Most television historians cite 1946 as the first year of network television. Early network program schedules relied primarily on sports, games, and variety shows as pioneers tested television's production limits. Sitcoms did not make a significant impact on network programming schedules until 1949, when several popular radio series made the transition to television.

CBS was the first network to make a serious investment in television sitcoms because it wanted to distinguish itself from NBC, with its emphasis on comedy and variety shows. Some of CBS's early efforts (*The Goldbergs*, *Mama*, and *Life with Luigi*) were ethnic comedies featuring Jewish, Norwegian, and Italian families. While *The Honeymooners* was not an ethnic sitcom, it showed a lower-middle-class couple in an urban setting.

On paper, early television sitcoms featured more diversity than did more recent shows. There were at least three sitcoms featuring African-American casts, *The Laytons* (on the defunct DuMont network), *Beulah* (ABC), and *Amos and Andy* (CBS). Of these three, *Amos and Andy* was the most popular and controversial; it had been a huge hit throughout most of radio's history, and CBS chairman William Paley saw the show as a potential television hit, too. The radio version had featured two white actors, Freeman Gosden and Charles Correll, as the voices of Amos and Andy. Two African-American actors, Spencer Williams and Alvin Childress, portrayed the characters in the television version.

Controversy erupted from the beginning of the program's run. The NAACP protested to CBS and the press that *Amos and Andy* "depicts the Negro in a stereotyped and degrading manner . . . It strengthens the conclusion among uninformed or prejudiced people that Negroes and other minorities are inferior, lazy, dumb and dishonest."[2] Others, including black actors and reviewers in black newspapers, praised the program for showing people of color on the television screen. Black actors may have been reluctant to protest the show because their objections could hinder the opportunities for African Americans in future television series.

There was truth in the arguments put forth by both sides. Stereotyped characters, including George "Kingfish" Stevens and his wife Sapphire, Lightin' the janitor, and lawyer Algonquin J. Calhoun, appeared on the show. The Andy character, who functioned as a philosophical narrator on the television version, was de-emphasized in favor of the "Kingfish" character, who always seemed to be involved in nefarious, get-rich-quick schemes.

People who argued in favor of *Amos and Andy* cited those characters depicting a growing black middle class. Most supporting characters were African-American shop owners, bankers, merchants, and well-dressed professionals. Individual episodes were morality plays, including the classic Christmas episode in which Amos took a part-time job to earn enough money to buy a special talking doll as a present for his god-daughter.

Although some historians give credit to the NAACP for the demise of *Amos and Andy* after two seasons, the major reason for the show's cancellation was the same one given for so many of the television industry's decisions—economics. The show finished thirteenth in the Nielsen ratings during its first season but dropped to twenty-fifth in its second year. Both Gerald Jones and Robin R. Means Coleman[3] believe that at a then-pricey $40,000 an episode CBS had suffered too much controversy for too little financial return.

One consequence of the controversy surrounding *Amos and Andy* was the elimination of black sitcoms for at least fifteen years, with few blacks appearing on television in supporting roles. Following the show's final airing, ethnic sitcoms in general faded away. Repeat episodes aired in syndication for at least another ten years, and ironically the show was seen in Washington, D.C., during the same summer that Dr. Martin Luther King gave his "I Have a Dream" speech.

A second major trend during television's first decade was the transition of big-name radio stars and sitcoms to television, where in many cases the shows underwent few changes for the viewing audience. Many of these shows de-emphasized the stars' financial status and made them middle-class characters. Such was the case for the mother of all sitcoms, *I Love Lucy*, which made the transition from radio, where it was called *My Favorite Husband.*

In addition to the writing, acting, and physical humor of Lucille Ball, part of this show's appeal was the fact that Lucy and her bandleader husband Ricky Ricardo (played by Desi Arnaz) were portrayed as middle-class people in a small New York City apartment. The producers decided that money was not funny: Middle-class people had problems and issues that rich people did not have. There was also Lucy's ongoing struggle to be something other than a housewife, as she tried to be part of Ricky's act at his nightclub. This led Ricky to say in one episode, "I want a wife that's just a wife!"—a sentiment of many males in the postwar United States.

Apart from the humor and the universal themes in *I Love Lucy*, the show set production standards for most sitcoms to follow. Instead of being broadcast live from New York City, *Lucy* was filmed in Hollywood before a live audience, with three cameras, in much the same way that theatrical films were shot. This technique, which was the brainchild of Desi Arnaz, provided a visual quality comparable to that of theatrical films and ensured that the show was preserved for future audiences.

Other shows making successful transitions from radio to television included *The George Burns and Gracie Allen Show* and *The Jack Benny Show*. The stars essentially played themselves, and audiences watched them in middle- or upper-middle-class homes. Sitcoms soon sought greener pastures. Many American families moved to the suburbs, and sitcom settings moved there as well, depicting what were supposedly positive family dynamics.

Suburbs and Siblings

Television's second decade began in the mid-1950s, when many new shows featured families in small towns and suburbs. These television families reflected what many real American families had done and still others wanted to do: move away from large cities to suburbs or smaller towns. By 1953, 20 percent of Americans lived in the suburbs, and the percentage grew steadily throughout the remainder of the decade and the early 1960s.

The suburbs distilled the essence of the American family to a nucleus of two young parents and their children. Gerald Jones writes that there was a change in family values as the suburbs became the cradle of a new secular religion: faith in consumer goods.[4] Most families moving to the suburbs did not want to take their old furniture or outdated household appliances with them and instead bought new replacements. More space also meant buying things they could not have in city life, such as barbecues, lawn chairs, and recreational equipment.

The new family model meant that grandparents and older family members usually stayed behind in the city. New parents now found advice on raising a family from other sources, such as Dr. Benjamin Spock's best-selling book, *Baby and Child Care*. Family sitcoms served as weekly models for raising a family. Three such shows, *The Adventures of Ozzie and Harriet*, *Leave It to Beaver*, and *Father Knows Best*, are the best-known and most enduring examples from this era.

The Adventures of Ozzie and Harriet was anything but adventurous. It resembled a well-produced home movie. The show featured the "real" family of Ozzie and Harriet Nelson and their sons Ricky and David. Critics have called the show one of the blandest sitcoms ever produced, yet it remained on the air for fourteen years and still holds the record for television's longest-running sitcom.

Most conflicts or problems on the show were relatively minor, usually involving difficulties in Ricky and David's love lives or an around-town search for a particular flavor of ice cream. Ozzie tried to problem solve, but it was Harriet who most often found solutions, or the problems solved themselves. Perhaps the strongest appeal of the show was that it lacked major conflicts or family problems, providing a numbing effect for men and women who had grown up during the Great Depression and World War II. There was comfort in watching this attractive television family solve minor mishaps and in seeing a father who was constantly around the house. It was unclear what Ozzie did outside the home; he seemed to have no discernible profession.

If *Ozzie and Harriet* presented any strong message, it was that of 1950s consumerism. When Hotpoint was the sponsor, many of the show's scenes took place in the kitchen. When the sponsor changed to Kodak, there was an emphasis on picnics and other outdoor activities. The show provides an early example of product placement.

If *The Adventures of Ozzie and Harriet* taught few lessons in family conduct and dynamics, *Father Knows Best* taught many. The program fits John D. Crossan's definition of myth by establishing and reinforcing the standards of WASP-like, middle-American family conduct.[5] Gerald Jones writes that *Father Knows Best* "flung itself into the task of demonstrating proper family conduct with all the ingenuous confidence of a Sunday school film."[6]

Father Knows Best featured the Anderson family: Jim and Margaret (played by Robert Young and Jane Wyatt) and their three children, Betty, Jim Jr., and Kathy (a.k.a. Princess, Bud, and Kitten, played by Elinor Donahue, Billy Gray, and Lauren Chapin). The show preached the middle-American value system, including hard work, respect for parents and others, and pursuit of dreams, within the confines of what was allowed—especially for females—in the 1950s.

One disturbing aspect of *Father Knows Best* was the underlying message that indirect communication and lying are acceptable in maintaining family harmony. On the show, arguments between Jim and Margaret Anderson were repeatedly dismissed as mother and father's simply "having a discussion." In one episode, a fight developed while Jim was trying to teach Margaret to drive. Princess came to the rescue by applauding her parents and thanking them for demonstrating what a "real" fight would be like in a less-than-ideal family. Jones writes of the "eerie undercurrent in a picture of family life that strove so hard to be wholesome, traditional, and Christian."[7] One of the central messages of *Father Knows Best* was that intelligent women, such as the Margaret Anderson character, ought to be content to limit themselves to doing household chores while wearing high-heeled shoes and button earrings.

Despite its shortcomings, *Father Knows Best* provided perhaps the most powerful images of family life to those who searched for answers about family dynamics. In *The Great TV Sitcom Book*, author Rick Mitz quotes one former fan of the show, who said, "Recently, I saw some episodes of *Father Knows Best* and found myself crying in the same places I had twenty years ago; my head knew better, but my heart didn't."[8] Mitz's book includes an image captured from one of the shows, depicting the Anderson family sitting around the kitchen table and holding hands, with their heads bowed in prayer over a plate of hamburgers.[9] If any image typifies the show while presenting a video version of Norman Rockwell's American family, this is it.

Leave It to Beaver provides another glimpse of the small-town family, with many values and lessons of *Father Knows Best* in a slightly different package. The show featured June and Ward Cleaver (played by Barbara Billingsley and Hugh Beaumont), older brother Wally (Tony Dow), and young Theodore or "Beaver" (Jerry Mathers). *Beaver* was in many respects more multidimensional than *Father Knows Best* because it presented universal problems that real children might face while also presenting less-than-perfect child characters such as the wisecracking Eddie Haskell (Ken Osmond). Flawed characters were featured, with the Cleavers as the eye of the storm in the midst of semidysfunctional families. Other parents were out of town or yelled at their children too much.

June Cleaver was one up on Margaret Anderson: She cleaned house while wearing pearls and always seemed to have time to serve cookies and milk to her boys. She also participated more in family decision making and problem solving, although Ward usually provided solutions to problems in the form of homilies delivered approximately twenty minutes into the show.

Family sitcoms such as *Ozzie and Harriet*, *Father Knows Best*, and *Leave It to Beaver* continue to affect American society and politics today. In her book *The Way We Never Were: American Families and the Nostalgia Trap*, Stephanie Cootz writes that when liberals and conservatives debate public policy about families, they frame their arguments in terms of how many "Ozzie and Harriet" families there are in America.[10]

Liberals contend that fewer than 10 percent of American families have a breadwinner father, a full-time stay-at-home mother, and dependent children. Conservatives argue that over one-half of mothers with preschool children are either not employed or are employed part time. They also cite polls showing that mothers want to spend more time with their children and that families like the Nelsons and Cleavers are making a comeback in public opinion if not in raw numbers.

Few critics of popular culture deny the impact of these shows on American culture, but when they appeared in their first runs they had in one sense only modest success. Each show had a significant number of

viewers and a long run (again, *Ozzie and Harriet* lasted for fourteen seasons, still the longest run of any sitcom) but limited success in the Nielsen
ratings. *Father Knows Best* was the only show of the three to finish in the
Nielsen top twenty-five for an entire season, coming in thirteenth during
the 1958–59 season and sixth in 1959–60. Furthermore, none of these
shows finished in the all-time Nielsen top one hundred series.

The three shows have enjoyed success in syndication and cable, and
here a new level of influence appears. Some may laugh at the unreal
worlds of the Nelsons, Andersons, and Cleavers, but for others there is an
element of nostalgia blended with the wish that their own families had
been like the television households.

In his *New York Times Magazine* article "The Triumph of Burbopolis,"
Michael Pollan writes:

> The Cleavers, Ozzie and Harriet, Donna Reed, and all
> the rest proposed an ideal of suburban life that every-
> one knew was unrealistic and silly; and yet as we
> made fun of it, we allowed the stereotype to exert a
> kind of normative hold on us. Your own family might
> be hopelessly dysfunctional, but maybe the Grables
> next door were getting it right.[11]

The dark side of the family sitcom and its influence on today's popular
culture are also in evidence, as Pollan later concludes:

> What's remarkable is how Cleaverism continues to
> organize so much of our thinking about suburbia.
> Now, though, it's the lie of Cleaverism—call it
> Cheeverism—that dominates the popular image,
> offering writers and moviemakers a cheap way to con-
> struct a gothic version of suburbia, to throw its dark
> side into sharp relief. Now behind every smiling lawn
> is a dysfunctional family: Donna Reed is sleeping with
> the woman next door, and Eddie Haskell's got a gun.[12]

Despite evoking a darker view of recent family life, these older sitcoms
continue to give reassurance and humor to new generations. Viewers
today laugh at the plotlines, but still hope that a family somewhere is
"getting it right." In future years, critics may observe that the true impact
of these and later family sitcoms is felt long after their first runs as they
provide visual servings of milk and cookies and surrogate Sunday school
lessons for new audiences.

Escape to the Country
and Other Fantasies

Television's sitcoms of the 1960s were less a mirror of culture, or what the
public wanted culture to be, than a cultural "antidepressant." These
shows did little to address the social and political upheavals of the 1960s
and early 1970s, but instead took viewers to rural areas or presented

fantasy situations complete with a witch or a Martian. Sitcoms were an escape from the six o'clock news.

Rural comedies such as *The Andy Griffith Show, Green Acres,* and *Petticoat Junction* and comedies with rural characters out of their element such as *Gomer Pyle* and *The Beverly Hillbillies* dominated the ratings during this decade. ABC may have planted the roots of this trend in the late 1950s with *The Real McCoys,* a sitcom about a family from West Virginia who traveled to California to seek their fortune, in a contemporary, humorous version of *The Grapes of Wrath.* CBS followed the ABC lead by producing rural sitcoms of its own.

An exception to this trend was *The Dick Van Dyke Show,* featuring Van Dyke as a television comedy show writer and Mary Tyler Moore as his wife. The show reflected the Camelot years of the Kennedy presidency, and many thought that Van Dyke and Moore mirrored the presidental couple. *The Dick Van Dyke Show* was one of the first sitcoms whose humor came from adult situations. In many ways, the show was "metatelevision": It showed the behind-the-scenes activities of writers creating a weekly script for a comedy show.

The Dick Van Dyke Show was such a surprise in the sitcom landscape that it suffered from low ratings in its early run; the show eventually became a hit and ran for five seasons, finishing near the top of the Nielsen ratings, but cast members wanted to move on from *Van Dyke* to pursue other projects.

The success of *The Dick Van Dyke Show* did not initiate a trend toward adult sitcoms; instead, networks developed more escapist programming. CBS maintained its strategy of rural and small-town sitcoms, while ABC chose to air animation in prime time. Four series, *The Flintstones, The Jetsons, Top Cat,* and *Calvin and the Colonel,* all aired during ABC prime time in the early 1960s. Network executives reasoned that children controlled television viewing early in the evening, and if families watched these shows together, adults might continue to watch ABC after the children had gone to bed. ABC employed the strategy of animation in prime time almost thirty years before Fox revived the trend with *The Simpsons* in the late 1980s.

The strategy was short lived, with *The Flintstones* being the only series to sustain a modest run; the others eventually moved to Saturday morning. If programming for families was ABC's intent during the early 1960s, it is interesting to note what children learned from these animated programs. Winston cigarettes was an early sponsor of *The Flintstones* and commercials showed Fred and Wilma Flintstone at home smoking Winstons. (This was before the 1971 ban on cigarette commercials on television.) *Calvin and the Colonel* was a thinly disguised animated version of *Amos and Andy,* featuring the voices of Freeman Gosden and Charles Correll (who had played these two characters on radio) as a fox and a bear who had migrated from the south to take up residence in a northern city.

Although prime-time animation did not survive the entire decade, sitcoms with live actors in cartoonlike situations certainly did. Shows featuring witches (*Bewitched*), a Martian (*My Favorite Martian*), and two series featuring monster families (*The Munsters* and *The Addams Family*) were typical of the decade. A talking horse, *Mr. Ed*, and some castaways "on a three-hour tour" to *Gilligan's Island* added to the overall silliness of the 1960s television world.

Despite the increased social turmoil of the late 1960s (the assassinations of Reverend Dr. Martin Luther King and Senator Robert Kennedy, race riots in major U.S. cities, intense protests over the war in Vietnam) television sitcoms were still reasonably benign. The overall strategy of sitcom programming soon changed, not for social reasons but for economic ones. Advertisers concerned with specific demographic information wanted to know which programs reached certain groups and who saw the commercials. Marketing research showed that although many viewers were older and lived in small towns and rural areas, the most dedicated consumers were in the eighteen- to thirty-four-year-old bracket and lived in cities and suburbs. This group of viewers spent more money than did those living in small towns and rural areas.

CBS resisted the information because they had the most to lose: Many of their highly rated shows were rural comedies. NBC and ABC, however, used the demographic research to develop younger and more diverse sitcoms. In 1968, NBC premiered the first black situation comedy since *Amos and Andy*: *Julia*, starring Diahann Carroll. ABC gave some recognition to the women's movement by airing *That Girl*, a sitcom about a small-town young woman, played by Marlo Thomas, who came to New York City to work as an actress.

Thomas's character was something less than an independent working woman; her father and boyfriend constantly came to her rescue. Still, *That Girl* was a precursor of sitcoms showing more independent women in the 1970s. Fighting to rise above its traditional place as the third-place network in the Nielsen ratings, ABC also developed sitcoms such as *The Brady Bunch* and *The Partridge Family* for younger audiences.

By 1970, the new CBS president Robert Wood urged the chairman William Paley to make necessary major changes in the network's lineup, especially with regard to sitcoms. Wood feared that the other networks were more progressive than "The Tiffany Network" (CBS) and that the network faced losing young urban audiences. In a drastic reversal, CBS canceled its rural ratings winners in favor of dramas that soon sank in the ratings. This move at first seemed regressive for the number-one network; however, the time had come for CBS to overhaul its lineup. When the dramas failed, a new breed of sitcoms ushered in the 1970s.

During the late 1960s, network television learned that program executives must turn at least one eye to the culture. It did not matter how many eyeballs watched their programs; they must be the "right" young urban and suburban eyeballs. This lesson helped to produce a second golden age of television sitcoms in the early 1970s.

One Step Forward
and One Step Back

Many television historians and videophiles point to the early 1970s as television's second golden age, especially with respect to situation comedies. After the major housecleaning of sitcoms at CBS came some of the most watched and remembered programs of television history. The network had been slow to react to cultural trends and preferences but rebounded with shows like *All in the Family (AITF)* (and its various spin-offs from Norman Lear such as *Maude* and *The Jeffersons*), *The Mary Tyler Moore Show (MTM)*, and *M*A*S*H*. By the 1974–75 season, these were five of the top eleven shows in the Nielsen ratings (*Rhoda*, a *Mary Tyler Moore* spin-off, was also in the top ten).

The Norman Lear comedies introduced new topics to network television, with *AITF* leading the way. The show's central character, Archie Bunker (played by Carroll O'Connor), became a cultural icon, and the Bunker household in the Queens section of New York City was a flash point for ideological and generational debate.

The first episode of *AITF* set the tone for the series when Archie and wife Edith (Jean Stapleton) came home from church one Sunday morning. Daughter Gloria and son-in-law Michael (the Stivics) had stayed at home, and it was implied that they were having sex while the Bunkers were at church. For the next seven seasons, debates about sex, religion, race, politics, and most other social issues took place for millions to see on a weekly basis. Archie's African-American neighbors Lionel and George Jefferson (Mike Evans and Sherman Hemsley) joined the Stivics in debating Archie, at times turning him into a human punching bag.

After a slow start in the ratings, *AITF* became a "water cooler" show: People gathered at work to discuss the previous night's episode. *AITF's* appeal to a mass audience was that it openly discussed social issues of the past ten years and that there was an eye-of-the-beholder phenomenon at work. Liberals and intellectuals could cite the wrongs of prejudice, while others could identify with Archie and cheer for him week after week as he battled the Stivics and Jeffersons.

CBS anticipated that most of the protests about *AITF* would come from conservatives and the Bible Belt; instead, most of the negative response came from liberals such as Laura Z. Hobson, who wrote an article in *The New York Times* criticizing Lear and the show for fostering bigotry and racism. At the same time, schoolteachers in many parts of the country requested *AITF* study guides in an effort to teach students about the wrongs of racism.

Whichever side of the fence viewers favored, *ATIF* opened the way for other sitcoms to deal with socially relevant issues. Archie's sister-in-law Maude (Bea Arthur) was his liberal counterpoint and got her own spin-off series, and George Jefferson got another Lear spin-off. Other non-Lear shows also engaged society's concerns and norms.

Gerald Jones describes Archie Bunker as "an archaic figure, lovable but unprepared for the brave new world, being trained by those more assimilated than he."[13] Archie was a blue-collar version of the network executives or "suits" who had been out of touch with the culture and had to be dragged into a brave new world of programming.

Archie Bunker's African-American counterpart on NBC was Redd Foxx, in *Sanford and Son,* a huge ratings winner for the peacock network. *Sanford and Son,* a Norman Lear-Bud Yorkin product, seemed to have appealing elements for almost everyone. Foxx was Fred Sanford, owner of a Los Angeles junkyard and father of thirty-four-year-old Lamont (Demond Wilson), who was always trying to better himself and to escape from the yard.

Many laughed at the broad humor of Foxx's Sanford character, but the message for millions of Americans was the struggle of Lamont to better himself despite being held back by members of his own race and class. People could identify with Lamont's character and could associate his strivings with their attempts to leave their own "junkyards" to strive for better lives.

As well as showing people of color, early 1970s sitcoms now included women with careers and in independent roles. *The Mary Tyler Moore Show* took up where *That Girl* left off by featuring Moore as Mary Richards, an associate producer for a newscast at a Minneapolis television station. *MTM* won more Emmys (twenty-seven) than any other prime-time program in television history, and television critics who reviewed the show praised it as being "an important one for women."

The Mary Richards character did seem more independent than Ann Marie in *That Girl* in that she had a steady job and was less dependent on a boyfriend; however, the show was not a strong feminist statement. Even head writer James L. Brooks stated that *MTM* was not a feminist vehicle. Mary Richards was the "nice girl" who, like Ann Marie, was suddenly independent. The difference between the characters is that instead of relying on her father and her boyfriend for support, Mary got her support from her colleagues in the workplace. Indeed, Mary's colleagues were her family and in the final episode of *MTM* she said that they made her feel loved and less alone. *MTM* was one of the first programs to show the workplace as a second home and co-workers as family.

*M*A*S*H** also featured the surrogate family theme, introducing strangers who eventually became "family" as they faced the horrors of the Korean War. Much has been written about *M*A*S*H** as a satire of the Vietnam War, set twenty years earlier, during the Korean War. In many ways, the show was a genre parable that deconstructed traditional sitcoms' structure and tone. Rick Mitz in *The Great TV Sitcom Book* writes that *M*A*S*H** was television's first "black" sitcom (obviously a reference to tone and mood, not race).[14]

The television version of *M*A*S*H** began where the movie version ended, showing the weekly efforts of medical officers such as Hawkeye

Pierce (Alan Alda) and Trapper John McIntyre (Wayne Rogers) to circumvent the military system and to pursue women during their off-hours. The show eventually became, in the words of Mitz, "a mini movie with a laugh-track" that could be classified as a "dramady."

Some episodes of M*A*S*H contained no laugh track and acted as minisermons on the horrors of war. One classic episode was shot in documentary style black and white: Members of the 4077 Mobile Army Surgical Hospital were interviewed by a stateside television news reporter. Another was shot from the perspective of a patient lying in bed and observing the action around him.

The show made a statement, often overlooked by critics, about organized religion. Father John Mulcahy (William Christopher) the 4077's chaplain (and once called the "resident celibate" by Hawkeye) was often viewed more as a mascot than as a spiritual leader and adviser. Chaplain Mulcahy eventually earned the respect and love of the 4077, not because of any theology he preached but because he was a good person doing good, showing his faith through works (including going on a mission to see the horrors of war firsthand and performing an emergency tracheotomy on a soldier with his Tom Mix pocket knife). The 4077's attitudes toward this cleric seemed consistent with popular attitudes toward organized religion during the 1970s and early 1980s.

The last episode of M*A*S*H*, in 1983, was the most watched single episode of any television show in history. The episode was filled with ironies; most characters went against type. The usually strong, wisecracking Hawkeye suffered a mental breakdown; the skirt-wearing, section eight (mental disability)-seeking Klinger (Jamie Farr) married a Korean woman; Hawkeye and his nemesis, Margaret Houlihan, said good-bye with a prolonged, passionate kiss; and in the ultimate demonstration of respect, Hawkeye and B. J. Hunnicut (Mike Farrell) saluted Colonel Potter (Harry Morgan) near the end of the episode.

M*A*S*H* took the attitudes of many who had protested the Vietnam War and fought against "the system" during the 1960s and early 1970s and made them mainstream for millions of viewers. The lessons learned were that the traditional good guys and defenders of freedom are not always good, that the system does not always work, and that working outside the system *can* work.

With the end of the Vietnam War came a return of escapist sitcoms similar to those seen in the 1960s, not only because of the end of more than a decade of turmoil (assassinations, racial unrest, Watergate) but because of economics. Advertisers and networks became less obsessed with demographics as they realized the difficulty of producing programs that kept well-educated, affluent people in front of their sets, and they reverted to their former strategy of trying to capture the greatest number of eyeballs.

ABC, following their program chief Fred Silverman, led this trend with shows reinforcing the myths of the 1950s, such as *Happy Days* and *Laverne and Shirley*, along with a space-alien-visits-earth concept in *Mork and Mindy*. The network rediscovered the importance of appealing to children and teens early in the evening and produced harmless sitcoms with one or two comedic "bones" thrown to adults during the twenty-two minutes. Parents began watching these shows over their children's shoulders and stayed tuned to ABC for adult fare later in the evening, such as *Soap, Three's Company*, and *Barney Miller*.

Soap, a prime-time satire of soap operas, featured a rich dysfunctional family and sexual innuendo of a kind not previously seen on television. The show drew numerous protests, and conservative Christians flooded ABC with over 30,000 letters during the summer of 1977. Word leaked about some of the show's content before its fall premiere; protests came before the public had seen a single episode. Fred Silverman called 1977 "the summer of *Soap*," as the protests fueled the general public's curiosity about the show.

Sexual innuendo was also obvious in *Three's Company*, in which a male character pretended to be gay so that a landlord would let him rent an apartment with two women. *Barney Miller* was another workplace-as-family sitcom about police officers in New York's twelfth precinct.

This escapist sitcom menu (along with Aaron Spelling-produced action shows and light dramas) took ABC to its first ever number-one ranking for an entire season. The late 1970s comedy *Benson* was counter to the ABC ethos, but provided a bridge to the shows of the 1980s.

Benson (the character's full name was Benson Dubois, perhaps a bit of coding hinting at W. E. B. DuBois), played by Robert Guillaume, was a spin-off from *Soap*; the character had been a butler for the Tate family. Matriarch Jessica Tate sent Benson to assist her widowed cousin, Governor James Gatlin, with his household affairs and the raising of his daughter Katie. After a couple of seasons, Benson was promoted to state budget director, upholding the American myth that any individual can climb the status ladder through hard work and determination. In reality, however, the ladder is steeper for African Americans and other ethnic groups. The show included episodes about numerous social issues, such as war. The potential consequences of nuclear war were brought home to Benson and the governor's family during a computerized war simulation at the governor's headquarters.

Benson served as a primary transition to a new era of sitcoms during the Reagan years. Nuclear television families made a comeback, whereas characters on nonfamily sitcoms found solace and comfort in places "where everyone knew their names."

Back to the Future and "Eat My Shorts"

The Reagan years brought a desire to recapture the American dream and to re-establish so-called traditional American values. One Reagan political campaign commercial (entitled "Morning in America") seemed to capture in a few seconds the essence of the Reagan administration. The commercial was shot in a small town in Northern California and showed the townspeople celebrating on the Fourth of July. The imagery was like a Norman Rockwell painting in motion, sounding a responsive chord for those who thought that America had lost its sense of direction over the past twenty years. Television reinforced much of the Reagan value system of the eighties, with sitcoms leading the way.

The 1980s did not start out as a sitcom-friendly decade. Rick Mitz asks the question "Whatever happened to 1979–80, 1980–81, and 1981–82?"[15] The Nielsen ratings of these years showed a growing preference for news and dramatic shows, with fewer sitcoms making the top twenty-five. Also, viewers were gradually turning to cable channels and purchasing VCRs for taping programs and playing movies in the VHS format.

A gradual resurgence of sitcoms started in 1982, when shows such as *Cheers* and *Family Ties* entered NBC's prime-time lineup. Both shows got off to slow starts but stayed on the network's schedule because of the patience of the network's programming chief, Brandon Tartikoff. Tartikoff was different from most network programming executives in that he allowed programs to develop and find an audience. He also recognized that although many of NBC's programs were not doing well in the Nielsens, they did capture the desirable demographics of educated urban viewers. This was not only the case for NBC's sitcoms but also for NBC dramas such as *Hill Street Blues*.

By the 1984–85 season, NBC was out of the ratings basement, thanks mainly to one program—*The Cosby Show*. Veteran comedian Bill Cosby's series about an upper-middle-class African-American family in New York City was an immediate ratings winner, finishing third in the Nielsens during its first season and first in 1985–86. NBC built its Thursday-night lineup on the foundation of Cosby with what would eventually be labeled "Must See TV"—a tradition that continues into the twenty-first century.

Cosby was in many ways a retro family sitcom, featuring a strong nuclear family with 1950s family values—the values that the Reagan era wanted to recapture. The Cosby (Huxtable) family was an African-American version of the Andersons or the Cleavers of the 1950s, with a few notable exceptions that brought the show into the 1980s and broadened its appeal in a way that cut across demographic lines.

Mother Claire Huxtable (Phylicia Rashad) was a lawyer who did not stay home serving cookies and housecleaning while wearing pearls and heels. In many episodes she was the voice of reason, the parent who solved the conflicts during the twentieth minute of the show and brought resolution to turmoil. Bill Cosby's character, Dr. Cliff Huxtable, was not a Jim Anderson or Ward Cleaver. Cliff had his moments of strong decision making, but he could also be the source of comedic conflict. Other evidence that Cliff was a less-than-perfect father was that he suffered from the Dagwood Bumstead syndrome of raiding the refrigerator for all the wrong foods. Claire was his constant dietary monitor.

Robin R. Means Coleman writes: "For both blacks and whites this was a new never-before-seen image of blackness."[16] Cosby's near-perfect upper-middle-class family sparked debate. Many thought that the show was a leap forward for African Americans. Who would not want to be like the Huxtables, no matter what one's racial or ethnic background?

Jhally and Lewis in their book *Enlightened Racism: The Cosby Show Audiences and the Myth of the American Dream*, however, write that *Cosby* made the American dream seem too easy for African Americans, ignoring the obstacles to upward mobility faced by many blacks during the Reagan-Bush years.[17]

Both positions have merit. While being a model family, the Huxtables did offer a small glimpse of African-American culture (black college and university sweatshirts, artifacts, jazz albums) for millions of Americans. One season's introduction segment featured the family dancing, superimposed on the marquee of the famed Apollo Theater. The counterargument is that during an era of "Willie Horton" and "benign neglect" of affirmative action and social programs, the American dream was unattainable for many African Americans.

Perhaps the real truth is that *The Cosby Show* represented a positive start with little or no follow-up in the way African-American families could be depicted on television. The Huxtables fell into almost anyone's latitude of acceptance as a family to emulate. Aside from the spin-off show *A Different World*, which offered much of the same philosophy and tone as *Cosby*, little in prime-time programming offered the spectrum of black experience.

Besides *Cosby*, NBC featured the nuclear family sitcom *Family Ties*, which benefited from being scheduled on the same night as *Cosby* and was another retro 1950s family sitcom with a strong mother figure, Elyse Keaton (Meredith Baxter Birney). The show was a microcosm of political debate in the 1980s set under one roof—the parents were liberal and the kids were conservative. President Reagan called *Family Ties* his favorite show.

Elyse and Steven Keaton (Michael Gross) marched in peace rallies and served sprouts on their sandwiches. Son Alex Keaton (Michael J. Fox) read *The Wall Street Journal*, worshiped William F. Buckley, Jr., and was the poster boy for the Reagan 1980s. Sisters Mallory (Justine Bateman) and Jennifer (Tina Yothers) were disinterested in liberal politics and spent their time in pursuits typical of young sitcom females (talking on the phone, going to the mall).

One family sitcom that maintained some of the elements of the non-nuclear family of the 1970s was ABC's *Who's the Boss*, which successfully combined a number of elements of other successful sitcoms. Tony Micelli (Tony Danza) played an ex-baseball player with an eleven-year-old daughter (Alyssa Milano). Micelli answered an ad placed by a career woman (Judith Light) and became her housekeeper, in a show that week after week presented the awkwardness of sex role reversal.

Another ratings winner for NBC was *Cheers,* featuring a Boston bar that was a Noah's ark for broken-down people, a place where "everyone knows your name." Ex-baseball player, recovering alcoholic, and Cheers bar owner Sam Malone (Ted Danson) was the bartender and resident ringmaster for an assortment of poor souls and wanna-bes. A major focus of Cheers was the unresolved sexual tension (U.S.T., as it is known in the television industry) between Sam and barmaid Diane Chambers (Shelly Long) and later bar owner Rebecca Howe (Kirstie Alley). *Cheers* was a throwback to the ensemble comedy of *The Mary Tyler Moore Show,* while foreshadowing a trend of workplace or social setting as surrogate home, which dominated 1990s sitcoms.

By the early 1990s, *Cheers* was the most watched show on television, appealing to a wide audience that not only appreciated the rapid-fire insulting humor of the patrons but identified with the characters' aspirations and loneliness. *Cheers* was the consummate sitcom for this period when people were increasingly more career minded and less family oriented.

The late 1980s brought another workplace-as-home and co-workers-as-family sitcom, with CBS's *Murphy Brown* (starring Candice Bergen), a show that seemed to be a *Mary Tyler Moore Show* on steroids. Murphy Brown was the liberal, hard-as-nails anchor of a television news show, *FYI.* Her home in the Georgetown section of Washington, D.C., seemed to be always under renovation. Eldin (Robert Pastorelli), the ubiquitous house painter, offered Murphy advice and was one of her best friends. Despite her success and wealth, Murphy always seemed to be one step from the edge (she was a recovering alcoholic). *Murphy Brown* presented the career woman in near-caricature form—what Bonnie Dow, author of *Prime-time Feminism,* called "the feminist as stooge."[18]

Fox provided alternatives to the more traditional sitcoms, in the form of *Married, with children* (MWC) and later *The Simpsons.* Fox had failed in its attempt to play by the traditional rules of programming in its competition against the established networks and decided to establish its own rules. *Married, with Children* was one of the first products of that strategy, making Fox a competitor of the established networks.

It is foreign to most observers to call *MWC* a sitcom parable; however, if we accept Crossan's premise: that parable tears down or deconstructs, *MWC* fits this definition.[19] Jones writes: "It wins its audience over by shouting, in sitcom form, that the sitcoms are a lie."[20]

MWC featured one of the most unattractive families in sitcom history, the Bundys, parents Al and Peg (Ed O'Neill and Katey Sagal) and children Kelly and Bud (Christina Applegate and David Faustino). Each episode contained insulting humor about Al's lack of sexual prowess, Peg's lack of sexual fulfillment, and Al's less-than-brilliant children's success in manipulating him. If family members showed any affection at all, it usually occurred during the final minute of the show before the last commercial.

Fox also pursued the antifamily in its animated sitcom *The Simpsons*, arguably Fox's most significant show in its less-than-twenty-year history. *The Simpsons* followed the *MWC* formula of the bumbling father Homer Simpson, but wife Marge is a benevolent soul despite her small world of Springfield. Lisa is the "good" daughter, and baby Maggie's only role on the show seems to be sucking on a pacifier. In early episodes, ten-year-old Bart Simpson was often the focus of the show, a self-proclaimed under-achiever who most of the time is a sharp-tongued, fourth-grade version of Groucho Marx.

Bart's rebellious behavior, however, seems to come as a last resort because he tries to play by the rules, only to be foiled at every attempt. He is an extension of his hapless father, but his wisecracking behavior and skateboard are weapons that Homer does not possess. Bart's lot in life can be appreciated by all ages. In recent seasons, Homer has become the focus of the show as he tries to enhance his middle-aged life.

The Simpsons goes much further than *Married, with Children* in that it is a satire about the system, not just the traditional nuclear family. The show takes on issues ranging from censorship to organized religion and can do so because the animation disarms viewers and serves as a yielding factor. It also demonstrates that the animated sitcom can succeed in prime time, and it ushered in a wave of animated shows in the early 1990s.

ABC's *Roseanne* was the ratings winner of the blue-collar family sub-genre. Roseanne followed *MWC* and *The Simpsons* in presenting a situation about which many viewers could say, "My family and situation are not that bad." Again, affection and love were usually demonstrated in the last minute of the show after twenty-one minutes of insults and put downs. *Roseanne* differed from past blue-collar sitcoms in that the mother was the central figure of the family and often the main decision maker.

The antifamily sitcoms of the late 1980s foreshadowed the edginess and attitude of many 1990s and early new-century sitcoms. Attitude was the watchword of the 1990s no matter what the setting for sitcoms.

In Your Face or "Nothing" but Attitude

Network television faced new challenges in the 1990s, including an increased number of cable viewers and channels, "self-programming" VCR users, Internet use, and two new networks—WB (Warner Brothers) and UPN (United Paramount Network). The established networks, along with the newcomers, adopted new strategies for all programming, including sitcoms.

During the 1990s, several identifiable trends surfaced: male characters attempting to survive the new rules of society; young urban professionals (in many cases working for media companies) involved in a social tribe; and, on the newer networks, African-American sitcoms. Although more black sitcoms were produced during the 1990s than at any other time in television's history, most other racial and ethnic groups were largely absent from the screen.

Two early examples of males trying to survive the 1990s were *Northern Exposure* and *Home Improvement*. *Northern Exposure* combined many successful elements of past sitcoms while being a throwback to the dramadies of the 1980s. Dr. Joel Fleischman (Rob Morrow), a recent graduate of Columbia University Medical School, was assigned to the small town of Cicely, Alaska, for four years to repay the state for financing his education. Fleischman was always trying to return to his home in New York City but could not find a way to escape his obligations. He was trapped in a world not his own, with assorted eccentric characters and a strong woman pilot, Maggie (Janine Turner), who provided on-again-off-again sexual tension. Cicely was a metaphor for the experience of many male viewers who were trapped in their own unfamiliar worlds of the early 1990s.

If any sitcom defined the plight of males trying to survive the 1990s, it was *Home Improvement*, a nuclear family show in 1990s packaging. The timing for *Home Improvement* could not have been better; Georgetown University linguist Deborah Tannen had just released her book on gender communication, *You Just Don't Understand*. Almost every episode of *Home Improvement* provided an illustration of a principle from this book about contemporary differences in gender communication.

Tim Taylor (Tim Allen) was Tim "The Tool Man" Taylor, host of a cable television home improvement show. He and his wife Jill (Patricia Richardson) had three sons. Jill's biggest challenge was trying to educate Tim in the ways of gender communication and to convince him that the meaning of life is not "More power!" (Tim's favorite phrase). Wilson (Earl Hindman) the Taylors' next-door neighbor and backyard philosopher, assisted Jill in her efforts.

Other examples of the "lost male" subgenre included ABC' s *Coach*, a show in which the central character, college football coach Hayden Fox (Craig T. Nelson), tried to redefine his masculinity and become a better father and husband. Later in the decade, CBS added a block of such sitcoms (all set in or near New York City), which included *Cosby* (in this new Bill Cosby vehicle, he played a laid-off airline worker), *Everybody Loves Raymond*, and *The King of Queens*. CBS tried to corner the East Coast urban audience with this menu of sitcoms.

The show that helped establish a second 1990s trend of young urbanites tribing together was *Seinfeld*, which eventually became the new cornerstone of NBC's Thursday night "Must See TV" tradition and paved the way for a flood of friends-hanging-out series on the network.

Standup comic Jerry Seinfeld says that the show was written not to please audiences but to please the people involved in the show. Much has been said about *Seinfeld* as the "show about nothing," and in most episodes life's little events (standing in line, trying to get really good soup from a nasty restaurant owner, throwing out someone's prized *TV Guide*) were explored in humorous detail. In a bit of metatelevision, a running plot device on *Seinfeld* was Jerry's trying to sell NBC a concept for a television show that was the same as *Seinfeld*.

Seinfeld set the tone for a decade when the U.S. economy soared and the quality of life improved for many Americans. It made no political statements and promoted an attitude of looking out for oneself even among one's own tribe of friends. Other sitcoms including NBC's *Friends* continued this theme throughout the 1990s.

Friends explores the problems of six twenty-somethings living and working in New York City in the 1990s. At times, the friends are less than friendlike as they continue the sitcom theme of "taking care of number one," stealing one another's lovers, apartments, or personal possessions. *Friends* is the lead-in show for NBC's strong Thursday night lineup of comedies.

If Generation Xers could identify with the characters on *Friends*, older baby boomers could laugh at *Frasier*, a spin-off from *Cheers*. Frasier Crane (Kelsey Grammer), a psychiatrist and former barfly from *Cheers*, decides to move to Seattle and start a new life as a radio talk show host. His father Martin (John Mahoney), a former Seattle cop, comes to live with Frasier in his high-rise apartment building, raising the baby boomer issue of how to take care of aging parents. The intergenerational conflict has been a running theme on *Frasier* since its first episode.

Frasier's psychiatrist brother Niles (David Hyde Pierce) is even more fastidious than Frasier when they attempt conflict resolution about such issues as having the right friends, dining at the right restaurants, and drinking the right wine. The running theme of the show seems to be "the paralysis of analysis" as Martin constantly scolds his sons for their over-analysis of issues. It is a theme that many identify with in the stressed-out 1990s and early 2000s. Ultimately, *Frasier* demonstrates that in an era of financial stability for many Americans life is not really so bad.

The workplace is the setting for other shows featuring young urbanites, such as ABC's *Spin City* (the New York City mayor's office) and *Sportsnight* (studio and headquarters of a cable sports show similar to ESPN's Sportscenter) in which characters form significant relationships with their co-workers. NBC's *Newsradio* and other sitcoms of the era seemed to imply that most urban Americans worked at a media-related organization.

Gay and lesbian characters were the focus in at least two sitcoms, *Ellen* and later *Will & Grace*. ABC's *Ellen* (Ellen DeGeneres) was in the mold of *Seinfeld* and other thirty-somethings comedies, featuring the Ellen character as a bookstore-coffee shop owner. Early in its run, *Ellen* had many of the same themes as other 1990s young-professionals-in-the-city sitcoms, but after the first two seasons a running plot device was Ellen coming to grips with her sexual identity.

When Ellen eventually "came out" by accidentally making the announcement over an airport public address system, it was a significant moment for many in the gay-lesbian community (there were numerous viewing parties the night of the "coming out" episode). Some critics believed that *Ellen* had developed into a one-joke show, because she had been dropping hints for over a season that she might be a lesbian. Once she revealed her sexual identity, the show had nowhere to go. *Ellen* also drew protests from conservative religious groups, causing concerns for advertisers, many of whom pulled their sponsorship of the show. Despite protests from DeGeneres and numerous others in the gay-lesbian community, *Ellen* was canceled in 1998.

In contrast to *Ellen*, NBC's *Will & Grace* debuted in 1998 to high ratings and few if any protests. Will (Eric McCormack) is a young gay lawyer, and Grace (Debra Messing) is his heterosexual, career woman, live-in (and later across the hall) friend. The secret of *Will & Grace*'s success may be that it premiered in the wake of several popular movies featuring the gay-man, straight-woman combination. This combination became one of the most successful formulas for films of the late 1990s. *Film and TV Magazine* reported that "the GM/SW duo has proved itself a pop culture fixture."[21]

Another late 1990s comedy that extended the urban young professional genre and sounded a responsive chord for many young professional women was Fox's *Ally McBeal*, one of the few Fox sitcom hits of the 1990s. Ally (Calista Flockhart) is a woman lawyer working in a Boston law firm, struggling with the issues of "finding Mr. Right," exploring the potential for motherhood, and solidifying her professional identity. A central theme (discussed later in this book) is that Ally should not be alone.

Ally McBeal features surrealistic moments that make it a sitcom for the postmodern age, including an imaginary dancing baby who haunts Ally in the middle of the night. The show often deals with issues of meaning, reflecting society's spiritual attitudes and interests at the new millennium. *Ally McBeal* was an immediate hit, especially with young women, and debate surfaced as to whether the show was redefining feminism. *Time* magazine ran a cover story asking whether *Ally McBeal* was the face of the new feminism.

The dominant sitcom programming strategy of Fox and the newer networks WB and UPN has been to create programs for audiences not being served by ABC, CBS, and NBC—in other words, attracting younger viewers and people of color. Fox earlier demonstrated the success of programming for younger viewers, because advertisers wanted to buy commercial time on programs appealing to those who had not yet made brand choices.

As mentioned earlier, Fox employed this strategy in the late 1980s when it had difficulty competing with the established networks. WB and UPN followed the Fox model in the 1990s. As a result, these networks became homes for dramatic programs appealing to young viewers and situation comedies seeking African-American audiences. Young non-African-American viewers who considered the urban scene, fashions, and lingo to be trendy also started watching these shows. Urban sitcoms with African-American actors were no longer just for blacks.

Unfortunately, many black sitcoms seemed to degrade African Americans, often presenting them in a unidimensional manner. In her book *African American Viewers and the Black Situation Comedy*, leading African-American television scholar Robin R. Means Coleman calls the era of the 1990s the "Neo-Minstrelsy Era," writing that black sitcoms have gone full circle and returned to the roots of *Amos and Andy*.[22]

Black actors such as Bill Cosby and Tim Reid, star of *Frank's Place*, a short-lived but critically acclaimed dramady of the late 1980s, have criticized Fox's "urbancoms." Reid says, "By depicting African American culture solely through the hip generation, Fox is making a tiny segment of us drive our entire TV image. Calling that 'cutting edge' is comical. It's more of a tragedy."[23] Cosby spoke out against one of Fox's urbancoms, *Martin*, calling it "crass and vulgar."[24]

Martin (starring stand-up comic Martin Lawrence) was a comedy-romance. Intraracial put-downs were a key element of the show, along with stereotyped characters played by Lawrence. One character, Sheneneh, featured Lawrence in full drag as a woman who drank forty ounces of beer straight from the bottle and was always ready for a fight. *Martin* lasted from 1992 to 1997.

Another Fox urban sitcom, *Living Single*, borrowed elements of successful 1990s shows by depicting the lives of six young, rising black professionals. Many blacks enjoyed the show, but others believed the use of black voice (slang/dialect) and intraracial insults limited the way in which African Americans were portrayed.

By 1996, UPN and WB continued the Fox trend with lineups of urbancoms. Means-Coleman writes that UPN's *Malcolm and Eddie* and *Good Behavior* are straight out of the *Amos and Andy* mold, featuring one classical "straight man character" pitted against a buffoon character.[25]

WB's most popular comedy, *The Jamie Foxx Show*, featured Foxx as a helper in a family-owned hotel. The show received criticism for overuse of broad physical humor and Foxx's impersonations of famous African Americans. WB's *The Wayans Brothers* showed the brothers getting into and out of numerous difficult urban situations. Gangster types were often glorified, and there was a liberal use of black voice. Numerous other urbancoms have come and gone throughout the 1990s and early 2000s, many of them not cracking the top 100 Nielsen-rated prime-time shows.

A major exception to most trends in African-American programs of the Neo-Minstrelsy Era was Fox's *Roc*. Charles S. Dutton played Roc Emerson, a hardworking, play-by-the-rules garbage man in Baltimore. His household included wife Eleanor (Ella Joyce), younger brother Joey (Rocky Carroll), and their strong-willed father (Carl Gordon). *Roc* presented the problems of maintaining family balance in the face of racial, intergenerational, and work issues (Eleanor worked as a night nurse, while Roc worked during the day, which contributed to a less than satisfactory love life).

Although it lasted only three seasons, *Roc* may have been one of the ignored classics of the 1990s. The show presented an African-American family trying to better itself while giving non-African Americans a glimpse of the culture in a nonpreachy manner. Also noteworthy was the fact that many of the episodes were shot "live," creating a high level of energy and spontaneity. Unfortunately for viewers of all races, there were very few *Roc*-like efforts in the 1990s, as African-American sitcoms chose instead to follow a cookie-cutter formula.

Roll Credits and Fade to Black

"And so it goes," as newswoman Linda Ellerbee has often said. Where is the sitcom going in the twenty-first century? Much has been written about the death of network television as we know it in the new millennium; however, *Washington Post* media critic Paul Farhi writes that without the networks and large conglomerates we can say goodbye to free episodic television.[26]

Network television will probably survive, providing programs not only over the airwaves but via Internet and other delivery systems. In the not-too-distant future, those who enjoy *Ally McBeal* or *Will & Grace* can watch this week's episode or past episodes whenever they want. It is already possible to go to some shows' websites and watch clips. Interactive sitcoms are currently in development at the networks and other sources. Cable television services such as HBO and Showtime will continue to produce original programs, although viewers are unlikely to see twenty-plus episodes of their favorite show a year. Also, quality cable programs come at a price for viewers.

The Internet may also provide greater diversity in program content and in the faces we see onscreen. Before its demise Digital Entertainment Network made an attempt to provide programs for those underrepresented on network television. Diversity of content rather than delivery systems may be the biggest challenge to the networks. In any case, the sitcom has survived as a genre for over seventy years on radio and television and will probably continue to survive. From *Amos and Andy* to *Ally McBeal*, the genre is one of the few constants in programming in the history of broadcasting. Although media critics and broadcast historians have more complex explanations for the survival of sitcoms, the simple reason may be that after a day of hard work people of all ages just want to laugh.

Of sitcoms of all kinds, it has been said that imitation is the sincerest form of television. It is ironic, given the conservative programming bias of television executives, that the shows that viewers and critics have loved the most were the ones that were different, took risks, and were trendsetters. These shows reflected what was going on in society instead of lagging behind and shooting at a moving target that had already passed. The shows we remember most dealt with life in a small row house in Queens, a television newsroom in Minneapolis, and a law firm in Boston, instead of the limited worlds of Hollywood or midtown Manhattan.

Sitcoms have established a major component of television as civil religion by providing clues about how to live our lives, what is acceptable behavior, and (most important for the networks and sponsors) what to buy. It is not only the nostalgia or "video yearbook effect" that appeals to us in classic or contemporary sitcoms; it is looking at society or ourselves in a little fun-house mirror and laughing at the reflection for twenty-two minutes. Perhaps in future sitcoms, we will see our reflection not dimly, but face to face.

ONE

Seinfeld

NOTHING BUT ATTITUDE

Again I saw that under the sun the race is not to the swift,
nor the battle to the strong, nor bread to the wise,
nor riches to the intelligent, nor favor to the skillful;
but time and chance happen to them all.

—*Ecclesiastes 9:11*

Sometimes we don't get what we want.

—*Newman*

Episode: **First aired:**
"The *Andrea Doria*"   December 19, 1999

If *Seinfeld* is the show about the "nothing" in our lives, the
"nothing" is the host of small and annoying circumstances that
bug us all and are perfect fodder for the comedy of daily neu-
roses and the characters' own recurring self-centeredness. This
show embodies the myopic drama of the trivial, the struggle
for worldly success, and the vague sense of existential angst
that wonders what it's all for—and we still laugh.

Called the defining sitcom of the 1990s, must-see-TV, and "the show
about nothing," *Seinfeld* lives on in syndication as one of the most lucrative comedy shows in history. It rejects warm fuzzies in favor of cool,
sharp observations about everything in life that is rude, unfair, and idiotic
and projects the proper postmodern attitude for those times when the
race goes not to the swift and people do not get what they want.

Jerry Seinfeld and Larry David, two stand-up comics with no agenda
other than to create an extremely funny situation comedy, sold *Seinfeld* as
a pilot to NBC in 1989. The first episode, entitled "The Seinfeld
Chronicles," did not make it to the network's regular fall 1989 lineup after

focus groups criticized it as "weak."[1] The concept found support, however, at Castle Rock Entertainment, which produced several additional episodes. Neither the pilot, which ran in July 1989, nor the four additional episodes made an impression in the ratings, and the show's future looked dark after that short, early run. NBC executive Rick Ludwin, however, believed in the show and obtained a half-season order for 1990–91.[2] By the end of that season, *Seinfeld* was highly rated, thanks in no small part to its position after the long-running sitcom *Cheers*. By that time, it was also a hit with television critics: *Entertainment Weekly* called it "probably the funniest show on television,"[3] and Tom Shales of the *Washington Post* called Jerry Seinfeld "a very funny fellow" and wrote the show was a "pleasantly bright idea."[4]

Co-producer Larry David left *Seinfeld* at the end of the seventh season, saying it was time for him to try something else.[5] His departure was a blow to the entire team because David's biting, dark humor had established the show's ethos. The exit left Jerry Seinfeld alone at the helm (until David's return to write and produce the show's finale in May 1998). Worries about David's departure dissipated after the show got into its eighth season and it became clear that the signature dark humor would continue to define *Seinfeld*, David or no David. By *Seinfeld*'s ninth and final season, it had become one of the most popular shows in television history, constantly rated in the top five prime-time network offerings and delivering that all-important "money demo" of eighteen- to thirty-four-year-old viewers to advertisers. In fact, the show brought in so much money that insiders joked that NBC's "fabled Brinks truck had backed up to Jerry's house" before the last season, unloading a million dollars per episode for his continued participation.[6] Well after its signoff in 1998, *Seinfeld* continues to thrive as "the most sought after show" in syndication, according to Columbia TriStar Television Distribution president Barry Thurston.[7]

On one level, a wildly popular and commercially viable show about individuals leading lives of futility and frustration brings up serious theological and philosophical questions, even though everything about *Seinfeld*—its creators, its writers, and its characters—demands that we not take it too seriously or try, as Seinfeld put it, to "take apart the frog to see how he jumps."[8] Yet media literacy principles demand that we pick up the scalpel, and so we dissect Episode 136, entitled "The *Andrea Doria*," written by Spike Feresten for the eighth season of *Seinfeld*.

Episode Synopsis

George Costanza (Jason Alexander) thinks he has snagged a terrific apartment ("You could fit fifteen people in that bathroom"), only to have his hopes dashed because the apartment superintendent decides instead to give the apartment to Clarence Eldridge (Ray Stricklyn), an elderly survivor of the *Andrea Doria* shipwreck. Later, George finds out from Kramer (Michael Richards) about the scope of the shipwreck and decides the disaster was not all that bad ("Only fifty-one people [died]? That's it?"). Jerry Seinfeld (Jerry Seinfeld) convinces George that if the apartment is awarded to someone on the basis of the degree of personal suffering, then George can certainly compete with a shipwreck survivor because he has endured much more suffering in his own life. With renewed confidence in his victim status after a short dinner visit with his bickering parents "to find out more about his childhood," George approaches the tenants' board to make his case, leaving them in tears.

Elaine Benes (Julia Louis-Dreyfus) waits in a restaurant for a "fix-up" date who the waiter finally informs her has been stabbed. She learns that an ex-girlfriend has attacked Alan Mercer (Tom Gallop), and Elaine decides that this makes him a passionate "stab-worthy" guy. Elaine later finds that he is one of the worst men to date: the bad breaker-upper ("You know how when you break up you say things you don't mean? He says the mean things you don't mean but he means them"). On their next date, after Elaine tells him she does not want to see him anymore, Mercer ends the conversation by saying, "See you around, big head." Elaine begins to obsess about the size of her head, especially after a taxi driver asks her to move it so that he can see out the back window and after a bird flies into her head in the park. ("Never seen that before," says an elderly bystander.)

Kramer has a bad cough but refuses to see a doctor. ("They botched my vasectomy. I'm even more potent now.") In the park, he spots a dog with the same cough. He decides to take the dog, and himself, to a vet because he believes vets are superior to doctors. He takes the dog's cough medication and ends up behaving just like a dog.

Jerry wants his mail carrier neighbor Newman (Wayne Knight) to remove eight sacks of mail he has cached in Jerry's storage locker because he is too depressed to work. Newman refuses Jerry's demand until he realizes that he must deliver the mail if he is to win his coveted transfer to Hawaii. Not only are eight bags too many to deliver, but Newman is temporarily disabled after getting into a fight in which Kramer bit him on the leg. The sworn enemies (Newman and Jerry) enter "an alliance" designed to fulfill Newman's dream of moving to Hawaii and Jerry's dream of Newman moving away from him. Jerry will wear Newman's rookie-year uniform and deliver the bags of mail. Unfortunately, Jerry does too good a job by delivering mail to nearly 80 percent of the recipients ("No one has ever cracked the 50 percent barrier"). The Postal Service discovers the ruse, and Newman loses the transfer.

In the end, Elaine arranges to have dinner with Mercer at the Old Mill Restaurant to show him her indifference to his "big head" remark. She vows to either shrug it off or "jam a fork into his forehead." During dinner, Mercer casually says that her "big head" goes well with the "bump in her nose," and she loses her cool. Kramer is summoned by a patron of the

Old Mill, who tells him to send for help because "there is a crazy, big-headed woman attacking a man with a fork." Kramer intervenes by hoarsely barking out "There's trouble at the Old Mill" to local police officers who end the melee.

A short time later, Mercer is the final winner of the coveted apartment that George fought the shipwreck survivor to obtain. George wonders whether he lost because of the suffering Mercer has endured—perhaps the stabbing or the "fork in the head" from Elaine. Mercer says no, he just gave the "super" fifty dollars. Mercer dismisses George with the quip, "Tough luck, chinless."

Narrative

Although *Seinfeld* may have reinvigorated the sitcom for many viewers, the show hardly reinvented the genre, despite such claims by hard-core fans. In many ways, *Seinfeld* is a typical situation comedy: Each episode contains approximately twenty minutes of content with two commercial breaks of three minutes apiece. What distinguishes *Seinfeld* from other sitcoms of its time are features such as overlapping subplots, rapid-fire dialogue (*Seinfeld* scripts are much longer than the average sitcom script), and numerous scene changes. The show also eventually shed opening credits and instead used its signature comic musical theme with the "popping bass" to announce the beginning of each segment.

Perhaps the aspect of *Seinfeld* that most contrasts with rival sitcoms is its insistence that the show have no higher purpose than to be consistently funny. It is a comedy of manners, with every mundane irritation of modern life taking on disproportionate significance. At least on the surface, no big issues or crises of meaning arise, in contrast to competing sitcoms such as *Home Improvement* and *Roseanne*, which often used comedy as a vehicle to make a point about family life or society at large. With *Seinfeld*, any connections made about values must come from the viewer after a careful analysis of the episode. The writers and producers were steadfastly committed to a "no hugs, no learning" philosophy[9] because as Jerry Seinfeld once put it, "Comedy needs a nice edge to it."[10]

The setting of *Seinfeld*, like that of many sitcoms before it, is contemporary Manhattan, with many scenes occurring in Jerry's apartment, restaurants, taxis, cars, medical clinics, and parks and the occasional scene shot in apartments of the other major characters. Many dilemmas on the show are directly connected with urban life, such as the search for the perfect apartment, the annoying taxi ride, and the neighbors we would like to help move away.

By the time the "The *Andrea Doria*" aired, the four main characters, Jerry, Elaine, George, and Kramer, were well established with viewers. Fans knew their quirks and sore spots. We expected George to act like a loser, Jerry to provide witty asides, Elaine to be obsessed with how people treat her, and Kramer to slide through Jerry's door to surprise us with another peculiar idea or scheme. Newman arrived in the third season (January 1992) to play "Lex Luther" to Jerry's "Superman," although we are never told why the two hate each other.[11] Every week, a number of secondary characters breeze in and out of the lives of the regulars. In "The *Andrea Doria*," Alan Mercer plays antagonist to Elaine (and eventually George), motivated by a desire to "keep the upper hand" in all matters, as George might say. "Keeping the upper hand" is a recurring theme in this series because for all the main characters, achieving their goals and appearing in a positive light in all circumstances are prime motivations. Antagonists are those individuals who get in their way.

Scholars of comedy and television are quick to point out that at least the three leads—Jerry, Elaine, and George—are archetypal Jewish characters. Jerry Seinfeld, both in real life and in the sitcom, is Jewish and acts as the straight man *schlimazel*—one to whom bad things regularly happen.[12] We cannot mistake the character of George Costanza for anything but the comic schlemiel—one who brings about his own bad luck through his actions and foolishness.[13] On this "Jewish Question," Lisa Schwarzbaum writes:

> Was there, dear friends, ever a more Jewish non-Jew in TV history than George Louis Costanza? The family name is meant to suggest Italian heritage, but no one's buying: Only begotten son of Frank and Estelle (they of the biblical-scale yelling and kasha eating), child of Queens, N.Y., a man weaned on the milk of Jewish neurosis, creation of inspired Semitic comedic misanthrope Larry David, George is, indubitably, the fretting prince of *Seinfeld*.[14]

The character of Elaine Benes is also technically *not* Jewish and is the butt of many jokes for her "schiks-appeal" and frequent mislabeling as a Jew. We can, however, see her as the epitome of the "Jewish-American princess," overly concerned with her looks, status, and ability to gain acceptance by men. The show's stereotyping of rabbis, Jewish mothers, and Judaism in general has caused some in the Jewish community to grumble that the show's humor fails when it takes on Jewish issues.[15] Examples of worrisome plot details include Jerry making out with his girlfriend during the movie *Schindler's List*; the cranky soup-stand proprietor nicknamed "the Soup Nazi"; and an episode in which Elaine wonders why Jewish men find her so appealing.[16] Television critic Tom Shales, who praised the show in its first few seasons, changed his tune in 1998, partly because of the show's portrayal of Judaism:

> It's ironic that the late Brandon Tartikoff, the NBC executive who put the show on the air, worried it would be "too Jewish" for the rest of the country— because what the show turned out to be was too self-hatingly Jewish instead.[17]

Just as in large Jewish families, relationships among *Seinfeld* characters are tightly intertwined and are key to the action, providing a never-ending source of fodder for Jerry's joke mill. Jerry is a high school friend of George, who is his source of comic relief and trouble. George is Costello to Jerry's Abbot (Seinfeld admits this is deliberate),[18] providing Jerry with an opportunity to use his comic wit to judge, advise, and console never-ending ineptitude and failure. Jerry is a favored character in the series, as one might expect because the show is loosely based on his experiences as a stand-up comic in Manhattan. He regularly gets the opportunity to put the less fortunate characters, such as George, in their place with a smart and wry retort. Jerry's former girlfriend and now-platonic sidekick, Elaine, is more his equal than is George, although Jerry never misses a chance to mock and expose her as vain and shallow. The two share tastes and a judgmental attitude about the tastes of others. Kramer holds perhaps the most-favored-character status. He is Jerry's brilliant but bizarre neighbor, a cut above the rest because he answers to no one. Described as "less idiot than savant,"[19] Kramer is almost magical—the "master of disaster"—a source of amazement and awe as well as a prolific generator of inane business schemes. Sometimes, as in his Lassie-like rescue at the end of this episode, Kramer saves the day, proving that, in *Seinfeld*'s world, you need not be reasonable or normal to prevail.

Notwithstanding the legendary standard of "no hugs, no learning," protagonists learn at the end of each episode not the usual sitcom lessons, but more likely lessons about the futility of life. The comedic narrative is established early on when a problem or set of problems arises: George's attempt to get the good apartment, Kramer's search for a cure for his cough, Elaine's quest for a passionate man, and Newman's desire for paradise (which coincides with Jerry's desire to be rid of Newman). These issues are affected by complicated interconnections among the main characters, the impersonal workings of fate, or the scheming of other characters. Sometimes physical violence (as in a fork to the forehead) supplies an emotional outlet, but more often confrontations are nonviolent, with the sardonic remark as the weapon of choice. Examples of plot resolutions featuring intertwining story lines are Kramer's rescue as Elaine attacks the "bad breaker-upper" at the Old Mill or Mercer's use of bribery to get the apartment of George's dreams, knitting George's and Elaine's dilemmas together as they both become victims of Mercer's manipulation and caustic verbal attacks.

Conflict is never satisfyingly resolved in *Seinfeld*. The main characters make stupid mistakes that seal their failure and misery: George never takes the obvious shortcut by simply paying the "super" more for the apartment as Mercer does; Elaine allows Mercer's "big head" remark to drive her to violence; Jerry's eagerness to help Newman escape to Hawaii becomes his downfall as he does "too good a job" to be believed. In the end, each of the main characters fails to reach the desired goal because, in the immortal words of Newman, "sometimes we don't get what we want." These characters live and thrive in an antagonistic world. Perpetrators—aside from George, who always suffers—generally do not suffer. The stabbing and the fork in the head may have slowed Mercer down, but they did not stop him. He exists to prove that hard work and nice manners are useless in a fight against a scheming, bribing manipulator. If we accept the characters of Elaine and George as archetypal Jewish victims in this episode, then Mercer is the momentary reigning Gentile.

Structure

The dominant message of this episode, and perhaps of the whole series, is that the world is cruel and people always suffer whether or not they deserve to, so we must enjoy life while we can. If "enjoying" means putting the "screw-gee" (as George says) to others, so be it. Just remember: Everyone else is out to put the "screw-gee" to us, too.

In this message is the notion that we can only rely on close friends to any degree. In this episode, a definite tension is explored between relying on friends and being vulnerable to their dangerous scheming. Friends are, after all, flawed and self-centered human beings, and it is likely that their inane behavior will lead to discomfort in our lives life, but beyond our immediate circle lies even more danger. In *Seinfeld*'s world, no one can be trusted, not even God, who appears to be absent, unconcerned, or antagonistic toward human beings. Comic relief—in observing the suffering of others and seeking a degree of comfort for ourselves and our buddies—is the only source of joy and meaning in life. Life is constantly shown to be cruel and unfair, both by the way the characters are treated and by the way they treat others. This episode ends on a note of futility about the limited possibilities for finding human fulfillment: finding good apartments, passionate lovers, doggedly loyal friends, and the joy of helping your enemies move away.

Seinfeld's worldview is cynical, feeding off those mundane details of life over which a person can gain a degree of control, as we see in Elaine's pre-emptive breakup with the bad-breaker-upper, Kramer's trip to the vet for a cough remedy, and Mercer's bribe to get the good apartment. When writers and producers of *Seinfeld* call it "a show about nothing," what they really say is that it is a show about nothing of real importance.[20] The characters are consumed by trivialities because they cannot find redemption or release in anything of value.

Seinfeld satirizes the American cultural myths of achievement, possibility, and hard work. Kramer, who never seems to have a steady job, gets everything he wants, while Elaine works very hard and gets very little, except perhaps contempt, for her efforts. The show mocks social institutions that seem to have so much control over our individual lives: the U.S. mail (in this episode), religion, family, and tradition. Repeatedly, these are depicted as corrupt, tasteless, annoying, ridiculous, inept, or alienating.

In one sense, *Seinfeld* can be considered a subversive or parabolic series. Baby boomers have been criticized for worshiping at the altar of their own well-being, serving only a god of success and material wealth. *Seinfeld* offers a minimalist alternative to these secular values of American culture. Yes, the characters strive for success, but they rarely achieve it on any grand scale. In many ways, the show demonstrates the futility of putting too much faith in the "work hard and you will succeed" credo. (We need only spend time with the working poor to understand the true destructiveness of that belief.) *Seinfeld* acts out the myth and turns it on its head in such a clever and humorous way that—if we are not careful—we do not even notice it. Because the satire is somewhat buried, the overall effect of the show is to reinforce the dominant value system, in that characters still strive for success. The media reports about the real lives of Jerry and the gang show that none of them is a poster child for economic justice in society. Jerry Seinfeld is a comedy club success story with a $4-million home, a collection of expensive cars, and a job as pitchman for American Express credit cards. In 1996, the entire cast negotiated to become among the highest paid television actors in history, a set of negotiations that drove salaries for all popular television actors higher as well. Seinfeld himself ended up making $1 million per episode in the ninth and final season. Even if *Seinfeld* does poke fun at society's obsession with success and materialism, making us think about how puffed-up and vain we have become, it does so as it rakes in ever more cash for advertisers whose jobs depend on our obsession with material wealth.

Signs, Codes, and Messages

The visual and auditory signs that make up *Seinfeld* derive largely from the genre of Jewish comedy known as *shtick*—old-fashioned observational humor filtered through vaudeville, movies, and old television and filled with references to other elements of popular culture. The gang revolves around Jerry—their centrifugal force—who is a neurotic boy in a man's body. His apartment is the center of their universe and his doorway the entrance to a small community of acceptance.

In homage both to vaudeville and to the fast-paced 1990s, *Seinfeld* cultivated its ability to move off a joke or comic line quickly. The quick cuts from scene to scene mirror the characters' quick pace in conversation, yet viewers are not disoriented in any way. Every interior scene follows an establishing shot that sets the scene of the narrative, and because outdoor scenes are not given such establishing shots, we are reminded of the show's "interior" nature. Almost everything happens in big, dull-toned urban buildings among people who inhabit rather small spaces (apartments, offices, booths at restaurants). This "interior-ness" gives the show a claustrophobic feel, representing the claustrophobic ambiance of urban life itself.[21]

Although critics are fond of calling *Seinfeld* a dark comedy, the lighting of the scenes in no way reflects the emotional tone. The show is brightly lit, indicating little mystery, but it cannot be characterized as warm. Somewhat drab colors in the urban landscape contribute to the overall feeling of detachment the series promotes. The characters treat outsiders with cold disapproval, delivering sneering, judgmental comments. The main source of warmth (and movement) is the character of Kramer, whose upbeat personality belies the grayness of the surroundings.

Very few special visual or auditory effects are in the making of *Seinfeld*. In "The *Andrea Doria*," a human-sounding cough comes from a dog, and a short segment with a happy-go-lucky Jerry—dressed in a postal carrier's uniform—delivering mail is set to whistling 1950s music that is reminiscent of *The Andy Griffith Show*. This video aside conveys "the world as it used to be," when urban life was simpler, and it is comic to us today because our world has become so cynical and suspicious of "the good old days."

Several visual signs repeatedly appear in the series. One is the doorway chat that symbolizes the exclusiveness of the gang of four. For example, in the *Andrea Doria* episode, when Jerry answers his door and sees Newman standing there, Jerry says, "I'm probably not going to let you in," and then shuts the door in Newman's face. If we watch *Seinfeld* on a regular basis, we notice that many scenes take place in or near doorways—thresholds to intimacy. Jerry does not want to let much of anyone into his world. Related to the doorway chat is Kramer's famous slide through the door (which *Entertainment Weekly* claims he did 284 times).[22] The door has become an icon for the magical Kramer to burst through, lifting the mood of everyone in the room. In this episode, Kramer makes his usual dash for Jerry's refrigerator, grabs food, and then coughs on it while noting there is no expiration date ("There is now," says Jerry). Without missing a beat, he proceeds to stump the gang with his knowledge of "Amazing Tales of the Sea" (the title of a book he wrote). Kramer's slide symbolizes an invasion of the lighthearted and unself-

conscious into a ridiculous, self-obsessed world.

Another recurring sign in the series (and this episode) is the messy Newman apartment—a symbol of all that is evil and slothful in Jerry's world. It exists in stark contrast to Jerry's compulsive neatness, a result of his need to find whatever small measure of control that he can. George's dismissive stance and behavior toward Eldridge, who was awarded the apartment because of his suffering in the *Andrea Doria* shipwreck, is another sign reminding us of yuppie self-centeredness and narcissism in the face of elders. At the tenant board hearing, George tilts his chair against the wall and absentmindedly thumps a drumbeat while Eldridge tells the story of his rescue. The tilted chair and bored thumping take viewers back to junior high school study hall, where restless and rebellious students used aggressive body language to annoy the teacher. It also shows that George cares for no one's story but his own.

An analysis of one shot in which Jerry and Elaine are at Monk's cafe discussing "the bad-breaker-upper" shows how visual signs are used to depict cynicism in *Seinfeld*. The two are discussing why "the bad breakup" is so heinous: Because all relationships break up, how one does it is of the essence. At one point, they both shrug and throw their hands into the air in a gesture indicating that they  believe what they are talking about is common knowledge and accepted by everyone. About a good breakup, Elaine says, "What's more important in a relationship?" Jerry replies, "Nothing." Of course, in the real world, some relationships do last, and some people try very hard not to break up, but in Jerry and Elaine's world, there is no such thing as hope for true love in a relationship; there is only companionship and sex. Their upturned palms and questioning facial expressions demonstrate how insular their world is.

Power and Ideology

Seinfeld was produced and written primarily by artists born in the last few years of the baby boom generation. This subset of the larger demographics is sometimes called "the television generation" because by the time these people were born, most middle-class families had at least one television set, and this generation never knew life without television. As the television generation grew to adulthood, they experienced the growth in disposable income earned by young people, increasing mobility and independence, fragmentation of families, and the rising influence of a media-saturated popular culture. *Seinfeld* portrays all that alienation and angst and in so doing delivers the upwardly mobile television generation to advertisers. Viewers eighteen to forty-nine years old are attracted to the show, but the demographics most sought after are viewers aged eighteen to thirty-four because advertisers believe they have the most disposable income and are most willing to spend it. Just as the show *thirtysomething* drew these attractive consumers to drama, *Seinfeld* drew them to a new style of comedy.[23]

Also like *thirtysomething*, *Seinfeld* made these yuppies the center of the universe. The prevailing point of view in the show belongs to Jerry, a member of this somewhat affluent "money demo" crowd. Jerry—a self-centered, judgmental, cynical, urban, Jewish New York man-child—holds the power of a quick wit. As the master of the verbal put-down, he is judge, adviser, parent, and ringleader to them all. The irony is that, much like his buddies George and Elaine, he has very little power over his own life.

Kramer, however, has a mysterious power to always succeed or "come out smelling like a rose." In this episode, the "bad-breaker-upper" Alan Mercer has aggressive power over everyone he meets, including the ex-girlfriends who attack him. As Elaine and George learn, there is great power in the ability to make someone *that* mad.

Rarely in *Seinfeld* do we see life from the point of view of an ethnic minority (apart from Jews). People of color are almost exclusively comic foils, as in the stereotyping of the Pakistani taxicab driver who humiliates Elaine by asking her to move her head so that he can see out the back window. Women, older people, children, and people who are poor are generally fodder for Jerry's, Elaine's, and George's humor.

Jewishness, however, is a central theme in the show, even though it is sometimes concealed from the view of the audience. To notice it, we must understand something about the narrative codes and stereotypical characterizations of which we spoke earlier. For example, in this episode, suffering is the theme, just as in Judaism the question of unjust suffering and the relationship with God (as "the chosen people") is of prime importance. If George is the stereotypical suffering loser, or the schlemiel, then Alan Mercer is the stereotypical gentile, the scheming outsider who manages to come out ahead despite being outside the "family of God."

Aside from Elaine, the favored female, women do not fare very well in *Seinfeld*'s world. They are good for companionship and sex, but they are criticized for being vain, largely unintelligent, and ignorant about trivial matters that are so important to "the guys."

Class differences are not portrayed as a major concern in the show. These young urbanites seem to be financially better off than their parents and grandparents.

Government workers like Newman are considered a step below the reigning elites (Jerry, Elaine, George, and even Kramer). People like Kramer, who seem not to work yet have enough money, are considered a step above the rest. The show tends to focus only on the upper middle class, that is, on people with disposable income much like the people advertisers are seeking to attract.

Functions

People watch *Seinfeld* largely because they recognize themselves, to some degree, in these alienated, cynical young urbanites and can laugh at what they see.[24] When *Seinfeld* was in its fifth season, one of the co-authors of this book remembers coming into the rock radio station where she worked and hearing a colleague describe in great detail how each of the characters is "just like" someone she knew in her own life. This colleague seemed to feel that the writers had insight into her life. Such recognition builds loyalty and "buzz"—the free promotion that a show gets only when viewers start repeating memorable catch phrases and lines of dialogue in their everyday lives.

Television critics and fans alike contend that a major reason people watch this show is that Jerry Seinfeld achieves his oft-stated singular goal of making the show funny. People want to laugh at themselves, at foolish behavior, and at ludicrous situations. This humor relativizes people's lives, which may be full of suffering and failure. The main characters serve as a collective "village idiot," which we need to feel superior. The audience also enjoys laughing at what they recognize in *Seinfeld* from other television shows. Intertextual pop culture references are a *Seinfeld* staple, and the Trivial Pursuit crowd among late baby boomers is fascinated by them. Part of the joy of watching *Seinfeld* reruns is to catch those references missed the first time around.

What then do we make of the short- and long-term effects of watching *Seinfeld*? In the short term, the show encourages us to laugh and release our expectations of a perfect world. That, in and of itself, is so therapeutic that many psychologists regularly prescribe laughter as a mood-lifter for their clients who harbor a gloomy view of life. In the long term, viewers attached to this show and its ideology may be confirmed in their life of self-promotion or "me-ism" at the expense of community and family. The writers may contend that they are only portraying life more realistically than a rival show like *Home Improvement*, but if people start to view their own world as one devoid of lasting relationships and hope for the future they run the risk of becoming rude, surly, and unpleasant. An insightful look into the *Seinfeld* worldview appeared in *Entertainment Weekly*'s special Seinfeld finale issue, in which writer Mike Flaherty creates what he thinks a fictitious episode number 939 might look like:

> None of them are married (natch). Jerry and Kramer still live in their respective apartments, with more frequent pop-ins from new neighbor Elaine, who inherited Newman's lease after he finally got his Hawaii transfer. As for George, he's contending with a nursing home, a roommate, *and* a common bathroom. Got the picture?[25]

Fans of the show who take a close, serious look at it, as we are doing, must ask themselves: Is what we find funny in *Seinfeld* indicative of what we want to become? Viewers need not assume any of the character flaws flaunted in *Seinfeld*. Knowing why we laugh at what we laugh at is the kind of awareness that guards against overidentifying with these characters. A good question to ask after we have enjoyed laughing at a character's antics might be: Was I laughing at something I saw in myself or in my culture, or was I laughing in spite of myself? If we laugh at something about ourselves, perhaps a foible or failure of our own, then we are using humor as a healthy way of confronting ourselves. We might then ask ourselves if a change is necessary. If we laugh at something despite ourselves, perhaps because a previously taboo subject is being treated lightly (a common *Seinfeld* comedic ploy), we might wonder if we are allowing our laughter to "normalize" a subject that we would prefer to keep off limits. Sometimes this reason for laughing alerts us to a conflict in our value system; at other times it shows us that our humor is more flexible than we thought. After all, some sacred cows are meant to be skewered.

Theological Analysis

Although a "show about nothing" may seem to offer us little to ponder theologically, we need only look at the Jewish tradition of seeking wisdom to see connections to *Seinfeld*. Even one of its main writers, Larry Charles, compares *Seinfeld* to "a dark *Talmud*" with "brilliant minds examining a thought or ethical question from every possible angle."[26] Jerry Seinfeld himself admits to a higher purpose: "[C]omedy is my mission. That's what I can do to make the world a little less bad."[27]

Seinfeld is, in many ways, the Ecclesiastes of sitcoms. In the Hebrew wisdom book of Ecclesiastes, the author, Qohelet, laments that "all is futility." The more common translations give us the famous catchphrase as "Vanity of vanities. All is vanity" (Eccles. 1:2). Hebrew scholars say that this key word translated as "vanity" can also be interpreted as "futility."[28] Either way, *Seinfeld* qualifies. The characters in *Seinfeld* are vain, and their lives seem futile. In their worldview, human beings are victims of the forces of fate that constantly puts their lives in danger. Suffering seems to define human life. Therefore, meaning can be sought or contained only within the very small, mundane things that make up everyday life. Just like Qohelet, the characters in *Seinfeld* decide it is best to enjoy life's little pleasures, such as the humor in the nagging irritants of modern life. And why not? Death, or failure, is always right around the corner. Also like Qohelet, the show depicts a God who is far away and unengaged. Both Seinfeld and the author of Ecclesiastes are solitary men. Of Qohelet, Carole Fontaine writes:

> Significantly, the author [of Ecclesiastes] never speaks of entering a meaningful relationship and so lives in a world where he is the only true subject. Nature, women, and other social inferiors remain objects for his use, so naturally he suffers the boredom of the elite who exist in a world populated only by themselves.[29]

The characters in this show find their salvation in the material things and activities that make up a mundane life: a nice car, going to the movies, eating out, having coffee with friends. In some ways, it would be "salvation" for many people to find significance, meaning, or even just humor in the ordinary, much as Jerry and his friends do. The ordinary can be a window into the divine. When people seek religious experience to lift them from their mundane existence, they refuse to see that God communicates in the dull and everyday probably more often than in mystical vision or rapture. Once a person has a mystical experience in the ordinary, he or she is much more able to laugh at and reject the bloatedness of our culture's need to acquire things. *Seinfeld* succeeds in stripping away the allure of materialism and self-centeredness by showing us how ridiculous it looks.

The producers of *Seinfeld* seem to say to us that life is full of suffering. Accept it, and get over it—you are not entitled to a worry-free life, so get on with your day-to-day routine and seek whatever happiness you can grab for yourself along the way (the Qohelet message updated). It is a bleak picture of society, but it captures that which *is* terribly bleak about contemporary life in urban America—its narcissism and nihilism. There may not be a hug in that message, but there certainly is a lesson.

TWO

The Simpsons

REDEFINING THE FAMILY SITCOM

Now I guess I'll have to give up my hopes and dreams and settle for being a decent husband and father.

—*Homer J. Simpson*

Episode: **First aired:**
"The Wizard of Evergreen Terrace"   September 20, 1998

A contemporary cartoon satire that gives us the distance we need to see ourselves close up, this episode is full of the over-the-top goofiness we've come to expect, along with the simple reassurance that "family" is once again our lives' best work.

The Simpsons first aired in December 1989 on the Fox network. As a series, it reintroduced, reinterpreted, and reinvigorated the subgenre of animated television situation comedy. In its first season, it became a flagship show for Fox, helping to establish the network's "edgy" identity. The show first entered the Nielsen top fifteen in March 1990, although ratings have fluctuated over the years. In a glowing review, media critic Ken Tucker wrote: "The Simpsons are the American family at its most complicated, drawn as simple cartoons."[1] The episode addressed here, "The Wizard of Evergreen Terrace," appeared on September 20, 1998, as the season premiere. Highlighting the satirical edge of the show, this episode is suffused with a broad array of popular cultural references, even as it deepens the development of the main characters on this most "pro-family" of television programs.

Driving home from work, a man listens to the "Five o'Clock News Flush" on radio station KBBL; each story is accompanied by the sound of a flushing toilet. He hears that the life span of the average American male is

76.2 years. Reacting in horror, he slams on his brakes, crashing into the highway divider. Apparently unscathed, he cries out: "76.2! But I'm already 38.1! Half my life is over, and what do I have to show for it?" He hops out of the car, crosses several busy lanes of traffic, and arrives at a call box. Then the scene becomes bizarre: As he picks up the phone, he starts complaining about how miserable and meaningless his life is, all the while assuming that the female voice at the other end of the line belongs to his wife.

Is this man in shock or insane? Such questions arise repeatedly on entering the weird yet familiar world of Homer J. Simpson and his cartoon family. Each week, *The Simpsons* teases and challenges viewers to look at their own lives as reflected in an animated mirror. Combining manic comedy with cutting satire, the series sheds humorous but critical light on the dominant institutions and values of American society. This attitude has been on display from the start, setting the show apart from standard sitcom fare. Since its debut as a pilot in 1989, *The Simpsons* has been a flagship program for the Fox network, emerging both as a darling of media critics and a magnet for criticism.[2]

The Simpson family, created by cartoonist Matt Groening (previously best known for his subversive comic strip "Life in Hell"), first appeared in a series of short bumpers between skits on *The Tracey Ullman Show* in 1987. The humor of these "cartoonettes" tended to be dark and "edgy." This offbeat bent inspired fledgling Fox, because it sought to attract younger demographics than the big three network rivals, to hire Groening and James L. Brooks (the *Ullman Show*'s producer) to create a weekly half-hour series. *The Simpsons* premiered as a series in January 1990, occupying the 8:00 P.M. Sunday time slot. It was the first animated sitcom to appear in prime time since *The Flintstones* and *The Jetsons*, although these earlier cartoons had disappeared from prime time by 1964 as networks found that so-called kiddie programming held little appeal to maturing baby boomers.

In 1989, the situation was different. Boomers now had children of their own: the new wave of Generation X, which provided a huge new market of media-savvy viewers for a network seeking to establish a niche. *The Simpsons* arrived in this altered landscape, becoming a ratings winner in its first year. By the end of that season, its artistic standards had improved as well. The drawing of the main characters was purposefully "softened," becoming relatively less grotesque and more inviting, while the comedy writing focused more on the relationships among family members and relatively less on "gross-out" gags. These alterations made it Fox's highest rated show in the early 1990s. In its second season, the series moved to Thursday night to compete with NBC's ratings juggernaut *Cosby*. It continued to perform well there, despite the unenviable task of competing with "Must See TV." By its sixth season, however, it had returned to 8:00 P.M. on Sunday, where it remains today, anchoring Fox's programming on that night.

Narrative Elements

At the start of the episode under consideration here, Homer's usually oblivious consciousness is jolted by the radio report that his life is "half over." This drives him into an existential crisis. As he arrives home from work after his "epiphany on the highway," he is bedraggled. Marge, his long-suffering wife, offers comfort, saying: "One thing you've accomplished [in life] is making me very happy." Homer responds: "Oh yeah, they'll put me on a stamp for that!" Then follows a dream sequence of his future funeral—replete with references to pop cultural artifacts—wherein he is characterized as a "real sack of crap."

> "Who invented this pile of junk? Was it you, Bart?"—referring to his unruly son. Daughter Lisa says, "No, it was Thomas Edison . . ."

Later, the family tries to cheer him up with a movie entitled: "Homer Simpson, Welcome to Your Life." In images from previous episodes, Homer is shown as an astronaut and a heavyweight boxer and playing with his children. None of these supposed "successes" alleviates his despair. Then, after an image of the car "Kit" from the 1980s television series *Night Rider* appears on the screen (momentarily impressing him), the projector breaks. Homer lashes out: "Who invented this pile of junk? Was it you, Bart?"—referring to his unruly son. Daughter Lisa says, "No, it was Thomas Edison," and recounts Edison's many other inventions. The rest of the episode shows Homer seeking to redeem his life by inventing as many gadgets as had Edison.

After numerous failures, Homer consults with a member of the "scientific community," Professor Frink, who tells him the "secret" of inventing: "All you have to do is think of things which people need, but don't exist yet." With this piece of information, he returns home to invent, blowing up his house a few times in the process, comparing his progress to Edison's with a "horse race" wall chart. The products of Homer's creativity are an electric hammer, a gun that blasts makeup at a woman's face, a constantly screeching "Everything's O.K." alarm, and a "Lazyman Reclining Toilet Chair." After he demonstrates them to his family, Marge tells him that these inventions are terrible: "No one will buy them or accept them as gifts!" He responds forlornly: "I guess I'm no better at being Thomas Edison than I was at being Homer Simpson." As son Bart mounts the toilet chair, there is a quick cut to commercial.

After the break, Homer is shown having dinner with his family. In apparent defeat, he says: "Now I guess I'll have to give up my hopes and dreams and settle for being a decent husband and father." Then, as he falls back in his chair, we realize that he has somehow managed to design something useful after all: leg brackets that prevent the chair from tipping. His family is amazed and proud, but he

> [T]his episode follows the generic sitcom pattern . . . Familiar status quo—Ritual error made—Ritual lesson learned—Familiar status quo.

becomes paranoid and thinks that they will steal his invention. Unfortunately, once he returns to his cellar to celebrate, he sees the same brackets in a photo of Edison. It seems that even the fruit of Homer's own "creativity" was unconsciously borrowed from his rival. In a fit of indignant desperation, he decides to go to the Edison Museum in New Jersey to destroy the original chair and claim the invention as his own. Along the way on the interstate, he intentionally runs over Edison's ghost, who implores him to abandon his plan.

Eventually, Homer arrives at the museum, but just as he starts to smash the chair with the electric hammer, he notices a familiar "horse race" chart on the wall comparing Edison with Leonardo da Vinci. He concludes that, compared with Leonardo, Edison was as much a failure as himself, and in good conscience he spares the chair. Sometime later, as he sits at home watching the television news, he sees a report that a remarkable discovery has been made at the Edison Museum: two previously unknown inventions—chair-leg brackets and an electric hammer. Edison's "already wealthy" heirs are shown dancing with money, and the Simpson family is disturbed by the injustice. Bart remarks: "You're taking this pretty well." Homer, reclining on his toilet chair, responds: "Let's just say I'm sitting in the right chair."

The narrative form of this episode follows the generic sitcom pattern described by David Marc as "Familiar status quo—Ritual error made—Ritual lesson learned—Familiar status quo."[3] Homer's ordinary life is disrupted; he conceives a ridiculous plan to cope (the ritual error); he is helped, hindered, and put in his place by outside forces and by his own (in)abilities (lesson learned); finally he returns to his normal status as one of society's "also rans." In a formal sense, nothing is new. The same pattern can be seen in Ralph Kramden's "get-rich-quick" schemes on *The Honeymooners* and in Tim Taylor's attempts to invent "more powerful" tools on *Home Improvement*. Nevertheless, as we see, a potentially subversive critique of culture does lie *between the poles* of the plot in *The Simpsons* in which the initial status quo is interrupted by the "toilet flush" of the five o'clock news, and the denouement finds Homer enthroned on his own invention, the toilet chair.[4]

In the series' first few seasons, Bart was clearly the hero; in this episode, Homer is the protagonist. This has increasingly been the case: Because of the show's success, it became unnecessary to rely on Bart's radical behavior to draw an audience. Homer's usual motivation is to immediately satisfy his urge to consume the good things in life, which consist primarily of beer, doughnuts, and television programs. In this episode, however, he is motivated to find meaning in life through inventing useful things—which, presumably, would provide him with more money, thus allowing him to feed his appetites even more.

The antagonist seems to be Homer's own limitations: his lack of creativity, his greed, his self-centered paranoia, and, ironically in the end, his troubled conscience. Each of these personal attributes, however, is in large part the product of cultural conditioning. Thus, the ultimate antagonist seems to be the competitive, materialistic nature of American capitalism (symbolized by Edison and the actions of his "greedy heirs"), which is passed on to individuals like Homer by social institutions (the media, the family, school, religion).

The character of Homer Simpson is that of a stereotypical working-class American male. He is employed, incongruously and unsatisfactorily, as a safety inspector at the local nuclear power plant. Homer is ignorant and lazy, governed by his appetites. He would rather hang out at Moe's Tavern with his drinking buddies than spend time with his family, yet he expects his family to serve his own needs. He is a clownish figure, representing in ridiculous fashion both the hubris and the weakness of the "typical" working-class patriarch.

Homer's wife Marge is charged with nurturing and serving her family. Her enormous blue beehive hairdo symbolizes her heavy burden. She is patient, caring, and relatively intelligent, with a heart of gold; still, her circumstances sometimes frustrate her, and she emits a guttural growl to signal her rage. She is the glue that holds the family together.

Ten-year-old Bart has become an icon of rebellion. In the early years of the series, a number of his slogans ("Eat my shorts," "Underachiever—and proud of it!") spread throughout the burgeoning youth culture in America and around the world. His name is an anagram for "brat," and his life seems to revolve around causing trouble at school, with his sister Lisa, and with authority figures of all kinds. Bart is an eternal preadolescent, who consistently spurns the dictates of his elders. Yet he is not all "bad" and occasionally shows signs of being a vulnerable little boy in need of—and capable of—caring.

Lisa is eight years old, the family genius. Her concern in life is eventually to escape the subservient status of her mother and to achieve success through her own merits. She has prodigious talents in many areas, particularly in her ability to play the saxophone. She is the intellectual power and conscience of the show (although, on occasion, she can be mischievous as well). If Bart simply defies authority, Lisa is a critical "muckraker" who uncovers hypocrisy and injustice at the heart of society.

The other members of the family include baby daughter Maggie and Abraham "Grandpa" Simpson. Maggie is often ignored by her family, her wishes expressed in the form of mime as she toddles along, silenced by her omnipresent pacifier. Grandpa is a caricature of a forgetful, incompetent, and slow elderly man. His nature is displayed in this episode when he is amazed that filmed pictures on a screen can actually move: "They're alive!" he exclaims.

The Simpsons live on a pleasant suburban street called Evergreen Terrace in the town of Springfield, which exists somewhere in the United States. Springfield itself is a stereotype, being perhaps the most common town name in America, as well as the locale of the 1950s sitcom *Father Knows Best*. Springfield's inhabitants include a whole range of social types. Among a myriad of others, they include autocratic, feeble nuclear plant owner Montgomery Burns; Waylon Smithers, his gay assistant; the drunken denizens of Moe's Tavern; Apu, the Indian owner of the Kwik-E-Mart; Mrs. Krabapple, Bart's repressed, resentful schoolteacher; "Kennedyesque" Mayor Quimby; cantankerous Krusty the Clown; and hyper-Christian Ned Flanders and family. Each of these characters recurs in the series, allowing an almost endless variety of plot lines to develop.[5]

The central relationships on the show occur between members of the Simpson family. In this narrative world, Homer usually initiates action—often stumbling onto a ridiculous new scheme to escape the tedium of life by feeding his appetites. Marge reacts, lending her support or mildly chastising her husband's behavior, always seeking to maintain stability in the family. Alternatively, Bart causes problems for authority figures, and Lisa attempts to solve problems caused by others by dint of her intellect or moral suasion.

Clearly, the male members of the family are favored in the narrative to the extent that they routinely initiate the action, but the female characters almost always display the virtues of clear thinking, moral strength, compassion, and caring. It is the women of the Simpson clan who get their men out of trouble—trouble that may threaten the continued existence of the family itself. The Simpson children are favored in that they are the explicit cultural critics on the show. Whether through Bart's rebellion or Lisa's moral outrage, the children have not yet been entirely socialized, have not "bought into" the mainstream of American culture. They are still relatively free. Because they never age as cartoon characters, they never become the fully complacent and compliant adults their parents apparently are.

Of course, *The Simpsons* is no purely "domestic" comedy. Also included in the action are the citizens of Springfield (and of numerous other places) and their social institutions. In this sense, society itself is a major player.

In this episode, it is society (in the form of the news media) that leads Homer to reassess his life. It is society again (the news media, as well as the "wealthy heirs" of Edison) that "puts him in his place" on the toilet chair in the end. In this way, *The Simpsons* portrays a range of relationships internal to the family, as well as external ones that place that family in its social context. Indeed, the most important relationship on the series may be that between the Simpson family and the broader society.

Structure

The dominant message of the series is: The only thing that really matters in life is having a supportive family. That family may seem totally dysfunctional—like the Simpsons—but whose family is truly "functional"? After all, antagonistic external forces constantly threaten its stability. These same forces also foil the attempts of its individual members to develop their talents and to achieve their goals in life. Such forces are entrenched in cultural values, expectations, and institutions and embodied by authority figures. On *The Simpsons*, almost any arena of society may be a target of criticism, including the workplace, the economy, marriage, friendship, religion, politics, law, medicine, even the family. "Cultural contradictions" appear at the heart of each of these institutions.[6] For example, in a society that preaches the value of work, individuals like Homer are encouraged to find fulfillment in leisure and consumption. In addition, patriarchal authority (in the home, at work, in school) conflicts with the virtue of pursuing individual autonomy and self-worth.

Despite these contradictions, in the end it is the family itself that always provides a (relatively) secure and nurturing place for the individual threatened by society. It is a haven in a heartless world. Ironically, the apparently "cynical" worldview portrayed by the series (which has been roundly condemned by its critics) actually promotes a positive view of the role of the family. This is obvious, for example, in Homer's own name. Even while he constantly seeks to escape his responsibilities as husband and father, the visceral, magnetic force of family always pulls him home in the end. Thus, Homer turns out to be a true "homer," making *The Simpsons* perhaps one of the most "pro-family" programs on television.[7]

The form of cultural critique on the show is satire: the exposure of the wickedness, absurdities, and inequities of human life with the intention of correcting them through the use of irony, ridicule, and parody. Although satire need not always be "funny," its force diminishes to the degree that it becomes too earnest and serious. One thing in short supply on *The Simpsons* is earnest seriousness, making it the perfect "counterprogram" to CBS's *Touched by an Angel*, which appears at the same time. Far from promoting a message that all is fundamentally "okay" with the world, *The Simpsons* shows a society corrupt at its core. Its animated form is a great strength, providing wide latitude for irony and satire.

The ironic distance achieved through animation is a function of its "pre-sentational" nature. That is, unlike live action shows that "re-present" what we already know to be real, cartoons present us with a new world that may or may not reflect our own. Viewers must make the connections between their own lives and the lives of the characters drawn by the animators. Yet although cartoon characters may appear odd and funny, at the same time they can be remarkably familiar, because animation, by its nature, thrives on stereotyping. Cartoons are not limited by the specific physical appearance or personality traits of human actors; thus they tend to produce exaggerated caricatures of what "typical" human beings are like. For example, the Simpson family *itself* is a stereotype of a "traditional" nuclear family unit: Homer works a nine-to-five job, Marge is a housewife, they have 2.5 children (if baby Maggie is taken to be a "half-child"), they live in a suburban house clearly beyond their financial means, and they go to church on Sunday. In this way, the traditional core of the show promotes a degree of comfortable recognition for the viewing audience in the face of unrelenting satire.

One of the strengths of *The Simpsons*, however, is that its individual characters do not remain mere caricatures. Through the years, they have become increasingly complex, much more so than most characters on live action sitcoms. As Owen puts it: "Because [the characters] are drawings, they can change and grow while remaining frozen in time."[8] For example, even though Homer looks almost the same now as he did in the early years, he has evolved from an autocratic jerk into a "dreamy dumbbell." Such development has allowed viewers to identify with the characters as individuals while maintaining stereotypical familiarity.

This development is in line with the goal of satire, which is to be both recognizable and fanciful. Thus, *The Simpsons* can continue to skewer the evils of society while not seeming to be too dangerous. As a cartoon, it can go where no live action show can, by creating unique locations, bizarre special effects, fantasy sequences, stylized violence, improbable feats of move-ment, and farcical behavior.[9] At the same time, its subversive potential is blunted when its characters and situations are seen purely as figments of imagination. As with the privilege accorded to the court jester, animation may thus seem "safer for children" than live action satire. This fact allows a critical show like *The Simpsons* to get on the air in the first place.[10]

Signs, Codes, and Messages

Each episode of *The Simpsons* opens with a sequence in which family members return home at the end of the day. This repeats a pattern seen on *The Flintstones*. The first shot is of clouds in the sky. As an angelic choir softly intones "The Simpsons," the clouds disperse to reveal the town of Springfield below. From the beginning, the viewer's perspective is tran-scendent, superior, and "godlike"—far above the mundane goings-on in the life of the town. The next few scenes establish the characters of the family members. As Bart is forced to confess to various misdeeds on the chalkboard at school (the content changes weekly), Homer gets off work at the nuclear power plant, casually tossing aside radioactive material that sticks to his back. Lisa is kicked out of band practice for playing jazzy riffs on her sax (again, the tune varies), while Marge and Maggie run errands at the grocery store. Each family member converges on home: Bart on his "magical" skateboard, Lisa on a bike, their parents in cars. As they arrive, they rush to the living room couch, only to encounter a novel, unsettling situation confronting them each week. Turning their attention to the television "hearth" in front of them, they settle in to watch, ironically, a show about themselves.

The impact of this manic sequence is twofold: While the viewer maintains a "heavenly" distance at first, the Simpson family is compelled to escape from the hazards of the world. They return to the safety of home, where the walls are painted in soothing shades of "rosy" pink and the comforting flicker of the television is always present. As they watch, however, a shift occurs: Members of the Simpson family themselves watch a show called *The Simpsons* and take on the perspective of the viewer. This shift implicates the viewer with the cartoon characters and vice versa. That is, the Simpsons have managed to gain the same distance from what they are watching as the viewing audience has, thus mitigating any distance that previously existed between us and them. The message is that the great American viewing public is now watching a show about *themselves*, in front of their own television hearths. A further implication is that, just as the characters we are watching are animated by forces beyond themselves, we ourselves are subject to forces of consumerism and conformity, which manipulate our own lives. Watching the show gives us an opportunity to "open our eyes" to this underlying reality.

In the episode under analysis, to gain a sense of the potentially subversive content situated "between the poles of the plot," it is useful to focus on the signs and codes of meaning encountered in three scenes: (1) Homer's moment of existential angst on the highway at the beginning; (2) his inventions, which establish his stereotypical working-class status; and (3) the closing scene, in which Homer is surrounded by his family in apparent defeat.

Following a commercial break, the first scene begins with an establishing shot (once again) taken from high above the transmitting tower of radio station KBBL. The call letters satirize the endlessly vapid character of so many contemporary media with their constant "babbling." There is also an implied reference to the biblical story of the tower of Babel, a symbol of arrogant humanity's perpetual attempt to supplant divine power and of God's decision to "confuse the tongues" of human beings and to scatter them over the whole earth, thus limiting the reach of their power forever (Genesis 11). KBBL is thus a double-edged symbol for the media's aspiration to arbitrate taste and truth and the evil and futility of this intent. This symbol is reinforced by the initial shot taken from "God's" point of view. Meanwhile, Homer is a passive recipient of the news (i.e., the "excrement," the meaningless garbage) that is "flushed" over him as he drives home from work. As an imbecile, he does not understand the referent for the word "website" in the first story on the news. This ignorance sets him up for the second story about the average life span of an American male—76.2 years. This apparently irrefutable, scientific fact contained in a number (with a decimal point no less!) overwhelms his fragile psyche. Suddenly, his whole life seems to have become a waste of time, to be "flushing away." It is unclear why the usually carefree Homer reacts in this particular way. Could it be that this flash of truth on the radio has led to an "epiphany" on the highway, waking him from his slumbering existence, shedding light on a path of potential transformation? If so, the meaning of the scene is highly ironic: The babbling flush of the media has opened Homer to the possibility of self-realization. As he emerges from existential despair, he is led to seek redemption, but how? How can he buy back his life?

Homer's quest for redemption involves patterning his life after that of the great hero of American inventiveness, Thomas Edison.[11] The way to find meaning in life is to be creative, but not just creative—inventive: "to think of things which people need, but don't exist yet." The key to finding meaning in life is thus to satisfy the human need for more and better consumer products. This idea has obvious appeal for Homer. What he invents epitomizes his status and consciousness as a working-class "Everyman:"

> The message is that the great American viewing public is now watching a show about *themselves*, in front of their own television hearths.

- The electric hammer: As Homer shows it to his family, the hammer promptly goes haywire, dragging him screaming all over his living room. There is no clearer proletarian symbol than the hammer, and to the extent that it is electric, it is both more powerful and potentially more uncontrollable—perhaps symbolizing the revolutionary potential of an empowered working class.
- The "Everything's O.K." alarm: an invention that points to Homer's role as protective patriarch. In ridiculous fashion, it is designed to continually squeal an alarm to show that all is right in the home. Soon it too breaks, bringing relief to the whole family.
- The makeup gun: a symbol of the subservient and vulnerable status of women in American culture. Homer shoots the gun at Marge who, he expects, will be pleased at the

hassle-free speed of beautification. Daughter Lisa says, "Women won't appreciate being shot at." Homer replies, "Women will like what I tell them to like, honey."

- The "Lazyman Reclining Toilet Chair": perhaps the greatest gift any stereotypical American working-class male can hope to receive. Never again must he rise from his chair and leave the television to go to the bathroom. It is indeed a triumph of consumer culture over the cruder requirements of the human body. Yet the chair is also an ironic symbol of the compliant position of the American male captive at the altar of consumption: the television set.

Marge tells Homer the bad news that his inventions are terrible, to which he responds forlornly, "But this is the best I could do." He leaves the room, only to have Bart climb onto the chair. Thus the boy is a budding man, already comprehending the utility of a reclining toilet in the living room.

The overall message of this scene, with its many symbolic overtones, concerns the degraded condition of the working-class male: Homer has done nothing more than invent things he thinks people "need, but don't exist yet." People just like him would want electric hammers and toilet chairs because that is what they are enculturated (i.e., "trained") to want. Thus, in exaggerated, stereotypical fashion, Homer's inventions satirize the debased tastes of the American working-class male who wants powerful tools, a secure home, a beautiful wife, and a little time off in front of the tube. Yet the particular way in which they seek to satisfy this urge for comfort blinds members of the working class to their oppression at the hands of consumerism and capitalism.

Finally, at the culmination of the narrative, Homer's apparent triumph in inventing the chair-leg supports is short lived; they were Edison's invention after all. His attempt to destroy the evidence in New Jersey is thwarted by his own guilty conscience, which recognizes in Edison a kindred spirit, a man, just like Homer, who "set the bar a little too high" when compared with Leonardo. In an action epitomizing the Marxian notion of "false consciousness" (the idea that workers and owners are really just the same), Homer goes home without hammering the chair and, unfortunately, without his electric hammer as well. On the surface, the lesson seems to be that Homer is really a softhearted person, aware of his limitations and willing to live with them. He returns to the warm embrace of his family, and there we expect the episode to end. In a last ironic twist, however, Homer is instead punished for his act of mercy. After its discovery at the museum, the seemingly useless electric hammer is suddenly an item of great value when its invention is attributed to Edison. This will "mean millions to Edison's already wealthy heirs," observes television newsman Kent Brockman. Thus, members of the monied elite once again expropriate a working man's invention. Homer's family recognizes the injustice, but he can do nothing but stew in his own excrement, once again the victim of social forces beyond his control.

An analysis of the symbolic content of these scenes reveals a harsh and graphic commentary on American society. Between the poles of a seemingly conventional sitcom plot, the narrative movement, which begins with a toilet flush, ends in a toilet enthronement (with the hero described, between the two poles, as a "real sack of crap"). From the start, as we look down from the heavens, we see the news media making a working man (Homer) view his life as meaningless. The path of redemption he chooses requires the stimulation of his creative nature, yet this action eventually leads him to embody some of the worst vices of competitive materialism: greed, paranoia, and cutthroat antagonism. He resolves to make a name for himself by destroying his adversary (Edison) but his guilty conscience finally forces him to back down. Yet his conscience ultimately betrays him. Once again, he becomes a victim of society, realizing that his quest for success is doomed to failure. The only thing he can rely on, in the end, is his long-suffering family. The question for Homer, or for us as viewers, is whether we realize that it is actually in the nuclear family *itself* that redemption is to be found. This is the overall message portrayed weekly on *The Simpsons*.

Power and Ideology

The satirical perspective of this episode addresses important issues and ideologies of contemporary society. Many Americans seem to worry about the "breakdown" of the traditional family and the relative scarcity of "true heroes" (such as Edison) in an era of "Monicagate." There are also concerns about the increasing level of wealth in postindustrial society, distributed unequally according to seemingly objective criteria that reward high-tech savvy and inventiveness. Responding to these realities, the producers of *The Simpsons* articulate a vision critical of the unjust distribution of power in America. The show represents a particular point of view, that of a "typical" white, working-class, patriarchal Protestant family living in North America. Absent from this view is much reference to the concerns of ethnic or religious minorities, of people over fifty, of cultural conservatives, or (not surprisingly) of economic elites.[12]

In the world of *The Simpsons*, Homer has explicit power over the members of his family, although there is plenty of room for Marge and the kids to oppose him. This reality lends an egalitarian cast to the family structure, which, along with its nurturing and accepting role, makes the idea of family appear to be "good" on the show. Yet outside forces dominate Homer and his dependents. In this episode, these include the media, members of the economic elite, and cultural values that drive Homer's competitive behavior as well as his guilty conscience. Such forces are a constant threat to a working man in the United States. Like so many other working-class persons, the show implies, Homer is hindered in his quest to find meaning in life by his "false consciousness," a state of mind that causes him to sublimate his striving for authentic power and creativity into lazy, sexist, and gluttonous behavior.

Women like Marge are enculturated to serve these men and fail to pursue their own goals apart from their mates. The process of enculturation can be witnessed when contrasting Bart—who is free and mischievous—with his father Homer, and Lisa—who is both creative and morally attuned—with her mother Marge. We, the audience, have a front-row seat to watch as Bart and Lisa learn to become working-class Americans, losing their creative spunk and dynamic potential in the process. This all happens in the course of a half-hour comedy that, perhaps not surprisingly, is devoid of a laugh track.[13]

Functions

Individual viewers of *The Simpsons* may or may not be aware of the scope of its satirical intent. The target audience of the series consists mainly of adolescents, college students, young professionals, and families with young children. The show is skewed to younger demographics (people born after about 1955), whose propensity to buy and consume products on a massive scale appeals to the Fox network and to advertisers. Such viewers are considered "hip." Reared on a steady diet of television, they are alert to the show's numerous references to icons of popular culture, which is part of the show's appeal. In addition, young viewers may enjoy the manic and outrageous antics of the characters (particularly Bart), with little knowledge of many of the references. Other viewers respond to the cutting satire, agreeing (in varying degrees) with its critical commentary on contemporary life, its perspective on the value of the family, or both. With a mix of satire, slapstick, and intertextuality, the show has become a ratings winner for Fox and a cash cow for sponsors (as well as for its creators).[14]

If the sitcom genre has historically *promoted* the consumerist values of American capitalist culture "in miniature," how does *The Simpsons*, which satirizes almost every aspect of that construction, affect viewers? If Nielsen ratings are any indicator, the antics and tribulations of the Simpsons clearly resonate with a large number of people, who are entertained and challenged by the characters and by the situations that confront them. Still, there is a question of whether the satirical tenor of the show actually causes viewers to look critically at their culture and at their own lives, which the show's creators clearly intend. Are audience members likely to agree with the series' overall message about the importance of having a supportive—if "dysfunctional"—family to shield individuals from the oppressive forces of society? If so, are we likely to react by trying to reshape alienating social institutions along more humane and egal-itarian lines? An analysis of this episode of *The Simpsons* demonstrates the critical, even subversive potential of the series as satire, but real viewers must respond each week in their own ways.

Theological Analysis

A number of theological issues arise in this episode, though they appear "between the lines" of the narrative. These include judgment, sin, redemp-tion, and grace. The opening shot, high above the KBBL radio tower, is a reminder of human-ity's constant striving to "reach the heavens"—to gain ultimate power, to be arbiters of truth—and of the divine judgment over and against this vain conceit. Of course, the "god" implicitly por-trayed on *The Simpsons* may or may not be the "God" of Judeo-Christian tradition. It may sim-ply be a transcendent critical presence that hovers above society, relativizing all of its cultural values and aspirations.

> A number of theological issues arise in this episode. . . . These include judgment, sin, redemption, and grace.

In this light, however, one conservative Christian scholar characterizes *The Simpsons* as "the most religious" show on prime-time television.[15] According to Bowler, the series is one of the few that "takes religion's place in society seriously enough to do it the honor of making fun of it." He points out that the Simpson family, as well as almost everyone else in Springfield, attends church or temple services regularly. They believe in God and often engage in prayer (as in the famous mealtime grace offered by Bart: "Dear God, we paid for all this stuff ourselves, so thanks for noth-ing"). Some episodes even directly address issues of religion, as when Homer sells his soul to the devil for a doughnut, and, in a parody of *The Devil and Daniel Webster*, Marge wins it back by showing that Homer's soul had already been pledged to her. In the episode under consideration in this chapter, as in most, theological issues are more subterranean.

The narrative opens from the perspective of God, which immediately puts all that follows in a position of judgment. That is, the satirical critique is from a perspective that transcends, and relativizes, the social reality portrayed. The first scene also establishes that Homer's life is in need of redemption. When struck by the "news flush," he somehow realizes that his life is without meaning because he has "nothing to show" for his years on earth. He has produced nothing of enduring value. He rejects Marge's suggestion that he has already "accomplished" making her and the kids "very happy"; this in and of itself is not enough for him. Therefore, he eventually decides to do something *really* important: to invent things people need. He will redeem his life by selling the fruits of his creativity on the market.

To "redeem" literally means to "buy back." In English, it has a rich biblical heritage. In the Hebrew Scriptures, it refers to God's buying back the people of Israel from slavery in Egypt and exile in Babylon. In Christian writings, redemption refers to the act of God that, through the death and resurrection of Jesus Christ, purchases fallen humanity from bondage to the forces of sin and alienation: "[W]e have redemption through his blood, the forgiveness of our trespasses, according to the riches of his grace" (Eph. 1:7). Thus, in the Judeo-Christian tradition, God purchases men and women from whatever forces interfere with the ideal divine-human relationship of mutual love, trust, and dynamic creativity. These forces are the root of the reality of sin, the engrained human propensity to become alienated from God.

In the Bible, redemption is an act of God. It involves a movement of divine grace (or acceptance), which does not deny the reality of sin or the necessity of judgment. For Homer, however, the search for redemption requires his own initiative. It will come, he hopes, from the development of his own creative capacities, which will earn him both money and reputation. Homer seeks to "buy back" meaning in his life by making a huge financial profit from his inventions, to "buy back" his public reputation and sense of self-worth. This attitude reflects the high value that American culture places on the individual and on individual achievement, initiative, and inventiveness. The paragon of this virtue is Thomas Edison, who invented so many useful (and profitable) things, seemingly all on his own. In this light, it is not surprising that Homer's hope for redemption follows a path set by a hero of his culture.

Such a path, however, also leads Homer to failure, to alienation from his family, and to despair. He is set up to fail because he is not capable of "being Thomas Edison." But who is? Certainly not the real (rather than the mythical) Thomas Edison himself, whose inventiveness was helped by hundreds of lab assistants and financial backers over the years. The real Homer, rather than the idealized "inventor" of his imagination, is not a "creative" person in this sense; thus his ill-conceived plan to imitate Edison is doomed. Worse than that, it leads him to engage in some of the worst forms of sin: greed, cruelty, and paranoia. The lesson, it seems, is that life cannot be "bought back" by becoming something one is not, even if this means denying the cultural value of individual achievement in the marketplace.

How can we achieve redemption? Ironically, the message of the episode, and of the series as a whole, is that redemption (to the extent that it occurs) indeed *does* involve an act of grace. Such grace may not be a gift from a divine being, in the Judeo-Christian sense, but in the world of *The Simpsons* grace is nonetheless an ever-present reality. Its locus is within the family unit itself. It is the family that always accepts its members back into the fold. In particular, Marge Simpson suffers a great deal of abuse and stress to support her brood and her spouse. In this, she is something of a "Christ figure" in the context of the show. She gives of herself, dying a thousand deaths in terms of realizing her full potential, to make a home where family members find unconditional acceptance. She is no fool: She understands that she is victimized and gives her guttural growl of protest. Yet she always serves as the soul of graciousness at the heart of the family structure.

In the end, when Homer's self-centered search for redemption ends in ignoble enthronement on a toilet, his family still surrounds him. They accept him as he is, not as society expects him to be. They are the source of grace in his life, the true path of redemption and meaning. Thus, his cruel statement of defeat—"I guess I'll have to give up my hopes and dreams and settle for being a decent husband and father"—ironically is both more truthful and hopeful than he thinks. His ultimate act of creativity lies in helping to create his family, both as procreator and nurturer. Authentic creativity is an act of love, not of competition or greed. The theme is articulated over and over again in the Bible, as well as in the cartoon world of *The Simpsons*.

Although many people might hesitate to label the show "pro-family," the analysis of this episode shows, at its heart, an affirmation of the family. The satirical tenor of the series may seem cynical, but there is still a great deal of hope in each episode. Because the cartoon characters never age, there is always the implied hope that, given a social transformation, things can change for the better in an ill-defined future. In the meantime, there is always the family to keep individuals going in a dehumanizing society. The family itself may be a target of satire; yet, as McConnell puts it, the genius of *The Simpsons* is that it "deconstructs the myth of the happy family, but wisely and miraculously leaves what is real and valuable about the myth unscathed."[16] In a world where individuals are constantly put "in their place," the family is the center of meaning in life. Thus, the family serves as a sort of divine presence, accepting each person as he or she truly is. This may be the ultimate significance of *The Simpsons* as a satire of contemporary American society.

THREE

Moesha

HIP-HOP FAMILY VALUES

Dang, Mo. You got more men than Wu Tang!

—*Niecy*

Episode 110:
"You Say He's Just a Friend"

First Aired:
October 2, 2000

It was created by and for black Americans; it features a central character who is a minority teenage girl; it is a network success story—all of these things make *Moesha* refreshingly unique. What we see is not the stylized Huxtables of *Cosby* but a functioning family thriving in the hip-hop world of the black middle class. We are treated to pop vignettes as we watch Moesha and her family and friends seek solutions on their own cultural terms: answers drawn from their own unique place in the world.

In fall 1999, when the NAACP was blasting Hollywood for failing to hire, promote, and feature people of color on prime-time television, the makers of *Moesha* must have been shaking their heads in frustration. Since debuting on UPN in January 1996, this lighthearted situation comedy has been produced and written entirely by ethnic minorities, mostly African Americans. *Moesha* stars Grammy award-winning pop singer and Cover Girl model Brandy and portrays the trials and tribulations of life as a young adult in a black, middle-class, Southern California environment. While this show will live on in syndication, its network announced in the spring of 2001 that it had been cancelled.

  Moesha is the creation of Ralph Farquhar, Sara V. Finney, and Vida Spears; Farquhar is best known for writing the screenplay *Krush Groove*, a major motion picture released in 1985 (many times referred to as the best break-dancing film ever made). Farquhar also spent many years as a supervising producer on the Fox hit *Married, with Children* and, along with Michael Weithorn, created the short-lived but critically acclaimed Fox dramedy, *South Central*. During its run, *Moesha* ranked consistently in the top 100 among viewers of prime-time shows and was the ninth most popular television show among blacks in the United States in early 2001. *Moesha* regularly commanded an audience of over three million people and was the sixth most popular show with adults eighteen to forty-nine in its heyday.[1] *Detroit News* television critic Michael McWilliams calls it "fervently upbeat, like a Gidget retread lined with guests from Ricki Lake,"[2] and *Entertainment Weekly* says, "*Moesha* sets a new standard for kid-friendly family entertainment."[3]

In this chapter, we apply the five analytical lenses to an episode from *Moesha's* sixth season, paying special attention to the role the show plays both in the lives of those who watch and interpret it and in the entertainment industry, as an example of a marketable show that successfully reaches out to young African Americans. In addition, we discuss how the narrative in this episode touches on the spiritual discipline of discernment—the art of choosing well when faced with ambiguous situations.

Episode Synopsis

As Moesha (Brandy Norwood) and Jamal (Bernard Stephens), her study partner at the fictional California University, tackle their economics homework, they begin to talk about their respective "long-distance relationships." Moesha's boyfriend, a rapper named Quentin but better known as Q, is on tour in Australia, and Jamal's girlfriend is at college somewhere "down south." A few scenes later, before another study session, Moesha dresses in tight-fitting, silky pants and a backless blouse, prompting her ex-boyfriend and longtime buddy Hakeem (Lamont Bentley) and her roommate Niecy (Shar Jackson) to remark that she has more than "studying" on her mind.

Moesha denies that her dress is inappropriate and goes to Jamal's apartment to study and watch videos. Jamal starts to flirt with her, but Moesha rebuffs his advances. After watching videos, they fall asleep side by side on his couch, and Moesha returns home the next morning. There she finds a perturbed Niecy, who has spent the evening fielding phone calls from Q. Niecy tells Moesha that if she really loves Q, then "love

should have brought you home last night." After Moesha receives a gift from Q in the mail and a video from yet another suitor, she realizes it is time to make a choice. To clear things up, she pays Jamal a visit to emphasize that they are just friends, surprising him and his visiting girlfriend. (As it turns out, Jamal considers the relationship long distance because the friend lives forty minutes south of Los Angeles and has a different area code.) Moesha allows Jamal to humiliate her in order to make things right with his girl-friend, then heads home to make a video for Q. She tells Q that she regrets missing all his phone calls because "a lot's been going on around here, but it's all O.K. now." On the tape, she says she loves him and no one else.

At Moesha's family's home, her little brother Myles (Marcus T. Paulk) needs a haircut, and their father Frank Mitchell (William Allen Young) wants to take him across town to an inexpensive barbershop. Dorian (Ray J), Frank's son and half-brother of Myles and Moesha, convinces Frank that he can cut Myles' hair for free because he learned to cut hair while in "boot camp" for car theft. When Frank considers the savings, he agrees and even gets excited at the thought of Dorian's turning a skill he learned at boot camp into a possible vocation. Dorian also becomes enthu-siastic about the thought of "legit" money and jumps ahead to printing out flyers promoting "D-Money's Barber Shop." In no time, Dorian's boot camp buddies are over at Frank's house, making themselves at home. Frank walks in to find his house is now a neighborhood barber shop and gets angry with Dorian, calling his friends "boot camp thugs." Dorian accuses his father of employing a double standard, treating Myles's and Moesha's friends with more respect than his friends. Frank shuts down Dorian's business, leaving Dorian to wonder where he went wrong as a new entrepreneur.

Functions

Moesha is the first successful network series in television history to revolve around a minority teenaged girl.[4] As such, it has changed the face of network television and has shown that giving such characters a strong and empowered voice can pay off. One fifteen-year-old, posting a review of *Moesha* on a website devoted to teen girls (www.smartgirl.com), says she watches because the plots "focus on serious, realistic issues without being too dramatic—the show almost always makes me laugh."[5] This response emphasizes what makes *Moesha* different from *Seinfeld* or *The Simpsons:* Although all three shows provide individual pleasure for the viewer by making him or her laugh, *Moesha* goes a step further and pro-vides a network-level platform for discussion of serious issues facing black teenagers, a demographic group that was all but ignored on televi-sion before *Moesha* aired.

In fact, all black demographics were ignored on the three big networks in the late 90s when *Moesha* first aired. To find shows produced and writ-ten by African Americans, one had to visit what broadcasting insiders call the "netlets"—Fox, UPN, and WB—which were cashing in on what advertisers had just discovered: that "African Americans spend more leisure income and watch more TV than other racial groups—an average of 40 percent more throughout the day."[6] What do they prefer to watch? Research by TN Media shows that "blacks are more likely to tune into shows that have black casts or lead characters."[7]

Television history is littered with stories of valiant attempts to capture authentic African-American life (without reducing it to what *Newsweek* calls "low-end slapstick," referring to shows like *The Jeffersons, Homeboys from Outerspace,* or *Martin*).[8] Frank Reid, the African-American star of *WKRP in Cincinnati* and creator of the 1987 CBS dramedy *Frank's Place,* took the failure of his dramedy particularly hard. In the aftermath of that experience, Reid has become Hollywood's toughest critic of racial issues, calling the television industry "one of the most segregated industries in America today."[9] Another show that had potential but did not last was Farquhar's *South Central,* a dramedy about life in a low-income urban neighborhood. Farquhar created it for CBS; but, after viewing the pilot, that network passed on it, allowing Fox to pick it up in 1994; it lasted less than a season. Farquhar speaks candidly about his choice to soften up the content of *Moesha* after his experience with *South Central,* a show he calls his most "startling and uncompromising."

> *Moesha* is different from a woman losing her job
> and her son going out and getting money from a
> dope dealer. It's not to say that middle-class kids
> don't have problems. Just that . . . *South Central* had
> an air of gloom. With *Moesha,* we've chosen not to
> go for the grittier side.[10]

Moesha may be a light comedy portraying the good life for middle-class African Americans, but it is not *The Cosby Show;* it contains no subtext designed to make white Americans feel better about black teens, and although *Cosby* sought to fit in with the status quo and be attractive to mainstream white audiences, *Moesha* is unabashedly created for black audiences. In fact, *Moesha* is so geared to the hip-hop audience that those out of touch with that culture need a translator to understand many of the characters' references. It is this aspect of *Moesha* that some non-African-American viewers appreciate. Watching the show gives them access to a culture that is alluringly different from their own, providing an education in African-American youth experiences. *Moesha* achieves Afrocentrism, however, without making the black experience seem sacred or untouchable. Moesha and friends have been known to poke fun at rap star Coolio, the Wayans brothers (a comedy team of brothers with a competing sitcom), and a former boyfriend who once told Moesha his African name, Ohaji, meant "conquering warrior."[11]

In further contrast to *The Cosby Show*, the family featured on *Moesha* is much less wealthy (although from the sets used for Moesha's family home we could hardly tell) than the Huxtables. The father works as a Saturn dealer, and the stepmother is a teacher.[12] Moesha attends a local state university, not an expensive private black college. Her half-brother Dorian runs with a rough crowd and has been arrested for stealing a car, something we cannot imagine Theo doing on *Cosby*. *Moesha* does pay homage to *Cosby* in that it explores the life of a loving, successful family who happens to be black. There is a commitment to the ordinary. There are no outrageous situations or outlandish behavior on the part of anyone in Moesha's immediate family (except perhaps Myles, who is after all a preteen boy and is expected to be somewhat out of step). For example, although Brandy is a pop-singing superstar, Moesha is tone deaf and does not sing on the show. All of the over-the-top characters are friends and guests who wander in and out of the Mitchells' life, such as—in this episode—Dorian's boot camp buddies.

One teen fan of the show says she especially appreciates Moesha's relationships with her father and stepmother. This portrayal of a strong family is precisely why *Moesha* won the 1996 Parents' Choice Silver Honor and was showcased with a salute by the Museum of Television and Radio during the sixteenth annual William S. Paley Television Festival in 1999. *Moesha* is the kind of show children can feel comfortable watching with their parents. There is a lot of youthful insider language, and some discussion of sexuality, but there is also a playful, relaxed tone. Moesha and her brothers generally show respect for their elders and eventually (after some fussing) do the right thing, which makes the show attractive and marketable to older viewers as well as young.

Moesha took on an additional function as of the 2000–2001 season. Although remaining a situation comedy, it evolved into a romantic soap opera, with stories that developed over several episodes. For example, in the episode we are considering, we are left with lingering questions about Moesha's relationship with Q. She says she loves only him, yet we see her smile with interest as Khalib (Ginuwine) tells her, in the video he mailed to her, that he wants to see her during the Thanksgiving holiday. Brandy tells *TV Guide* that this new "soap opera" element allows the show to focus on all the ups and downs of romantic love for young people.[13]

Structure

Moesha is a comedy that highlights and defends middle-class African-American family life in the United States. The dominant message behind this series is that positive, healthy family values thrive in the hip-hop world of the African-American middle class. "We like to say stuff," says Farquhar, "but we're not preachy about it."[14] In the episode we are considering, the dominant message is that responsible relationships require discernment in the family and community, and that we need the wisdom of others to help us make careful choices.

With a stable and reliable father, an intelligent and independent working mother, and two well-adjusted children, *Moesha* could almost be a new-century *Father Knows Best*. The addition of Dorian forces the family to cope with some elements of African-American life that too often make the news, because "D-Money" has a criminal record. Dorian ran away from his Oakland home to hide at the Mitchells' house in Leimert Park, a middle-class black suburb of Los Angeles. In a plot development that some viewers found shocking, Moesha and Myles found out the truth about Dorian in the 1999 season: He is not their cousin (as they grew up believing), but is actually Frank's son by another woman. This discovery causes some distress; however, within weeks Dorian is taken into the Mitchell fold and becomes a respectable, albeit somewhat marginalized, member of the family, driving his uptight, middle-aged father to distraction. Frank's discomfort with having a child full of surprises (as in D-Money's home barbershop) whom he cannot always depend on creates considerable tension in the series.

In one respect, *Moesha* has a touch of parable to it, challenging the standard Eurocentric narrative typical of situation comedies. In this world, African Americans are empowered, intelligent, lively, and self-supporting. We are about as likely to see a plot about the upscale, white, yuppie world of *Friends* on *Moesha* as to see Brandy replace a major character on *Friends*. *Moesha*'s world is not contemptuous of white America, but does not need its acceptance, which is refreshingly new for television.

There is a lot of satire in *Moesha*. In "You Say He's Just a Friend," Moesha's friend Niecy gets some of the biggest laughs when she uses sarcasm and sassing to pull Moesha into line. When Niecy wants to make the point that she cannot keep lying to Q about where Moesha is (because she is with her handsome study partner), she tells Moesha: "You got me lyin' more than Halle Berry in traffic court," comparing Moesha to the famous black actress who was accused in February 2000 of leaving the scene of an auto accident in West Hollywood. Niecy implies that this time Moesha has gone too far. Niecy also pokes fun at Moesha's attraction to rap musicians: "Dang, Mo. You got more men than Wu Tang (a six-member Staten Island-based rap group)."

Narrative

Being a soap-opera style romantic comedy, *Moesha* has an extensive background story that precedes the episode under consideration here. Moesha attends the fictional California University in Los Angeles and now lives on campus after living at home until season five. She returned to school after her boyfriend, Q, tried to get her to drop out and accompany him on tour with his rap group. Q (who does not appear in this episode) is one of Moesha's on-again, off-again love relationships that heated up at the end of the 1999 season.

In the Mitchell home, Dorian is still adjusting to life outside boot camp (a juvenile detention program featuring military-style rehabilitation) and to the fact that his Uncle Frank is really his biological father. Dorian has become a big brother to Myles, although Myles often shows more common sense than Dorian. Myles floats through life at the Mitchell house as many youngest children do—with an easygoing style, positive attitude, and a witticism for all occasions. Frank must make many adjustments in the 2000 season. His wife Dee (who does not appear in the episode we are discussing) has taken an educational consulting job in Jamaica, leaving him at home to raise the two boys while he continues to run his Saturn dealership.

"You Say He's Just a Friend" focuses on Moesha's attempt to stay true to Q in the face of her loneliness and attraction to other men. Motivated by a desire to have fun at the university, Moesha "hangs out" with her tall, brawny, and handsome study partner Jamal, who is the physical opposite of the short, wiry, bald Q. Jamal seems attracted to Moesha, even though he admits to being in a long-distance relationship; by suggesting that the two of them watch the film "Love the One You're With," Jamal hints that his philosophy on "long-distance relationships" might differ from Moesha's. Jamal then becomes the seductive antagonist (although a sympathetic and attractive one) to Moesha. Moesha's major issue in this episode, her fidelity to Q, is resolved when she is made aware of her own "creeping around," thanks to her friends Hakeem and Niecy, and decides she wants to make clear to everyone that she is devoted to Q.

Dorian's dilemma (the secondary story in the episode) centers around his enthusiasm for the haircutting skill he picked up in boot camp. Without bothering to ask his father's permission to use the house, Dorian launches into "D-Money's Barber Shop," based in the beloved Mitchell kitchen. His first customers are friends of the family, like Hakeem, but he quickly invites his boot camp buddies Dirt, Bullet, Jake, and friends, to his home for cuts. When Frank finds young former criminals in his home, he argues with Dorian for taking such bold initiative; Frank makes it "crystal clear" to Dorian that he cannot cut hair in Frank's house. Dorian is the protagonist in this story line, and Frank appears as the antagonist, thwarting Dorian's attempt to become responsible. Frank's motivation is from the heart: He is only trying to protect his home and family from young men he perceives to be a threat. He does not see the elitism in his stance, but to Dorian it is "crystal clear."

Frank uses his parental authority to teach Dorian a lesson about balancing his enthusiasm for running his own business with common sense—there's a time and place for everything, and the Mitchell family kitchen is not the place for "D-Money's Barber Shop." Left open is the question of whether Frank would support Dorian cutting hair in the garage or perhaps at the local community center. Because of time constraints, a show like *Moesha* cannot attend to all the questions brought up in an episode like this one, which leaves us hanging. We wonder whether Frank rejects Dorian's business because he wants a more upwardly mobile career for his son or just because he does not want strangers getting their hair cut in his house.

The Dorian haircutting story brings up the larger question of the use of stereotypes in *Moesha*. Some viewers of this episode may find the depiction of Dorian's boot camp friends too broad for their tastes. One young viewer told us she thought the episode made Dorian's friends look unrealistic, ridiculous, and offensive. She bristled at their jokes about "coming back and robbing" Dorian if he got too successful and at a remark about a girl who had "the cutest little bullet hole in her left thigh." In a situation comedy, certain characters are drawn just for laughs, but in this case, the viewer felt that these young people were made to look like violent criminals when, in fact, many young people do make mistakes, pay for their crimes, and then go on to live respectable lives. Dorian's friends are depicted as fools, using exaggerated body language, mispronouncing words, and making light of serious situations. Yet because they are Dorian's friends, and Dorian is such a likable character, they have a lighthearted air; their jokes are meant to be tossed off as silly remarks that make Dorian look smarter. Somehow, though, these casual jokes about bullet wounds come off as disrespectful to young black men from lower-class neighborhoods, a social class that gets no respect on television these days. Even though he is on the show to bring an "edge" to it, Dorian's character is much less offensive because he is not one-dimensional like the so-called thugs who surround him.

Power

The power elites in the entertainment industry are slow to recognize and embrace diversity. African Americans who wanted to be seen and heard in television in the 90s repeatedly had to approach the newer networks (UPN, WB, and Fox) after the powerful Big Three turned down their ideas. Some shows, like UPN's *The Hughleys*, began on a Big Three network only to find new life, as well as more artistic freedom, at a netlet. During the last few years, UPN has made an effort to stay on the edge, not only continuing its "urban-leaning" programming on Monday nights but also reaching out to generation-X men, demographics it feels are underserved, with shows like World Wrestling Federation *Smackdown!*[15]

Although not a top-ten show in the overall rankings, *Moesha* managed to capture a respectable share on television. During its run, the show had an excellent placement, airing at the start of prime time on Mondays. *Variety* reports that "Monday zoomed ahead last year [1999] to consistently rate as the night more Americans are planting themselves in front of the tube—making it an even more important battleground for the nets."[16] Also, *Moesha* was followed by *The Parkers*, a *Moesha* spin-off that has become the number one television show in black households.[17] (As mentioned earlier, *Moesha* ranked number nine among black viewers in 2000.) In addition, *Moesha* has been sold into syndication by Paramount Domestic Television, giving African Heritage Network the right to barter sales to national advertisers. With all these advantages, the show could *not* be unattractive to advertisers, especially those who want to reach its core audience of African-American teenagers.

Most plots on *Moesha* are concerned with the everyday issues facing young adults and their social systems: family, friends, school, and jobs. Now and then, these story lines bring up larger sociopolitical ideologies at work in American society. In "You Say He's Just a Friend," Moesha experiences not just the usual tension caused by a long-distance relationship, but also the greater tension faced by young people who choose to pursue a college education when so many forces pull them away. At the end of the 1999 season, Moesha told Q she was going to stay in school rather than work as a manager for his rap act. In the African-American community, there is a strong trend (personified in *Moesha* by Frank and Dee) to encourage young people to stay in school and prepare for a career that can be competitive in the marketplace. Working against this trend is the allure of high-paying, glamorous fields such as sports and entertainment. The episode tells us that staying in school when one's fiance is a touring rapper may be difficult, but the strong, like Moesha, can survive and be better off for it.

In Moesha's story, power resides in the one who is most persuasive, which, in this case, is her best friend and roommate, Niecy. She helps Moesha see that time spent with Jamal, her study partner, may not be as innocent as Moesha claims. Hakeem also tries to enlighten Moesha about her own intentions, but is less effective. He points out that Moesha's choice of a backless shirt for a study date may send the wrong signals, but Moesha dismisses his concern. Niecy persuades Moesha to make a choice: If she loves Q, she will spend less time with Jamal. After hearing that from Niecy, Moesha takes steps to end the flirtation.

The ideology at work in Dorian's haircutting story line is more complex and troublesome. As mentioned, some viewers were offended by the portrayal of the young boot camp graduates as criminals who were not very bright. This story brings up the greater social question: Have we abandoned our at-risk young black men? Do we believe rehabilitation efforts like boot camp really work? Are we, as a society, going to treat young people who make mistakes in the same way Frank treats Dorian's friends—with suspicion and fear? If we do, what are the consequences of that rising fear?

The class issue of how an upwardly mobile middle-class African-American man (Frank) views streetwise at-risk young black males (Dorian and his boot camp friends) is paramount in this episode. In one scene, Frank is in his kitchen, surrounded by Dorian's friends, who tease him:

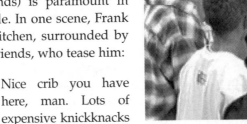

Dirt: Nice crib you have here, man. Lots of expensive knickknacks and what-not.

Jake: Oh, man. You think this is nice? You should see what they got upstairs.

Frank: Dorian—Your friends are gonna have to leave!

Frank: [articulates his fear to Dorian after his friends leave the house] You had a bunch of strangers in my house. Who knows what those boot camp thugs were doing upstairs?

By labeling Dorian's friends "thugs" (painting Dorian with the same brush), Frank lets his classism show. Dorian realizes he has been branded.

Dorian: Oh, I see the real problem.

Frank: Oh, do you? What is it?

Dorian: You don't think my friends are good enough to be in the house. I bet you wouldn't trip if Mo or Myles' friends went upstairs.

Frank: They don't have any friends named Bullet.

Dorian lives between the smart, financially sound, upstanding world of Frank, Moesha, and Myles and the harsh world of street gangs and school dropouts. In the dialogue and acting, we can detect how the producers of this show probably relate to boot camp graduates. Frank, Myles, and Moesha are polished, somewhat sophisticated, and urbane (much like the creators of the show). Dirt, Bullet, and Jake are made to look stupid, silly, and criminal. When Dirt jokes that if Dorian continues to be successful at cutting hair, he might have to come back and rob him, Jake reassures Myles that this remark was just a joke because they are "re-*hab*-ilitated." Jake cannot even pronounce "rehabilitated," which makes us think he has not completed the process. Putting the boot camp boys out of his house, Frank is hoping to rid his family of the influence of the streets. No doubt the influence of gangs and street criminals on middle-class African-American neighborhoods is a serious issue, as it is in neighborhoods of all ethnic varieties in the United States; however, in a show as important to the black community as *Moesha*, one hopes for a more sensitive depiction of young men who have gone through rehabilitation programs like boot camp.

The power in Dorian's story lies not with Dorian (his business is shut down), but with Frank, who uses his parental authority to clamp down on Dorian's attempt at financial independence. At the end of the episode, Dorian tells Frank, "I can't wait 'til I'm 18 and can move on out of here," a refrain heard by parents everywhere. In the end, Frank reaffirms his control, and Dorian resigns himself to following orders. Although parents can relate to Frank's "tough love" attitude, a sadness emerges in the story as we watch Dorian's enthusiasm for haircutting squelched. Frank uses his power autocratically, with no opportunity for negotiation or compromise.

Race, gender, and socioeconomic class play key roles in *Moesha*, although this episode focuses mostly on gender and class conflicts. Because the context is an all-black environment, race at first appears not much of an issue. (Many other episodes of *Moesha* do make clear statements about racism and its effects on society.) Of course, for African Americans, race is always an issue. As Dr. Daniel Collins, the founder of the Bay Area Urban League says:

> Being a black person, you live with white people on your mind 24 hours a day. I have to figure out where I fit into an environment, and white people don't because they own the environment. It keeps my consciousness on razor's edge all the time.[18]

Because the entire worldview of this show—a young woman's life in a middle-class African-American household—is itself a radical statement about the status of both blacks and women, *Moesha* makes a strong statement that Afrocentrism in the entertainment world is both necessary and healthy. Perhaps when race is not part of *Moesha's* story line, such as in this episode, the producers imply the point that some issues, like gender and class, transcend race.

Moesha is nationally recognized as a sitcom that treats sexuality with openness and honesty. In October 2000, *Moesha* won a SHINE (Sexual Health in Entertainment) award for its portrayal of family planning, sexuality, and reproductive health issues.[19] Parents of young children might want to watch the show with them, simply to be on hand to explain some of the situations. *Moesha* places extramarital sex in a positive and nonjudgmental light; parents who want to teach a different view of sex need to be aware of this.

Although the character of Moesha certainly controls her own sexuality, males do not necessarily appear in the most positive light in this episode—they are reduced to pursuers and seducers of women. Moesha acts naive about Jamal's fairly obvious advances. She acts and dresses in a flirtatious manner and appears to enjoy her effect on Jamal, Hakeem, and Khalib (the three suitors on this episode). Moesha needs her friends to enlighten her about her naïveté, so that finally Moesha regains control, deciding that she prefers to give up Jamal rather than lose Q. Jamal's reaction to her decision is feigned innocence. Before his girlfriend, Jamal claims he had no designs on Moesha (even pretending to forget her name at one point). As Moesha loses her naïveté, Jamal seems to develop his, a depiction that stereotypes young men as duplicitous when it comes to sex.

Dorian's barbershop story line also includes dialogue about sex. The boot camp boys are looking at what appears to be a girlie magazine and talking about which women they would "get with" if they could. Myles, a curious fourteen-year-old, enters the room and wants to take a look, and they debate whether he is old enough to see the pictures. Dorian decides he is not, but Myles learns that gazing at pictures of nude women is a privilege a male acquires as he grows older.

Not to be outdone by the boot camp boys, Niecy also enjoys a copy of *Hunks* magazine, which is in keeping with her sexually assertive personality. In a comic interlude, giving her the opportunity to field yet another phone call from Q while Moesha spends time with Jamal, Niecy caresses and talks to the magazine while giving herself a facial. When Moesha tiptoes in at 7:00 A.M. after falling asleep at Jamal's apartment, Niecy gleefully assumes they "got butt naked, covered in honey, making the mattress pop a wheelie!" Her facial expression and body language indicate her vicarious approval of the idea, although Moesha assures her that "nothing happened."

Signs and Codes

Moesha is not particularly subtle in its use of signs and symbols to convey major messages. The dialogue usually perfectly matches the visual cues. During the opening song, performed by Brandy (the only time Brandy sings on the show), we see a dancing Moesha singing about how she's "gotta move on." Her motions are fluid, graceful, and understated, just like her character. As the opening song begins, she is dressed in colors of the sunset, aqua and tangerine. Behind her is a moving photo montage of her co-stars. Later in the song, Moesha stands in front of what appears to be a lovely California sunset, and emanating from her arms and upper torso are rays of light. The message: Moesha is so bright and cheerful that she radiates light, a symbol of wisdom, understanding, and divinity.

Clothing and decor are always important in television shows for and about young people. Because she is usually a fairly conservative dresser, Moesha's backless shirt in this episode sends the message that she is now grown up, sexy, and available—a message that Hakeem and Niecy pick up immediately. The boot camp boys' baggy pants and loose shirts, knit caps, baseball caps turned backward, and designer sportswear are symbolic of urban youth. Baggy pants signify rebellion; oversized outfits drive parents like Frank crazy because they make no sense to them, and boys wear them for that very reason. Frank is noted for his tightly fitting three-piece suits and cannot help making fun of Dorian's pants "not fitting." Loose clothing is also sometimes worn by gang members to conceal weapons, although because so many young people have adopted the look as a fashion statement, it has lost much of its effect as "gang wear."

The decor of Moesha's university apartment provides a number of important visual clues that reinforce the upward mobility of Moesha's middle-class status. The spacious apartment looks well beyond the means of the average twenty-year-old college student; it has hardwood floors, a leather couch covered in sunset-hued pillows, an oversized plaid-covered chair, bay windows with seating, and a fireplace.

The actors in Moesha are adept at using body language to reinforce dialogue. When Hakeem urges Moesha to "cut off" her relationship with Jamal, he makes precise scissorslike gestures with his right hand as he says the words. As Niecy loses herself in the thought of Moesha and Jamal's "making the mattress pop a wheelie," she raises her arms into the air, sways back and forth, and looks toward heaven, as if cheering on her favorite sports team. When Moesha realizes Jamal is coming on to her, she frowns with disgust, pulls her hands away, moves to the opposite end of the couch, and puts a pillow between the two of them, signifying that she intends to keep her distance. Body language reinforcing verbal cues is part of what makes the messages in Moesha come across so loud and clear.

An important icon—a symbol that carries us beyond the material into the realm of beliefs and values—is the Mitchell family dinner table, situated in the foreground of the kitchen. The kitchen table is a staple in the family sitcom (think of Roseanne, The Cosby Show, and All in the Family) because it reminds us of all the gatherings around food that our families have experienced over the years. Bringing us to the kitchen table makes us feel that we are part of the television family. When Dorian starts cutting hair at the Mitchell family kitchen table, he creates chaos in the safe haven, making Frank's tirade somewhat more understandable. His statement that Dorian has invited a bunch of strangers into his home (made in full view of the kitchen table) may also mean, "You invited a bunch of strangers to my kitchen table—the central location for fellowship and nurturing in this household."

Theological Analysis

There is no way to produce a television show about African-American life without in some way touching on the influence of religious faith, and Moesha is no exception. Sometimes there is mention of church attendance on the show, and Brandy has publicly stated: "I think it's because of God that I am where I am today. And I think he's the cause of all of us being here. I don't ever want to forget about him."[20] However, as with most television shows, the theological messages of the show are muted and between-the-lines rather than overtly stated. When we cull theological messages from commercial television, we do not imply that the writers and producers intentionally place these messages in a show. We look for embedded theology—the practical belief system that emerges in the ethical behavior of the characters. Rarely do we find any reference to dogma or doctrine on commercial television. Instead, we find a theology that starts with the human experience, and if we believe humans are "offspring of God," the theology is incarnational. These theological conclusions arise from a combination of analysis and intuition—and they are not meant to be the last word on "the meaning of an episode."

With that in mind, "You Say He's Just a Friend" seems to center on the theme of discernment, a spiritual discipline used when we face choices that may not be clear-cut. More specifically, the show is a lesson in discerning within community. Neither Dorian nor Moesha makes a choice alone—they are helped by family and friends who care about them. The theological message here is: Life is full of choices. Choose deliberately and choose well. Allow those who care about you to share their wisdom on the choice.

Discernment is a multivalent term. Some people refer to the making of any decision as discernment. The Jesuits, however, teach a form of discernment that is involved and technical, based on spiritual practices promoted by Ignatius of Loyola almost 500 years ago. Pierre Wolf, in *Discernment: The Art of Choosing Well*, says

> Discernment is the process of making choices that correspond as closely as possible to objective reality, that are as free as possible from our inner compulsions, and that are closely attuned to the convictions of our faith (or to our value system, if we have no religious belief).[21]

When a Jesuit speaks of a "discernment process," he does not refer to casual decision making, but instead to discovering what "spirit" or motivation is at work within a person (and within systems) and then choosing to follow the "spirit" that produces the most freedom, joy, kindness, and compassion in the world. A person might spend a month or so in retreat "discerning" between several choices that seem good when only one is best. We speak of "discerning" the right choice in this episode of *Moesha*, but it is clear that neither Moesha nor Dorian uses any formal pattern of discernment. Instead, they are discerning in the way that most of us are on a daily basis: evaluating our choices, listening to our hearts, listening to our friends, and then making a decision, hoping for the best.

To begin with Dorian's choice, coerced as it is, Dorian seeks financial freedom and independence through starting his own haircutting business, which conflicts with his father's desire to teach him responsibility. Dorian's choice to cut his friends' hair in the Mitchell family home seems like a good idea at first, but when Frank comes home, a "spirit" of fear emerges in him and he refuses to accept Dorian's business. Dorian has not thought through the consequences of his actions, and he fails to get permission to use the family kitchen in such a manner. Frank, using his parental authority, helps (coerces) Dorian to decide that now is not the time to start a haircutting business. Dorian probably feels he has no choice at this point, but he indicates at the end of the episode that he is resigned to accepting his father's choice (no business) by making a joke at Frank's expense: "Afros went out in the 80's!" This lighthearted ribbing after Frank takes him to task shows that Dorian will weather this storm with a good attitude. In his heart, he has agreed to abide by his father's house rules—even though he knows his father acted out of fear and elitism. Dorian discerns that he will live by the rules, even if it means giving up his newfound business. He sacrifices his dream for the good of the family.

Moesha's discernment is not at all coerced. She is already leaning in the direction of emotional fidelity to Q when Niecy helps her realize she must stop seeing so much of Jamal. Niecy's motivation is not entirely selfless; she has spent enough time fielding Q's phone calls and lying on Moesha's behalf, and she wants some resolution. Niecy's sense of sexual ethics enlightens Moesha and leads her to discern faithfully. Before Niecy's intervention, Moesha's attraction to Jamal seems unintentional, as if she does not understand that she is susceptible to his charms. After spending the night at his house, she realizes—with Niecy's help—that she is in over her head. Moesha finally follows her heart and declares her love for Q. We know she has done the right thing (at least for now) because we see joy in her face and hear warmth in her voice, indicating the confidence that comes with resolution.

When speaking about discernment, teachers in the Christian faith often point to Romans 12:2: "Do not be conformed to this world, but be transformed by the renewing of your minds, so that you may discern what is the will of God—what is good and acceptable and perfect." In any discussion of discernment, the question "How do we know what God's will is?" always comes up. The most honest answer is usually "We do not." We have no clear-cut, easy way to discover God's desire for us in any given situation, but we do have clues. We can test our choices by the "fruit of the Spirit" (Gal. 5:22–23): "love, joy, peace, patience, kindness, generosity, faithfulness, gentleness, and self-control." If we look at Moesha and Dorian's dilemmas in light of that list, we see that Dorian's choice exhibits (in the end) self-control, and Moesha's choice is based on love and faithfulness. Dorian even exemplifies generosity when he points out Frank's intolerance of the boot camp boys. Not all of our choices involve sweetness and light, and Dorian is generous in explaining to Frank that he shows prejudice against strangers when he refers to the boys as "thugs." Frank is simply not in a position to experience this as a gift.

Discernment is never done alone. Like Moesha and Dorian, we are all members of various groups: family, church, school, workplace, and society. Every decision we make affects the lives of persons in those social systems. Every time we assist another person in discerning the road that leads to spiritual freedom, we participate in God's movement in the world. Imagine a world where we graciously accept the wisdom of elders now and then, as Dorian does in this episode, or cherish the times our friends speak the truth in love to us, as Niecy does with Moesha. Our lives would not be as neat and clean as the sitcom world of *Moesha*, but we might discover considerably more freedom than we ever expected.

FOUR

Will & Grace

CHANGING SOCIAL VALUES

Why don't you just dress me up in fishnet stockings and thigh-high boots!?

—*Will*

You'd do that?

—*Grace*

Episode:
"Saving Grace"

First aired:
April 29, 1999

A straight woman and a gay man are roommates with characters of every persuasion on either side of them. We are presented with a wide range of sexual identities, gentled by humor that allows us to struggle with our own stereotypes. We are encouraged to exercise our will to see new ways of relating and offered the grace to laugh not only at them but at ourselves.

The Shot and Scene

Grace is on her knees before Will. She holds his hands and at one point puts his hands up to her face. Will is turned so that he does not face Grace directly, and the arm of the hand she holds is limp. Disgust, or perhaps just frustration, crosses Will's face. Grace as the supplicant takes a posture with Will that we all recognize. The bent knee, the imploring face elicit from us recognition of an intimate moment between lovers. When we look again, however, we realize that this version of the sign, the bent knee of supplication, does not fit our understanding of cultural codes. This posture reminds us of the classic marriage proposal, but it is not Grace's plea to Will for matrimony. It *is* a request for a radical new step in their relationship; Grace does not proclaim her undying love for Will, but instead asks him to prostitute himself. She asks him to go on a second date (and possibly a third) with Nathan Berry, a famous publicist who is also arrogant, obnoxious, and sought after by Grace as a client. The first date between Will and Nathan ended disastrously, with Will grateful that he will not have to encounter Nathan again. Then Grace strikes in this scene.

This shot seems to indicate that Grace is at the mercy of Will, beseeching him to have pity on her unfortunate circumstances, and at a superficial level, she is. She has seen how Nathan responds to her colleague Karen's wealth and prestige. She has seen how Nathan responds to Will's attractiveness. She has seen how Nathan disregards her presence, to the extent of insulting her when she offers him a drink: "Oh God no. I'm having drinks with *friends*." She senses she has little power in seeking Nathan as a client; she is at the mercy of Will's generosity to make her professional success possible.

Yet, as Grace asks Will to help her once more in her quest for Nathan's business, she holds power over him. She chooses to put her own needs first in their relationship. Her power in this situation comes from the tacit acknowledgment that both characters value the prestige and financial success that Nathan's business would bring; Will and Grace both buy the ideology of success; Will is caught in a dilemma between his commitment to his own integrity and the power of his friendship with Grace. The story reinforces the American cultural ideals of success and the behavior and values acceptable in reaching it. The myth of the American ideal is reinforced, applauded, and perhaps even defended (as in apologue) through ironic humor.

What is the effect of such a benign shot, an apparent sign of professed love, in its initial presentation? We laugh. We assume the role the directors have planned for us and laugh at Will and Grace's antics. Grace begs Will to make one additional date and then adds the possibility of a third. Will is appalled at her audacity and insensitivity. He asks her in a raised voice, "My God, Grace, why don't you dress me up in fishnet stockings and thigh-high boots?" The audience is given a split second to reflect on the comic visual image of Will thus attired as well as the profundity of Will's implicit accusation. Then Grace responds incredulously (camera shot close in on her face with wide-open eyes), "You'd do that?" And, we laugh. In many ways, this silly exaggeration is nothing more than entertainment. The audience's sympathy is caught, however, between Grace, who feels her own success is at the mercy of others, and Will, who feels Grace is stretching the bounds of their friendship too far. Never wanting us to think too long about these issues (for fear of losing the laugh), the director ends the scene. Will walks away, and Grace is left kneeling.

Using the five lenses of analysis on this show as we have on this one shot, we discover how this rather socially daring sitcom gently pushes the cultural envelope.

Narrative

Will and Grace, the two characters for whom the show is named, are best friends from college, who are both on the rebound from serious relationships. Will Truman (i.e., true man, played by Eric McCormack), is both openly gay and incredibly straitlaced. He is a gay man who "passes" for straight and is "about as queer as fresh milk."[1] His friend Jack McFarland (Sean Hayes) does not pass for straight and in fact offers the series a caricature through which to whimsically explore gay stereotypes. Grace Adler (played by Debra Messing) is straight. "Addled," from which "Adler" could be derived, means muddled or confused. Perhaps even more significantly, Alfred Adler was an Austrian psychiatrist who formulated the theory that feeling inferior causes an individual to change his or her behavior in an attempt to counteract this perceived inferiority. Grace, who is an interior designer, shows in this episode the degree to which she compensates for her insecurities and less-than-logical approach to life. Despite, or maybe because of, such compensations, Grace appears to be professionally successful. Her success is hardly due to her assistant, Karen Walker, who is useless in the office. Karen (Megan Mullally) is a New York socialite who admits that she married for money. She manages to spend her days at work filing her nails, browsing through fashion catalogs, and going to lunch. She is firm about not using the computer, fax machine, or photocopier; she barely operates the phone. We question Grace's judgment in hiring her, but Karen lends comic relief to Grace, who takes her professional identity very seriously. Just as the duo of Grace and Will carries the thrust of the social issues, Karen and Jack form a duo that makes a mockery of social and political controversies. For them, it appears that little is sacred or taboo.

Early in the first year of this series (produced by James Burrows, David Kohan, and Max Mutchnick), Will and Grace decide to live together, and Grace moves into Will's apartment. The show follows the further development of their relationship. Neither Will nor Grace is involved in a serious romantic relationship. Thus, the romantic tension of the series turns on their own relationship. We know that Will is gay, and yet we find ourselves hoping for a consummation between Will and Grace, which is likely never to happen. Though the relationship becomes ever more intimate, it remains unique for its striking absence of sex.

In this episode, Grace is desperate to capture Nathan Berry (played by Miguel Ferrer) as a client. The show begins as she leaves the apartment for an interview with him. She is clearly nervous, consulting with Will twice about her clothing and proceeding to leave wearing mismatched shoes. At Nathan's, we are introduced to his difficult personality. He has already sent one prospective designer away in tears and is about to dismiss Grace when he recognizes Karen, who belongs to his social circle and is not intimidated by his rudeness. Karen convinces Nathan to come to Grace's home to decide whether she deserves his business.

During his visit, Nathan meets Will. Clearly attracted, Nathan privately agrees with Grace to accept her as his designer if Will goes out with him. When Grace informs Will that she has volunteered him, he is furious at the thought of having to spend any more time with Nathan.

With assistance from Karen, Jack teases Will about his impending date. Will makes it clear that it is just one date, a favor for Grace. The evening is a disaster: Nathan is rude and pompous, and Will eventually cuts the evening short. When he arrives home, he finds what he expects, an upset Grace. He quickly learns that she is not disturbed about losing her client, but nervous about how Will may respond to the *second* date with

> Just as the duo of Grace and Will carries the thrust of the social issues, Karen and Jack form a duo that makes a mockery of social and political controversies.

Nathan, which she has arranged. Will is furious and refuses, despite Grace's pleading. (See earlier shot description.) The next day, Grace begins packing up her designs at Nathan's apartment in anticipation of losing his business. When Karen finally understands what is happening, she helps Grace see that Nathan hired her because she is a good designer, not because she knows Will. At that moment, Grace shows some self-confidence and indicates that she can function without Will's help.

In typical sitcom fashion, however, Will arrives at Nathan's as Grace makes this self-discovery and declares that he will help her. Immediately, Grace reels with relief, saying, "He would have fired my ass just as sure as I'm standing here." Will subverts Nathan's control by being overly effusive about his affection and his plans for their relationship. Nathan is instantly turned off, dismisses Will, but retains Grace as his designer. The episode ends with Will elated by his subterfuge; as he leaves the scene, he revels in how much Grace will appreciate his efforts.

In this episode, Grace stretches the limits of friendship, commitment develops, and we witness Grace's great dependence on Will. It is a fine illustration of the manner in which sexual orientation can be a plot device, source of humor, and impetus for character development.

Power

In this episode, the depth of Grace and Will's relationship is expressed in several clear yet understated ways. They are more than simply roommates as they dance on the thin line between friendship and romance. When Grace panics about wearing the right clothes and getting Nathan as a client, Will offers her a pep talk. Many of his lines are to be expected, but the scene has an overall familiarity and intimacy. When Jack points out that Will has just sent Grace off in mismatched shoes, Will dashes out the door to catch her. Jack laughs, but we accept how deeply Will cares. In another scene, Will returns home from his disastrous date with Nathan to find Grace sitting on the couch, clearly upset. Will infers that because of his rejection of Nathan earlier that evening Grace has lost her job. Grace assures him that her job is still intact, with *twice* the budget. Will hears this good news and sits down beside her. He notices that Grace is eating a Ding Dong. Because he knows her so well, he immediately knows the Ding Dong is a sign of something wrong. When confronted about the Ding Dong, Grace admits to setting Will up for a second date. Will is familiar with Grace's behavior and has cared enough about her to learn how to interpret it.

As titillation increasingly becomes the standard way to attract television viewers, sex has become the shorthand method of depicting intimacy. Of course, intimacy is rarely achieved because efforts at titillation override character and relationship development. *Will & Grace* goes beyond this pattern by depicting how Grace and Will grow closer throughout the season without ever sleeping together. In this way, the series challenges standard commercial practices, altering the status quo of market tactics—that part of culture that television so easily "manufactures"—and attempting to blur standard lines.

In addition to expanding television's depiction of intimacy, this series blurs the cultural distinctions between straight and gay. In a culture extremely preoccupied with sexual orientation, blurring these lines is a clever and bold plot maneuver. In one of the earliest episodes, Jack meets Karen for the first time in Grace's office. Having been previously informed of Jack's sexual orientation, the viewer is confused by his behavior and comments—he ogles Karen's lovely body and is impressed that her breasts were "not purchased." He finally convinces Karen to touch stomachs, and they both raise their shirts and touch flesh to flesh—something they clearly enjoy and are a bit embarrassed about afterward.

In the episode described in this chapter, Jack and Karen again blur the physical lines between gay and straight. Jack tries to teach Will the skill of visualization, "visual-eye-zation," as he terms it. He uses Karen as his model to show Will how he can kiss Karen by picturing her as James Vanderby from *Dawson's Creek*. Although Jack's point in this escapade is to show how he can kiss Karen without really kissing Karen, the physical contact and humor are there. After Jack and Will leave the office, Karen swoons from the kiss and collapses to the floor. From Karen's response, it appears that gay men can give women a good time. This scene reinforces stereotypes: that women are really whores who accept advances from anyone; that gay men are really heterosexuals who have not yet found the right woman. However, Jack and Karen play with such assumptions by using them to make a joke. Viewers laugh, and amid their laughter they can rethink their stereotypes.

Will & Grace portrays the diversity of gay life. Jack is undoubtedly a caricature of the gay man: His conversation is flamboyant; he is not interested in the mainstream Puritan work ethic; and he seems to have a new lover in every episode. Will is as reliable and steady as Jack is not. He is a successful lawyer who has just ended a seven-year relationship, and the breakup has left him out of sorts. Jack and Will act as foils for each other, and in that sense they are simply useful tools in driving the plot. The presence of both men on the show, however, portrays breadth and inclusiveness in the gay community.

In the same way, the humor of the series is egalitarian. In contrast to sitcoms of previous generations, *Will & Grace* offers humor *for* the gay community, rather than always at the expense of gay and lesbian people. As in the show *Ellen*, the gay and lesbian community gains voice in middle America when gay and lesbian characters speak for their own community and express life from a perspective that is something other than heterosexual. After Jack kisses Karen, he responds to Will's revulsion by saying, "I know what you mean. Politically, I'm tolerant of the heterosexual lifestyle, but the actual act is rather revolting."—an obvious take on the same line often used about homosexuality. In another scene, after Will finds out that Grace has arranged a second date, he informs her: "I would rather go out with an ebola-ridden gibbon monkey than go out with this guy. Hell, I'd rather go out with *Pat Buchanan* than this guy!"

Both gay and straight characters are the source of humor and the butt of jokes. There is a distinctly level playing field. In an unexpected and somewhat backhanded way, *Will & Grace* demonstrates an inclusivity not always seen in American culture. Of course, nothing is done or said to make a political point. The only goal, as with any television production, is *profit*, and successful sitcoms produce profits. Thus, Grace is a woman with her own business who at the same time seems not to know her own mind. Will is a successful lawyer who at the same time seems incapable of being in a relationship with anyone but Grace. The two title characters represent cultural underdogs in solidarity—women and gay men working to make a safe place for themselves in this world. The show offers nothing too bold and prophetic, but still exhibits a certain acceptance through a somewhat backhanded form of inclusiveness.

Structure

To a degree not often seen in other television genres, sitcoms relish the tensions their plots provide. It is tension that provides occasions for comic relief. In the element of surprise, of the unexpected, humor draws attention to the tension, heightens it even further, then releases it in the punch line and the laugh. *Will & Grace* is replete with these tensions in its physical humor, individual scenes, and overarching themes (such as intimacy versus sex, normalizing gay life versus trivializing it with humor).

Will & Grace is also successful because of the way it fits in the larger frames of the television industry and American society. Launched in fall 1998, the series has been very successful. As an article in the national gay and lesbian newsmagazine *The Advocate* described it, NBC's scheduling choice was "brave but calculated."[2] ABC had just canceled *Ellen* (a show featuring an outed lesbian) at the end of the 1997–98 season. Following on the heels of *Ellen*, many thought that *Will & Grace* would be too controversial to be successful. *Ellen's* open discussion and expression of lesbianism raised the ire of conservative groups across the nation, whose outcries prompted ABC to print a warning at the beginning of each *Ellen* episode, to caution viewers, and particularly parents, about the adult content of the show, despite the absence of any material usually deemed "adult." There was rarely any profanity, never any explicit sex, and never any violence.

Perhaps *Will & Grace* is more successful because, as one critic quipped, "NBC is not owned by Disney (as is ABC, which canceled *Ellen*) but by General Electric, which can drop a refrigerator on anyone who complains."[3] Although humorous, Richard Natale's comment highlights network ownership's immense influence over programming. Of course, there are many other possible reasons for the different reception of these two shows. As one reporter pointed out, Eric McCormack, who stars as Will Truman, is "only playing gay,"[4] unlike Ellen DeGeneres, who in *Ellen* featured her own personal life as a lesbian. Perhaps acceptance has been more easily attained because the focus is on the heterosexual appearance of the relationship between Will and Grace rather than on Will's sexual orientation. "[T]he gay-man/hetero-gal duo has become . . . a safe, lucrative way to package gay characters for the heartland."[5] As pointed out in the overview to the sitcom genre, this pairing has proved to be immensely successful as "a pop culture fixture." Perhaps *Ellen* was a martyred pioneer for shows to follow, or maybe with four characters in *Will & Grace* to carry the humor, the show is funnier. Whatever the multiple reasons for its success, the show crosses old boundaries of acceptable material for television and has created a receptive audience for what was once a taboo subject. In this manner, the series has been able to challenge subtly (and sometimes not so subtly) the status quo. As a sitcom, the show's primary loyalty is to the laugh, to the entertainment factor. If it makes a point about gay life, it does not do so at the risk of losing viewers. Gay and lesbian civil rights are divisive topics that help fuel partisan politics and appear in almost every discourse in the American public forum. Network executives look for ways to intrigue or excite viewers, but not to alienate them. Thus, *Will & Grace* must walk a delicate line.

Despite loyalty to the laugh, sitcoms play an interesting role in pushing the envelope because the viewer never quite knows whether a serious point is being made. Nothing is of ultimate importance except getting folks to laugh. Scott Seomin, executive media director of the Gay and Lesbian Alliance against Defamation, describes this loyalty in reference to *Will & Grace* in the following manner: "Let's remember this is a sitcom, and it needs to be funny to keep the audience. If it didn't, it would be off the air . . . and then we wouldn't have that means of educating the public about gay people in general."[6] He recognizes that the show has potential for creating a new cultural tolerance, but that it must always be mediated through humor. In a sense, the medium of comedy becomes an ally for creating cultural awareness and tolerance. In *Prime-Time Feminism*, author Bonnie Dow states: "Comedy offers space for representing social controversy and social change that might be too threatening when encoded as realist drama."[7] Perhaps *Will & Grace* offers an opportunity to examine the controversy about sexual orientation in American culture in a way that avoids the usual factions and tired accusations. Even though, and maybe because, *Will & Grace*'s ultimate devotion is to the punch line and not to a particular dogma, gay life is not a lightning rod for controversy. Instead, this show takes the course of American debate in a new direction.

In Crossan's terms, *Will & Grace* functions primarily as myth, reflecting back to the viewer what are regarded as safe and acceptable cultural norms. Yet, Will and Jack are two openly gay men, demonstrating diversity in the gay community. Their characterization by the clever use of humor pushes the limits of cultural acceptability, helping *Will & Grace* dance between myth and satire. Even as it reinforces the status quo, *Will & Grace* raises questions about the credibility and justice of established systems and about our culture's assumptions about and treatment of sexual minorities; it asks us, ever so lightly, what we value in human character and friendship.

Signs, Codes, and Messages

This episode asks us to pay attention to the character of Grace. As we laugh at her exploits in trying to get Nathan as a client, we also witness heart-wrenching scenes of her sacrifice of human dignity to gain what she claims as success. Repeatedly, Nathan treats Grace with great disdain. He rarely looks at her. The attention he gives Karen stands in stark contrast to his interactions with Grace. With Karen, he is clearly engaged, responding to her with questions to further their conversation. He accepts Karen's tough approach when she confronts him with the question of whether Grace has the job.

> As we laugh at [Grace's] exploits . . . we also witness heart-wrenching scenes of her sacrifice of human dignity to gain what she claims as success.

By contrast, during many moments of his visit to her home, Nathan mistreats Grace. He walks by her hand extended in greeting, whereas he later greets Will warmly, shaking his hand and offering extensive eye contact. At another point, without looking at Grace, he extends his arm behind him to have her take his coat and drops it. He scorns her hospitality when she offers him a drink.

Perhaps Nathan's disdain for Grace is shown most blatantly when he is seated with her on the couch. His back is turned to her so that his conversation is directed toward Will, as if Grace were no longer in the room. Toward the end of the conversation, Nathan asks where the washroom is. It is uncertain to whom he directed the question. Nathan looks only at Will, but Grace is his host. Grace answers his question by saying, "It's behind you," an ironic allusion to her position as well. Grace Adler is no more significant than a washroom. Nathan's interactions with her are replete with signs and codes informing us that we should—at best—pity her.

> [M]any camera shots accentuate Grace's character in this episode, lending her an off-balance and unreliable air.

In addition, many camera shots accentuate Grace's character in this episode, lending her an off-balance and unreliable air. Throughout much of this episode, she is shot farther away than other characters and slightly off center. The distance makes her appear smaller and more vulnerable. Keeping someone off center is a technique used when a character is shot alone, to provide balance in the frame composition. On several occasions, however, Grace's placement seems to exaggerate this technique of balancing by keeping her focus directly off-screen. Framing Grace by the camera in this way makes her appear "addled" and depicts her as someone who deserves Nathan's disdain. This camera approach emphasizes her need for help from Will—the strong, centered male who can see her through any trouble. In contrast to Grace, Will is usually shot in ways that accent his strength. Often he is shot in close-up, and when alone he is always centered in the shot. These signs help us understand that Grace cannot succeed on her own. Although we experience regret for Grace and her apparent ineptitude, we are also encouraged to laugh at her *because* of her failings.

Function

It is troubling that the directors are so adept at wielding their cameras that we laugh when we know we should not. Neil Postman challenges our easy acceptance of humor by asking, "To whom do we complain, and when, and in what tone of voice when serious discourse dissolves into giggles? What is the antidote to a culture's being drained by laughter?"[8] Not only are Grace's struggles crafted comically, but the implications of Grace's actions are also often masked by humor. As described earlier, Grace is on her knees before Will imploring him to do just one more favor for her and go out again with Nathan. We can see that, despite all his fervent arguments against it, Will begins to weaken. Just as he softens, Grace adds, "Or maybe a third date if he [Nathan] wants it." And we laugh. Will responds angrily with a sarcastic rhetorical question, "Why don't you just dress me up in fishnet stockings and thigh-high boots?" Grace answers as though he were serious, "You'd do that?" And we laugh again. Through his sarcasm, Will tells Grace that she is asking him to prostitute himself for her own gain. Perhaps his point is not entirely lost in the punch line, but its impact is seriously diminished. As Postman reminds us, we lose our ability to address cultural assumptions and to correct cultural problems when we have "dissolved into giggles." We become collaborators in Grace's degradation as we laugh at this scene. Our role as viewers is significant. Without our laughs, it simply is not funny. As consumers of comedy, we must also recognize our complicity. As collaborators in the laugh, we must examine that which we find humorous for what it says about human dignity.

At the end of this *Will & Grace* episode, we are informed that all is well. Yet a caricature of gayness wins the day in Will's scheme to rid himself of Nathan. This caricature is funny in its absurdity, but his success in getting out of the relationship with Nathan—which in itself is a complete farce—does not come through mature, direct discussion, but ironically only by becoming "more gay," by becoming effeminate and overly emotional. Neither is all well with Grace. She does not have to address her own growth and self-discovery by facing Nathan and her demons of insecurity.

Theological Analysis

What, if anything, can this episode show us about the growth of the human spirit? It is troubling that we find Grace's loss of human dignity funny. Throughout the episode, and running as a theme in the series, Grace is the lost one—the one who needs Will and even Karen to keep her on track, to keep her strong in spirit. Grace aggressively tries to assert her will toward Nathan and the world. The irony of this story is that in her pursuit of his business, she becomes like Nathan. Nathan uses Grace to get Will; Grace uses Will to get Nathan. In this circuit of logic, Grace can be criticized for causing her own demise. In contrast, Will is cast as a hero. He demonstrates grace in his loyalty and sacrifice for Grace. Through him, we get a glimpse of friendship that is not based on personal gain from the relationship. Will is solidly there for Grace even when her requests are unreasonable, but he is there on his own terms. He goes out with Nathan once, and it ends in disaster. When he discovers that Grace has used him again for her own gain, he still manages to rescue her in the end, without having to back down about his feelings about Nathan; he is self-aware and remains in control.

> Perhaps in the balance between Will and Grace, one can find fuller, more complete glimpses of the human predicament . . .

Perhaps Grace is kept weak to uphold Will: the sacrifice of the female character for the glory of the male. This old sexist dynamic is complicated, however, by the addition of Will's sexual orientation. Because he is gay, he does not assume the usual male presence and dominance in the culture; instead, he is placed low in the social hierarchy. This placement could make us see him as far more disadvantaged than Grace. However, playing Will's strength off Grace's weakness helps Will gain masculine credibility and pass as straight, as a "true man." In fact, Will's "passing" is so complete that sometimes he is written as being embarrassed by Jack's effusive "gayness." This makes it easier for the average American viewer to accept Will and to sympathize with him. Such acceptance can also send the dangerous message that the straighter he is, the better.

Neither one of these characters alone speaks fully of humanity. Perhaps in the balance between Will and Grace, one can find fuller, more complete glimpses of the human predicament: that we are all given to selfishness, that we are all capable of selflessness. It is troubling that this episode reinforces stereotypes of women—unreasonable, manipulative, weak, unable to stand on their own. Likewise, it is troubling that the male must remain strong and capable to maintain order in the midst of the world's chaos. These are heavy burdens for any one character to carry all the time. William Fore critiques this type of character manipulation:

> The good news [of liberation] requires that communication in the community take into account all persons, and the whole person, and that it deal with them as sons and daughters of God. Communication that does otherwise, that treats persons as objects, is in fact oppressing them.[9]

In the world of sitcoms, however, it is unlikely that any character will be well rounded, and thus sexual stereotypes abound. Instead, we might consider how the duo of Grace and Will depicts a balance in the human condition and an encouraging picture of commitment to another person. As the comedy plays with us and encourages us to laugh, the subtext speaks loudly of the absurdities and complexities of human life, which make us so frail and so easily laughed at. Can God be found in these comic frailties? Will does show us and Grace a glimmer of *God's* grace as he remains steadfast in the face of the wild demands made by his friend.

Yet true to sitcom form, the glimmer is tentative. As viewers, we are also captured by the tension of comedy, knowing that there are dangerous messages encoded in the positive ones. "Comedy is a more flexible form than drama because it can create multiple, conflicting and oppositional realities within the safe confines of the joke."[10] Everything can be explored, and yet everything is kept at arm's length. Sitcoms push the boundaries of what is acceptable while they never take the last step of committing themselves to what they propose. Despite nicely wrapped plots with clear finishes, sitcoms' propositions are like dangling questions left in front of viewers. What will we do with such a carrot dangling before us? Can we capture the positive in some way, even at the risk of losing the humor?

This is *our* tension as viewers. We watch in the tension of provocative inclusivity and human belittlement, of will and grace, of hope and doubt, where we mirror the predicament of our culture:

> Our ironic worldview may simply be the response of a culture which feels a deep need for a salvation it can't bring itself to believe in . . . . We feel the need for salvation from without, but we are secularized enough to doubt it exists . . . . Both the prayer and the doubt are present.[11]

Will & Grace presents both the prayer and the doubt: the prayer that the gay and lesbian community may truly be seen as part of mainstream American culture—the doubt that it can actually be seen so; the prayer that human nature may rise above petty self-indulgence—the doubt that human life can be more than self-centered interest. All the while, we laugh at the uneasy human predicament.

FIVE

Ally McBeal

IS FEMINISM A BYGONE?

*If women really wanted to change society, they could do it. I plan
to change it. I just want to get married first.*

—Ally McBeal

Episode: **First aired:**
"I Know Him by Heart"   May 24, 1999

The new face of feminism may be wearing a bewildered look
these days as Ally struggles along with the rest of us between
intimacy and independence. In the well-dressed, well-coiffed
world of urban success, we watch Ally and her law office
mates alter the romantic daydreams of our childhood by
embracing the hard work of creating relationships with imperfect people, including ourselves.

As soon as *Ally McBeal* was introduced in fall 1997, the critiques of its take on
feminism came rolling in. So did great ratings. The show rapidly made its
way into the Nielsen top twenty-five for Fox's Monday night lineup and won
Golden Globes for best comedy series and best actress. Although the series
opened to critical acclaim—*Newsweek* called it "the successor to *The Mary
Tyler Moore Show*"[1]—later in its first season *GQ* television critic Terrence
Rafferty called Ally "the thinking man's sex kitten—if only she had a brain."[2]

Ally McBeal features a successful young career woman who is lost and
confused in her personal life. One week she is a strong litigator, and the
next week she intentionally trips a woman in a supermarket to get the last
remaining can of Pringles. She kisses the boyfriends and husbands of her
co-workers. She worries that she will never marry. She proudly
announces, "I like being a mess—it's who I am." She is a hit with women

in the age group she represents, eighteen to thirty-four. Something about her life resonates with theirs. In this chapter, we ask what that resonance might be and look theologically at Ally's predominant dilemma: She feels lost without a man. The episode discussed here, "I Know Him by Heart," first aired May 24, 1999, as the season finale.

Episode Synopsis

Ally McBeal's friends and co-workers wonder whether she's losing her mind. The attractive-but-lonely twentysomething attorney thinks she sees recording artist Al Green singing to her, first in court and then in her bedroom. Ally's fantasy life has always been vivid, but it now seems to hold her hostage. Her close friend John Cage—a partner at Cage and Fish where she works—has recently advised her to give up looking for the perfect man and join the real world. This thought throws Ally into a cloistered depression; she prefers the daydream in her bedroom to reality.

The women she works with do not subscribe to Ally's it-takes-two-to-make-one mind-set and tell her they have given up hope of finding the perfect man. Her roommate Renée (also an attorney) convinces Ally that she has not tried hard enough. When a short experiment in frantic dating fails, Ling (another attorney in her office) rounds up a number of available hunks to come to the office during lunch hour so that Ally can "look them over" and take their phone numbers. Although initially excited by the prospects, Ally rejects them all on the premise that she does not want a man who answers a cattle call to meet her.

Meanwhile, John finds love at the office with fellow attorney Nelle as they decide to work on a less-than-perfect relationship that embraces the difference between them. Ally ends her bad day by entering into her favorite fantasy—riding a carousel with her perfect imaginary lover: the one, as the final song indicates, she "knows by heart."

Narrative

A one-hour weekly series produced by Emmy winner David E. Kelley (*Chicago Hope, Picket Fences, The Practice*), *Ally McBeal* is a drama with comedic touches, known in the entertainment industry as a dramedy. Pioneers in this subgenre were *Lou Grant, Moonlighting,* and *Northern Exposure. Ally McBeal,* however, is the first successful dramedy with a woman in the lead. Television critic Steven D. Stark writes that *"any semi-realistic drama about a modern woman, especially one that forsakes constant action to focus on her private life, would generate an enormous amount of attention."*[3] Previous prime-time successes with female stars were either situation comedies like *The Mary Tyler Moore Show* and *Murphy Brown,* or pure dramas such as *Cagney & Lacey* and *Dr. Quinn, Medicine Woman*. The actress who portrays Ally, Calista Flockhart, says:

> It's not the norm to have a woman protagonist. It creates a fervor. On top of that, Ally is somebody who wears her heart on her sleeve. . . . She tells her intimate secrets; she's vulnerable; people want to take care of her, protect her—or kill her [*laughs*].[4]

Fox's website promoting the show claims: "This law series takes the oath to deliver one of the most compelling and sensitive portraits of a young professional woman ever rendered by a man."[5] Indeed, the gender of the writer and producer is no small issue. Some television critics find it scandalous that this delicate, sad bundle of emotions called Ally is a male creation. Alyssa Katz, a Generation-X critic writing in *The Nation*, says:

> It's just completely appalling for Kelley to have created a matched set of his-and-hers shows, one celebrating the ingenious heroics of a male Boston lawyer and the other this lite dramedy about the self-destructive neuroses, childish foibles and desperate romantic needs of a female character who appears to be fully grown even if she does weigh about 100 pounds.[6]

The series contains multiple subplots that explore a variety of social issues, frequently gender-based controversies leading to court cases involving the law firm. It is misleading, however, to call the show a law series because in many episodes the court cases take a back seat to Ally's personal life and emotions.

Kelley adds an unusual touch (though not original with him—as viewers of HBO's *Dream On* series will note) in allowing us to see Ally's fantasies and hear her thoughts. The sequences in which Ally's imagination comes to life before us are sometimes serious, as when we see arrows shot through her heart, and sometimes ludicrous, as in the case of the dancing computerized baby who follows her around, reminding her that

her biological clock is ticking. The invitation into Ally's inner world makes the drama seem more real to us. Each of us has an inner voice that says what we never dare say aloud, but in Ally's world we can hear that voice, which simultaneously amuses us, horrifies us, and urges us to relate to her as "one of us."

This episode's ultimate concern echoes the ultimate concern of the entire series: Will Ally ever find true love? We are led to believe that Ally lived in the hope of finding her soul mate until John admonished her (in a previous episode) to join the real world and forget the quest for the perfect match. Ling similarly chastised Ally for her wishful thinking.

> Ling: Do you think you're just going to bump into him at a book-store both reaching for Balzac? It doesn't work that way . . . . You don't really *want* to meet anybody. Since nobody can measure up to this mythic dreamboat you've concocted for yourself, it's easier to be alone and just pretend you haven't met him yet.
>
> Ally: I'll meet him, Ling!

Ling, a wealthy, litigious, spoiled, and often egocentric character, usu-ally serves as comic relief, yet in this scene she acts as a reality check for the idealistic Ally. Playing the "wise fool," Ling tells Ally the truth about finding a mate: Many times it is a combination of availability, attitude, and attempts at dating, not the stuff of fairy tales.

Throughout the series, various characters have suggested that Ally actually *has* met a soul mate in John. Ally's relationship with John is depicted as close, tender, nourishing, but platonic. They seek each other for affirmation and comfort in their self-confessed strangeness. However, when John starts to live outside his imaginary world, making changes that give him more self-confidence, his relationship with Nelle begins to grow, causing anxiety for Ally because she distrusts and dislikes Nelle. Nelle, who is not fond of Ally either, tells John she is fearful that if Ally influences him to keep looking for a "perfect" lover, she (Nelle) may not qualify. The conflict is real for Nelle and John because they are so different. For all the jokes in the show about Nelle's being cold and unfeeling (hence the nickname Sub-Zero), her character is unashamedly honest, ready to take risks, and eager to confront reality head on. Her choices stand in the narrative as a stark contrast to Ally's flight from reality.

Of all the characters on the show, Ally is the most developed, and yet the viewer gets the feeling he or she does not know Ally very well. She is a woman full of surprises, given to high emotion, impulsive behavior, and sometimes deep compassion. She is driven by fears from her past, of which we get occasional glimpses.

One important narrative element in this episode is the implicit role of religious faith in Ally's life journey. It is not unusual for issues of faith to surface on *Ally McBeal*. Regular viewers have seen Ally attend an African-American worship service, because she wanted to be sur-rounded by forgiveness, and speak at the funeral of a teacher with whom she once had an affair. She was shown in the confessional, telling all to the man behind the screen. In one 1999 episode, Ally befriends Eric, a little boy dying from leukemia, who asks her to represent him in a lawsuit against God. Eric tells Ally he is not sure there is a God but he wants to sue God in case God is real, so that when he dies he can ask God "what's up" with all the sorrow in his life. In a conversation with Eric, Ally reveals that she lost a sister to an illness when she was eight years old and she stopped believing in God that day. Later, her mother pointed to a blimp in the sky and told her the blimp was God. Ally did not believe that, but her mother then told her that God had people make the blimp to remind us that God was up there watching, because that was all blimps do. They just look down.

Ally's description of a God who "looks down" on us humans recalls the popular image of the Old Man in the Sky who watches but rarely touches our lives. After the boy dies (and is escorted into the otherworld by a disembodied hand), Ally again doubts the existence of God but believes she met her angel in Eric. For Ally, the messenger is more credible than the source of the message.

Although it is speculative, viewers can infer a character's faith by examining where that character's deepest desire, joy, gratitude, and wholeness occur. In Ally's case, this episode and many others show us someone who chiefly desires a lifelong relationship with a man she can consider her soul mate. Because she lacks that, she is bereft of joy, and no wonder. Ally seems to be her own worst enemy, dwelling negatively on her single status, with mantras such as "I am a strong workingwoman whose life is empty without a man." Ally has no awareness that the emptiness in her life arises from more than the lack of a romantic relationship. In this episode, there is no resolution of any of her unhappiness, except her faint and unexplained smile as she rides on the carousel in the last two seconds of the episode. For the most part, we are left with a lost and lonely Ally.

Structure

The dominant message of this and other similar episodes is: "It is not good for Ally to be alone." This is classic dramatic myth, in which the tension between Ally's life as an independent career woman seemingly cannot be reconciled with her desire to find a life partner. It is not that she technically *cannot*, because we all know lots of twentysomething career women with partners; it is that she continues to run into obstacles, some of her own making, and that she has come to define herself as a "mess" in the love department. Many fans believe that for the drama to work, this difference must remain irreconcilable, because if Ally suddenly became happy, she might also become less interesting. It has not been that long since *Rhoda*'s marriage and *Moonlighting*'s romantic coupling of the lead characters marked a serious decline in these shows' ratings. Even in newer situation comedies like *Dharma and Greg*, in which the lead characters are happily married, the relationship has built-in conflict to keep story lines humming. If Kelley were to suddenly make Ally functional in love, he would lose part of the myth he has built into the show.

In this episode, Ally—finding herself alone—prefers a fantasy romance life to a real one because she believes she has failed at real love and that it may never come her way. A normal, healthy desire for a help-mate or spouse turns into a vision quest in which the vision is always elusive. This episode defends the worldview that love is difficult and painful, especially for young women who grew up in an era of feminism and learned that they could and should "have it all." *Ally McBeal* questions the view that women can have it all. By putting the spotlight on a woman who has every reason to think she can attract a mate—she is beautiful, intelligent, humorous, and makes decent money—and then not allowing her to find love, Kelley questions the view that feminism gives women true freedom. The show is satirizing what many young women have come to believe is feminism's unintended negative side effect: Women may have brilliant careers, but it may cost them the perfect lover.

Signs, Codes, and Messages

Ally McBeal is rife with visual and auditory cues that enhance each plot-line. The creative touches that make up the style and setting of this series (the mise-en-scène) tell us that we are in an upscale, urban, professional, modern and hip world of lawyers in love. Most scenes in the law office are bright and cheery, frequently featuring colors of the sun, sky, and jewels, giving the set a fresh, upbeat look. Nighttime scenes in Ally's bedroom or at the local bar where the lawyers gather are filmed in tones of blue and gray. Her apartment appears to be painted in corals, golds, and reds, giving it a warm glow.

Scenes of one person talking with another predominate, and the focus is usually on the person talking, with the one listening out of focus. These are generally head and shoulder shots; however, we frequently see full-length views of Ally. The director's preference for close-ups and two-person scenes gives the show an intimate feel, which is appropriate for the scenes about relationships. There are a few panoramic views in which many people are shown together, especially in courtroom scenes. These long shots are less personal and remind us that we are now in the public arena, dealing with societal issues rather than personal ones.

Popular music, much like a movie soundtrack, highlights the drama in this series. In the episode we are analyzing, we hear the 60s pop song "Did You Ever Have to Finally Decide?" as Ally looks over the handsome men Ling has rounded up for her to consider as dates. Most of the songs used in the series are either well-known popular hits from the 1960s and 1970s or adaptations and original songs by recording artist Vonda

Shepard. All are used in almost every episode to emphasize how Ally is feeling.

Special effects play a significant role in the program. When Ally sees a man she is attracted to, her tongue may grow long and spill out of her mouth. Once she was uncharacteristically happy and appeared to be walking on air. When she is embarrassed, Ally's face sometimes switches to black and white while the rest of the shot remains in color. In the episode we are analyzing, a shrinking Ally scurries away from a humiliating situation as we hear the sound effect of a car racing away. The fact that Ally's emotions are given a myriad of effects, both visual and auditory, while other characters get only a signature effect here and there, draws the viewer closer to the main character, making her decisions, dilemmas, and emotions dominant.

One of the most important semiotic devices in this series is Ally's physical appearance and body language. Messy hair, childlike pouting, and a nervous habit of touching her fingertips to her lips tell us this is a vulnerable woman-child who needs protecting. Ally is a klutz who falls down in almost every episode, as if she constantly thinks about something other than the task at hand. She is frequently shown flailing at someone for one reason or another, giving even her best friends an occasional sucker punch. This communicates that she is on the edge, nearly out of control, and highly aggressive. Just looking at her, we know she is the mess she embraces as "who she is."

Power and Ideological Issues

The creators of any television show are acutely aware of the race, ethnicity, gender, age, and socioeconomic makeup of the target audience. Fox's target audiences for all prime-time programming are people eighteen to forty-nine years old. The core demographic that *Ally McBeal* intends to reach and is quite successful in delivering to advertisers is women eighteen to thirty-four: prime consumers.

What are these viewers being sold? During the May 24, 1999, airing of "I Know Him by Heart" in the San Francisco market, there were commercials for vehicles ranging from compact cars to sport utility vehicles; for fashion (mostly unisex clothing; one for cosmetics); for other features on Fox; for soft drinks, computer-related items (including websites for electronic job hunting and stock trading), films playing in local theaters, gasoline, an amusement park, a grocery store chain, and a new cable network. From the lineup, it is difficult to tell whether advertisers are specifically targeting women. Only three commercials appeared to have a clear gender bias: an ad featuring the World-Cup-winning U.S. women's soccer team, a cosmetics ad, and a soft drink ad starring soccer star Mia Hamm (and Michael Jordan). No doubt advertisers are confident that *Ally McBeal* reaches the eighteen- to thirty-four-year-old female market and believe it also attracts its fair share of men of that age group.

Another clue that this show is directed toward the eighteen- to thirty-four-year-old professional is that the main characters all happen to be in that age group. They are attorneys in a small Boston law firm that is fully staffed, smartly decorated, and constantly busy. Although the characters are somewhat diverse, there is no class diversity. Without exception, all the main characters are highly educated and professional. They are extremely well groomed, with tailored suits for the men and high-fashion suits and dresses with smart accessories for the women—details indicating they have money to burn. No one in this firm, with the possible exception of the office secretary, has any financial worries. Everyone can afford to go out for drinks every night after work, buy expensive clothes, visit their therapists, and live in the nicest gentrified urban neighborhoods. Perhaps we are supposed to believe that they are average Americans, but judging by their material wealth the characters presented here are in the top 10 percent of wage earners in the United States. Because most Americans perceive themselves to be more upwardly mobile and wealthy than they are in reality, the producers of *Ally McBeal* have chosen to portray well-off characters who have the luxury of worrying about more in life than how far their next paycheck will stretch.

Ally McBeal is recognized in the television industry for showing at least an awareness of racial diversity. Although most of the main characters are white, Ally's best friend and roommate Renee, as well as Ally's ex-boyfriend Greg, are African American. Nelle's friend and co-worker Ling is Chinese American. All are treated as equals, and race is hardly ever discussed, as if racism were not a problem in the world of Ally McBeal.

Functions

Ally McBeal comforts many young professionals, helping them feel understood in their aloneness, vulnerability, and confusion about life. It validates female anger about relationships that are unsatisfactory because women work too hard at their careers. It touches nerves. For example, *American Demographic* magazine's October 1998 issue ran a cover story by Seema Nayyar and Jennifer Lach, in which the writers describe overhearing a conversation in a New York City elevator between two fans of *Ally McBeal*. One said, "It's really great. You know I hate it when I fit someone's demographic group. But, they're right! They're absolutely right on this one."[7]

Even though we are not privy to exactly what the show got "absolutely right," it is clear that viewers use this series to compare their own experiences of life with Ally's. This does not mean that all viewers agree with her outlook. One viewer might interpret her loneliness as a lesson about the consequences of bad choices. Another might interpret her quest for love as an affirmation that feminists *can* seek to have it all: a smashing career with all the financial benefits that come from it, and also a traditional female role in the home—marriage, children, and putting the family first.

For most viewers of *Ally McBeal*, the show probably functions mainly as comedic entertainment—a pleasant diversion. At the same time, it serves to validate a number of lifestyles, most of them privileged. It celebrates the high-paying career in the culturally diverse urban setting. It celebrates individual quirks and unusual viewpoints. It also celebrates the modern woman with all her choices in sexual partnering and living arrangements. All these themes are entertaining to the viewer, but they serve an even more important motivation for the creators and supporters of the show: By glorifying an upscale, individualistic, diverse way of life, the show promotes the lifestyle of a person who wants and needs the many consumer products advertised in commercial breaks in the show. Viewers who subconsciously connect this program with hearty laughs and warm associations between Ally's life and their own are more likely to connect with the advertisers' stories as well. This motive is not limited to products explicitly advertised. When women see the Clinique makeup bottles on Ally's bedroom dresser and notice that her clothes appear to come from the designer sections of a department store, their existing views that expensive makeup and clothing are what successful career women need to wear are reinforced. That reinforcement then compels big budget advertisers to spend more on a show like *Ally McBeal*.

Theological Reflections

When Ally laments that she is alone and feels incomplete, she taps into a worldview that has been legitimized for centuries by the Jewish, Christian, and Muslim faiths. The message "It is not good for Ally to be alone" is commonly promoted by a literal and conservative interpretation of Genesis 2:18: "The Lord God said, 'It is not good that the man should be alone; I will make him a helper as his partner.'" Ally internalizes the message, which now reads: It is not good for Ally to be alone; she needs a helper fit for her. In the episode under discussion, Richard Fish makes a crude reference to the creation story:

> Richard: That's why God gave man the handle, for women to latch onto. Fishism.
>
> Ally: *God* gave man the handle?
>
> Richard: Suck it up, Ally, and get a grip. [*a few moments later*]
>
> Richard: Here's the thing. You need a guy. You want sex. You need a guy to fulfill all your emotional needs—with an above

average handle, and you feel bad for wanting all that because you think that makes you weak—a bad feminist—when in truth every woman out there is exactly like you. They're all weak. God made you that way and it's sacrilegious to deny it. Go out there proud, Ally. You're not strange! You're not different. I am woman; hear me whimper!

On one level, Richard makes sense: Ally's desire is normal. Many people want someone special with whom to spend their days and nights. The danger comes when the "helpmate" concept is carried to extremes. The statement "It is not good for Ally to be alone; she needs a helper fit for her" is not the same as saying "It is bad that Ally does not have a lover; she is incomplete without one," or that, as Richard puts it, she is weak. This episode does not strongly emphasize that Ally needs a loving, healthy community of people around her so that she feels less lonely and needy.

One subplot presents a lesbian character, Margaret Camero, who challenges Ally on the statement that her life is empty without a man. Margaret is played as a sympathetic character; however, she is not allowed to say much in the episode. Like Ling with her Balzac remark, Margaret serves as a truth teller who embarrasses and upsets Ally by confronting her with reality. Her shining moment comes when she manages to get Ally to crystallize her dilemma into one pithy, emotionally charged statement about her life without a man: "It's only half empty!" This half-empty image is the centerpiece of this episode and brings up key theological questions.

If Ally truly believes that her only way out of depression is a perfect lover, and if that lover cannot be found because "all the good ones are taken," then Ally is subject to the proverbial catch-22. Of course, Ally's dilemma is nothing new. Women who came of age in the 1970s and 1980s will recall a series of magazine and newspaper articles that decried a shortage of eligible men in the marriage pool. Some articles speculated that if a woman had not married by the time she was thirty-five, her odds of finding a marriage partner were shockingly low. Young, single women began to panic and lose hope, assuming the statistics quoted in the articles to be true.[8] The problem was that, as Susan Faludi points out in *Backlash*, the statistics were flawed from the beginning, but the reporters covering the story failed to adequately question the numbers. Even a year later, when the numbers were shown beyond a shadow of a doubt to be skewed, the less shocking news about the myth of the man shortage was not heavily covered.[9] Just like Ally, single women in the 1980s bemoaned the fact that "there are no good men" and were willing to believe they would be losers in love, forced to go through life partnerless.

Feminist theologians warn of the danger in people's feeling incomplete without partners, pointing out that "feminist spirituality proclaims wholeness, healing love and spiritual power."[10] What does it say about our core belief in God if we declare that we are not whole persons until someone comes along to complete us?

According to feminist and other liberation theologians, wholeness and healing come in relationship to all of creation, not just in the aspect of sexual partnering. Reverend Marsha Wilfong says the story about the creation of Adam and Eve "declares that human creation is complete only when human beings exist in community."[11] There is certainly mutuality in the concept of human beings acting as helpers for one another, which many biblical scholars believe is the real point of the statement in Genesis 2:18. A less rigid interpretation of the Genesis passage leads to a different conclusion for women who seek to be in a just and loving relationship with a man, not as halves of a couple but as complete and independent persons.

People of faith always ponder the mystery of what it means to be made in the image of God. However, we can say with conviction that as human beings created in the image of God we are created to have the same desire as God, which is to be in relationship, and especially with those who are different from us—as different as male and female, as different as divine and human.

This episode carries a secondary theological message as well, and it is linked to the primary one: Relationships are enhanced by embracing "otherness" and diminished when we seek perfect images of ourselves in a mate. The story of John and Nelle demonstrates how humans can embrace the mystery of the other. Ally's discontent with her lack of a mate and John's discovery that his relationship with Nelle is enhanced by their diversity are contrasts illustrating that a search for the perfect extension of ourselves is futile; we will always "go around in circles" like Ally on the carousel, failing to enjoy the abundance of life God gives us in other people.

The two worldviews portrayed in this episode by Ally (it-takes-two-to-make-one) and Nelle (together-alone) are at odds with each other, and we may wonder which worldview is promoted as the norm. We could argue that because Ally is the title character, her worldview is privileged. Then again, who finds love in this episode? Nelle, the "anti-Ally." I may prefer Nelle's worldview, but another viewer may find Ally's more convincing or true to life. Kelley may even have his preferences, but once the video narrative is aired, the question of whose worldview has priority is the intellectual property of the viewer. Viewers understand that like stories from real life, stories that are invented do not always add up. The dueling worldviews are part of what keeps many viewers returning to *Ally McBeal* even when they are most frustrated. Viewers who discuss the show with one another invariably take sides with one character or another, arguing over these submerged "theological" issues about Ally's autonomy, self-esteem, and romantic standards. As in many well-written postmodern television dramas, everyone can find a side to take. This style of narrative fits nicely with our pluralistic, individualistic world.

For many viewers, there appears to be some healing or salvation in this episode's story. It comes to us by way of a glimpse of Nelle and John's budding relationship as they adapt to meet each other's needs, having no delusion that their relationship is or ever will be perfect or that they will be "soul mates." They are content to live in the moment and let the relationship take on a life of its own. Not maintaining Ally's unreasonably high standards for a man, Nelle gravitates to a man she finds interesting and amusing. Her openness to change in order to compromise and experience John's "otherness" shows Ally a new approach to relationships that has a much better chance for success. Nelle can be an agent of healing and salvation for Ally, but only if Ally can see the contrast and want the conversion.

The plot line involving John and Nelle has much to offer all of us in our relationships. How often do we embrace the strangeness and otherness of human beings who are different from us? Do we look for friends and lovers who are carbon copies of ourselves? Perhaps when we can embrace the otherness of beings as different as males are from females we have a model for embracing the otherness of the mystery we call God. Our wholeness comes as we are in a growing relationship with God, which in turn positively affects our relationships with others. This cyclical embrace of otherness helps make us whole.

Conclusion

Whenever someone brings up old business on *Ally McBeal*, Richard quickly moves them onto a new topic with the exclamation, "Bygones!" It is tempting to wonder, as *Time* magazine did in its cover story of June 29, 1998, whether feminism as a movement is a bygone, especially if Ally is the "new face of feminism."[12] Ally may very well be the new face of *post*feminism, a term defined by communications professor Bonnie Dow in *Prime-Time Feminism* as an attitude among young women that promotes competitive individualism, in contrast to 1970s-style radical feminism, which focused on sexual politics. One component of postfeminism is the (old-fashioned) notion that choosing the right man can solve most of a woman's problems.[13] Judging from "I Know Him by Heart," Ally is a poster child for this retro brand of feminism.

Feminists cannot agree on whether the character of Ally McBeal helps or hurts the cause of equality for women. Representing the Women's Freedom Network, Cathy Young hails Ally as "a capable lawyer" who "stands up for principle, confronting her colleagues when she thinks they're doing the wrong thing."[14] Young insists that men feel just as incomplete without a partner as Ally does and that they identify with Ally's confusion over her love life. Ruth Shalit of *The New Republic* is not as generous in her review of television's "betrayal of post-feminism." She says shows like *Ally McBeal* with weak and insecure but sexually aggressive leads are "really nothing but a male producer's fantasy of feminism, which manages simultaneously to exploit and to deplore, to arouse and to moralize."[15] Actually, both critics are correct. Ally is a strong woman in some instances and a weak and insecure one in others. Some fans say that is part of her charm.

If we look only at sad Ally, Shalit's assessment rings true. The character of Ally may be guilty of buying into the old, patriarchal view of what it means to be a woman, but in the opposing plotline, her nemesis Nelle has no problem being strong and complete with or without a man, at least not in this episode or this season. Nelle's strength, openness, and practicality in her relationship with John demonstrate that feminism in television narratives still has a fighting chance, as does the idea that all human beings are made in the unique and living image of God. Keeping an eye out for evidence of *that* on television makes for fascinating theological detective work.

Interlude

So Where's the Sex and Violence?

Public criticism of commercial television usually focuses on two issues: too much sex and too much violence. Television executives cry foul and claim that the first-amendment right to free expression is sacred. They label any talk of nationwide cultural standards for television as a call for censorship. Instead, they promote a rating system for parental guidance, as if only children and minors need protection from a demeaning and harmful media culture. "Watching what we watch" means being careful what we watch and understanding what we watch, because people of all ages are shaped by watching.

We concur with the critics: Much sex on television demeans men and women and depicts a dream world of pleasure without commitment or consequences. Much violence on television is little more than comic make-believe and fails to show the consequences of violence in the lives of either the victims or the perpetrators. Rather than depicting violence as a last resort, many programs glorify violence as a first resort. Hollywood presents annual awards to companies like George Lucas's Industrial Light and Magic for blockbuster pyrotechnics that ratchet up the level of violence in film and on television.

Nonetheless, in our view the major problem is not sex and violence, but the drive for profit maximization that fuels the industry in a more-is-better culture of consumerism. In the highly competitive quest for ratings, television goes as low as the market permits, as the winter 2001 show *Temptation Island* illustrates.* This section is called an interlude because the primary emphasis of this book is not on sex and violence but on the commercial forces in our media-dominated culture. (See Part IV.)

---

*The Fox network has crossed another moral line in this show, encouraging sexual infidelity in young couples as a way of testing the strength of their commitment.

Prime-Time Sexuality and the Search for Intimacy

So God created humankind in his [God's] image, . . . male and
female he [God] created them. . . . God saw everything . . . and
indeed, it was very good.

—*Genesis 1:27, 31*

I slept, but my heart was awake. Listen! my beloved is knocking.
—*Song of Solomon 5:2*

What does it mean to be made in the image of God in a televised world
inundated with images that occasionally affirm but mostly deny our best
sexual selves? How do we sift through the multitude of sexual stories and
make healthy choices for our own relationships, choices that honor both
the other person and ourselves? Our brains may "sleep" through the constant barrage of sex that appears in prime-time content and commercials.
We may believe we have tuned them out!—but our hearts are still awake,
waiting and listening for "the knock," those characters and story lines
that tell us something meaningful about ourselves and those we love.

Changing Gender Roles
and Sexual Relationships on Prime Time

In the years since prime-time television began, we have watched as
both gender roles and sexual relationships have evolved "on the tube."
Since its debut in our homes, television has broadened its reflection of
human relationships as we—as individuals and as a society—have
expanded our own roles and ways of relating to one another. We still
remember the idyllic families of *Ozzie and Harriet* and *Father Knows Best*,
and yet looking back from the perspective of thirty years, we now find
something sterile and surreal about a relational dynamic that was so
proscribed. Still, early prime-time roles did include Rose Marie on *The
Dick Van Dyke Show*, a single working "girl" always on the lookout for
a man. The shows' writers softened that quest with humor but occasionally interjected a poignant scene of tenderness and truth when Rose
Marie chose the integrity of her single existence over a "fella" who
could not give her the relationship she wanted. Then came *That Girl*,
and we watched a single Marlo Thomas make her way as a budding
actress in the Big Apple, but never without her fiancé, Donald, and her
"Daddy" (as she still called him) just behind to occasionally bail
her out.

Through the late 1960s and early 1970s when so much of our stable
postwar world turned topsy-turvy (including our sexual lives and roles),
television reflected those changes. Diahann Carol, a woman and a person

of color, starred in her own program about a single professional mother. Mary Tyler Moore hit the newsroom in Minneapolis as Mary Richards, a single professional in a male-dominated field, and held her own even with the crusty curmudgeon, Lou Grant.

"You've got spunk," Lou told her once, then paused: "I hate spunk." We did not believe that punch line, nor did Mary Richards. She knew, as we all did, that she had won his respect. Mary's show spun off at least two successful series, starring her friends Rhoda and Phyllis, one a wisecracking working woman, the other a widow whom the writers allowed to march to her own quirky drummer. We were treated to *Laverne and Shirley*, a retro slapstick show set in the 50s but with a decidedly liberated undertone.

"There is nothing we won't try. Never heard the word 'impossible.' This time, there's no stopping us," they sang in the opening title, celebrating "girl power" two decades before the Spice Girls.

Prime time broke all the rules when Norman Lear's *All in the Family* hit the airwaves (and spawned two successful spin-offs), cramming into one half-hour all the political, sexual, and religious topics that were dinner table taboos. Meathead and Archie had regular shouting matches about Nixon and Vietnam. While Edith and Archie waxed nostalgic in "Those Were the Days," the show's opening title song, Meathead did his best to drag Archie into the modern age, going toe to toe with his father-in-law about benevolent social policy, "women's lib," and even the sexual orientation of a few walk-on characters, which left Archie cringing. Gloria tried with limited success to coax her mother into feminism. It was a mystery to the devoted and ditzy Edith, but audiences in the studio and at home cheered wildly the few times she gently lectured Archie to bring him to a working-class epiphany or proclaimed in her high-pitched voice, "No!" and exited their drab living room to make her beloved bigot fetch his own beer.

By the end of the 1970s, prime-time television was full of small moments and large leaps. "Right-on Maude" strode larger than life into her own spotlight, a middle-aged woman, big boned but dressed to the nines, who gave no quarter and asked for none from her husband, daughter, or friends. Years later, actress Bea Arthur's reincarnation with Betty White and Rue McClanahan on *Golden Girls* gave us attractive widowed and divorced female characters in their late fifties and early sixties, independent and most definitely sexually active.

The Evolution of Male Roles

We saw more evolution in women's television roles than we did in the roles for men. Males were forced to share the spotlight and occasionally the child care with their female counterparts, and they were put on notice that the good ol' days of ruling the roost were over. Prime-time television left them with precious little else to do except be macho cops or mildly clueless foils for their increasingly evolved sisters. Two early exceptions to this male marginalization were *The Courtship of Eddie's Father* starring Bill Bixby and *A Family Affair* starring Brian Keith. Both shows gave us our first peek at the softer side of fatherhood. We saw men as single fathers and caregivers, spending "quality time" with their children beyond the brief bedtime kiss. They offered gentle observations that heretofore had come only from mothers. It took a few more seasons before we recognized that men, too, had new roles to forge and just as much distance to travel on their way to full prime-time personhood. We waited for the 1980s before male characters were allowed to be both vulnerable and strong, both determined and doubtful. It was still longer before prime-time romances were populated by both the drop-dead handsome and the endearingly pudgy, by men with full heads of hair and others with almost none. What fan of *L.A. Law* can forget the "Venus butterfly" episode in which the tender, short, and stocky mensch, played by Michael Tucker, knows the secret but powerful sexual technique that has his on- and off-screen wife, Jill Eikenberry, smiling for days. The culmination of this change perhaps surprised us all when the backside buns we saw on *NYPD Blue* were not those of the devastatingly sexy Bobby Simone, played by Jimmy Smits, but those of his not-so-svelte partner Andy Sipowicz, played by Dennis Franz.

Prime-time television reveled in the excesses of the 1980s with soaps like *Dynasty*, full of sex and sleazy business practices. With their halfback shoulder pads sewn sternly into their glittering power suits, Linda Evans and Joan Collins were just as ruthless and cunning as their historically male counterparts. The consumerist, perfect-bodied *Beverly Hills 90210* followed, and on its heels came the steamy *Melrose Place*.

The 1980s also gave us *thirtysomething*, an ensemble cast of baby boomers settling down, some married and some not, struggling with the ambiguity of the relationships in their lives. If we dismiss *Dynasty* as caricature, *thirtysomething* came knocking on our front doors, bringing into the homes of many in that age group their own dilemmas about family, friends, and lovers. The program was not afraid to ask the hard questions.

Gratuitous Sex

Gratuitous sex persists on television, outside the commitment and monogamy that our faith points to as ideal. Sex is present in the content of the programming and in the commercials that tell us, however subtly, that the slim and the beautiful and the strong succeed, that the right beer and the right car and the right makeup get us the girl or boy of our dreams. Time between the sheets is what we are shown, which leaves us wondering what these characters do during the other hours of their day. By its very nature, television telescopes time. With a little less than twenty-three minutes to wind up a sitcom and somewhere around forty minutes for a prime-time drama, we are left to discern on our own what constitutes the rest of the daily story of the hard-won intimacy in our own lives. In many shows and their commercials, sex is a commodity used to sell entertainment and e-commerce. As a commodity, it has been stripped bare of its context of relationship, its multidimensionality, and its role as a God-given gift proffered to help us travel the tender and sometimes ambiguous lifelong journey toward fulfillment. We see intercourse without commitment, pleasure offered and accepted without an underlying respect and honoring of partners.

The Sexualization of Youth

A troubling aspect of our culture is the sexualization of ever younger children. This is not a big issue in prime time. One doubts that such story lines and styling would get past even today's network "Standards and Practices," the behind-the-scenes panels that still keep an eye on ever-changing and often amorphous "community decency" ideals. Yet with the proliferation of cable and satellite came the rise of channels—MTV's outlets being the most prominent—that have become conveyors of youth culture. Not only the music but also the videos and styling and special programming have become increasingly sexual. One can argue that music itself in all its forms can be an intensely sensual experience; the accompanying costuming and dance can be sensual as well.

One startling example of this is the music career of singer Britney Spears. As of this writing, she is still a teenager but attracts girls as young as nine and ten years old to her concerts, youngsters who want to look like Britney and wear the clothes that Britney wears; but what may be appropriate for a young woman entering her twenties may not be suitable for a prepubescent girl. How do parents deal with this cultural phenomenon and the pervasive peer pressure to imitate a celebrity who is the current rage? Ms. Spears told an interviewer that she plans to save sexual intimacy for marriage. She subsequently appeared on the 2000 MTV Music Awards in an elegantly beaded and body-hugging costume to sing one of her latest hits and proceeded to shed most of the outfit. "Nothing wrong with good entertainment," say some, but if we examine the image and message as we do elsewhere in this book—Ms. Spears' comments to the press juxtaposed with her subsequent performance—we see a cognitive dissonance. In fairness, it may not be a dissonance for Ms. Spears herself. One can argue in good faith that a woman can choose to be "virtuous" and sensual. Indeed, that choice is open to men as well. But what of her younger fans? Can they digest this seeming paradox? Creative artists cannot reasonably be held responsible for all the actions and impulses of the community of fans who admire them, but as members of the "village" who raise our children, we are the ones who must set limits. We may be the ones to help the young people in our lives distinguish between entertainment myth and everyday reality, television image and true personhood, objectification and a healthy sense of a nascent sexual self.

Yearning for Intimacy

Even if we have become used to titillation, many of us find ourselves yearning for "The Relationship." Who can forget the on-again, off-again romance of Sam and Diane on *Cheers*, the humorous cat-and-mouse play between Bruce Willis and Cybill Shepherd in *Moonlighting*, the bickering and affection of Maggie O'Connell and Dr. Fleischman on *Northern Exposure*, and the respect between the polar opposites of Mulder and Scully on *The X-Files*? We cheered the courting and the sparking, engaged in the romantic suspense, gathering around our own versions of the water cooler to dissect both the dialogue and the dilemmas of human interaction.

Strong, integrated, and holistic characters do exist in the hours of prime time, but there are still prime-time reflections (and perhaps they are valuable) of our fears and insecurities about living in a "coupled" world: The message remains that none of us is complete without "another." Each week we watch on the Fox network the antics of Ally McBeal and her ongoing search for that "completion": a man. We laugh as her cartooned and animated tongue unfurls across the room when she spies an attractive male. It is one more paradox of our faith that we are called to community in all its forms and are also called to be content in whatever circumstance we find ourselves.

Is our real challenge to embrace both solitude and relationship as we move through the stages of our lives? We live in early singlehood through our teenage years and early adulthood. We may choose intimate and committed partnership and perhaps parenthood. We may move through the tragedy and aching questions of divorce and separation. As parents, we must let our children go, turn back to an emptier house, and make a new home for ourselves there. We eventually lose the life partners we cherish to illness and death as we move toward the end of our own lives. Fortunately, in the last ten years prime-time television has begun to address all these transitions, and we can be grateful for the storytellers who have named and dramatized these journeys for us.

An author and a poet have separately named both our need to be complete in and of ourselves with our God and our yearning for affection and connection in the context of an all-powerful love that embraces solitude and relationship. French Catholic priest Michel Quoist offers a dialogue between God and a young man who is searching and yearning for the love of his life:

> I need to love. All my being is desire. My heart, my body, yearn in the night towards an unknown one to love.

And God gently answers him:

> Listen, son, stop, and at the very end, deep within
> you, you will meet me. For I call myself Love. It is
> I who made you to love. Set your mind at rest; she
> is on your way, and since you hunger for love,
> I've put on your way all your brothers to love.
> Believe me, it is a long apprenticeship, learning to
> love.[1]

This dialogue offers Ally McBeal and all of us who yearn to love an option of apprenticeship in the discipline of loving well. We are given friends and acquaintances and family along the way to learn this holy and happy art. Quoist suggests that all forms of intimacy and loving are cut from the same cloth.

In her book *The Cloister Walk*, author Kathleen Norris has a chapter entitled "Celibate Passion," a seeming contradiction that is anything but. She discovers a "celibacy that works, practiced by people who are fully aware of themselves as sexual beings . . . they manage to sublimate their sexual energies toward another purpose." Norris admits that she has come late to Christianity, and she writes about her time as an oblate in the Benedictine order and her relationships with men and women "religious" who have embraced celibacy, not as a renunciation of intimacy, but as a choice to channel deep intimacy in other ways. Yet she is fully aware of a culture that still generally believes celibacy to be an aberration, a culture in which "orgasm becomes just another goal; we undress for success." Norris could be writing about a host of prime-time plotlines. She discovers "wise old monks and nuns whose lengthy formation in celibate practice has allowed them to incarnate hospitality in the deepest sense." She suggests that celibates have "learned to listen without possessiveness, without imposing themselves. With someone who is practicing celibacy well, we may sense that we're being listened to in a refreshingly deep way."[2] How refreshing indeed if we could offer that skill, that option, to our teenagers and to all in our community who are in transition, and finally to ourselves.

Norris and Quoist offer the possibility of an expanded definition of human intimacy, one that is disturbing but perhaps ultimately liberating. This possibility looks not just to the self—as so often depicted in prime time—but to a connection that nurtures both the self and others.

Few of us want to return to the days when sex was not talked about in any context, when it was considered "dirty," when it was a cause of shame and embarrassment. Somewhere perhaps between "prudishness and promiscuity" is the wholeness, the "shalom" we yearn for in our intimate lives. Returning to Genesis, we read that at first Adam and Eve were naked and were not ashamed; God blessed their companionship and their intimacy, both physical and emotional. Many of us, across denominational lines, can agree that at our best we seek committed and monogamous relationships, blessed by the daily discipline of love and undergirded by the strength of mutual respect, equality, and compassion. In this context, human sexuality can be celebrated and becomes a source of joy and deep connection, echoing the intimate yearning for the best lover of our souls, our God. Sometimes prime time reflects those values; sometimes it does not.

Intimacy and "Holy Attention"

At the close of the century and after forty-something years of prime time, we are presented with the widest range yet of both gender roles and intimate relationships. The 1990s gave us the gamut: Ellen DeGeneres's coming out as a lesbian; the almost-divorced characters of *Once and Again* taking their first faltering steps back toward the physical and emotional intimacy shattered by failed marriages; Camryn Manheim from *The Practice* claiming her Emmy award "for all the fat girls"; and Will and Grace living together as straight woman and gay man, both single but perhaps not for long. Along that gamut, both today and historically, we as viewers can see ourselves, our parents, our children, and our friends. Such is the nature of "evoked response," the power of shared meaning that allows us to identify with the people we watch. Today, characters and story lines are far more nuanced than ever before. These images and situations can make us uneasy, and yet they can affirm and even inform the undefined and perplexing areas with which we struggle in our own lives.

Our solution as persons of faith may lie in the ancient but renascent concepts of "discernment" and "holy attention." We are called by our God to be wise with God's wisdom, to live our lives intentionally by faith (not mindlessly by the "tube"), to pay attention to this world of prime-time television that "is too much with us." The information and analysis in this book and the suggestions for further study can serve as a starting point for developing a healthier relationship with the "black boxes" in our homes. We can use television to educate ourselves and our children in the discipline of visual and dramatic literacy and to understand the driving forces of prime-time programming and the advertising that supports it. The debate will continue about what is and is not acceptable in prime time, but in the end we must make those decisions for ourselves. Indeed the images and stories we choose to reject may be just as important as the ones we can affirm and embrace: Our "no" is just as vital to us and to our children as our "yes."

In the midst of the hearty passion and startling joy of the Song of Solomon, we have this surprising caution from the author, from the female voice: "I adjure you, O daughters of Jerusalem, . . . do not stir up or awaken love until it is ready!" (3:5). We are warned even by this exuberantly aroused woman to be wise in our passion, and we are reminded to pay holy attention to the desires of our hearts. These desires, if we choose to sanctify them by our faith, to recognize and accept their Godgivenness, lead us in our human yearnings toward greater knowledge of ourselves and greater intimacy with those we love and with our God.

Prime-Time Violence

Violence is everywhere on prime time, from the evening news and *Monday Night Football* to *Smackdown*, documentaries, and late-night horror movies. Because public concern focuses on the violence in crime shows, this discussion is limited to that genre of programming.

Functions and Gratifications of Crime Shows

Crime shows are among the most popular programs on television. One in seven characters on television is connected to law enforcement, and one in five programs is a crime show.[3] These include whodunit mysteries, hard-boiled detective programs, action cop shows, and lawyer and court-room dramas, as well as almost-extinct Westerns. What functions do crime shows serve, and why are they so popular? The answer to this question lies in what crime shows do to and for the audience. Scholarship on this issue is divided. Do crime shows *teach* us how to behave and *inform* us about the nature of the world around us? Do they *arouse* and *cultivate* our anxieties and fears, or do they *alleviate* them? Or can they serve all of these functions?

Morality Plays: The first task of every society is public order; without order no society can function for very long. Most crime shows are morality plays that define good and evil, teach right and wrong, establish norms and sanctions, and model good and bad behavior. In underscoring society's first moral, "Crime does not pay," they provide hope that the social order will be maintained and that justice will prevail.

Public Information: According to the realist school, art reflects life. Crime shows are dramatizations (docudramas) of the local nightly news reports. These shows depict life as it is on the mean streets of urban America and serve as a cautionary tale for society. They probe the criminal mind and provide us with an understanding of what makes criminals tick. Crime shows also demonstrate the law enforcement system at work, thus fostering trust in government.

Arousal and Cultivation: Art does not always reflect life. The reverse can also occur: After a time, life begins to imitate art. The audience may believe the real world is like the virtual world of television and expect real police to look and act like television cops; law enforcement personnel may sometimes take on the personae of their favorite television police officers.

We can infer from studies on the relationship between television and violence that for some people crime shows arouse and exacerbate fears, anxieties, and belligerent behavior. Studies have shown more likelihood of aggressive behavior on the part of some viewers if the violence depicted on television is realistic and exciting, succeeds in punishing the bad guys, and "includes situations or characters similar to those in the viewer's own experience."[4]

In the 1970s and 1980s, George Gerbner and his colleagues at the Annenberg School of Public Communications at the University of Pennsylvania developed extensive empirical studies to test their hypothesis about the long-term effects of television violence on viewers who watched television frequently. Noting that television depicts a fictitious world far more dangerous and violent than the actual world, these researchers developed a program "violence profile," an elaborate system for counting the number of violent acts per episode, in genres ranging from cartoons to crime shows, to support their contention that crime shows exaggerate the dangers of crime in society and thereby cultivate anxious and fearful people.[5] Their studies show that people who watch more than four hours of television a day are more fearful than those who watch fewer hours. They infer from this finding that television causes fear and makes violent behavior more likely among heavy television watchers. Activists in Britain make a similar claim: "Broadcasting and the media are breeder reactors. They help to generate the kind of activity on which they thrive."[6] In 2000, a study by Stanford University professors of medicine indicated for the first time that reducing the amount of television watched by elementary-age children—especially those with signs of hostility—reduces their level of violent behavior.[7]

The depiction of a scary, dangerous world also provides fertile soil for the growth of public attitudes supporting a repressive and punitive criminal justice system. The shows with mean streets where our television crime-fighting heroes refer to poor people—especially poor people of color—as thugs, creeps, scumbags, and roaches provide justification for public outcries of revenge when real crimes are committed and also contribute to the flight of the wealthy to gated communities in the suburbs. In the 1999–2000 season opener of *Law & Order*, the district attorney Adam Schiff (Steven Hill) and his assistant Jack McCoy (Sam Waterston) debate the charges they will bring against a defendant in a mass murder trial. Schiff favors a more modest charge, saying, "Victims' families need closure, not blood." McCoy, who is the plot device for expressing the audience's righteous outrage, raises his voice in rebuttal: "They are entitled to an eye for an eye!" Perhaps it is scenes like these that cause Colin Sumner of the Cambridge Institute of Criminology to speculate: "It may be that the public thirst for punishment is refreshed on a daily basis by television crime drama."[8]

In spite of the commonsense appeal of Gerbner's cultivation theory, which helps to explain the public's support of the construction of more prisons, the "three strikes law," and the re-establishment of the death penalty, Gerbner's view has several weaknesses. It contains a rather mechanistic notion of viewing, a simplistic understanding of how narratives function, and imprecise definitions of violent program content.[9]

Catharsis: Perhaps the theory's most telling weakness, however, is that it does not answer the question, Why are crime shows so popular? Why are crime and punishment such perennial themes on television, and why is prime time "crime time" for so many people? The fearful audience theory does not explain the popularity of crime shows among less fearful people; to explain this we need a broader and deeper understanding. Richard Sparks provides it by developing a theory of alleviation or catharsis, which first originated with Aristotle. We all suffer, he says, from diverse anxieties. Some are of known origin, but most are of unknown origin. Like a lightning rod that collects the electrical charges in the air and directs them in a particular path, crime shows channel a whole array of obscure, existential anxieties, many of which are unrelated to crime and punishment, into an exciting drama with a neat resolution, which reassures us that the world is ordered and just. "As Adorno says, they 'charm away' the challenge of disorder."[10]

From this perspective, crime shows are rites of exorcism and purification. They evoke our anxieties to alleviate them. Crime shows play on the underlying tension between anxiety and reassurance. Anxiety is the hook that captures and holds the audience; resolution of the crime provides the pleasure of reassurance and keeps the audience coming back for more. Television frightens with the news show and consoles with the cop show.* The triumph of justice is pleasurable and relieves anxiety.

This argument is the reverse of Gerbner's: Crime shows do not create fear; fearful people create the audience for crime shows. We are not faced with an all-or-nothing situation, however. Each of these four functions contains part of the story. They are mutually reinforcing rather than mutually exclusive. A cop drama can contain elements of each function, serving simultaneously as (1) a teacher of morals, (2) a description of real life, (3) a fear-producing fantasy, and (4) an anxiety-reducing cathartic. At the same time, some viewers may watch merely for the enjoyment of the tension and struggle as police deal with conflict and ambiguity.

American Television Cop Shows since the 1950s

Television is the contemporary American bard par excellence.[11] Like storytellers in oral societies, television programs *rehearse, test,* and *revise* our common beliefs and values, our collective intentions and aspirations. A brief look at several representative crime shows over the past half-century illustrates the interactive character whereby television reflects and at the

---

*In recent years, news shows like *The Verdict* on CBS and *Dateline* on NBC have been packaged like cop shows, playing up audience fears while also seeking to alay those fears and competing with cop shows for audience ratings during the same time slots.

same time shapes our view of ourselves and of the world around us. This applies particularly to issues of crime, punishment, and political attitudes toward outsiders (the "other").

The precursor to crime shows was the Western, a fictionalized rendition of the thirty-year period between 1865 and 1895, when cowboys fought Indians for control of the western United States. The simplistic and self-righteous battle between good and evil, order and chaos, civilization and savagery provided ideological support for the doctrine of manifest destiny and an expansionist foreign policy. We emerged from World War II with this self-understanding intact, and our government began putting in place those institutions (Central Intelligence Agency [CIA], International Monetary Fund, World Bank, the international monetary agreement signed at Breton Woods in 1947) that would solidify the United States as a world power. In 1950, the Truman administration codified this American self-image in a classified National Security Council document (NSC-68) that the president and his cabinet used to persuade certain leaders in Congress to fund the cold war. NSC-68 compared American virtues to Soviet vices and urged a crusade against Communism. Later the cowboy president, Ronald Reagan, demonized the Soviet Union as the "Evil Empire." During the ensuing decades after NSC-68, the cold war crusade fueled the nuclear arms race, justified intervention in a civil war in Vietnam, and supported repression by U.S. client regimes all over the third world.

Dragnet was adapted from radio in 1951 and is considered by some to be the most successful crime show in the history of television.[12] Its first run ended in 1959, but it enjoyed a revival from 1967 to 1970; reruns are still shown on cable stations. *Dragnet* ushered in a new era of crime shows. Filmed in black and white with ominous shadows of light and dark punctuated by the now famous musical score "dum de dum dum . . . dum," *Dragnet* quickly became a cultural icon, the classic realist cop drama with a gritty cinema *vérité* feel to it. The stories were based on real crimes, and Sergeant Joe Friday (Jack Webb) wanted "Just the facts, ma'am." Good and evil were represented by good people and bad people, but unlike the Western, in which the battle was waged on the frontiers of society, *Dragnet* depicted civilization itself—represented by the city—as the locus for the conflict between good and evil. In addition, the bad guys were no longer outsiders (Indians, outlaws, foreigners), but insiders, almost indistinguishable from other members of society. With evil in our midst, close at hand, cop shows titillate our fears of contagion and give rise to the need for purification. Senator Joe McCarthy capitalized on these fears in his made-for-television anti-Communist congressional witch-hunt in the early 1950s.

Another show, *The Untouchables* (1959–63), epitomized the archetypal attitude of police toward criminals. This show dramatized a fictionalized version of the actual 1920s contest between Chicago mobster Al Capone and U. S. Treasury agent Eliot Ness. The incorruptible Ness and his forces of right regarded Capone and his mobsters as refuse—thugs, punks, low life—to be swept off the city streets. The camera built dramatic tension with closeups of Ness's mounting anger at each frustrated attempt to nail Capone. If one had to choose a particular program to illustrate the contention that on television "evil resides principally in evil people, not generically in the human race"[13] or in evil structures and systems, *The Untouchables* would be a prime candidate.

Crime policy shifted in the 1960s, reflecting the liberalism of John Kennedy's "Camelot," the Civil Rights Act of 1964, and Lyndon Johnson's "War on Poverty." Cop shows of the time capitalized on this new popular recognition of the social origins of crime and the accompanying therapeutic emphasis on the rehabilitation of criminals. The police officer as social worker joined hands with the police as moralist on shows like *The Bold Ones* (1969–73), *The Mod Squad* (1968–73), *The Rookies* (1972–76), and *The Streets of San Francisco* (1972–77). Television cops became more introspective, sometimes questioning their own motives and even the assumptions of the law itself.[14] Reading suspects their "Miranda rights" was incorporated into the act of arrest on most shows during the 1970s.

This liberal view of police work lasted only a decade or so and was never uncontested. In response to the social upheaval caused by the growing protest movement against the Vietnam War, Richard Nixon campaigned for the presidency in 1968 and 1972 on a law-and-order platform. State legislatures passed "get tough" laws, which lengthened prison sentences; television reflected the spirit of the times in plotlines about cops handicapped by the legal constraints of decisions passed in the early 1960s by the liberal Supreme Court headed by Chief Justice Earl Warren. Criminals were shown going free on technicalities, and justice went begging.

Events of the 1970s injected energy into the political left. The humiliated Nixon resigned in 1974 after the Watergate hearings, and the CIA assisted the Chilean military in the overthrow of the socialist government of Salvadore Allende. Saigon fell to the North Vietnamese army in 1975, and the satirical comedy *M*A*S*H* (1972–83) depicted the futility of war and ridiculed life in the military. President Carter charted a more modest role for the United States in world affairs, negotiating the historic Camp David peace accord between Israel and Egypt in 1978–79 and introducing human rights into the calculus of American foreign policy. Then the Iranian hostage crisis (1979–81) broke the back of the American left. When Carter was unable to secure the release of fifty American hostages imprisoned in the U.S. Embassy in Teheran for over a year, the voters replaced him with a mythic movie star who promised to "stand tall" against America's enemies around the world.

Again police shows were quick to reflect the change in popular perspective. The most acclaimed show of the 1980s, Steven Bochco's *Hill Street Blues* (1981–87), first aired during the week of Ronald Reagan's inauguration. Media critic Todd Gitlin labeled *Hill Street* the first post-liberal cop show.[15] Gone are the cop as social worker and the liberal dream of improving the human condition. All we can hope for from our protectors is an uphill battle to maintain order in the midst of decay. *Hill Street* embraced a part of the Reagan revolution—its critique of liberals and its irrational fear of the multicultural diversity in American cities—while undermining Reaganite optimism and moral certainty. The setting is the seedy, rotting core of an unnamed midwestern city where everything breaks down, including phones, electricity, vending machines, toilets, squad cars, cops, and the criminal justice system itself. "Breakdown" is a metaphor for the reactionary message of the show: chaos and purposeless violence that can be contained only by the assertion of repressive counter-violence. On *Hill Street*, the station house is referred to as "a two-bit outpost on the edge of civilization" besieged by "your Third-World brown types," and the neighborhood as "a walk through the Third World." The underexposed and overdeveloped film produces a dirty look and the smell of fear.[16] Nonetheless, *Hill Street* was hardly a mouthpiece for the Reagan revolution. Its depiction of moral ambiguity reflected the public cynicism that emerged during the Vietnam War experience. On *Hill Street*, those who break the law were often portrayed as having more nobility than those who uphold it.

Another 1980s hit, *Miami Vice* (1984–89), produced by Michael Mann, merged the cop show with MTV and was even more cynical than *Hill Street*. Borrowing from the classical style of film noir, this show wallowed in moods of claustrophobia, paranoia, despair, and nihilism. Prominent among the themes of *Miami Vice* was the threat to the nation from the Latin American drug trade. This show featured cops who looked, talked, and acted much like the criminals they pursued and whose public duty was sometimes eclipsed by personal vengeance. Often the forces of good and the forces of evil were indistinguishable, and the weekly enigma turned on whether the moral fabric of society will hold together.[17] During this period, the Reagan government pumped millions into the Contra rebel forces in Nicaragua in an attempt to bring down another socialist government.

Reagan left office in 1988, and the following year the Berlin Wall came tumbling down, taking with it the neat division of the world into opposing camps and removing any structural support for projecting evil onto the "other." Moral ambiguity emerged as a dominant theme in the 1990s, as the graph on the next page illustrates.

Crime shows featuring lawyers and court proceedings are usually filled with ambiguity: uncertainty, circumstantial evidence, intense arguments about the nature of the law, and what justice requires in complex situations. During the early 1950s, less than 10 percent of crime shows featured lawyers and court proceedings. That number peaked at almost 30 percent at the height of the Vietnam War, dropped to 0 percent during the

Percentage

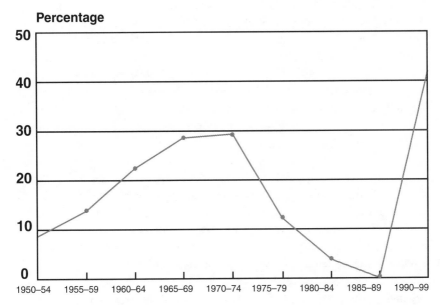

Law programs 1950–1992 as a percentage of crime shows. Source: *Morality and Social Order in Television Crime Dramas* © 1996 John Sumser by permission of McFarland & Company, Inc., Publishers, Box 611, Jefferson, N.C. 28640. www.mcfarlandpub.com

Reagan years, and is now near the 45 percent mark. At the same time, the percentage of good cops to bad cops dropped from 10:1 in the 1960s to 3:1 in 1995.[18] When *NYPD Blue* first aired in 1993, producer Steven Bochco explained that the hero Andy Sipowicz and his colleagues had "situation ethics":

> When you tell stories about cops who are in power, victims who are disenfranchised, and criminals, you are in a world where the rules are complex and changing. . . . If you do it fairly and properly you are going to tell stories that are disturbing sometimes—stories about good, moral cops who believe in the constitution and the system, but who sometimes don't play by the rules. I take some pride in not shying away from moral ambiguity.[19]

NYPD Blue builds on some of the postmodern themes of *Miami Vice*—distrust of institutions, resentment of authority, heightened awareness of life's ambiguities, the absence of a coherent social vision—but perfects the subgenre of nighttime cop soap with psychologically well-developed characters. Dennis Franz has won three Emmy awards for his lead role as Detective Andy Sipowicz, the cynical and tormented reformed alcoholic who seeks to exorcise his own demons by combating the contagion of urban evil. Deeply flawed and wounded by a bitter divorce and the murder of a son and a second wife, Sipowicz treats every crime as a personal insult. He pounces on suspects like an angry bulldog, intimidating and coercing confessions with little concern for civil liberties and legal niceties. Yet there is more to Sipowicz and his colleagues at the precinct on the Lower East Side of New York City; they exude class hatred, disgust, a loathing of the rot and refuse of urban chaos. "Scumbag" is one of Andy's favorite words to insult his suspects. In the establishing scene that introduces the program each week, we see a rotting tenement being dynamited but never replaced by urban renewal. This scene is a metaphor for the human and environmental deterioration that these television cops must deal with on a daily basis.

NYPD Blue provides its audience more pleasure from the drama of the characters' personal lives than from their police work. The weekly murders are usually solved in forty minutes, whereas the fraying personal lives of the detectives unfold from episode to episode with suspense but without final resolution. In the midst of the social disorder of a disintegrating urban life, this show creates a workplace family of the 1990s in which caring colleagues—women who are tender and tough and men who temper machismo with emotional vulnerability—support one another through various personal crises. The show creates intimacy with minimal dialogue by close-ups of exchanged glances and tender sexual scenes. The theme of the show is maintaining sanity and personal integrity in a world gone awry: Salvation is personal, not social. In one episode, a criminal complains that if he were rich Sipowicz would not have hit him. Sipowicz's reply epitomizes his attitude toward society in general: "Hey, this is America. I would hit you whether you were rich or poor."

In the midst of this cynicism, complex shows like NYPD Blue often have the ring of Lamentations or Psalms. At the end of the hour, we are left with the victim dead, witnesses too scared to come forward, compromised police work in some cases, and a sneering suspect who seems to get away with it. These shows no longer consistently wrap everything up with a Christmas ribbon at the end of an episode. The American viewing public is finally being presented with the archetypal idea that sometimes there is no justice, and we cry aloud to God with the psalmist for the restoration of righteousness.

Four other cop shows of the 1990s merit brief mention because of their contrast with Hill Street, Miami Vice, and NYPD Blue. The first, Walker, Texas Ranger, an action cop show in cowboy boots and Stetsons by Bruce Cervi and John Lansing, is a simplistic vehicle for exhibiting special effects, especially the kick-boxing talents of Chuck Norris. It is a throwback to the moralistic tales of the 1950s. The second, Nash Bridges, is an action whodunit starring an aging playboy with an ego the size of San Francisco bay, who tools around San Francisco in a yellow Barracuda convertible, waiting to rescue the next damsel in distress. Written and directed by (and starring!) Don Johnson, Nash Bridges explores white, midlife male fantasy. For Bridges as for Sherlock Holmes, crime fighting is an amusing adventure. One almost expects to hear him call out to his partner Joe Dominguez (Cheech Marin), "Come Bubba, the game's afoot."

More significant was a show that aired on and off for a couple of years in the late 1990s on ABC, entitled *Vengeance Unlimited*. Produced by John McNamara, this show starred Michael Madsen as Mr. Chapel, a private citizen (not a private detective) with a vendetta against evil. On his own initiative, this 1990s style urban Lone Ranger sought to punish criminals who have escaped prosecution because of legal technicalities or the ineptitude of the criminal justice system. Using techniques of film noir, *Vengeance Unlimited* examined one basic human emotion—revenge—over and over again. The hero was motivated by a deep and insatiable desire to avenge the brutal murder of his wife. In one typical episode, he loaded onto an airplane a captured right-wing Salvadoran general responsible for the slaughter of many peasants. After they were airborne, he introduced the general to family members of his victims. The episode ended as the airplane door opened and the general contemplated his death from 30,000 feet. *Vengeance Unlimited* did not get high enough ratings to stay on the air, not because it was too simplistic—if simplicity were the problem, *Walker, Texas Ranger*, and *Nash Bridges* would have died long ago—but probably because audiences preferred a more veiled and nuanced portrayal of vengeance, a fundamental motivation that drives all cop shows.

Critics hailed the fourth show, *Homicide: Life on the Street* (1992–99), as "one of television's all-time best police series" and "the best police series ever produced by American television,"[20] but its postmodernism was too enigmatic and philosophical for a mass audience. After seven years, this superb NBC drama of the conflicted lives of cops on the mean streets of Baltimore could not match the ratings of the hackneyed CBS offering, *Nash Bridges*, which aired during the same 10:00 to 11:00 P.M. time slot on Friday nights. One icon on *Homicide* is worth mentioning as a metaphor for the worldview of cop shows in the 1990s: the close-up of the scoreboard at the station house on which a hand writes a name in red (an unsolved murder) and then changes the name to black when a case is solved. In each episode, when a body was discovered, the scene switched to this board for the recording of a new name as the phone rang to report yet another murder. The Sisyphean message is that crime is always with us, but the living have a covenant with the dead to avenge their murders.[21]

PART II |

An Overview
of Prime-Time Dramas
Fables of Stability in a World of Change

Definitions, Origins, and Characteristics

This chapter gives an overview of the genre of programming known as *melodrama* or *drama* and provides a brief history of its development on prime-time television in the United States. For our purposes, drama programs can be described as *fictional narratives with recurring characters that air on a weekly basis and usually run for sixty minutes.* Weekly dramas can be divided into two broad categories today: *series* and *serials.* During television's early "golden age," teleplay *anthologies* were also common. Subjects for prime-time melodramas have included the Old West, the medical and legal professions, crime fighting, science fiction, and family life.

Television melodramas can be traced back to nineteenth-century stage plays that were considered a low form of opera. Derived from the Greek words for "music" and "deeds," these plays had songs and instrumentals with maudlin, highly contrived plots and happy endings. A stereotype of these dramas featured the villain who tied the heroine to railroad tracks and the hero who saved her at the last minute. Like an opera, the structure of a melodramatic play included a highly compressed introduction, a dramatic plot, and musical accompaniment that provided emotional cues.[1]

Dramatic *series* on television have adopted this plot structure. Each series usually has one main hero-character—often a white male—along with recurring supporting players. These programs are heavily action driven; "stuff happens" on these shows. There is usually only one main plotline that develops throughout the episode, reaches a climax, and achieves closure through the hero's victory over evil. This rising action-climax structure is repeated in miniature in each of the four twelve-minute acts that make up a weekly program. Because action is the narrative element driving these shows, the personality traits of regular characters change little from week to week. In syndication, we can view episodes out of their original broadcast order and notice no difference. Typically, dramatic series are shot on film with a single camera, like miniature Hollywood movies.

These were the characteristics of virtually all prime-time melodramas until the 1980s. During that decade, however, traits of daytime *serials*—most notably, soap operas—began to infiltrate prime time. Whereas dramatic series are propelled by action, serials are *character driven*. Action fans may even complain that "nothing ever happens" on these shows because relationships are what they "about"; even when they are filled with action sequences, the people and their relationships to one another dominate. The characters who populate these shows can change and grow over time; as in real life, they are affected by the things that happen to them. Consequently, it can be both confusing and frustrating to watch these shows out of their original sequence when they move to syndication. Prime-time serials typically have many regular characters as opposed to one main star, and they usually depict situations that function as extended surrogate families. They have many plotlines that intertwine in and between episodes; frequently, these individual story lines do not achieve closure for several weeks or months. Robin Nelson has coined the term "flexi-narratives" to describe these dramas.[2] The only technical difference between these prime-time serials and their daytime counterparts is that soap operas are always shot in sound studios on videotape with three cameras, whereas evening shows are shot on film with one camera.

Hal Himmelstein notes that television melodramas are conservative by nature in that they tend to reinforce the status quo through the hero-figures that populate them. These hero-figures function as "social types" along with villains and fools. "Within the television melodrama, these social types operate as signs, constructed according to our society's dominant values, reinforcing commonly held concepts regarding the 'proper order of things'"[3] He adds that melodrama is "highly significant in an age of surface complexity and contradiction . . . for it provides us with models of clear resolution for highly personalized, intensely enacted conflict."[4]

Himmelstein also shows how the myth structure of television melodramas is derived from ancient Greek epic poems such as *The Odyssey*. Typically, the hero finds himself in a situation where the equilibrium has been disturbed. Through his own outstanding abilities (and a little help from the gods), he overcomes a series of obstacles and eventually restores the natural order of things. As a prominent feature of these stories, the hero usually resorts to violence to accomplish "redemption." New Testament scholar Walter Wink has pointed out that this myth of redemptive violence is so deeply entrenched in Western civilization that it is a feature of most creation stories (but is conspicuously absent in the Hebrew book of Genesis).[5] The hero myth structure has been an essential ingredient in television melodrama from the beginning.

History

The Early Years of Live Drama

Melodramas made their earliest appearance on television when several popular radio soap operas—so called because their original sponsors were detergent companies eager to court domestic audiences of women—made the move to the little screen. Early versions of shows such as *The Guiding Light, Days of Our Lives*, and *As the World Turns* were performed live, as was nearly everything on television. Long overlooked by critics, these shows have been among the most durable in the medium, and they have since lent their serial structure and relational sensibility to a host of prime-time "quality television" programs as diverse as *Hill Street Blues* and *ER*. Live plays also made the move from radio to television and featured the work of such distinguished writers as Paddy Chayefsky, Rod Serling, Reginald Rose—and Shakespeare!—on shows like *Playhouse 90, The Kraft Television Theater,* and *Studio One*. This was the legendary "golden age" of television.

These anthology-shows featured different actors every week—giving many future Hollywood stars like James Dean and Paul Newman their first national exposure—and enjoyed a brief shining moment from the late 1940s through the 1950s. Confined by bulky cameras, television had to limit itself to studio performances that were broadcast live, and for the most part, the studios were located in New York City. Because Broadway's theater district was nearby, stage plays or specially written "teleplays" were ideal fare for television. These live dramas had an elitist appeal to the upscale purchasers of the first television sets. Their producers were willing to deal with more mature themes than did later "episodic" television, resulting in such classics as "Requiem for a Heavyweight," "Marty," and "Twelve Angry Men." Reginald Rose's "Thunder on Sycamore Street" even dealt with the issue of racism, although the nervous sponsor and network muted the incendiary potential of the program by changing the black protagonist into a white ex-convict.

The limitations of live television dictated the very "look" of these early programs in ways that are still with us. Hollywood movies are typically filmed with only one camera that is repositioned again and again until an entire scene has been shot. Careful editing then stitches the various angles together into a coherent whole. Because early television was "live," this approach was impossible; of necessity, story lines were acted out in continuity like stage plays. To vary the shots in a given scene, multiple cameras (usually three) were employed. Typically, two cameras were focused on each main character while the third was reserved for establishing or "wide" shots. The two close-up cameras were tightly cropped to avoid inadvertently showing the other cameras. This approach tended to favor close-ups with uncomplicated, out-of-focus backgrounds so that characters could be easily "read" on the small television screens in use at the time, and this format is still used in the productions of daytime soaps and some prime-time sitcoms.[6]

Recognizing a serious threat to its entertainment monopoly, Hollywood had imposed a virtual ban on cooperating with television when it first came on the scene, but that resolve began to weaken in the 1950s. When *I Love Lucy* debuted in 1951, one of its innovations (besides being structured around a woman who did everything in her power to get out of the house) was to substitute *film* cameras in Hollywood and then to edit the film to simulate the look of a live show. That same year, Walt Disney struck a deal with third-place ABC and launched *Disneyland*, an ingenious show that recycled his library of old films and drummed up excitement for his new theme park at the same time. One of the early programs Disney produced for this show contained several episodes about the legendary woodsman *Davy Crockett*—in effect, adapting the old Hollywood movie serial to television. (More than a decade before color television became widely available, Disney also had the foresight to produce all of his new programs, including *Davy Crockett*, in color.) Warner Brothers followed Disney's lead in 1955 and soon began churning out television Westerns, again for ABC.

The economics became clear. Whereas a live show disappeared into the ether as soon as it hit the airwaves (except for kinescopes shot off television monitors), original film series could be broadcast over and over. It was only a matter of time before all of television moved to Hollywood, where populist fare like Westerns and crime shows—which had a greater appeal to the working-class consumers who now purchased most televisions sets—could be produced quickly and cheaply. These factors soon spelled the end of the live teleplay anthologies.

1950s

TV's first *crime show, Dragnet*, appeared in 1951, the same year as *I Love Lucy*. Also filmed in Hollywood, it quickly established a perennial television genre. Its no-nonsense style was typified by its somber nine-note musical trademark and Jack Webb's flat, staccato delivery. Filmed and broadcast in black and white, *Dragnet* portrayed a society with clear rights and wrongs, where the tranquil stability of decent folks was momentarily threatened by criminals who were eventually apprehended by police Sergeant Joe Friday. He was a new kind of institutional, corporate hero for the era of the man in the gray flannel suit, a striking contrast to the lone rangers of Hollywood Westerns and the fringe-of-the-law private eyes of film noir. The name of the show itself was suggestive. Whether Webb intended it, the "dragnet" refers to a parable of Jesus in which good and bad are gathered together and then systematically separated—a metaphor evidently meant to represent the criminal element being isolated from the innocent population at large.

Besides being a hit with the public, *Dragnet* was important for another reason. As Steven Stark points out, its law-and-order ethos was an ideal vehicle for commercial advertisers.[7] Consumers want to know that their world is safe and secure before they part with their money, and *Dragnet* and its numerous offspring conveyed that message. This is no small point: Commercial television in the United States is a potent medium for creating desire for the products and services of free market capitalism. Ultimately, all of its programming is geared to support consumerism to insure its own survival and that of America's economic system. Just as melodramatic heroes bolster the status quo by providing models of socially approved behavior, so do melodramatic plots help to maintain a stable psychic environment for a robust consumer society.

Westerns were among the first shows to appear on television when it was a new medium, although these preliminary efforts were specifically targeted at children during daytime hours. As early as 1949, William Boyd converted all sixty-six of his Hopalong Cassidy "B" movie Westerns into a weekly series that became a ratings and merchandising hit for NBC. (Walt Disney undoubtedly paid attention to this phenomenon when he later marketed *Davy Crockett* and his famous coonskin cap.) "A" grade Westerns did not appear in prime time until after the major Hollywood studios began to make their peace with the networks. *Gunsmoke* led the way on CBS in 1955 and ran for twenty years—long after its many imitators had disappeared.

The first prime-time Westerns were classic shoot-em-up affairs, and they became instantly popular. During the 1958–59 season, there were nearly thirty such shows on the air, with titles like *Wagon Train, Maverick,* and *The Rifleman,* and seven of the ten top-rated shows were Westerns. Even then, critics complained about the amount of gun violence used to resolve conflict on these shows, and in 1961, the Federal Communications Commission (FCC) chairman Newton Minow singled out Westerns as major contributors to the "vast wasteland" of American television. Consequently, new programs set on the frontier became more domestic (*The Big Valley, Bonanza*), and, as Steven Stark observes, the concerns of the suburbs were simply transplanted to the ranch.[8]

Between 1955 and 1965, television Westerns managed to be most things to most people. Set in America's mythic past, they provided a reassuring sense of nostalgia for a nation that was undergoing a seismic shift in population from the cities to the suburbs while under the shadow of the hydrogen bomb. As Shakespeare had done in his historical dramas, television writers could use the distance of the western frontier as a safe canvas onto which they could project and examine contemporary concerns. Its "good guys and bad guys" not only fit the structural needs of the melodramatic form, but could serve as proxies for the drama of the cold war that was brewing. Advertisers loved Westerns because their plots reinforced the message of their commercials: No matter what the initial problem, it can always be solved in relatively short order.[9] The same is true of the format of most prime-time series.

The first *hospital drama* on television was *Medic*, which debuted on NBC in 1954. Produced with the cooperation of the Los Angeles County Medical Association, it began a symbiotic relationship between television and the health care establishment, which saw television as a powerful ally in bolstering the image of doctors. Medical dramas first caught on with a public that was in awe of the scientific and technological breakthroughs transforming America after World War II. Because health crises can happen to anyone, such programs reassured viewers that they would be in safe hands should their "time" ever come. With dramatic situations that were literally about life and death, doctor shows also had heroes tailor-made for the melodramatic form.

Perry Mason debuted on CBS in 1957 and remained on the air until 1966, during which time it attracted more than thirty million viewers a week. A hybrid *legal-detective* show, it is still considered one the most popular lawyer series in television history. It was noted for formulizing to maximum dramatic effect the segmented act-structure caused by commercial breaks. Each episode began with a murder and the wrongful arrest of the person who would become Mason's client. Through a mixture of detective work in the first half-hour and brilliant courtroom theatrics during the second, Mason always exposed the true perpetrator and exonerated his client. David Thornburn characterizes what he calls the "mythic or ritual content of Perry Mason" as "an endlessly renewing drama of murder, justice perverted, justice redeemed."[10] In marked contrast to *Dragnet*, *Perry Mason* displayed an implicit lack of confidence in the ability of the police to apprehend the right suspects, a distrust of public institutions that increased throughout the 1960s.

This skeptical animus was part and parcel of *The Twilight Zone*, the first *science fiction* program to make its mark on the popular imagination, which ran on CBS from 1959 to 1964. It was the creation of Rod Serling, a respected author of numerous live anthology dramas, including "Requiem for a Heavyweight"; he wrote more than half of the scripts for this filmed anthology series as well. Discouraged from exploring timely or controversial themes in his earlier work by nervous network executives and sponsors, he turned to fantasy and the surreal because he guessed that "the suits" would not take him as seriously and so would grant him greater creative freedom. It worked, as it did a generation later for the creators of the animated sitcom *The Simpsons*. Serling used *The Twilight Zone* to explore all manner of dis-ease just below the placid exterior of popular consciousness at the time, including the climate of distrust over McCarthyism and the cold war, as well as the latent fears occasioned by the nuclear age and the space race. *The Twilight Zone* was ahead of its time in that it was not as popular with critics or the public during its first run as it was later, in syndication. Nevertheless, with its distrust of the accepted wisdom of the day, it presaged such postmodern shows as *The X-Files* by more than forty years.

1960s–1970s

The Kennedy administration ushered in a brief era of idealistic optimism, when it was in vogue to tackle social problems at home or abroad, as with VISTA or the Peace Corps. Several shows in the 1960s were in keeping with this spirit. On NBC, E. G. Marshall and Robert Reed played a father-son legal team on *The Defenders*. Airing from 1961 to 1965, the show explored such controversial topics as abortion, euthanasia, capital punishment, and blacklisting. Two of the most popular medical dramas ever, *Ben Casey* and *Dr. Kildare*, both debuted in 1961, featuring a pair of handsome and idealistic young doctors who seemed cast in the mold of the new president. Dr. Casey in particular displayed a crusading zeal, and in the wake of Newton Minow's "vast wasteland" speech, both he and Kildare served as evidence that the networks were seriously trying to curb television violence. In *East Side/West Side*, George C. Scott played a social worker who dealt with all manner of urban ills in New York City; it ran for only a single season on CBS in 1963. Even *Star Trek* (1966–69) used the vehicle of science fiction to examine issues such as racism and war. With its multinational cast, it was a United Nations updating of the Western—complete with the mythic fascination of the boundless frontier.

Virtually invisible during the 1950s, a stream of *spy programs* burst onto the television landscape in the mid-1960s with such titles as *The Man from U.N.C.L.E.*, *The Avengers*, *Secret Agent*, *I Spy*, *Mission: Impossible*, and even the spoof *Get Smart*. These shows featured sophisticated heroes, techno-gadgets, and often glamorous settings, and they flowed out of the confluence of several timely factors. True to the demands of melodramatic form, their heroes were generally virtuous agents of goodness, truth, and the American way (or its British counterpart). These shows tapped into the zeitgeist of the cold war, but with the "hip and cool" trappings of the era so astutely satirized in the *Austin Powers* movies of the 1990s. The dusty Westerns that had been so popular only a few years before suddenly felt out-of-date, and spy programs seemed more in keeping with the times.

In an era when the CIA staged coups in foreign countries and even attempted to assassinate Fidel Castro, the genre rarely questioned the purpose or the methods of the government's foreign intelligence agencies. One notable exception was an import from Britain titled *The Prisoner*. Starring Patrick McGoohan as a former secret agent (a role he had played in an earlier series by the same name), *The Prisoner* was an extended allegory about the struggle of the individual to assert autonomy in the face of the anonymous bureaucrats who increasingly controlled his fate. Rather than being a captive in an Orwellian police state, the prisoner was a "guest" in a pleasant resort where all his needs were fulfilled—just like a modern capitalist society—and the program implicitly questioned whether citizens in countries like Britain and the United States could ever be really "free."[11]

The placid surface that inaugurated the 1960s began to crack by mid-decade with the assassination of the Kennedy brothers and Martin Luther King, Jr., race riots in decaying urban centers, and protests against the Vietnam War. A huge "generation gap" opened between parents and authorities from "the greatest generation" and their baby boomer children. Teenagers experimented freely with sex and drugs. Women and homosexuals began to demand equal rights. Divorce rates went up. By the early 1970s, abortion had become legal, and the Watergate scandal occasioned cynical distrust in government and in elected officials. Conservative by nature, commercial television was slow to respond to the social and political turmoil of these years, and prime-time melodramas rarely dealt directly with the issues roiling the day—unlike sitcoms such as *All in the Family* or *Maude*. Even *M*A*S*H*, set during the Korean conflict, tackled the Vietnam War obliquely.

Instead of addressing the issues head on, television served up soothing reminders of the good old days with such shows as *The Waltons* and *Little House on the Prairie*. Set during the Depression in rural Virginia, *The Waltons* featured a large stable family living in a world that was the virtual antithesis of the zeitgeist of the 1970s. There was no divorce, no generation gap, and no war of the sexes. The Waltons trusted *their* president, while the Watergate/Nixon debacle was unfolding on the evening news. African Americans and whites got along pretty well on Walton's mountain, and the only war that people went off to fight was a "good war" to defeat Hitler. Bedrock American values were affirmed: love of God, country, and family; hard work and the Jeffersonian ideal of the rural life. The Waltons reminded Americans of who they "really were" underneath all the turmoil of the late 1960s and 1970s and provided a comforting place to escape to each week. Other genre shows like *Marcus Welby, M.D.*, and *Owen Marshall, Counselor at Law*, did the same thing.

Commercial television's other strategy was to serve up a host of crime shows during this period. A brief catalog of the more successful programs aired throughout the late 1960s and 1970s gives an idea of how prime-time melodrama attempted to counterbalance uneasiness in U.S. streets and living rooms by restoring law and order on its television sets: *Mannix*,

Ironside, Columbo, The Streets of San Francisco, Kojak, Police Woman, Starsky and Hutch, Charlie's Angels, CHiPs—even *Dragnet* reappeared for a few years. Few of the newer characters followed Sgt. Friday's example as by-the-book police officers, however. In keeping with the growing distrust of authority figures during this period, many of these crime-fighting heroes operated on the edges of the law enforcement establishment or had quirky, unorthodox idiosyncrasies (Columbo's trench coat and cigar, Kojak's lollypop). Nevertheless, justice always caught up with the bad guys, so that these shows told Americans, "Fear not, things are really under control." By focusing their stories on *individual* villains rather than on systemic problems, these shows could reassure viewers at home even though the larger social problems remained unsolved.

The Prime-Time Serial Comes of Age

Cable television first appeared on the horizon in the late 1970s and began its slow, steady assault on the dominance of the "big three" broadcast networks. By segmenting the broad audience into niches, cable created possibilities for innovation in program content and style that reverberated across the television landscape. During this time, two new shows heralded a different way of structuring prime-time dramas: *Lou Grant* (1977) and *Dallas* (1978).

Lou Grant was the last spin-off from *The Mary Tyler Moore Show* and the first hour-long drama produced by MTM Enterprises. It brought to the melodramatic form many of the features that had made its sister sitcoms so innovative, notably a depiction of the workplace as an extended family. *M*A*S*H* had explored this terrain effectively throughout the 1970s, and even though it was billed as a comedy, its underlying serious sensibility earned it the label "dramedy"—and provided a fitting precedent for a full-blown ensemble drama like *Lou Grant*. Thomas Schatz says that *Lou Grant* "marked a crucial new direction for . . . hour-long drama . . . because of its primary focus on the workplace . . . and its aggressive treatment of 'serious' social and work-related issues."[12]

Dallas got off to a slow start in spring 1978, but it became one of the most popular television shows in the world and stayed on the air for thirteen years. Its principal claim to fame was to import the subject matter and serial form of daytime soap operas into prime time. On the former score, it spawned a swarm of imitators, from *Dynasty* and *Knots Landing* to *Beverly Hills 90210* and *Melrose Place*. More important, with its multiple plot strands that carried over from one episode to the next and its myriad characters who changed and evolved over time, *Dallas* paved the way for a new breed of ensemble serial dramas dubbed "quality television."

Dallas was also a seminal show in that it gave delicious expression to the spirit of its age: *Dallas* portrayed a dog-eat-dog world of high finance and high living that perfectly reflected the dominant ethos of the Reagan era. It fused the family-values appeal of *The Waltons*, with the rural can-do spirit of the frontier and added the ruthless credo of the Wall Street high rollers who were the new "Masters of the Universe" (to borrow Tom Wolfe's phrase from *Bonfire of the Vanities*). Oliver Stone's *Wall Street* made this explicit in the words of its antihero Gordon Gekko: "Greed is good. Greed works." *Dallas* tapped into this creed perfectly.

The precedents of *Lou Grant* and *Dallas* helped prepare for the appearance of *Hill Street Blues* in 1981. With this MTM drama, the prime-time ensemble serial came of age. Created by Steven Bochco and Michael Kozol, *Hill Street* was the first of a string of innovative dramas in the 1980s and 1990s, which Robert J. Thompson has titled "Television's Second Golden Age" because of all the characteristics they share.[13] These features include workplace settings that function as surrogate families, multiple story lines that extend over several episodes, realistic set design and production techniques, and plots that explore serious issues intersecting with the personal lives of numerous regular characters. These shows also deftly interwove comedy with their thoughtful themes. Together, they revitalized each of their respective genres: medicine (*St. Elsewhere*, *ER*, and *Chicago Hope*); law (*LA Law*, *Ally McBeal*, and *The Practice*); police (*NYPD Blue* and *Homicide: Life on the Streets*); family (*thirtysomething*, *Sisters*, and *Once & Again*); even science fiction (*Star Trek: The Next Generation*). Some of these shows defy easy classification and are hybrids of two or more genres: *Northern Exposure* (Western + magic realism); *Picket Fences* (family + law/court); *Ally McBeal* (law + feminism + magic realism).

The ensemble dramas of the 1980s and 1990s are starkly different from the classic melodramatic series of the 1950s, 1960s, and 1970s. *Hill Street Blues*, for instance, depicts a cold, ragged world in which police officers have all they can do to keep the urban decay of "the hill" from spinning out of control. The precinct's two desk sergeants (played successively by Michael Conrad and Robert Prosky) neatly summarized the show's attitudes toward new social realities with the following bits of advice after each morning's roll call: First, "Let's be careful out there"; and then, "Go out there and do it to them before they do it to you."

The old certainty about the social order taken for granted on *Dragnet* or *The Waltons* was replaced by a wary humanism. *Hill Street*'s large and eclectic group of detectives and uniformed beat cops were basically good people trying to make the best of an ambiguous and chaotic world. While political ads stated that it was "Morning in America," *Hill Street* may have more accurately reflected how Americans felt during Reagan's presidency. U.S. citizens had been held hostage in Iran during the year before Reagan's election, his first term was marked by a persistent economic downturn and farm crisis, and the cold war was rekindled by increased military spending that sent our national deficit soaring. Homeless people began filling the streets of major cities, and a strange new disease called AIDS made its first frightening appearance. In this context, the gritty realism of *Hill Street* probably mirrored our collective psyche more than we realized, and despite the economic prosperity of the 1990s, prime time's subsequent ensemble serials followed its groundbreaking lead.

1980s–1990s in Fast-Forward: Odds and Ends and Trends

Although ensemble dramas such as *St. Elsewhere* and *NYPD Blue* have earned critical reviews and awards during the past twenty years, other shows and trends during this period, which do not fit into the same category, are worth noting. One of them is *Cagney & Lacey,* which aired on CBS from 1982 to 1988. Conceived in the 1970s as a feminist counterpoint to the buddy police dramas typified by *Starsky and Hutch* and *CHiPs* (and in contrast to the rather blatant sex appeal of shows like *Police Woman* and *Charlie's Angels*), it was originally turned down by all three broadcast networks. The series began as a made-for-television movie in 1981, starring Loretta Swit and Tyne Daly in the title roles; encouraged by its success, CBS launched the show later that season with Meg Foster instead of Swit, who was unavailable. Because of poor ratings, nervous network executives feared that its tone was too stridently feminist and that its leads were not feminine enough, so they fired Meg Foster in favor of more conventionally beautiful Sharon Gless—over the loud protests of women's groups. After another season of poor ratings, they canceled the show in 1983. When it won a surprise Emmy at the end of the summer, CBS reversed course, and the publicity that had been generated by all the controversy helped build a better audience base. Jeremy Butler has written that *Cagney & Lacey* "challenged the genre's patriarchal underpinnings in fundamental, unprecedented ways" and "confronted women's issues that the genre had previously ignored: breast cancer, abortion, birth control, [date] rape . . . and spousal abuse."[14]

Another show was *Miami Vice,* which premiered in 1984. On the one hand, its partners Crockett and Tubbs were mere variations on the standard buddy formula of 1970s crime series. On the other hand, these agents ventured so deeply into the underworld of drug smuggling and dealing that it was often difficult to tell which side they were on—quite the opposite of the genre's typical moral rectitude. With its pastel wardrobe and set design and up-to-the-minute rock music soundtrack, *Miami Vice* also reflected MTV's stylistic influence on more traditional entertainment vehicles during the 1980s.

Ironically, 1984 also saw the debut of *Murder, She Wrote,* a veritable throwback to the Ellery Queen detective mysteries of the 1950s. What was most notable about it was its enormous success with older audiences on Sunday evenings, a time slot it occupied for more than a decade. (More on demographic programming below.)

Previously, we mentioned that *M*A*S*H* merited the label "dramedy" because of its combination of comic characters and situations with the serious issues and pathos of drama. Other half-hour dramedies have appeared on the air since then, most notably *The Wonder Years* (1988–93) and *SportsNight* (1998–2000). Several hour-long shows deserve the designation as well, specifically *Northern Exposure* and *Ally McBeal*, which we have examined under the category of situation comedy.

Since the end of the cold war, a number of prime-time dramas have explored territory staked out in the 1960s by *The Twilight Zone* and *The Outer Limits*, as if the collapse of old bipolar animosities released a host of free-floating anxieties with nowhere to go. Delving into shadowy conspiracies and the paranormal have been such shows as *Twin Peaks, The X-Files, Millennium,* and *Profiler*. At the opposite extreme, the late 1990s saw the emergence of a number of shows that dealt specifically with religious themes. Notable among them have been *Nothing Sacred, 7th Heaven, Promised Land,* and *Touched by an Angel*, which has regularly scored ratings in the Nielsen top ten.

Since 1990, NBC's *Law & Order* has gradually established itself as a solid hit with critics and audiences alike. A hybrid of the law and police genres, its rigorously formulaic structure has maintained the show's quality and ratings even as its cast has undergone numerous defections and replacements. The first half-hour always begins with the discovery of a murder and follows two New York police detectives as they narrow suspects before making an arrest. The second half then follows two district attorneys as they build their case and prosecute the suspect in court—often with surprising twists. The cases depicted on *Law & Order* always spring from controversial headlines and explore the issues behind them with thoughtfulness and nuance. Although the show deserves the label of "quality television," it eschews the characteristics of most ensemble dramas by rarely delving into the personal lives of its characters or carrying plotlines from one episode to the next.

As noted earlier, the presence and influence of cable transformed television programming in the 1980s and 1990s and is primarily responsible for what are known as "niche channels." During the reign of the "big three" broadcast networks, shows were pitched to the largest possible audience because competition was small, but cable systems multiplied the number of available channels from which viewers could choose. Today, niche channels on cable aim their programming at specific audiences, and the traditional networks have followed suit by tailoring shows to demographic groups valued by their advertisers. For example, NBC's "Must-See TV" lineup on Thursday nights has been successful in attracting the desirable eighteen- to forty-nine-year-old market, and *Murder, She Wrote* did equally well with senior citizens on Sunday nights. On cable, the WB network has clearly staked out turf with teens and has been responsible for shows such as *Dawson's Creek* and *Felicity*. Other niche channels have included Lifetime and Oxygen (for women), BET (for African Americans), and Odyssey and PAX (for families and those with a religious orientation).

The influence of cable has nudged dramatic series in stylistic directions they might otherwise not have gone. This can be seen in the distinctive visual and storytelling styles of shows such as *Twin Peaks*, *The X-Files*, *OZ*, and *Homicide: Life on the Streets*. Premium movie channels have also been able to produce shows that push the dramatic envelope because they need not worry about the same decency standards as broadcast networks. HBO has been particularly successful at this with shows like *The Sopranos* and *Sex and the City*.

Against these developments, prime-time dramas still fail to explore the world of ethnic and racial minorities—or women—in any meaningful way, except where they appear in ensemble shows. One program that followed two families during the Civil Rights years—one white and the other black—was *I'll Fly Away*. Despite glowing reviews and several critical honors, however, it was canceled after only one season. Stephen Bochco's *City of Angels* debuted as a mid-season replacement in 2000. Set in an urban hospital with a mostly African-American cast, it was the first such prime-time drama in years to go after a mainstream audience.

Another interesting omission in recent prime-time dramas has been any evidence of the high-tech industry and culture fueling the tremendous economic growth of the 1990s. Although the advertising and entertainment industries have been visible on both sitcoms and dramas from *Frasier* and *Just Shoot Me* to *thirtysomething*, television seems not to know what to do with new technology like the Internet—just as motion pictures did not know how to react to television when *it* was a new medium.

Metanarrative and Theology

As noted earlier, television melodramas exercise a stabilizing function in American culture by holding up heroes worth imitating and by reinforcing the myths that undergird the structure of American society and its economic system. As such, they *reflect* attitudes and beliefs in the general culture; they *follow* trends rather than inaugurate them. They also work to re-establish equilibrium in society when it has been disrupted.

Accordingly, television's initial prime-time dramas reflected the sense of moral certainty that emerged from having endured the twin crucibles of the Great Depression and the Second World War. At a time of tremendous social and economic relocation with the growth of corporate America and the migration to the suburbs, television melodramas provided reassuring narratives of law and order, stability, and the triumph of medical technology over the chaos of disease and death. Later, as the prosperous postwar society began to question itself at home and abroad, prime-time dramas responded with tales of idealism or surrealism or hi-tech espionage. When the old verities of the postwar years no longer "worked" and this vacuum of values threatened to undermine the fabric of society, television crime fighters symbolically battled the forces of chaos and won, and television families reminded Americans that they had survived hardships in the golden past.

The world that emerged from this upheaval was one of moral ambiguity, and television drama has been struggling to accommodate it ever since. In their more cynical moments, television's melodramas threw morality out the window and reveled in the thrill of unrestrained greed, revenge, or sexual gratification. In their better moments, they have embraced a cautious humanism based on a generic sense of decency, even in the face of unremitting chaos. It is disappointing that prime-time television has yet to devote many programs to the concerns of racial minorities or women with the same innovation and nuance given to other social themes during the past two decades.

As this book goes to press, two of television's most acclaimed dramatic series are NBC's *The West Wing* and HBO's *The Sopranos*. While *The West Wing* has garnered more Emmys than *The Sopranos* and is smartly written and handsomely produced, it is still essentially a very traditional network drama. All of its characters are morally upright and try to do the right thing at the end of the day—no one more so than Martin Sheen's President Josiah Bartlett. On the other hand, *The Sopranos* forges new ground by exploring characters and plots of startling nuance and ambiguity, with people who are as capable of acts of generosity and tenderness as they are of self-interest, brutality, or fear. In other words, they are deeply human characters who are full of complexity and self-contradiction. They are us. And, like us, they are allowed to *remain* in their ambiguity and to experience the consequences of their actions, to occasionally learn from their mistakes, and to live another day. We see these characters as God sees them—as fallible human beings who, despite their best intentions, are still in need of redemption. This is not the way television usually works. But in not serving us heroes to emulate, *The Sopranos* may provide the bracing look in the mirror we've needed all along.

SIX

Law & Order

The Cop Show Prescription for Containing Evil

Episode:
"Loco Parentis"

First aired:
January 5, 2000

The hallmark of *Law & Order* is its practice of recasting news as fiction. Knotty moral and legal issues are "ripped from the headlines" by executive producer Dick Wolf, who regards the show as a chronicle of our times. Each week, New York City cops and district attorneys use straightforward linear detective work and the judicial process to explore the ambiguities of human responsibility and the flaws of the legal system.

Overview of the Show

Law & Order premiered in 1990 and is currently the longest-running cop drama on television. This show has been nominated for over seventy awards; in 1997, it won the Emmy for best drama series. At a production cost of $1,700,000 per episode, *Law & Order* is a real moneymaker for NBC, ranking consistently in the top fifteen programs. In the week of February 14–18, 2000, it ranked twelfth among programs and got a 12.5 rating, which translates to 12,600,000 viewers. In the same week, the number one program, *ER*, got a rating of 20.9 (21,067,200), but it cost 7.7 times as much to make. Universal Television provides the capital for *Law & Order* and holds distribution rights. The first seven years' episodes are in syndication and are aired in forty countries.

The initial voice-over describes the show's weekly formula of police work (law) and court work (order): "In the criminal justice system the people are represented by two separate and equally important groups: the police who investigate crime and the district attorneys who prosecute

the offenders. These are their stories." The camera puts the audience in the shoes of the detectives during the first half of the show and the prosecutors during the second half, so that we see the criminal justice system from the perspective of law enforcement. During the past ten years, actors have come and gone, providing movement to disguise the program's repetitive formula. The cast for the 1999–2000 season included six main characters. Detective Lennie Briscoe (Jerry Orbach), cynical but driven to rid the streets of scum like those who murdered his daughter, feels his age and fears others may think he is over the hill, yet is determined to do his job even from a wheelchair, if necessary. Briscoe's younger partner, compulsive and passionate Detective Ed Green (Jesse L. Martin), can charm a teenage girl into a confession just as easily as he can frighten hardened toughs into fingering an accomplice. Their no-nonsense boss, Lt. Anita Van Buren (S. Epatha Merkerson), hassles her men for more facts and clues until she is satisfied she can give the district attorney sufficient evidence to bring a case to court. The complex and charismatic Assistant District Attorney, Jack McCoy (Sam Waterston), unravels the legal puzzle of the week and preaches moral rectitude to judge, jury, and audience. McCoy's young (under thirty) and attractive partner, Assistant District Attorney Abbie Carmichael (Angie Harmon), combines the skills of detective, social worker, and prosecutor. Finally, the seen-it-all District Attorney himself, Adam Schiff (Steven Hill), embodies enough wisdom and compassion to inspire grateful trust and make any New Yorker proud of the local law enforcement establishment.*

The show always has an introductory tease or prologue, four acts, and an epilogue. The tease is usually a brief scene in which a crime (most often a murder) is discovered; Acts 1 and 2 show detectives Briscoe and Green as they follow the clues that lead to a suspect; Act 3 depicts assistant district attorneys McCoy and Carmichael building a case against the suspect; Act 4 takes place in the courtroom as the case is brought to trial; and the epilogue consists of a brief scene in the district attorney's office with McCoy, Carmichael, and Schiff, to bring closure to the moral dilemma of the week. The hallmark of *Law & Order* is its practice of "recasting news as fiction." Knotty moral and legal issues are "ripped from the headlines" by executive producer Dick Wolf, who is fascinated by the life and death issues law enforcement must engage.[1] Over the years, the audience has

---

*In 2001 Dianne Wiest replaced Steven Hill as District Attorney Nora Lewin.

been treated to fictionalized versions of celebrated cases like those of Rodney King, Bernie Goetz, Tawana Brawley, Dr. Jack Kevorkian, Gavin Cato and Yankel Rosembaum, the Crown Heights riot, and many others. Wolf himself regards the show as "a chronicle of our times. Everything you want to know about America can be found in the 180 episodes of *Law & Order*."[2] The tone of the show is definitely contemporary, but it claims continuity with high-quality shows of the past by its use of realist techniques. Most notable is the technique used to signify a change of scene: a three- or four-second shot of a black screen with words in white giving the time and location of the next bit of detective work. Then comes a sound right out of *Dragnet*. The audience hears a simultaneous blending of the slamming of a prison door and the banging of a judge's gavel, placing *Law & Order* in continuity with the most famous cop show in the history of television.

The worldview of *Law & Order* is strikingly different from that of other 1990s shows. This is a good cop show, a white-Republican-upper-middle-class show. The world is fraught with legal and moral dilemmas—yes, even moral ambiguity—and sometimes the good guys lose, but the cops act with restraint—no corruption or rot in this NYPD unit. The district attorneys are poster people, models of respectability, wisdom, ingenuity. Waterston carries an intertextual halo from the role he played in *I'll Fly Away*, a television drama about segregation in the South. Harmon looks like the svelte model she is—the NBC website proudly announces: "At the age of 15, Harmon beat out 63,000 entrants to win (the) *Seventeen* model contest"—and Hill exudes the aura of a modern-day Solon. The district attorneys are Ivy League folks, and the high-quality production values emit an air of *The New Yorker* version of cop shows. These people are in charge of the justice system, and even though life has its dilemmas, they find a way to cut the Gordian knot most of the time. By borrowing the rationalism of classic whodunits, *Law & Order* allows the audience to examine the intellectual side of contemporary crime without emotional trauma or cynicism.

The introductory visual in stark shades of black and white gradually changes into a red, white, and blue halo around the words "Law & Order." Then an imposing shot of the front of the Supreme Court is draped by the undulating red and white stripes of Old Glory, establishing an aura of patriotic awe and respect for the criminal justice system. Wolf is forthright in his praise of cops, describing the show as "the classic good-guy story. You read a lot about bad things cops do, but I've spent an inordinate amount of time with them, and the reality is that the vast, vast majority of cops do not go out and shoot people in the street. And that's the side I tend to portray in *Law & Order*. In nine years of the show, the two lead detectives have never fired their weapons. Not once."[3] His praise of the American criminal justice system is even more effusive, suggesting an insensitivity to how poor people of color experience life on the inner city streets of the United States. Explaining that he grew up in Canada and is familiar with the civil code of justice in Quebec and France and with the British style of justice, Wolf declared: "On the whole it's probably the fairest system that anyone has thought of so far. . . . Based on (my) experience I can tell you that though imperfect, the American justice system is, as Cinderella's Godmother said, 'the fairest of them all.'"[4]

The "Loco Parentis" Episode

The episode that we examine aired on January 5, 2000, and must be put in the context of the Columbine High School killings that occurred in spring 1999 and other recent incidences of youth violence. Two earlier episodes in the 1999–2000 season deal with related issues. In the season premiere on September 22, 1999, entitled "Gun Show," the district attorney's office tries but fails to hold a gun manufacturer legally responsible for a mad gunman's slaughter of fifteen new female medical students attending an orientation discussion in Central Park on gender issues in medicine. This episode struggles with the issue but ends up endorsing the ideology of the National Rifle Association. The following week's episode, entitled "Killer," explores whether or not a ten-year-old girl with a psychopathic hatred for little boys should be sent to a mental institution for murdering a classmate, or whether the mother should be given another chance to socialize her daughter. This episode ends with the judge's disregarding the advice of the prosecution's psychiatrist and taking a stand for freedom and another chance. At the same time, it suggests that the legal system shields neglectful parents and their criminally inclined children from responsibility for the consequences of their actions.

The January 5, 2000, episode picks up the theme of parental responsibility explored in the earlier show; in this episode, however, not only is the teenage son locked away for killing a classmate, but his father is also sentenced to prison for training his son to act in violent ways. The story opens (the tease) with trash collectors discovering the body of teenage Chris Skinner wrapped in a blanket and stuffed into a plastic bag left on the street for pickup. Detectives Briscoe and Green carry out the investigation (Acts 1 and 2) by interviewing the victim's mother, his closest friend, a schoolteacher, a neighborhood grocer, the superintendent of the building outside which the body was found, neighbors in the building, and high school classmates who are members of gangs called the Freaks and the Skaters. Finally they narrow this list of suspects to a member of the Freaks. After obtaining a search warrant, they discover the likely murder weapon, a scythelike knife that is banned in the state of New York, and arrest the sixteen-year-old boy, John Telford.

Act 3 opens with a judge setting bail at a measly $20,000, symbolic of the prosecutors' weekly uphill battle to prove the guilt of their suspects. As Assistant District Attorneys McCoy and Carmichael go about building a case against the teenager, they interview another boy, Leo, whom John intimidates on a regular basis. Leo tells them of the storage room where John practices his martial arts on a mannequin that his father has brought home from the department store where he works. When McCoy and Carmichael report that John's father has armed him and trained him in violence, District Attorney Shiff stuns them with the command, "Charge the father" (with the murder of Chris Skinner).

Act 4 takes place in court, where McCoy builds a case on a little-used law of "depraved indifference." Mr. Telford is charged with murder because he has trained his son to be violent. The camera keeps returning to track the rising emotions in Mrs. Telford. When her husband is put on the witness stand and denies any responsibility, declaring, "Where do you get off telling me how to raise my kids? I love my  boys. I did the best that I could," she can no longer restrain herself. She erupts with the accusation: "He did not. It's not true. He ruined him." The judge gavels her into silence while the defense lawyer asks for a mistrial, which the judge refuses to give. Back in the district attorney's conference room, the mother offers to testify and confronts her husband: "See what you did to John? You're not gonna do it to Jimmy [John's younger brother]." To the father's chagrin, John confesses, and McCoy and the defense lawyer work out a deal whereby the father and the son both serve time. The epilogue puts it all in perspective. Carmichael speaks to Schiff: "Sandra Telford had her husband served with divorce papers at Rikers [correctional facility]." McCoy adds: "Sacrificed her marriage to save her sons." Schiff replies: "If she'd spoken up sooner she might have saved Chris Skinner." McCoy, still surprised at the successful strategy of holding a parent responsible for the actions of his son, asks, "You want to put *her* in jail too?" "Don't tempt me," Schiff responds. Thus the issue of parental responsibility is wrapped up neatly by tough prosecutors, who expand legal precedent and give the audience and our lawmakers something to think about as society struggles with how to prevent teen violence.

Part of the attraction of the show is that the villains are often folks like us, without evil motives. This fact adds to the realism and the audience investment in issues that we ourselves might encounter. We have neighbors like these people. Mr. Telford is a bit extreme, but representative of many fathers who want their sons to stand up for themselves and fight back. The heroes are also like us, giving expression to our attitudes and feelings.

Character development on *Law & Order* must be integral to the story lines of the criminal investigations because, unlike work-family dramas such as *NYPD Blue* or character studies such as *Homicide: Life on the Street,* this show has no subplots involving the personal lives of the characters. The turning point of this episode takes place in the district attorney's office when Schiff tells McCoy and Carmichael to charge John Telford's father with the murder of Chris Skinner. Character development is achieved in this scene through shot-countershot close-ups depicting the emotional reactions of McCoy and Carmichael.

McCoy:	[Charge the father?] On what basis?
Schiff:	Depraved indifference.
McCoy:	Hold the father responsible for the criminal acts of his son?
Schiff:	You don't think he's responsible?
McCoy:	Morally, maybe. . . .
Schiff:	It's good enough for me. It's about time we knocked some sense into these parents.
McCoy:	You're wielding a pretty big stick.
Schiff:	They don't do the job? Puts it on us.
McCoy:	Does it?
Carmichael:	Nobody's ever tried it.
Schiff:	That ever stop you two before? [McCoy and Carmichael exchange doubtful glances. Then Carmichael rises to the challenge.]
Carmichael:	What do you think?
McCoy:	[hesitates as the camera closes in on his perplexed and troubled face. After a long pause he says] It makes me nervous.
Carmichael:	I don't know. Telford encourages John's aggressive behavior; he arms him to the teeth. Jury might buy it.
McCoy:	That's what makes me nervous.

In a later scene, McCoy reiterates his hesitation: "Suppose we pull it off, who's next?" Although the district attorney's office holds the doubt in abeyance while they vigorously prosecute the case, the audience is left pondering the complexity of justice and the trade-offs in law enforcement.

In one court scene in this episode, the audience gets a sympathetic insight into the character of Lennie Briscoe and what drives his police work. At the same time, we see how his colleagues in the district attorney's office seek to protect him from more personal pain. After cross-examining him about circumstantial evidence in the case, Telford's defense lawyer turns to the central issue, parental responsibility.

Defense: You have children, don't you, Detective?

McCoy: Objection.

Judge: [to Defense] Where are you going?

Defense: The prosecution has raised the issue of parental responsibility. I'd like a little leeway to address their argument.

Carmichael: Fine, Judge, but with this detective?

Judge: I'm going to give it to him, Miss Carmichael. You're the ones pushing the envelope.

Briscoe: I had two daughters. One of them was murdered.

Defense: Because she turned state's evidence in a drug case?

Briscoe: She was going to testify against a dealer.

Defense: So she was selling drugs herself.

Carmichael: Objection.

Judge: Overruled. [The camera closes in on the agonized face of Briscoe.] Yeah, she was selling drugs.

Defense: And as her father, shouldn't you be held criminally responsible for her drug dealing?

Briscoe: [closes his eyes in pain, almost breaking down, and murmurs] Criminally responsible? No. [Then in anger he squints his eyes and blurts out] But I didn't give her the pills and teach her how to sell them!

Reading *Law & Order* through a Theological Lens

Law & Order constructs a modestly progressive, almost politically correct view of race and gender relationships among law enforcement personnel. "Race is still the single most explosive issue that we as a country have to deal with," observes Dick Wolf.[5] Two of the six regulars on *Law & Order* are African American (Detective Ed Green and Lt. Anita Van Buren), and Detective Green is one of the most likable characters on the show. In a December 1999 episode, Briscoe and Green go to a run-down housing proj-

ect looking for a Hispanic teenager suspected of murder. Talking with the white superintendant, Briscoe vents his disgust, saying: "They multiply like roaches." Then the camera shifts to the face of Briscoe's new partner, Ed Green. In a turn-the-other-cheek gesture, Green absorbs the comment with pain, but does not respond in kind. Although Green is portrayed in a more favorable light than his white partner Briscoe, and their boss is a winsome African-American woman, the more interesting tasks of prosecution are reserved for the all-white cast in the district attorney's office.

The program does a bit better with gender, presenting Lt. Van Buren as a strong, decisive, and fair policewoman. Although Jack McCoy is the stock plot device to voice the moral outrage of the district attorney's office (and of the audience), his partner Abbie Carmichael goes head to head with him in thinking through the intricacies of moral dilemmas. In spite of their age difference, he treats her with respect as an equal. Unlike most female cop show characters, she never dresses suggestively, and the visual script never makes her a sex object. Nonetheless, the leading roles on *Law & Order* are reserved for two white male characters, Detective Lennie Briscoe and Assistant District Attorney Jack McCoy.

We have already referred to Lennie Briscoe's denigration of lower-class people of color who live "like roaches" in housing projects. A similar disdain for the super rich is expressed by Jack McCoy in an episode entitled "Merger," which aired on October 13, 1999. These expressions of class antagonism are rare on *Law & Order*. For the most part, within the constraints of their character traits (e.g., Briscoe's cynicism, McCoy's moral outrage), the heroes on this show are consistently respectful even of those they arrest and charge with murder. Decency and common courtesy are marks of the program. However, the class system appears as a benign given, never a source of oppression or a contributing factor in crime. The powerful economic structures of society are ignored. Crimes are individual aberrations that do not call for social solutions or structural changes. In this sense, crime and punishment are privatized. By and large, this also applies to the television cop show genre itself.

Law & Order functions as a myth (see Introduction, pp. xv–xvi) that reinforces confidence in the existing social system, "the fairest of them all." Aimed at an upscale audience—the key ads for the episode examined in this chapter were for Toyota Avalon, Pontiac Bonneville, Weight Watchers, Internet services, cell phones, HDTV, and the following movies: *Magnolia, Snow Falling on Cedars, The General's Daughter, Hurricane,* and *The Cider House Rules*—this show turns horrendous crimes of passion into intellectual puzzles. This transformation gives the audience and those who control society reassurance that in spite of all the threats to social order, we need not lose our rational equilibrium. As stock plot devices, the characters represent our anger but not our fear. They are motivated by duty and a clear sense of right and wrong; thus, this is a modernist, not a postmodernist show. It owes more to the whodunit genre than to the action-cop or the hardboiled-detective genre. It contrasts significantly with the cynical urban survivalist genre exemplified by *NYPD Blue,* which is much more working class, depicts rot everywhere, with no hope of turning crimes into puzzles, and with characters who try to keep themselves a little clean and avoid emotional collapse and psychological degradation. The value of *Law & Order,* however, is that by looking at all the intricate aspects of criminal behavior, it sometimes explores new legal resolutions.

According to Christian tradition, the law has three major functions and purposes: law defines right behavior and thus serves as a moral guidebook; it is, in Martin Luther's words, a "dike against sin" to prevent and restrain evil; and it punishes evil. *Law & Order* portrays the American criminal justice system as a workable moral guide that restrains and punishes evil and thereby provides security for law-abiding citizens. By wrestling with the moral dilemmas of the law, this program also attempts to improve the criminal justice system. However, *Law & Order* and other television cop shows find it difficult to take the next step beyond the law to forgiveness, repentance, and reconciliation. With the reinstitution of the death penalty and the introduction of harsher penalties, including "three strikes" laws, our legal code has moved back in the direction of an eye for an eye, fueled partly by the moral outrage of cop shows. One could argue that plea bargaining and the discretion given judges in the sentencing process represent structural forms of social forgiveness and rehabilitation. Yet most cop shows, including *Law & Order*, arouse audience animosity at these aspects of the criminal justice system by depicting the frustration of prosecutors at every obstacle that softens the punishment of criminals they convict. One consequence of this animosity is the broad public support for a dramatic increase in prison and jail populations over the past two decades as the following numbers from the U. S. Bureau of Justice Statistics illustrate:[6]

Year	National Prison and Jail Population
1980	501,900
1985	742,600
1990	1,148,700
1995	1,585,600
2000*	2,014,000

*Estimated year-end

The U.S. rate of incarceration is 672 per 100,000, which is second only to Russia and six to ten times the rate in most industrialized nations.

Christian tradition also recognizes the inadequacy of the law. As the apostle Paul noted repeatedly, without grace (forgiveness) the law becomes a harsh judge that kills rather than restores.[7] The title of Bishop Desmond Tutu's recent book on the end of apartheid in South Africa captures this Pauline dynamic: *No Future without Forgiveness*.[8] By limiting their treatment of social evil to crime and punishment, cop shows reinforce the vicious cycle of tit for tat. Victims and their families who settle for revenge when their victimizers are punished sometimes do gain a measure of relief, but deeper healing eludes them. Only forgiveness can open the way to inner freedom and a hopeful future. A society that feeds on a cop show culture of revenge ignores the things that make for peace and ends up punishing itself along with the criminals. The meanness of spirit that permeates our public life is due in part to the television cop shows we ingest.

The central symbol of Christian faith is the cross. The cross points both to the necessity for forgiveness and the agonizing process required to bring it about. We can understand the satisfaction parents or spouses get from watching the execution of their loved ones' murderers, but Christian faith and human experience teach that only forgiveness can heal and rehabilitate both the victims and the victimizers. One action step that religious communities can take is to pressure the networks and the cop show writers for shows that depict the struggle to forgive. This struggle involves painful movement through grief and anger to a withdrawal of projections and an acknowledgment of the potential for violence in each of us. This change may lead to a degree of empathy for the victimizers and a recognition of the mystery of evil, the absence of justice, and the necessity to oppose evil without objectifying it or thinking we can ever completely vanquish it. The failure of *Law & Order* to depict the struggle to forgive accounts for its tone of self-righteousness and superficial resolution of the pain that crime and punishment inflict on people and on society. Dick Wolf, we believe you have missed an opportunity to redefine the cop show genre. You have written a good show, and you can write an even better one. We wager that shows that depict the struggle to forgive would also increase your audience!

SEVEN

ER and Medical Dramas

MOMENTS OF GRACE IN THE MIDST OF CHAOS

Episode: **First aired:**
"Leave it to Weaver"   September 30, 1999

Since fall 1994, NBC's *ER* has been one of the most successful prime-time dramas in television history, finishing its first season with an average audience of more than twenty million viewers, second only to *Seinfeld. Newsweek* called it a "S*M*A*S*H" and described it as an "adrenaline rush of trauma, pathos and heroism."[1]

Why is its appeal so enduring? Does it fit the hospital drama genre? How does it differ? What does *ER* tell us about grace and redemption? Does its adrenaline-charged pace tell us anything about life in the United States at the millennium?

[Pandemonium reigns in the ER as a young doctor carries in a wounded little girl.]
Dr. Kovac: Have you ever been to the circus?
Young patient: No.
Kovac: You have now.

A very pregnant woman lumbers into a train on the platform of the Chicago "El" and is forced to stand because it is full. Another passenger tries unsuccessfully to coax a surly, earphone-wearing teenager to give her his seat, but she gently asserts that it is all right. Once off the train, she gingerly makes her way down the street and is nearly run over by two novice skaters on rollerblades. At a coffee shop, an elderly woman asks her if she may touch her stomach, but the mother-to-be thoughtfully declines. An obnoxious grade-schooler tells her that the warm milk she is about to drink is "nasty" and orders a double-tall vanilla latte of his own.

Just as she leaves the coffee shop—her day already off to a bad start—people start screaming, and before she has a chance to react, an out-of-control truck smashes through the store's plate glass window.

Welcome to the crazy, out-of-control world of *ER*, where chaos can break out at any moment—and usually does.

Narrative

Continuing the "lens" approach we have been developing throughout this book, we begin our exegesis of *ER* by looking at the *narrative elements* that characterize the show. For simplicity's sake, we focus on one episode, the season opener for 1999–2000, entitled "Leave it to Weaver."

As with almost every episode of *ER*, the action is set in the emergency department of County General, a fictitious urban hospital meant to resemble Cook County Hospital in Chicago. The main plotline revolves around the resignation of County General's Chief of Staff, Dr. Donald Anspaugh, and the changes this will precipitate for the rest of the hospital's staff. As victims from the coffee shop-truck crash are brought in, the staff buzzes with rumors about Anspaugh's resignation and his replacement by the acting chief of the ER, Dr. Robert Romano. The ER staff has not enjoyed Romano's abrasive style, and senior doctors Mark Greene and Kerry Weaver decide to be candid about their reservations in a meeting with Dr. Anspaugh and doctors from other departments. In the meeting, however, it becomes clear that all those called to the meeting by Green and Weaver support Romano. When asked his opinion, Mark's is the lone voice of dissent, and when it is Kerry's turn to back him up, she smoothly jumps on the bandwagon and endorses Romano's appointment—explaining later that she wanted to save the ER from Romano's wrath once it became clear which way the vote would go. Having thus feathered her nest, Weaver is promptly invited by Romano to take over as ER chief—a position she has unsuccessfully sought before.

ER is an *ensemble* show in which the narrative strands of recurring characters interlace in a single episode as well as from one episode to another, and the show presents diverse characters in terms of race, gender, ethnicity, and job description—a noteworthy feature since its inception. The "Weaver" episode introduces two new members to the ER staff: a svelte, athletic African-American pediatrician named Cleo Finch, and a general internist from Croatia named Luka Kovac. Subplots in the episode include the growing romance between divorced Mark Greene and British surgeon Elizabeth Corday; Dr. Romano's intrusive references to a previous romance between Corday and African-American surgeon Peter Benton; nurse Carol Hathaway's ongoing pregnancy with twins (she is the woman featured in the opening tease); the desire of physician's assistant Jeanie Boulet—who is HIV positive—to adopt a baby who also has the virus, and her indecision about policeman Reggie's proposal of marriage; young, rich, handsome resident John Carter's treatment of and subsequent interest in the divorced wife of one of his cousins; and a court-ordered mediation session between Peter Benton and Carla Reese, the mother of his deaf son, to determine whether the boy will be allowed to move to Germany with her and her new husband.

Numerous patients from the coffee shop-truck crash are also followed in this episode, including the grade-schooler who hated warm milk, the teenager with headphones who would not give up his seat, and the grandmotherly woman who wanted to touch Carol's stomach. One man loudly stomps around the ER demanding attention for a migraine headache, to no apparent effect. "What kind of bush league joint is this?"

> [T]he show presents diverse characters in terms of race, gender, ethnicity, and job description—a noteworthy feature since its inception.

he demands. When Luka arrives for his shift, he discovers a little girl named Michelle huddled in an ambulance outside—her mother has been seriously injured and is already on a respirator and heart-bypass machine in the ER. Suddenly, a fire alarm goes off, and chaos ensues. Everyone rallies to evacuate patients, shouting from room to room and running from one place to another. Drs. Benton and Carter crack open the headphone teenager's chest to save him. In the midst of this din, Randy the receptionist discovers that the man with the migraine has set off the alarm, and she hits him in the face, knocking him to the floor. As Carter and Benton prepare to wheel their patient upstairs, a cylinder of oxygen accidently falls off the gurney, the nozzle comes off, and it becomes a miniature missile. It hurtles through the reception area and slams into a phone booth as Luka walks in carrying little Michelle. "Have you ever been to the circus?" he asks. "No," she replies. "You have now."

Structure: Genre

ER readily fits into a long-established formula that has been around since television's earliest days: the *doctor-hospital melodrama*. Because it airs weekly with a recurring cast of characters, the show is easily recognized as a *series*, although with its frequent character-driven plots, multiple intertwining story lines, and workplace-as-family environment, *ER* also resembles an *ensemble serial* or soap opera. Using the terminology spelled out by John Dominic Crossan, the show has characteristics of an *action* story that exists as a "field" of activity for the way things are, but it also veers in the direction of *satire* because many of its plots question and undermine the current state of the health care system. For example, Carol Hathaway discovers Dr. Kovac saving a partially used suture kit at the end of the day. "I know you don't keep the open ones, but the scissors haven't been used, or the forceps," he says. "It seems such a waste to throw them away." As we shall see, the characters on *ER* often subvert the rules and regulations of the medical and public health establishment when such codes seem counterintuitive or get in the way of timely and compassionate care.

A Brief Overview of the Genre's History

Television's first medical drama was *Medic*, which debuted on NBC during the 1954–55 season and starred Richard Boone in his first television role. Borrowing the case-history format of *Dragnet*, the show was distinguished by a graphic realism that included the use of real doctors, nurses, and operating rooms. Scripts were supervised by the Los Angeles County Medical Association, a collaboration similar to those the American Medical Association (AMA) itself had with subsequent hospital shows such as *Dr. Kildare* and *Marcus Welby, M.D.* For years, this arrangement assured that television's portrayal of doctors reinforced the image promoted by organized medicine.

Medic established a formula that nearly every medical drama has imitated in some way ever since: the doctor as mythic hero. In a 1994 story on *ER*, *Time* magazine summarized the predominant ethos of these earlier shows:

> Doctors are television's perfect heroes. . . . With a flick of a scalpel, they can make decisions of life and death, and with a consoling word reconcile people to either. They are privy to their patient's closest secrets, deepest fears, most traumatic moments. Dressed in white, they watch over them like angels. And when they make their bedside pronouncements, they do it from above, like God.[2]

In his chapter "Medical Melodramas," in the book *TV Genres*, Robert Alley points out that science and technology had played a tremendous role in fueling the nation's economic boom following the Second World War. Thanks to antibiotics and new vaccines, medical wonders were occurring every day, and the public naturally transferred its awe of science to doctors. *Medic* capitalized on this mystique by beginning each episode with a description of the doctor as "guardian of birth, healer of the sick, and comforter of the aged."

Medic introduced two other features that were common on medical shows for almost thirty years. Each episode revolved around only one "case," which was followed from beginning to end and structured like an ancient hero-story. Typically, the patient started out in a state of equilibrium that was interrupted by an accident or illness. Doctors then entered the plot, took time to diagnose the malady and prescribe a remedy, and eventually—often against great odds (especially when surgery was involved!)—effected a cure. Thus, the original equilibrium was restored. These two characteristics—the "single case" episode and the cure of most patients—were standard in nearly all medical dramas until the 1980s.

Although *Medic* focused on medicine per se, its two successors—both of which premiered in 1961—focused as much on the drama of hospital politics and interpersonal conflict as on medical expertise. Richard Chamberlain and Vincent Edwards starred in the title roles of *Dr. Kildare* and *Ben Casey*. Like President John F. Kennedy, who had captivated the nation with his youth and idealism, both of these doctors were crusaders battling bureaucratic caution and tradition while combating disease.

1969 introduced *Marcus Welby, M.D.*—the most successful medical series in Nielson history at the time—and *Medical Center,* both of which ran until 1976. Robert Young's Dr. Welby resumed the genial persona he had played in *Father Knows Best* as a kind, competent doctor who still made house calls. In *Medical Center,* Chad Everett played young surgeon Joe Gannon and was paired with elder counselor Dr. Paul Lochner, much as Marcus Welby was teamed with the younger Steven Kiley. These "youth versus experience" duos, in turn, were similar to those in *Ben Casey* and *Dr. Kildare*—no doubt a deliberate strategy, even then, to lure different demographic viewers (and their advertisers) to the same show.

In 1972, Jack Webb recycled the semidocumentary style of *Dragnet* into a show about paramedics in *Emergency!* Featuring several intertwining case histories per episode, the show was surprisingly popular with children and lasted until 1977. *M*A*S*H* debuted the same year as *Emergency!* but, in the midst of the Vietnam War, represented a brief departure from most doctor shows by veering in the subversive direction of satire. Originally billed as a comedy, the show quickly manifested more serious overtones by depicting the absurdity of heroic (what else!) doctors trying to heal soldiers during the Korean War—only to send them back to the front lines to be killed. A new word emerged to describe this genre-hybrid: *dramedy.* Unfortunately, *M*A*S*H*'s bite did not last as long as the series did. By the time of its demise in 1983, the show was more notable for how far it had developed the "ensemble" style pioneered by *The Mary Tyler Moore Show (MTM)* than for bucking the establishment. When *Trapper John, M.D.,* debuted as a vague spin-off (1979–86), the satire was replaced by the standard doctor-hero formula of medical dramas, with a *MTM*-style ensemble cast.

Aside from reinforcing the myth of the doctor-hero, all of the medical shows mentioned so far bolstered the other predominant myths of the health care establishment in the United States. All of the patients depicted in these programs had ready access to first-class medical treatment with cost never being a significant factor, and high technology was always readily available and nearly always worked for the patients' benefit. The predominant messages of these shows: Everyone has access to health care; drugs and technology are superior to alternative therapies; one can expect to get well under this system of care. Prime time's next medical drama began to chip away at this mythological monolith.

St. Elsewhere debuted on NBC in 1982. Like M*A*S*H and Trapper John, M.D., it was an ensemble show. Alexander Nehamas points out in his article "Serious Watching" that unlike previous hospital dramas, St. Elsewhere depicted its doctors as fallible human beings, subject to the same fears and venalities as the rest of us, and whose patients did not always survive. William Daniels' Dr. Craig may have been a brilliant surgeon, but he was also an imperious boor who was a lousy father and whose marriage eventually ended in divorce. The show also adopted the interwoven, multiepisode plot structure that had been developed by such prime-time serials as Dallas and Hill Street Blues. More important, the fictitious St. Elegius Hospital served as a prism through which a variety of contemporary issues could be viewed and examined, including new medical procedures and the nature and ethos of the health care system itself. Toward the end of the series' run, St. Elegius Hospital was even purchased by an HMO.

After the conclusion of St. Elsewhere in 1988, no new medical dramas appeared on prime time until 1994, when both ER and Chicago Hope made their debuts. With its emphasis on high technology, weighty issues, and almost exclusively male, imperious doctors, Chicago Hope was the more traditional of the two new shows. By comparison, ER's breathtaking, frantic pace and mixed-gender, multiethnic, multiracial cast gave it a ratings lead that it has never lost. Continuing the trend begun by St. Elsewhere, ER is a decidedly more earthbound medical drama compared with its television predecessors. Its doctors are competent professionals who want to practice medicine well, but they are also portrayed as fallible human beings—many of whose lives are, well, messed up. As with St. Elsewhere, the situations on ER have served as vehicles for examining issues in health care and the wider culture.

Signs

For anyone who has ever watched ER, the plotlines traced in the narrative section above barely manage to convey the roller-coaster sensation of viewing an actual episode on television—the almost cathartic experience of moving from heart-pounding action in one scene to tender pathos in another. How do the producers of ER use their cameras and manipulate sound to carry us along on the ride they want us to have? How do they use signs or what we might call "cinematic language" to suggest meaning for us? Of the many tools at their disposal, the four that ER's producers use most distinctively are sound, camera movement, editing, and visual icons.

Sound

Sound is an often-overlooked aspect of cinematic language, which can be highly effective; every episode of *ER* makes great use of sound effects and music. It seems hard to believe that the emergency department of County General is not in a real hospital at all but on a set on a sound stage in California. One reason for this is that the assorted beeps and buzzes that we associate with hospital equipment are audible in the background of nearly every scene. In our episode, we hear the shouting of doctors and nurses when the fire alarm suddenly goes off. We hear the sound of Dr. Carter suctioning blood from the chest cavity of the "headphone guy." We hear the quick beeping sound of the heart resuscitation machine as Carter readies the paddles on the sides of his chest and the jolt of electricity as it passes through his body. All the while, we also hear the relentless syncopated "whah" of the fire alarm. Because we have been forced to listen to that alarm for nearly two minutes, we feel a surge of frustration, anger, and exhilaration at seeing the culprit punched to the floor. *Sound* does that to us. By the time the canister of oxygen has rocketed into the phone booth and Luka has carried Michelle into the ER, the alarm has sounded continuously for two minutes, 45 seconds. Its persistence helps to communicate the sense of anarchy that prompts Luka's comment that the ER is a circus.

Music, of course, can be another powerful cue for our responses during a sequence. In the fire alarm scene, the music consists of an ominous-sounding bass coupled with chords that vaguely sound like choir voices. They by no means dominate—the fire alarm does that—but the music contributes to a sense of urgency, tension, and poignancy all at once. One signature musical feature of *ER* is the use of mellow chords to signal a "heartfelt moment." In the current episode, Carol Hathaway escorts the grown children of a woman killed in the coffee shop to the operating room so that they can spend time with her. As she brings them into the room, strings begin to sound a single, tender chord followed by several plucks of a harp. We see that the dead woman is the same person who had asked to touch Carol's stomach. The music—which lasts a mere fifteen seconds—and Carol's reaction are all we need to feel the pathos of the moment. The producers of *ER* intentionally try to keep such moments brief and to a minimum, but the musical cues enable them to "punch up" the emotion despite this scene's brevity. We notice this effect again toward the end of the chapter.

Camera Movement

Nearly every episode of *ER* has at least one sequence—and often more than one—that has been shot with the use of a Steadicam. This is a combination camera and harness device that allows the camera operator to walk with the actors as they move through a scene. First used in *Rocky* when Sylvester Stallone made his famous jogging run up the steps of the Philadelphia Museum of Art, Steadicam produces an image that is smooth and fluid, and it completely eliminates the jerky movement typical of hand-held cameras. Before Steadicam, cinematographers had to rely on cumbersome tracks, dollies, and cranes to achieve gliding camera movements. With a Steadicam harness, the camera can move in and out of a scene as easily as one of the characters.

On *ER*, this puts the viewer in the midst of the action, and the effect can quicken one's pulse. In the fire alarm sequence, Mark Greene and Kerry Weaver are in an empty operating room conferring about Dr. Anspaugh's departure when the buzzer goes off. Still on camera, they go through the door, through another operating room, and into the hall and begin to shout directions about evacuating patients. Peter Benton meets Greene as one of the orderlies runs into view and tells Benton that their patient is "crashing." Benton calls Carter, who runs past the camera that follows him into the operating room. There, the rest of the team has readied paddles to shock the patient's heart back to life. We see Carter execute this as the camera glides behind him for a better view. Now Benton makes an incision and opens the chest with a rib spreader. Carter then suctions out the excess blood. This entire sequence, which lasts nearly a minute, has taken place without a single edit. The effect of this, which no doubt required careful choreography to pull off seamlessly, is that viewers, along with the rest of the *ER* staff, have been swept up in the chaos caused by the fire alarm.

Other camera tricks that *ER* uses to great effect rely on time-tested techniques: close-ups and zooms. Without shifting the camera at all, close-up shots and zoom lenses permit the viewer to get closer to an actor. Psychologically, this has the effect of bringing us into a zone of intimacy with the characters. We see reactions and emotions register on their faces and are drawn into what they are feeling. In one scene, Carol Hathaway hears voices coming from a mostly empty operating room. She sees Luka inside, with Michelle still in his arms, explaining all the scary equipment that is keeping her mother alive. Each time the camera cuts between Luka's explanation and Carol's thoughtful reaction, it gets closer. Techniques like this are especially important in television because of its small screen size. Close-ups enable viewers to see as much of a character's facial expressions as possible given the medium's size limitations.

Visual Icons

ER's producers also rely on assorted health care "icons" to quickly establish a medical ambiance. For example, the show's title sequence uses shots of gurneys, X rays, stethoscopes, and operating masks, all of which are visual shorthand for "doctor," "nurse," or "hospital."

We mentioned above that the sound effects of *ER*'s medical equipment are very convincing. Another reason that it is hard to believe that County General is not an actual hospital is that it *looks* so real. The producers originally spent about $700,000 reproducing the abandoned hospital where they made the show's pilot on a Hollywood sound stage. They went so far as to include ceilings, even though these make lighting particularly difficult, and each week they spend thousands of dollars on disposable gowns, gloves, and syringes—just like in a real hospital. In fact, however, this manufactured *ER* is not like real emergency departments at all. Patients on the show never have to fill out insurance forms or endure questions about their ability to pay. Typical ERs are not as hectic as County General's, nor do patients' families have unhindered access to examination and operating rooms as on the show. Yet because *ER*'s look and sounds are so authentic, when they are combined with a Steadicam that allows gurneys and patients to walk in and out of the picture frame as we "move" through the halls, we are convinced that *everything* depicted on the show is realistic and true to life.

> *ER*'s producers also rely on assorted health care "icons" to quickly establish a medical ambiance.

Editing

We have already mentioned that *ER* makes extensive use of multiple, intertwining story lines throughout every episode, and this is achieved through *editing*. Particularly *during* fast-paced sequences, editing keeps the camera from lingering anywhere for very long, cutting quickly from character to character. One sequence shows little Michelle's mother being hooked up to the heart-bypass machine, and the duration between most of the cuts is one to two seconds. Together with delicately pulsing music underscored by one or two bass chords, this quick intercutting subtly suggests urgency and suspense. Once we hear the beeps slow down on the heart monitoring equipment and the musical chords resolve to a pleasing harmony, we realize the patient is all right by the time Dr. Corday says, "She's stabilizing." In this one scene, editing, music, and sound effects invisibly combine to convey a sense of tension followed by resolution.

Editing keeps the pace brisk *between* scenes as well. In *Television's Second Golden Age*, Robert J. Thompson has observed that in the era of the remote control "clicker," these frequent shifts from one scene to another on *ER* effectively do the clicking for us and thus trick us into forgetting to check out what is playing on other channels. In the episode we have been examining, the length of each scene varies during each of the show's four acts. In Act 1, all but two of its sixteen scenes are under a minute, with most lasting about forty-five seconds (and some as brief as ten and twelve). This rapid intercutting between scenes conveys the sense that many things are happening at once and is meant to hook viewers into watching the entire episode. That goal achieved, the pace slows down in Acts two and three, in which most of the scenes last more than a minute, with one lasting as much as two minutes thirty seconds—this is the meeting attended by Mark and Kerry to determine Dr. Romano's suitability to be the new chief of staff. The pace in Act 4 quickens again, with most scenes lasting around forty seconds.

Power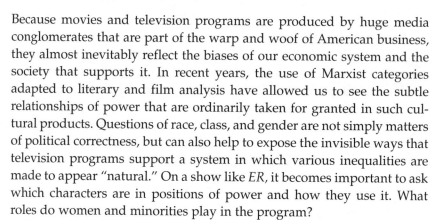

Because movies and television programs are produced by huge media conglomerates that are part of the warp and woof of American business, they almost inevitably reflect the biases of our economic system and the society that supports it. In recent years, the use of Marxist categories adapted to literary and film analysis have allowed us to see the subtle relationships of power that are ordinarily taken for granted in such cultural products. Questions of race, class, and gender are not simply matters of political correctness, but can also help to expose the invisible ways that television programs support a system in which various inequalities are made to appear "natural." On a show like *ER*, it becomes important to ask which characters are in positions of power and how they use it. What roles do women and minorities play in the program?

From its very first episode, *ER* broke new ground with a large ensemble cast that featured as many women and people of color as it did white men. Female doctors and medical residents abounded; most were white, but not all. Jeanie Boulet, for example, is not only African American, but one of the first regular characters on prime time to have HIV and to be portrayed in a sympathetic light. Another recurring female psychiatrist is gay. Kerry Weaver, a strong, assertive doctor and administrator, has a disability that requires her to walk with a crutch. A Chinese-American medical student featured in the first season has returned in a regular role. Virtually all of the nursing and support staff are played by minorities, most of them African-American, Hispanic, and Asian women—except for Carol Hathaway, the head nurse, who is white.

It must be admitted that in the hierarchical chain of command, most of the key positions are still held by white men, with people of color mostly relegated to jobs farther down the pyramid. (Peter Benton was a noticeable exception until the arrival of Cleo Finch.) This color line may reflect the current state of affairs in most urban hospitals, but it is unfortunate that *ER* has not "pushed the envelope" more on this subject. Another significant gap is that although the ER is always filled with people from a wide range of racial and class backgrounds, poor people and patients of color are almost always seen from the point of view of the better-educated doctors and nurses.

In our episode, four characters in positions of power are Drs. Anspaugh, Romano, Greene, and Weaver. How do they wield that power, and for whose benefit?

As the hospital's chief of staff, Anspaugh is clearly the character with the most authority. Yet as the episode begins, we see him chafing because the bureaucratic "detritus" he must attend to as an administrator keeps him from taking care of patients; he wants out. As chief, he is obviously in a position to do a lot of good, especially in establishing hospital policies and serving as a liaison between his doctors and HMOs or lawyers suing for malpractice. This episode shows him making a decision for what he considers to be a "greater good"—namely, the hands-on care of patients.

"Rocket" Romano is a thorn in the side of nearly everyone in the ER. In earlier seasons, we saw him play what amounted to mind games with both Peter Benton and Elizabeth Corday. As the sponsor of their residency and fellowship programs, Romano clearly has power over both of them; his exercise of that power is often autocratic and bullying. He seems to enjoy seeing people squirm. His leadership grates on the ER staff because he seldom seems to have their best interests at heart. His is a portrayal of power as ego trip.

As one of the senior doctors in the emergency department, Mark Greene uses his position to represent the staff's feelings about Romano to Dr. Anspaugh and even goes out on a limb to do so. His use of authority on behalf of those under him may ultimately cause him grief, but the staff applauds his efforts because he has acted with integrity on their behalf.

In many ways, Kerry Weaver's character is the most complex of the four we have examined. A competent administrator, she often seems torn between organizational efficiency and compassionate health care delivery, and in the words of *The New York Times*, "the audience rarely knows whether to like or dislike . . . her character."[3] Our current episode bears this out. On the one hand, her own self-interest and ambition clearly get the best of her when she leaves Mark as the lone voice of dissent. On the other hand, past experience with Dr. Romano indicates that her fear of a backlash against the ER is well founded. In many ways, hers is the most realistic portrayal of someone in power, with an ambiguous combination of personal ambition and a professional desire to look out for the common good.

When we shift our lens slightly, a fifth character emerges as one worthy of examination—Jeanie Boulet. Although she is "only" a physician's assistant, her commitment to compassionate health care is such that she is willing to subvert ethical guidelines and legal regulations for the benefit of a patient. In this episode, a young mother with end-stage AIDS is brought in with her infant son. As a person with HIV herself, Jeanie is concerned to find out whether the child has the virus so that, if he does, he can be started on the "triple cocktail" as soon as possible. Legally, the hospital may not test a minor for HIV without the approval of a parent or guardian. In this case, the child's mother is incapable of speaking and will soon die. Rather than wait out the lengthy process of going through the Department of Children and Family Services to find a foster family, Jeanie orders an HIV test for the boy—behind Dr. Finch's back and specifically against her orders. Later, she tells a nurse in the pediatric ward to start the boy on the antiviral cocktail. This is one instance when someone with power uses it on behalf of a marginal person—a minority child with a stigmatizing illness.

Jeanie's dilemma and her subsequent actions play out a frequent theme on *ER*: Legal regulations and insurance restrictions can get in the way of compassionate health care delivery. In this case, the real "power" is held by faceless executives and bureaucrats whom we rarely meet on the show—as indeed we seldom do in real life. As a recurring "counternarrative," we see how bureaucratic agencies and regulations can produce realities that take on lives of their own and that sometimes prove detrimental to the very people they were set up to help.

Functions

Why is *ER* so popular? What does the audience "get out" of watching it each week? Perhaps more important, what benefits or gratifications do its producers, network, and advertisers reap?

Producer, Network, and Advertiser Gratifications

At the macrolevel, an obvious first answer to our question is that NBC (which broadcasts the show) and Warner Brothers Television and Amblin Entertainment (which produce it) want *ER* to be a hit. Because it has been number one in the ratings for so long, Steven Spielberg, Michael Crichton, John Wells, and Lydia Woodward (ER's creators and producers) can charge NBC hefty prices for future installments of the series—and get them. As of the 1999–2000 season, NBC paid Amblin Entertainment and Warner Brothers Television $13 million *per episode.* Such a windfall has "trickled down" to *ER*'s yeoman performers, many of whom were unknown before the series began. With the defection of George Clooney from the show during the 1998–1999 season, there has been greater incentive to retain other cast members, and they have been rewarded handsomely for their loyalty—some of them to the tune of $27 to $35 million for additional three-year contracts.

During *ER*'s first season, it attracted more than twenty million viewers each week. Even during its sixth season, it still pulled in an average audience of more than fifteen million. As the drama with the largest weekly following on television, *ER* can attract a bevy of advertisers interested in reaching customers in the eighteen- to forty-nine-year-old market. In January 1999, NBC could charge $565,000 for a thirty-second commercial during the show. The episode we have been exploring comes packaged with a total of thirty-two ads, with several more between the end of Act 4 and the closing credits. The commercials include pitches for cars, movies, grocery items, and retailers, as well as a variety of promotional spots for NBC programming and local news. Most of the ads are aimed at middle-class family households, some of which are presumed to have children (Jif, PlayStation). A few ads are geared to more upscale consumers (Lexus, Chrysler, Motorola wireless web connections). A 1997 article in *Billboard* magazine notes that music industry executives had determined that, based on survey data, they should advertise on *ER* if they wanted to appeal to women shoppers.[4] A 1998 article in *Variety* about the racial gap between programs watched by whites and African Americans has obvious ramifications for advertisers.[5] Whereas *ER* is a consistent ratings bonanza among white viewers, it finishes nineteenth for blacks.

A further beneficiary on the macrolevel is the health care establishment. As noted earlier, the AMA has had a longstanding advisory relationship with the producers of medical dramas, no doubt because it recognizes that heroic depictions of doctors on television can translate into public esteem and financial rewards in real life. In addition, medical foundations have been known to lobby *ER*'s writers and advisers to dramatize new medical procedures or public health issues to educate viewers.[6] For example, one episode during the seventh season featured a teenage girl who discovered—much to her chagrin—that it is indeed possible to contract gonorrhea through oral sex.

Audience Gratifications

On the microlevel, what do viewers get out of watching *ER*? Obviously, this varies from person to person, but a careful look at the program's "formula" reveals that each episode has something for everybody. Thus, every show has a few scenes of heart-racing action followed by slower scenes of human interaction. In addition to story lines that examine a medical condition or situation, others follow the personal lives of characters we have come to care about or to dislike. Among these story elements lie the gratifications for various members of the audience.

In our current episode, the fire alarm scene with its chaotic swirl of activity is the *action sequence* for thrill seekers. (In earlier seasons, the producers even went so far as to include one "gross-out" scene per show, such as when an ambulance crew brought in a man with huge shards of glass protruding from his chest!) Our episode has a few slower scenes that deal with some *medical situation:* Luka stitching the "latte boy"'s arm and later doing the same for Carol; Jeanie and the Hispanic child with

HIV; the emergency delivery of a baby whose mother dies at the same time. Sprinkled throughout are scenes that deal with the human interactions or *personal lives* of the ER staff: Mark and Kerry putting their heads together to fight Romano's appointment as hospital chief; Carol trying to pull information out of Mark about his dating relationship with Elizabeth; Peter Benton and Carla in their mediation session over their son Reese; Luka confiding to Carol that he feels Weaver and Greene do not trust him because he is foreign; Carter's romantic stirrings for his cousin's ex-wife Elaine. Such scenes enable viewers to "catch up" on the lives of characters they have come to love or dislike. (Let's not forget the "heart-throb" appeal of characters such as Doug Ross, John Carter, and Luka Kovac!)

On another level, every audience member is also a potential hospital patient in real life. Medical dramas like *ER* can help ease anxieties about going to the hospital by reassuring viewers that they will be well cared for by competent and compassionate professionals.

Balancing Expectations

ER's creators must be careful to gratify the needs and expectations of the network and its advertisers on the one hand and the audience on the other. With so much money at stake, characters are unlikely to venture far beyond what the audience has come to expect or tolerates. For example, Carol Hathaway is one of the benevolent angels of compassion in the ER. Fans expect this from her and love her for it. When she becomes pregnant with twins by Doug Ross, who then leaves town without her, she faces the prospect of being a single mother. In the United States today, women who find themselves in such situations may consider abortion as an option, but because it is a hotly contested issue, it was unlikely that *ER*'s writers would script this scenario for such a beloved character. Viewers might revolt or, worse yet, boycott the show. By the same token, because so many people distrust HMOs and insurance companies, it is permissable to feature stories that are critical of the decisions they force on doctors with regard to patient care. The fact that a prime-time drama such as *ER* exists in a commercial environment means that market forces *and* audience demands can subtly dictate which story lines are acceptable and which are not.

Audience Role Models

Viewers may enjoy seeing characters like themselves and the values they hold dear mirrored by the fictional people they care about, but the choices these characters make can also subtly influence attitudes and expectations viewers might have for their own lives. *ER*'s actors seem sensitive to this possibility. The April 1999 issue of *Jet* magazine quoted actor Eriq Lasalle explaining why he asked to end his character's inter-racial romance with white doctor Elizabeth Corday: "We have to take care of the message that we're sending as African Americans or any other group of minorities, that we have the exact same type of exchanges with our mates that we get to see our White counterparts have."[7] The article noted that before Dr. Benton's relationship with Corday, he was shown to have had two troublesome relationships with African-American characters. Similarly, actress Laura Innes asked that her character Kerry Weaver be developed more fully: "[P]eople with disabilities are marginalized all the time. And I don't just mean sex, I mean romance and intimacy. I'm obviously not the hot sexy one. But I just want her to have a fuller life."[8]

With this in mind, what choices do some of *ER*'s characters make and why? In our current episode, Dr. Anspaugh voluntarily steps down from a hospital position of considerable prestige, authority, and financial reward. Why does he do this? Because it seems important to him to have more direct hands-on contact with patients. Viewers are given the unspoken message: "Money isn't everything; sometimes it's worth it to sacrifice wealth or prestige for more satisfying work with people,"—not a bad message. To complicate matters, we must remember that this message is put forth by producers who charge $13 million per episode to a network that charges more than half a million dollars to advertisers who spend many thousands more to encourage audiences to buy their products and services. What does it mean when an altruistic message is delivered via such a system of money chasing? Do *ER*'s writers and producers really believe that money and power are not everything, or is it a cynical way of making us feel good while they smile all the way to the bank? Is the *real* message, "It's okay to *want* to be rich, but you might as well accept that you never will?"

This episode also shows that Mark Greene and Kerry Weaver make contrasting choices in voicing their opinions about Romano's selection as chief of staff. It raises an implicit question for us as viewers: "Which is more important, to act with integrity (even when you might suffer for doing so), or to compromise for the sake of political expediency and personal ambition?" The episode takes an ambiguous position on this and leaves it up to viewers to decide for themselves: The ER staff applauds Greene for sticking up for them, but Weaver gets the promotion.

Theological Analysis

Now we can use the insights we have gained from our various lenses and fields of view to arrive at a deeper interpretation of what *ER* might be saying about life and our society. In our plot analysis, we noticed that there is an underlying sense of chaos in certain scenes. The truck that wreaks so much havoc in the opening tease comes out of nowhere and nearly takes

Carol with it. Had she delayed coming out of the coffee shop for only a minute, she might have been one of the victims—along with her twins. In the ER itself, the sudden blare of the fire alarm not only takes everyone by surprise, but puts them in crisis mode. Life and death are at stake, and the doctors and staff must operate under far-from-ideal conditions. Other episodes of *ER* have put the medics through power outages and water failures, and in each instance, they have been forced to muddle through with courage, good humor, and ingenuity.

Others have noted this underlying sense of chaos as a recurring theme of the series. In its 1994 cover story, *Newsweek* observed that "*ER* mixes trauma and soap opera in a setting of permanent crisis. The emergency room is its Vietnam. When the choppers land on the roof of the hospital, you half expect one of the young residents to shout 'Incoming!'"[9] A 1995 article in the *Progressive* commented:

> ER . . . takes as its controlling metaphor not the hack-neyed, high-modernist, cliche of the Healer as Godlike Genius, but the more contemporary view of the hospi-tal, and the health-care system, as a war zone. There is no effort whatever to explain or analyze the system here. "Stuff happens and someone has to deal with it," seems to be the show's guiding intellectual principle.[10]

In the premier episode of *ER*'s sixth season, the truck crash and fire alarm sequences effectively recapitulate this "chaos theory," and the words of new doctor Luka Kovac make this explicit when he refers to the ER as a "circus."

How we interpret this "ER-as-crisis" motif also depends on our under-lying model for thinking about disease. One traditional way to understand illness is to think of it as an anomaly: We presume that peo-ple are basically healthy; sickness disrupts health; Godlike doctors cure the disease and restore the patient's equilibrium. As a metaphor for America, the disease-as-anomaly model was operative in medical dramas before the mid-1980s. As miniature "metanarratives," those traditional hospital shows reinforced the notion that life in America was basically all right, that the few things that went wrong could be isolated and fixed without indicating that the whole was fundamentally faulty. In an essay on another genre, "TV News as Narrative," Sharon Lynn Sperry notes:

> Av Westin, former president of ABC News, says that he expects an audience to come to his news programs asking "Is the world safe, and am I secure?" There is clearly a link between the question and the answer provided by a news structure that plots events directly along the lines of the hero story: The world at peace is disrupted by some event . . . [and e]ventually, the dis-ruption is settled or forgotten, and the world returns to its original state of rest and security.[11]

Sperry continues, "There is a primary problem with this structure . . . as hero story. The world . . . [is] never really at rest or in security."[12]

Indeed, the events of the last half of the twentieth century have made this abundantly clear. We live in a postmodern world, no longer assured that human ingenuity and technical progress will make life better and better. After a century in which modern technology made both Hiroshima and the Holocaust possible, we are no longer certain that human beings are basically good. In the United States, events such as the assassinations of the Kennedy brothers and Martin Luther King, Jr., the quagmire of Vietnam, race riots, and Watergate all contributed to a loss of trust in the old verities of the post–World War II era. Years of runaway inflation in the 1970s, the loss of small farms, and job layoffs because of the restructuring of the global economy all remain powerful memories even in times of prosperity. With the end of the cold war, Americans have watched in horror as ethnic tensions flared in places like Rwanda, the Balkans, and East Timor. Tucked away in suburbia, we realize that in our brave new world no place is safe.

How do we respond to such a world? Is it enough to circle the wagons, stick our heads in the sand, and hope for the best? The writers and producers of *ER* seem to suggest that the appropriate response is to reach out with compassion and care and do the best we can.

How do we know this? As the writer in the *Progressive* noted, on *ER* "[s]tuff happens and someone has to deal with it." Indeed, compassionate humanism is a hallmark of the series. The doctors and nurses may be fallible and even have miserable personal lives, but most of them seem to want the best for their patients. With the fire alarm blaring in their ears and people running in every direction, the medics still

> The writers and producers of *ER* seem to suggest that the appropriate response is to reach out with compassion and care and do the best we can.

manage to jolt their patient back to life—and even open his chest to do it. Jeanie's care for the baby with HIV means that he will get a head start on drugs that can prevent him from developing full-blown AIDS—even if she has to break a few laws to do it. Luka takes the time to explain to little Michelle how all the scary machines and tubes are keeping her mother alive. Several characters have consistently manifested compassionate care for the folks who wander through the ER's doors—most notably Jeanie, Luka, Carol Hathaway, and John Carter—and even Peter Benton shows that he has a tender side at times, especially with his deaf son Reese.

We have already observed that story lines regularly deal with the catch-22 situations of managed care and public health regulations. Their human compassion in the face of suffering leads the doctors and nurses of ER to break a few rules now and then. Not only do these story lines lead us to this conclusion; the "semiotic codes" do as well. When Carol or

Luka is moved with pity for some poor soul, we see it in their close-up faces or hear it in the gentle musical chords we alluded to earlier. Such visual or musical cues are there to alert us to what might be called "moments of grace." In the Christian tradition, "grace" is the word used to describe a free gift of God's goodness "breaking into" the world. Such moments punctuate episodes of *ER* with regularity. They underscore the reality that in a harsh world where things can go wrong—and often do—the human heart can still be moved with pity and concern, and people can go out of their way to help those in need. Such moments can be transformative for patient and healer alike.

In an emergency room, everyone is in the same situation: Doctors, staff, and patients all inhabit an environment of "permanent crisis," which may be why it is as good a metaphor as any for these postmodern times. In this world of chaos, we can only do our best with care and compassion, which is exactly how the doctors and nurses of *ER* face each day. "If I only manage to help just one person," said med student Lucy Knight in an episode in Season six, "that's enough for me to feel that the day has been a success." Compared with the self-confident Kildares and the reassuring Welbys of earlier times, *ER*'s doctors, nurses, and staff practice heroism on a diminished, human scale. As we look with uncertainty at a brave new millennium, this may be as salvific as prime-time television is likely to get, and that can be good news indeed.

EIGHT

Beverly Hills 90210

THE WORLD ACCORDING TO TEENAGE SOAPS

If I can get on with my life, you can get on with yours.
—*Kelly to Donna*

Episode: **First aired:**
"That's the Guy"   May 19, 1999

90210 is only one zip code after all, and a small and insular
world where diversity is different hair color and everyone is
slim, beautiful, popular, and monied. It is full of the urgent
geometry of love triangles and intersecting plotlines, the first
Generation-X soap. It does not shrink from the tough issues of
teenage life but answers all questions in the quick time frame
of tensely edited scenes and scripts, keeping viewers coming
back to see intimacy and intrigue up close but not too personal.

The episode "That's the Guy" was the finale for the eighth season. This
episode reflects the genre of soap opera (daytime drama) while demonstrating the innovations to the genre that prime-time positioning initiated.
Because this season finale focuses on rape and eating disorders, it is more
melodramatic than usual, and it lacks some of the series' well-known
humorous qualities. Nonetheless, the shape, content, and pacing of the
episode are clear examples of the genre.

Shot and Scene: Bulimia and the Fragility of Life

Gina and David are having a cozy evening together, playing childhood
games like dominoes and Old Maid. They seem casual and at ease with
each other, as though perhaps every evening together is spent in this fashion. Dylan, David's roommate and Gina's former boyfriend, arrives on

the scene, and the tension mounts. As Dylan enters, David belatedly warns him not to slam the door so that the dominoes do not fall. After Dylan slams the door, there is a pregnant pause as the three wait to see whether the dominoes tumble. When it is clear the dominoes will remain standing, Dylan responds, "Well, some things are stronger than they look," referring not only to the dominoes but also to Gina herself. Gina has explained earlier in the episode that dating Dylan was bad for her mental health, because Dylan was in love with someone else. In this encounter, David tries to protect Gina from Dylan as she flees from the room and from the tension Dylan creates.

After David warns Dylan to leave Gina alone, we watch Dylan brood about the situation, while ostensibly staring at the dominoes. Despite David's cautionary words or maybe because of them, Dylan slams the door when he leaves the house. Only the viewer is left to witness the dominoes in their rapid collapse. As the last domino falls, it catapults a maraschino cherry onto a melting sundae.

Dramatic tension among the characters is accented by the tension between the innocence of the children's games and the adult anguish symbolized by falling dominoes. They fall in a moment, but the memory of their fall lingers. An innocent pastime has pointed to the fragility of life and the manner in which Gina and Dylan both experience loss. Likewise, Gina and David's attempt to create security in a homey, confined environment is only as stable as a row of dominoes. As no one domino stands or falls alone, neither does Gina or David. Outside forces pummel them and knock them over. In the face of great insecurities, Gina's desperate attempt to control her life has led to an eating disorder, bulimia. The scene closes with a graphic sign of her agonizing struggle: a close-up of an uneaten, melting ice cream sundae.

Beverly Hills 90210 (often referred to in this chapter simply as *90210*) has a notable history of tackling difficult issues such as eating disorders. However, the complexity of such issues is often diluted by the manner in which they are depicted. In this scene, Gina returns to her location of powerlessness—one cannot help but wonder why. Rather than facing Dylan in a moment of strength, she flees the room the minute she feels awkward. David is left to fight her battle for her. Gina's eating may be stabilized at the moment, but it appears that her health is now dependent on a second man. A reference to Old Maid in the conversation between Gina and David further underscores such dependence. Gina's words about her experience of bulimia depict an informed struggle to overcome negative images of herself. However, the *signs* and *codes* of the narrative send a *message* of her great sense of powerlessness. Without the right look, she too will wind up a stereotypical old maid—alone, disliked, and discarded. The handling of this issue ultimately does not empower Gina (or the show's female viewers) with the greater self-awareness and inner strength needed to overcome such a painful situation.

In spite of these serious criticisms, young women watching this episode learn about an experience that exists in many of their own lives. Eating disorders are a significant health threat for women in the United States. Having someone on national, prime-time television give voice to the emotions and context that create an eating disorder no doubt helps countless young women to begin expressing their own struggles. However, as with so much on television, this scene also glamorizes bulimia. Gina says that she has been bulimic for a long time, and yet physically she shows no signs of the stress that this illness puts on the human body; instead, she remains an image of the beauty to which so many women aspire. Ironically, even in her presumed state of bulimia, Gina's image sets an unrealistic goal for many young women and thus creates the dissatisfaction about body image that can cause eating disorders. The role model who should raise awareness carries the very image that potentially creates poor health among women. The threat to health that bulimia presents is completely undermined by Gina's apparent beauty. Awareness is raised about a significant issue, but awareness, in this case, has a price.

Thus, this scene walks a complicated path between myth and parable. Much of what it portrays is a commentary on the strength of the human will to survive in difficult times. Yet as the dominoes fall, the myth is quietly undermined, and the fragility of human nature is exposed. When Gina shares her story of bulimia with David, the ugly side of societal pressure on women's body image is revealed and at the same time called into question. Although such questions are raised, Gina still continues to appear outwardly healthy and beautiful. Her physical presence only reinforces the myth that bulimia is not a significant health issue or threat to women's lives, which merely reinforces the status quo.

Using the interpretive lenses, we now turn to an examination of other story lines in this episode and series, which represent quintessential prime-time soap opera.

Narrative: Techniques of the Soap Genre

Although a scene like the one with Gina, David, and Dylan (played by Vanessa Marcil, Brian Austin Greene, and Luke Perry) is easy enough to describe, the nuances behind it are often not. These are built on years of relationships among characters. The same characters and their relationships are used to propel the show's plot through scores of episodes. It is assumed that viewers have a vested interest in keeping track of the history of relationships, encounters, conflicts, and crises, just as one does with friends and relationships in real life. All human relationships, all interactions between good friends, carry within them the scars and joys of other interactions. Thus, any attempt to summarize a soap opera plot forces one to mention countless other episodes in which necessary information was relayed. Defining a particular relationship requires elaboration of all the characters and the ways in which they connect to this particular relationship.

The most common technique for creating complex, intertwining story lines is the "relationship triangle." *90210* intentionally and repeatedly creates stable two-person relationships that are challenged by a third person. The dominoes fall after conflict between David and Dylan over Gina.

The triangles among the nine characters on *90210* are dynamic and always changing. The characters are Gina (Vanessa Marcil), David (Brian Austin Greene), Dylan (Luke Perry), Kelly (Jennie Garth), Matt (Daniel Cosgrove), Donna (Tori Spelling), Noah (Vincent Young), Janet (Lindsay Price), and Steve (Ian Ziering). In this episode, the major triangles are as follows: Dylan loves Kelly, but Kelly is confused about her feelings for Matt (first triangle). Instead, Dylan dates Gina, but Gina gets tired of always playing second fiddle to his true love and eventually breaks up with Dylan (second triangle). In the aftermath, Gina begins spending time with David, who also happens to be Dylan's roommate (third triangle). The continued presence of Dylan becomes increasingly confusing for Gina despite her growing relationship with David. This tension comes to a climax when David discovers Gina and Dylan together in bed.

Donna is also caught in a love triangle in which she finds herself attracted to two men (fourth triangle). There is Noah, the reliable boyfriend whom she knows well and who wants her to move in with him, and there is Wayne, the mysterious handsome surfer who has recently appeared in her life. Donna finds herself strongly attracted to Wayne at the risk of losing Noah. Kelly, Donna's roommate, tries to give her advice, but Kelly is reeling from her own personal trauma of rape and is not very available or very wise. Kelly is also emotionally caught between Matt and Dylan, both of whom she finds attractive. The advice Kelly gives Donna could be just what Kelly herself needs. Eventually the advice leads Donna to lose Noah and then realize that she does not know Wayne as well as she thought she did.

These triangles are an effective narrative device used in soap operas. Extensive theories in the field of counseling address the dynamics of triangulation. When triangulated, both the relationships and the individuals involved in them become vulnerable to intensified conflict, sticky tension, blaming, and deceptive manipulation. Rather than two people addressing their problems directly, both deal with their issues by embroiling a third person in them. As most therapeutic systems note, this is neither healthy nor effective.[1] However, as the television industry has discovered, it does make for great stories. Triangles create tension. Tension propels plot. Like most serials, soap operas are *character* driven. Thus, they revel in the use of this character technique.

Because the format for soap operas demands a never-ending story line, there is ample time for building up and tearing apart relationships. The development and dismantling of triangles is the predominant method used. However, unlike daytime dramas, which usually appear five days a week, *90210* aired only once a week. To keep continuity and to ensure a high level of audience comprehension, the cast remained comparatively small. As a result, relationships on *90210* were even more insular than those commonly found in daytime soaps. Thus, the movement of characters within these triangles seems even more pronounced.

Structure: *90210* and Trends in the Characteristics of Soap Operas

Although defining the characteristics of a soap opera is difficult,[2] when we bump into one we usually know it. We recognize the complex and intertwining plotlines, the characters' confused relationships with one another, and the exaggerated sense of conflict. This highly developed genre did not suddenly appear but evolved slowly, always mirroring the subtle changes occurring in the target audience. Daytime soap operas sprang directly from the serial radio shows of the 1920s and 1930s, which were created solely to advertise (to women) soap and other home cleaning products. Today's daytime soap operas, like their predecessors, have low production costs and generate enormous revenues by providing twice as much time for advertising as evening television. Historically, these ads and the story lines were created to entice the female homemaker. Even today, many of the sponsors of daytime soap operas continue to be companies focused on selling to the female consumer products to make her life more beautiful and glamorous.[3] In the beginning, soap operas were slow-paced shows with long, extended scenes. The plot lines were safe and only barely more exotic than the lives of the homemakers who listened to or watched them.

In the late 1970s, many daytime soap operas intentionally updated their look to regain contemporary relevance. Speeding up the dialogue, inserting more sensational issues in the narrative, and creating more elaborate and exotic sets and background music were some of the techniques used to help achieve this. Many such characteristics of daytime and prime-time soap operas, taken for granted today, were initiated in the 1970s.[4]

Prime-time soap operas (including *90210*) share these similarities with daytime shows, but they have had to evolve in some particular ways to survive prime-time competition. In the 1980s, shows such as *Dynasty* and *Dallas* rose to great popularity as their subject matter became more and more daring. As the market began to show an interest in this genre, the television industry sought to widen the demographics of its audience. Fox, a relatively new "netlet" at the time, decided to try a new variety of evening soap opera appealing to teenagers and debuted *Beverly Hills 90210* on October 4, 1990. Creator Darren Star wanted the show to address the emotional lives of teens. *Beverly Hills 90210* was one of the first shows to capture the imagination of Generation X.[5] Although television critics did not greet the show with enthusiasm, it was an instant success among its target audience.

The story of *Beverly Hills 90210* begins with the Walsh family moving from Minnesota to Beverly Hills. Their twin daughter and son are in high school and must cope with all of the cultural changes that such a move creates. Each subsequent year of the series follows the characters through another year of high school until their graduation at the end of the 1992–93 season. These seasons provided ample opportunity for the show to address the weighty social issues that teenagers faced then and that they still face today. Over time and through careful writing, "true characters emerged from the stereotypes."[6]

As the characters have aged, the show has become more typical of the daytime soap opera—fewer social issues, fewer artistic efforts. Some changes in style and script have been made as the writers and creators intentionally followed the developing interests of their audience. Some of these changes evolved naturally as the characters began to resemble more and more closely in age and occupation the characters most typically seen on daytime soaps.

Despite these trends in the series, *90210* still has features that separate it from its ancestry of daytime soap operas. The show moved much faster than most daytime, or even earlier run prime-time soap operas; to keep its teen appeal, *90210* tried to be unusual and to do the unexpected. There is a strong effort at humor in the show's dialogue and editing. These quirky and unique characteristics are, in part, what led to the show's long life. Panned by critics when it first began, it lived a remarkable nine years.

Such innovations and attempts to be less conventional do not prevent *90210* from resembling all soap operas in promoting a world that is assumed to be the quintessential American dream. The beautiful and thin are successful. It is easy to make money and live comfortably. Community is narrowly defined as a close-knit group of friends. Viewers are tantalized by the easy life—sunshine, sandy beaches—and are invited to achieve such goals themselves. As a result of this focus, diversity on *90210* means that among the female characters there is sure to be a redhead, a brunette, and a blonde. Characters other than the main nine remain peripheral and only assist in the action between the leads—rarely do they create action themselves. The characters who really matter are white, wealthy, attractive, and in their teens. Such characteristics point to the ways in which *90210* is a myth upholding the typical American dream of wealth, luxury, and comfort.

Perhaps because it caters to a teenage audience raised on television and savvy to its persuasive ways, *90210* also appears at times to undermine the American myth of success—never to the extent of entirely abandoning such a worldview, but still calling into question the very messages it seems to promote. For example, while Gina and David are handling

Gina's eating disorder and creating a safe haven for themselves, the dominoes fall, and we shudder at the stark reality that self-sufficiency *is* myth. In this manner, *90210* cleverly plays to the form of parable. Although it never fully adopts such a structure, it does willingly participate in questioning the values it seems to espouse.

Signs, Codes, and Messages

The settings of all soaps are remarkably insular, and never is this more the case than in *90210*. We are prepared for this in part by the opening credits, which boast a photo montage of the stars. Each member of the cast is featured independently on a full screen for a significant time. Woven into these sexy shots of each actor is a hectic and chaotic collage of poses of different combinations of characters. These images are shown rapidly and convey the message of a community in movement—connected to and disconnected from one another—and thus are dynamically interesting. However, it is clear that *they* are the extent of the community. The final scene of the opening credits shows Kelly and Donna, who begin by holding hands as dance partners. As they back away from each other, their hands are pulled apart. The ambiguity of that visual comment is intentional, pointing to the tension that makes the show: To what degree and in what fashion are the characters truly loyal to one another? The answers vary from week to week.

Following a series of ads is another set of introductory material that reminds the viewer of a slightly larger setting. We see street scenes, supposedly depicting Beverly Hills; there are bikers, rollerbladers, bikinis, traffic, sunshine, palm trees, beaches, large homes, beautiful clothes, and lots of movement. These are all clear signs of the context of the show, easily recognized as standard images of the glamorous California life. Beyond these opening scenes, little attention is paid to this outside world throughout the course of the show; again, this is a way to insulate the characters. Although these introductory shots tells us that the story is set in a particular place, in truth the wider community seldom plays any significant role in the plot.

The world of *90210* is really only the world of these nine characters, who must somehow make it on their own. At one point in this episode, the music group Collective Soul sings at the nightclub After Dark. In the background of the action we can hear the lyrics: "I am acquainted with your suffering. All your weight falls on me. It brings me down." As a commentary on the burden the characters carry, these lyrics could not be more profound. Later, Collective Soul sings: "Are these times contagious? I've never been this bored before. Is this the prize I've waited for? Now that the hour's passing. . . . Is there a cure among us?" Such despair highlights each character's own struggle, and we watch as the camera pulls away to show Noah, Kelly, Matt, Steve, and Dylan standing still in the midst of the crowded dance floor. Their lack of movement sets them apart. They stand alone, not giving one another much solace in their small community, yet they are also unable or unwilling to let others join them.

At a specific moment in the introductory material, the viewer is further prepared for such struggles by a powerful metaphor that points to the remainder of the show. Amid the rapid images, we see a traffic light indicating when pedestrians may cross the street. The walk and don't walk signs flash on and off in quick succession, not working in "real" time. Perhaps the seeming indecision of the signs alludes to the flightiness of the culture, in which every day means a new fad, every day holds the question of whether one will still be fashionable and part of the "in" crowd. On a more basic level, the flashing walk and don't walk signs foreshadow the tempo of the episode. There is no time to pause, to rest, to process; one might lose the window of opportunity. If one does not move quickly, one is likely to get run over, literally by the traffic, and figuratively by the stresses of life.

This theme is *technically* depicted in a scene in which Dylan is in town hanging signs that read, "$100,000 Reward for Rapist." In a previous episode, Kelly was raped by a young man, Joe Patch (played by Cliff Dorfman), in an alleyway in town. Dylan feels frustration over the failure of the police to catch the rapist. Because of his complex emotions for Kelly—frustration at not being able to solve her problem, despair at not being her chosen love—Dylan takes matters into his own hands by posting reward signs. An anonymous older woman, her clothes suggestive of homelessness, approaches Dylan as he finishes hanging the signs and tells him that she heard Kelly screaming and struggling the night she was raped. The woman can point to the place where it happened. She tells Dylan that she tried to get help that night but no one would listen to her. Dylan tries to get more information from her but she begins to leave. Just before she exits, she turns around and says, "God bless you for what you're doing."

Technically, this scene begins like all the others; however, after the woman repeats that she heard Kelly scream, the scene is filmed with a handheld camera. Often this technique makes the product appear like someone's home video. The handheld camera results in a jumpy picture as the videographer walks; often the camera does not remain level, so that actors are shot off center and at awkward angles. Using the handheld camera gives a realistic feel to a fictional story, as though it were a documentary. In addition, this filming "more closely approximates human movement"[7] and helps viewers feel they are experiencing the scene just as the character is.

Use of the handheld camera, sets this scene apart from the others in this episode. It has a more frantic quality, depicting Dylan's desperation and frustration. It also gives an air of vulnerability. With the handheld camera, we lose all sense of being omniscient viewers, and instead we are intimately thrown into the precariousness of the character's story. Dylan and the anonymous woman are on their own, while the woman describes her inability to make anyone listen. The typically unnoticed chief narrator of ordinary filming, the omniscient viewer, is removed, and as a result the viewer is forced to pay attention to *how* the story is told. Dylan appears isolated as he fights a system he senses does not care about his concerns and problems, and thus he seeks to take care of Kelly's problem himself. Ruth Rosen's words about the daytime soap *General Hospital* ring true for *90210* as well: "This mythic community, turned in on itself, is obsessed solely with its private agonies, drawing unity only from its individual pains."[8] The plot of *90210* is driven by individuals and their personal traumas.

Power: The *90210* Treatment of Rape

Such insularity and fragility are most pronounced and most disturbing when social issues are treated only with regard to the way they affect the nine main characters. Issues such as rape and bulimia are presented as private matters whose societal causes and cures are irrelevant. Because of this, there is little room in the text of the show for social analysis. As mentioned earlier, in this episode Gina admits to being bulimic. When she confides to David why she passed out in the bathroom, Gina describes her bulimic behavior as a way in which she tries to maintain control over her life. Before she finishes her last word, David responds, saying "Thank you for telling me." This is his only initial response. Through musical cues and Gina's expression, we are led to believe that this issue is now resolved— at least between these two. Although the subject does come up between them again, it is frightening how quickly a deep psychological problem is presumed resolved merely because a peer has acknowledged it. David's insufficient response may *reflect* typical twentysomething male behavior, but left uncriticized by any character on the show it also *shapes* male behavior by modeling it.

The way in which the episode handles Kelly's rape experience is another example of the manner in which social issues are kept personal. Early in the episode, Donna reminds Kelly that rape is "a crime of violence, not of sex, not about wearing provocative dresses; [your rape] wasn't about anything you did." This is a positive message—a clear statement that victims of rape are not "asking for it" but instead are victims of a system that allows or even promotes such treatment of women. However, except for the briefest reference to a rape support group later in the episode, little is said to help the viewer ponder a social milieu that allows for and even promotes such criminal behavior. To offer such a critique would call into question a worldview that encourages seeing women as objects of beauty to be acquired—indeed, a worldview promoted by the characters and story of *90210*. Instead Kelly, in a moment of stubborn courage, says to her roommate Donna, "If I can get on with my life, you can get on with yours." They will pick up the pieces, wherever they may have fallen, and continue on with relationships. The only assistance Kelly receives in this episode is from her two heroic knights, Matt and Dylan. These two, who are disgusted with the slow police investigation, join forces to take matters into their own hands. They mount a search for the rapist and offer a generous reward for information leading to his capture. Outside authority is not consulted. What is lacking is a sense of a greater community that is not only culpable in this problem but might also be of assistance. In reality, these issues are too large for these individuals to cope with on their own. They cannot single-handedly change the institutional and systemic realities of American culture. Perhaps their inclination is to try—along with the help of a few friends. Social reform is not what rape victims initially need, and thus the focus in this episode is more on Kelly and the ways in which her friends can help her. However, because this is a season finale and the series did little to address such a systemic issue, this episode only further helps to disconnect the characters' experiences from their context.

The result is alarming. Matt, Kelly's boyfriend and one of her chief defenders in this episode, unknowingly sends the rapist to Kelly's shop. Joe (the rapist) is a client of Matt's legal services. Originally, he comes to Matt for defense in a case of theft. Early in the episode, Joe asks Matt to take his case: He is suing the police for brutality. Joe is depicted as a shifty character. In a later scene, without knowing she is speaking of her rapist, Kelly challenges Matt about how he can defend a client (Joe) who is guilty of theft. Despite this conversation, Matt has agreed to take Joe's case. As Joe is leaving Matt's office, he asks Matt where he might buy his mother a gift. Matt suggests Kelly's shop, which is downstairs in the same building.

When he enters her shop, Kelly and the rapist recognize each other; she demands that he leave. Instead, Joe locks the door and pulls out his knife. In fear and panic, Kelly takes a gun from her purse and shoots him again and again and again, continuing to pull the trigger of a gun long empty of bullets. Then the screen fades to black. Clearly shot for drama and tension, the sound script laying a pounding beating ominous music, this scene closes both the episode *and* the season.

When Joe first enters the shop, Kelly is holding her cordless phone. She could have easily called 911 or even Matt upstairs. Because Joe is armed only with a knife, no match for her gun, Kelly could have held him at bay while crying for help in the crowded mall. However, sometimes the natural response is not as rational as this, and a victim lashes out at her assailant. In this scene, *90210* promotes the American ideal of self-defense and depicts a woman who is strong enough to protect herself. Yet it does so with a twist of irony, for it is one of her defenders, Matt, who sends the rapist back to Kelly, thus necessitating the act of self-defense. Even though we want to cheer at the villain getting his due, we realize that Kelly shoots only because of Matt's first act. He has unwittingly embroiled her in an act of further violence.

"We can make it on our own." It is a misleading and dangerous myth to suppose that our actions and choices are independent of all others in this world. Although the plot of *90210* seems to suggest such rugged individualism, the undercurrent, exemplified by the mixed implications of Matt's actions, modifies this theme.

Function

As mentioned earlier, the narrative of *90210* is rather insular, keeping to a fairly narrowly focused cast. The viewers of the show appear to be the only outsiders allowed into the private community of *90210*. They quickly become part of the insular world created by the nine characters. Viewers get drawn into a story and walk this endless journey with the characters. A connection develops, which wraps viewer and narrative tightly together. Part of what draws us in is the ambiguity of characters' lives. The world of the soaps is a place where right and wrong flourish side by side and where there are few absolutes. Rosen writes, "Soaps offer continuity. People don't just watch soap operas; they live with them. . . . [Soaps] seem intimate but are safely remote."[9] The open-ended story line, one week flowing into the next, allows the viewer to create his or her own meaning and at the same time, voyeuristically, keeps these issues and traumas at arm's length.

The tempo of each scene and the editing between them reinforce this remoteness. On the one hand, we are sometimes thrown obscenely into intimate moments between characters; yet this intimacy remains at best elusive and at worst false, as the format of the show never allows for serious reflection by cast or by viewer. Instead, events always remain in a mode of urgency. We must keep moving to stay ahead. In this mode, the focus is on survival; what is valued is an ability simply to cope. Reflection is unnecessary and even a liability, as it can make one appear weak and vulnerable or distract one from the *real* task at hand, which is getting something done. This urgency becomes all the more vivid for cast and viewer alike when it is compounded with the philosophy that success depends entirely on one's own ability and determination. Characters and viewers have little time to process their choices with one another; moments for connection are eliminated.

The editing of *90210* dictates this sense of urgency, as the pacing of scenes is dramatic and quick. When time for commercials and the introductory material (including both initial montages and scenes from the previous episode) is subtracted from the sixty minutes of airtime, this episode runs for roughly forty minutes. In that time, there are twenty-nine scenes, so that on average a scene runs eighty-three seconds. Story lines are told in little bite sizes as we jump around among several subplots at once. This teenage soap opera may take its cues from music videos and commercials; both of these genres share that distinctive rapid-fire pacing, as though the editor wished to construct a collage. The practice stimulates and moves the viewer by bombarding her or him with input. Thus, we can explore the issues of a particular story line during several scenes throughout the episode; however, there is no moment in the narrative when in-depth reflection is permitted or required. "On evening soaps there is no time to experience the consequences of stupid or sinful behavior."[10] The primary task of each scene is to convey information and elicit a response that motivates the viewer to continue watching. Reflection is secondary, and when it is done, it appears inauthentic because of its hurried nature and its reliance on stereotype.

Urgency is used throughout this particular episode in the tension surrounding Kelly's postrape trauma, increasingly heightened through the plot's unfolding without reflection. First there is a scene in which Donna urges Kelly to talk to Matt about what has happened. When Kelly does tell Matt, he responds by saying, "Listen to me. I want you to tell me everything. I want you to know that I love you. I love you. And I'm right here. And that this changes nothing. Do you hear me? Changes nothing." A sweet and compassionate response, but denying the truth that for Kelly everything has changed, a truth that goes unsaid.

In another scene, Kelly encourages her roommate Donna to get on with her life as Kelly is trying to do, but Kelly's "getting on" is simply that. It is not the road to recovery that one would hope, but instead consists of fits and starts. Such a pattern is typical of the recovery process, but it also lends itself well to creating tension in the story line. In a scene following her conversation with Donna about getting on with her life, Kelly thinks she sees her rapist at the nightclub and publicly panics. In another scene, she wakes up screaming from a nightmare, after which her only reflection to her roommate Donna is, "It won't be [over] until he pays for what he did to me." No response ensues from Donna. Throughout these scenes, the viewer is not allowed to forget the fragile state of Kelly's mental health. The culmination of all this tension building, then, is no surprise. In the frightening moment when Kelly actually does meet her rapist again, she whips out the gun and shoots and shoots and shoots. No doubt, in any situation so grave one would want a woman to do what was necessary for self-protection. However, given that Kelly has taken no visible steps toward healing, we are witnesses to the exaggerated effect of the gun firing again and again and again. The camera shot has the viewer looking down the barrel of the gun. As the gun is shot, the viewer is in the direct line of fire. We watch as Kelly continues to pull the trigger long after she has run out of bullets. This solution does not help Kelly heal. She destroys her destroyer, but such revenge does not necessarily bring peace or justice to the situation. It certainly does not allow for Joe's healing and redemption. Instead, this intense season finale plays deftly into our society's understanding of how to deal with a criminal and supplies a rush of adrenaline that comes from such sweet retribution.

This rapid editing lends itself to the exciting delivery of plot. As viewers, we are not meant to spend too much time deliberating over appropriate and necessary actions, justice, forgiveness, or retribution. Instead, we feel intensely in the moment with our characters. Getting swept up in the urgency, we look down the barrel of the gun, and we feel and react, just as the characters do. We are not called on to reflect: on what it means for Gina to sleep again with a man who does not love her; on what it means for Dylan to sleep with Gina as a power move over David; on what it means for Matt and Dylan to compete in a macho way for Kelly's affection, when the real issue is her traumatic experience of rape; on what it means that Kelly has been given a gun and thus an apparent opportunity for self-protection, but also an invitation to dangerous violent acts of her own.

Theological Analysis

What is the significance of the fact that there is no pause, no rest, no sabbath available in this show, in this genre? It means that as we rush from one scene to the next, we are encouraged to focus on our doing rather than our being, on acting rather than on reflecting. It means that success is measured by our list of achievements rather than our character and ability to respond to another in need. No doubt it is unrealistic to expect television to imitate the rhythm and pattern of a spiritual life; that is not its purpose. However, television's prevalence in our lives speaks of our dangerous loss of a deep spiritual practice. Faith takes dedication, discipline, and responsibility. Spiritual insights are seldom given to us on a palatable platter but are rather mined from the hard earth of practice, and time is needed for such growth and discovery. Television—entertainment by nature—generally does not encourage this, but instead asks us to sit back, relax, and get swept up in the stories we see.

This is especially true of a show like *90210*. When the story line never ends, the viewer has no opportunity to pause to reflect on the characters and their choices because the chaos continues the following week. We are prompted to guess at the future, not reflect on the past. This tendency is both explicitly and implicitly supported by the creators of the show. The cliff-hanging endings are designed to pull viewers into potential scenarios for the upcoming week—or season. In the writing itself are also subtle clues that reflection is unnecessary. For example, David initially comments when Gina tells him about her bulimia, "Thank you for telling me." These five words cannot replace the long, difficult spiritual struggle of coming to terms with this painful, destructive behavior.

Another example of this lack of reflection is the handling of Kelly's postrape trauma. In Matt and Kelly's relationship, we see little of the psychological anguish that rape triggers. There are occasional brief conversations that usually end with Matt or Donna looking pensive. Matt and Dylan each seek to defend Kelly rather than help her get the therapy she needs. Healing requires slow, careful work and is far from entertaining. Could it be that the all-male team of writer, director, and producers had something to do with this rather insensitive handling of postrape trauma?*

Lack of reflection on the part of the characters means that they devote their time to accomplishing things. This can be a positive image of ability and drive and a compliment to human imagination, but it also has a foreboding side. Over time, the viewer comes to think that all problems are solvable, no hurdle is too high. We just need to work a little harder to pull ourselves up by the bootstraps. Such expectations send to the audience a destructive message that any problems any viewer might have are a result of the viewer's own incompetence. The burden on the individual is immense. Mirroring the success-driven orientation of American culture, we are faced with the question of whether we have any need for God, because our own ability to take care of ourselves is so strong. Like the television characters we emulate, when we face significant trauma, there remains nothing to fall back on but our own rugged self-sufficiency.

This is not to say that we are not each responsible for the direction of our lives. However, we should not overemphasize our need and even our ability to control the chaos of the world. Strong television messages of independence run the risk, at the very least, of creating outsized expectations for one person and, at the worst, of blaming the victims of trauma for their own suffering. Theologically, this message drowns out the possibility of receiving grace. It also overinvests in the power of humanity, thus ignoring any help God might provide; God seems useless.

The power of God also seems diminished by the portrayal of the world and the lack of human diversity on *90210*. Although most religious traditions attempt to expand their concept of God through the practice of reflecting on the diversity in creation, this is absent from our episode. The world is full of diverse cultures, climates, economic conditions,

---

* John Eisendrath wrote this episode, and Michael Lange directed it. The executive producers were Aaron Spelling, E. Duke Vincent, Paul Waigner, John Eisendrath, and Jason Priestly.

educational standards, language systems, and so on, but the world of *90210* is very small. Quietly and slowly we are persuaded that these nine characters point to what a complete creation is or perhaps should be. Because the white, wealthy, professional world is the center of this show, and because these characters turn only to one another for comfort and help, the great diversity of creation is truncated. God's creativity seems to come up lacking. Humanity becomes the answer, and only a tiny portion of humanity at that. In this fashion, the life experience of these characters is the answer, is powerful, is the clear image of who and what we should seek to attain.

This theological weakness feeds on itself throughout the show and is clearly depicted in this season finale. Reliance solely on humanity does not provide solace or a wider view of the purpose of life. The more that the characters attempt to control their problems themselves, the greater the problems become. Kelly accepts a gun from Dylan for her protection. She is not licensed and apparently not trained to use it, but it gives her a sense of security. Eventually, in her panic, she uses the gun, with devastating effect.

These are the theological risks of this episode and series. However, at its conception, *90210* offered attention to teenagers who were seeking answers to some of life's most serious questions. *90210* was able to address these issues without condescension and without raising the skepticism of its teenage audience, known to be keenly sensitive when adults offer less than the truth. In this way, this series gave credence to the experiences of teenagers in our culture and validated them as members of society with significant issues. At the same time, despite appearances, television cannot and should not substitute for real conversations, interventions, therapy, friendships, or legal counsel. In the end, television is only a masquerade, with all the necessary lights, costumes, and pretense.

NINE

Touched by an Angel

POPULAR RELIGIOUS DRAMA

Sometimes I still shake my head and wonder at the things that human beings are capable of. And then I remember the most human hour of my own life.

—Monica the Angel

Episode:
"Black like Monica"

First aired:
May 2, 1999

If God is explicitly referred to anywhere in prime time, it is on this show. *Touched by an Angel* consistently brings up questions about how God works in the world, transforming hearts and minds, one person and one episode at a time. It offers a comforting dose of generic spirituality, but like everything else constrained to the prime-time clock, it has little room to deal deeply with the ongoing and untidy realities of our lives or the ambiguities in our faith.

You need not look hard to find theology in *Touched by an Angel*. The show has single-handedly proved to Hollywood that stories about God's action in the world are marketable. It has made it much more likely for us to see a television character pray, worship, or speak about God on prime-time television today than ever before.

When *Touched by an Angel* debuted on a Wednesday night in September 1994, opposite the sitcom *Roseanne*, the hour-long drama featuring three angels was not the hit it became in the late 1990s. In fact, it had little hope of survival.[1] The *San Francisco Examiner* called it "another example of why America is the stupidest place on earth," and *Entertainment Weekly* snorted "Halo, I must be going."[2] An amazing turnaround took place in its second season, partly because of a new producer, Martha Williamson, and the loyalty of viewers who participated in a letter-writing campaign when CBS considered canceling the show. By the time the episode "Black like Monica" ran some four years later, *Touched by an Angel* was more than surviving—it was thriving in its new time slot, right after *60 Minutes* on Sunday evenings. By the turn of the millennium, more than twenty million people were tuning in to the show each week.

"Black like Monica," which originally aired on May 2, 1999, shows how deftly this series raises theological questions and attacks social problems such as racism while selling a spirituality that never challenges the status quo of another societal problem: consumerism.

Episode Synopsis

In the small town of Aynesville, Illinois, a black man known only as Mooney has been viciously murdered near a local graveyard on the same day that civil rights pioneer Rosa Parks arrives in town to celebrate the recent discovery of the diary of an underground railroad hero. Monica, an angel, discovers the body and reports it to the town leaders. Fearing that publicity about the hate crime on such a monumental day will upset Parks's visit, an ad hoc committee of the city council votes to withhold information about the murder until after the celebration. Believing that truth is more important than image, Monica speaks out against the cover-up and is thrown into jail. As an angel, she is divinely freed from jail, but leaving the cell she notices an amazing change: She is now black, with curly hair, brown skin, and a Southern accent. She experiences racial prejudice firsthand and realizes that color makes quite a difference in this human world. The white killers search for another black person to murder, and see Monica. She knows that as a black woman she is marked for murder, and she runs. When she falls and cuts herself, the sight of blood makes her realize that she has become human and can die. She prays that God will make her white again, and in the twinkling of an eye she is transformed back into a white angel and is left alone. Monica returns to the site of the murder and meets Andrew, the angel of death, who tells her that Mooney was in the cemetery the day he was murdered because he wanted to set the record straight: The person who helped with the underground railroad was not a white man, as the town historian believes, but a free black woman, a relative of Mooney's, who is buried there. Monica returns to town to tell what she knows, to confess her own human weakness of racism and to receive forgiveness. Then she reveals to the town leaders that she is an angel and asks them to confront their racism, be reconciled, and tell the truth about Mooney's murder. The murder suspects, the notorious racist Foley brothers, are arrested once clear evidence against them is found.

Narrative

Touched by an Angel was created by John Masius, known for his Emmy-winning writing on *St. Elsewhere* and for creating the new NBC hit *Providence* in January 1999. Masius had a marketable idea but apparently failed to execute it well in the early days of the show, and CBS brought in Williamson to make major changes. She looked at the show and saw what was missing: the presence of God. "Instead, he was the butt of some jokes," she says. Under Williamson's wing, the show has come to life with the message that God exists and loves us and wants to be part of our lives. "If you can get that simple but absolute truth across every week, you have changed television," she says.[3] Williamson, an evangelical Christian, says she strives to "make truth more and more the deciding factor in [her] actions."[4] She did not like the show's early emphasis on the supernatural attributes of the angels, particularly a scene in which one of the angels raises a dog from the dead. Williamson's angels have no wings; they do not fly around (they just mysteriously materialize) or perform miracles on command.

Touched by an Angel has a relatively simple narrative structure. Each episode has a clear beginning, middle, and end, and each is self-contained, with no arcing story lines to remember. The series has made history in the genre of drama, being one of the first successful prime-time television series to focus on spirituality every week. This is not the first show ever to portray religious subjects. In a 1997 cover story about God on television, *TV Guide* listed five religion-based dramas that preceded *Touched by an Angel: Father Murphy, Hell Town, The Father Dowling Mysteries, Heaven Help Us,* and *In the Beginning.*[5] Most of those featured an interesting lead character who was a priest; however, *Heaven Help Us* was about humans who died and became angels. The obvious antecedent to *Touched by an Angel* is Michael Landon's *Highway to Heaven,* in which Landon played an angel who swooped down and fixed people's problems. Williamson wanted to travel a different road:

> We take the next step. We don't treat angels as a fantasy, which most angel shows and movies do. After doing a good deed, the angel disappears into the night, and someone says, "Who was that winged stranger?"
>
> It's very, very difficult to write. People think it's easy because you have this built-in deus ex machina:

God is going to come in and fix everything. That's not true. With any other series, you can have people talk about both sides of any question, and they end up with it up in the air. Fade to black. We can't do that. We ultimately have to come to a decision from God's point of view, which is tremendously difficult sometimes.[6]

As *Touched by an Angel* rose in the ratings, Hollywood became more interested in plots about God. A *TV Guide* poll conducted in 1997 by Peter Hart Research Associates found that 56 percent of the people who were asked "How much attention does religion get on primetime TV?" answered "Not enough."[7] In the same survey, 61 percent wanted more references to God, churchgoing, and other religious observances in prime time, and 68 percent wanted more prime-time spirituality, defined by the poll as "belief in a higher being, but not necessarily an affiliation with a particular organized religion." Eighty-two percent said they wanted television to make more reference to moral issues.[8]

Touched by an Angel touched a nerve in the American viewing public, and producers responded with a number of new shows about religious values, including ABC's critically acclaimed but short-lived drama about a Catholic priest, *Nothing Sacred;* the WB network's *7th Heaven;* and CBS's *Promised Land.* As *Touched by an Angel* made it more acceptable to mention God in prime-time drama, other dramas not centered on a religious figure or spirituality copied the idea. It is now common to see plotlines with elements of a variety of religious traditions on shows like *The X-Files, ER, Star Trek: Voyager, NYPD Blue,* and *Ally McBeal.*

Touched by an Angel's popularity relies on the likeability of its three regular characters and its predictably upbeat narratives. Episodes feature three angels: Monica, the attractive thirtysomething apprentice caseworker with the Irish accent (Roma Downey); Tess, the nurturing mentor and mother figure (Della Reese); and Andrew, the angel of death who appears when people are on the threshold between life and death (John Dye). Much as in *Fantasy Island* or *Love Boat,* various well-known guest stars appear each week in stories that are set all over the United States and occasionally in other parts of the world.

In "Black like Monica," the action centers on Monica and her intervention in Aynesville's time of trial, when a hate crime threatens to mar the town's black history celebration. Monica appears to be a stereotypical all-suffering woman: joyful, kind, loving, sweet, and compassionate. She smiles a lot. Downey has perfected the sincere, earnest look of understanding that Monica bestows on all people with whom she interacts. Her job is to plead with people to follow God's way; pray for wisdom; beg the despondent not to give up on life; and suffer along with those who are suffering. Monica is not devoid of anger and frustration or even panic, when humans do not see the light; but she tries to tame those emotions with gentle, kind persistence to make her point. Throughout this episode, we are privy to Monica's thoughts via voice-over narration, allowing us to enter her situation as she struggles to seek out and reveal truth in a town where racial tensions remain submerged.

The other main characters in this episode are Tom McKinsley (John Ritter), the charming and respected small-town sheriff, and his deputy James (Rick Worthy), whose last name is never used in the episode. In standing up for what is right, Sheriff McKinsley speaks out against the cover-up of Mooney's death and is consequently not allowed to vote as part of the ad hoc committee that decides to keep the murder quiet. Sheriff McKinsley is portrayed as a hard-working, honest, and well-meaning man who is philosophically against racism yet has a hard time acknowledging his own racism. As he becomes more and more disgusted with his mandated complicity in the cover-up, McKinsley is drawn to Monica both for absolution and for camaraderie (they share the secret knowledge of Mooney's death).

James is the most intense and pivotal character in the episode. The archetype of the black man living in two worlds, playing the white man's game when he must, James knows deep in his heart that racism still oppresses him and other black people in his town. An incident like Mooney's murder kicks all of those feelings around until they explode in righteous indignation. James is a man of few words, but when he does speak, he says something important. At the beginning of the episode, he is portrayed as a supportive second-in-command, chuckling collegially at the sheriff's awkward portrayal of a local hero in the town's black history pageant. He and the sheriff look like a pair, working on the murder investigation and openly discussing their differing points of view about the town's race problems. James accompanies the sheriff and a few other key townspeople as Monica takes them to the site of the murder; James is outraged that the town leaders, both black and white, would vote to keep it a secret.

Communication between the sheriff and James on racial issues is at the heart of "Black like Monica." In a scene outside Rosa Parks's "Pathways to Freedom" bus, a tearful Monica begs the two men to "search the dark corners of their hearts" and "confess it to each other and to God."

James: [*crying*] I hate it when you call me Jimmy. I'm not your boy. I'm a man. And I hate it that every time I walk into a nice store or a fancy restaurant everyone looks at me like I'm from another planet. . . . White people, they got something in them that wants to see us put down.

Sheriff: Every one of them?

James: Every one of them.

Sheriff: I . . . I try to be a good man. A fair man. I think racism is wrong and I try to keep up with what I'm supposed to say, black, African American, people of color. I don't pull a black man over just because he's driving a Mercedes. I contribute to the Negro College Fund. But I still don't get why you've got one language for us and another for each other. . . . I have a lot of black friends in this town. But you know what? God help me, every time I shake the hand of a black man, something deep inside, something I can't explain; something involuntary makes me want to wipe my hand on my pants, and I don't know why. [*crying*] I'm sorry. I know it's terrible and I am sorry. I pray to God that He will cut it out of me because I don't even know where it's coming from. So. That's the truth. I don't know where we go from here but at least I know where we stand.

Rosa Parks: [stepping off the bus] Yes, I think you do. You're standing on God's side now.

This climactic scene brings some resolution to the tension in an earlier scene in which James tells McKinsley that he gives the racist Foley brothers credit for one thing: "At least I know where I stand with them." After the confession, the sheriff and James appear to be more at ease with each other. We see them looking each other in the eye and finishing each other's sentences as close friends often do. More important, we hear the sheriff call his deputy by his preferred name, James, not Jim or Jimmy as he did previously in the episode—an indication that the sheriff has heard James's request and is willing to change his behavior immediately. The episode ends with signs of hope for racial reconciliation in Aynesville.

Structure

People either love *Touched by an Angel* or they hate it, mostly because the dominant message is about God and it is simple: God exists, God loves us, and God's love can transform us into better people. *Touched by an Angel* does not create a world for us; it defends a particular worldview, in which God is alive and active in our lives. The angels, as representatives of God, teach people how to live with God's transforming action each week.

In "Black like Monica," the human failing that upsets God's equilibrium is racism. We are told that racism surrounds us and can be detected in both individual and structural ways. We are also warned that denial and secrecy hurt communities but that there is freedom and reconciliation in facing up to our role in the continuing pervasiveness of racism.

In the end, the corrected story of the town hero—that in fact *she* was a black free woman (not a white man as the town's historian thought) who supplied safe housing for travelers on the underground railroad—prevails, and justice is done. The viewer also finds comfort in the arrest of the murderers, the valuable lesson Monica learns, and the reconciliation between James and the sheriff.

Signs and Codes

It is perhaps only fitting that a show about angels has an "otherworldly" look about it. Sometimes its sets and scenery look too clean and neat to be real, perhaps because some of them are not real, but instead are computer-generated covers. Most of the show is shot in Utah and sent to the CBS studios in Los Angeles for postproduction touchups. CBS's animators often use computer technology to basically "rub out" the existing scenery and paste on scenery that is more appropriate to the setting of the story. On a visit to these studios in June 2000, animator Chris DeChristo demonstrated how a shot of the desertlike brushland around a railroad tunnel in Utah could be digitally transformed at the click of a computer mouse into one with lush, green terrain from Pennsylvania. When CBS senior vice-president Charles Cappleman was asked if this was done to save money on location shoots he replied, "Absolutely." Cappleman says the decision to produce *Touched by an Angel* in Utah (where nonunion labor is available) saves CBS thousands of dollars per episode.

Not a lot of spectacular bells and whistles appear in *Touched by an Angel*. Williamson is quoted as saying, "God doesn't use a lot of special effects."[9] The primary signs used to present a divine point of view are the angels themselves. We know these characters are angels because they tell us each week that they are and because a halo of light appears around them as they reveal their heavenly identity. Light is an ancient symbol of divinity, and light shining on and within a person universally signifies enlightenment or knowledge of a higher nature, a key concept in all major religions. But there are a number of ways to signify the divine in a dramatic series. Why haloed angels?

Angels are exceedingly popular and have been for several years, as anyone who works in a bookstore or gift shop knows. Today's believer in angels is as likely to be a practitioner of New Age religion as a Christian, Jew, or Muslim (three religions with sacred texts attesting to angels). Many people believe that they have a guardian angel or that an angel at one time or another has helped them out of a tight spot. Stories of angels rescuing people in danger are widespread and as varied as the people who tell them. Also, angels are mysterious and supernatural, two elements with proven marketability in television and movie stories these days.

In biblical terms, an angel is a messenger of God. In the Hebrew scriptures, the angel sometimes speaks on behalf of God and sometimes is understood to be the human representation of God.[10] In the Gospels, angels make announcements (Luke 1:11; 1:26), minister to Jesus in his time of distress at the Mount of Olives (Luke 22:43), and sit in the empty tomb telling visitors "he is not here" (Mark 16:5). In each case, the angel is on hand to make a pronouncement. According to *Harper's Encyclopedia of Mystical and Paranormal Experience*, angels are immortal beings who live in the spirit world and serve as intermediaries between God and humans.[11]

In an opening scene of "Black like Monica," we are explicitly told what this show's angels do:

> I am Monica: an angel sent by God as a messenger of hope and peace and truth. I am not magic. I cannot predict the future. I cannot alter the past. Whenever I am on this earth I always come in human form, to appear more like you.

In addition to the angelic signs, this episode uses a number of other signs and codes to get its message of reconciliation across. If we look only at the visuals used in the scene in which Sheriff Tom McKinsley and Deputy James confess their racist failings (see dialogue above), we find the two standing close together in front of Rosa Parks's "Pathways to Freedom" bus. Tom is on the right, signifying the white, traditional views on race, and James is on the left, signifying the left-leaning civil rights movement. They are crying and looking each other in the eye—two signs of intimacy. A portion of the word freedom, FREED, is seen between them as they make their confessions. The bus itself is a sign of the unjust system that once forced blacks "to the back of the bus," a symbolic way of marginalizing a group of people. This particular bus is decked out in red, white, and blue, the colors of the U.S. flag, reminding us of the goal of "liberty and justice for all," a key message in this episode. In a single frame of one pivotal scene, without any words or music, we can see two men from different backgrounds brought closer together and "freed" by that togetherness.

Power and Ideology

Touched by an Angel often champions the little guy, the down-on-her-luck single mother, or the terminally ill person. Rarely, however, does the series seriously challenge the status quo. As with any television series, the power lies in its sponsors and the show's ability to deliver the right kind of viewer to those sponsors. During the April 2, 1999, airing of "Black like Monica" in the San Francisco market, there were commercials for the male potency drug Viagra, Post's Shredded Wheat, Ensure, Advil, St. John's wort, Levitz Furniture, and a host of ads touting gifts at major department stores for Mother's Day.

Judging from the commercials, this series is aimed at the older person who is or wishes to be as healthy and active as a younger person and is willing to spend money to achieve this. The Viagra commercial features a romantic older couple dancing. The DiscoverBrokerage.com ad ridicules ageism by giving comeuppance to two dismissive young financial wizards who come slumming into a dark neighborhood bar only to realize that the older man bartending is in reality a dot-com millionaire. The Ensure commercial is not for persons wasting away from a degenerative disease, but is advertised "for healthy people" and stars athletic, retirement-age persons pursuing outdoor activities with such vigor that they look too busy to stop and eat and instead drink the high protein supplement. All these commercials suggest that *Touched by an Angel* helps sell the good life to older adults.

> All these commercials suggest that *Touched by an Angel* helps sell the good life to older adults.

Another indicator of whom this series tries to reach is the setting. The characters in *Touched by an Angel* live in the very best neighborhood—heaven! They wear human clothes that appear to come off the racks of fine department stores. Monica is frequently decked out in flowing, romantic Laura Ashley-style dresses and nostalgic hats with flowers or other frilly ornamentation. Tess looks the part of an upscale older woman, usually outfitted in bright, flowing silky costumes that highlight her vibrant and spunky personality. Andrew, the angel of death, ordinarily sports a *GQ* look with tailored casual slacks, perfect shirts, and every hair in place. The characters are costumed according to their "assignments": For example, if Monica portrays a nurse in a hospital, she dresses like a nurse. When the angels visit a poor household, they are generally dressed "down."

Although the targeted audience is one with expendable income, the series tells stories about people at a wide range of income levels. The casting of an older African-American actress as the "head angel" fond of dispensing her wise "mother-wit" indicates an interest on the part of the producers in elevating the role of African Americans on television. In various interviews with the cast and producer, it is clear that Della Reese, an ordained minister who founded the Church of Understanding Principles, has a strong voice in the writing and production of the show. In addition, the show regularly features African Americans in strong guest-starring roles and highlights problems of racism and classism.

The plot of "Black like Monica" challenges the assumption that the civil rights movement of the 1960s and 1970s eliminated racism on a structural level. This episode asks the viewer to confront his or her own complicity in the systemic sin of racism, by using Monica as the character through whom we learn about the pervasiveness of white privilege and prejudice against black people. The show seems to want to confront viewers with the idea that if angels can fall prey to racism, maybe we are guilty as well.

Spirituality and ethics also affect the social location of the series. The series is written to highlight the importance of knowing there is a higher good that must be attained. Viewers initially interested in the show are those who already believe in a God who created heaven and earth and believe that God expects us to live in a way that leaves the world a better place. Advertisers are greatly interested in these people because they generally care about quality-of-life issues and can be persuaded to purchase products that claim to enhance the quality of life. As crass as it sounds, spirituality sells if it subtly taps our deepest desires for life to be full of vitality, comfort, and material abundance.

Touched by an Angel is a success because it has done just that: sold us on stories about a good God who wants abundant life for us.

Functions

The romantic notion that a kindly and attractive angel intervenes in our lives makes the series a popular as well as a commercial hit. It is "feel-good" television. Fans of the show describe it as "uplifting." Some critics call it easy religion: A person need not get dressed, attend a communal worship service, or even interact with other human beings.[12] Although the angels in this program sometimes deliver tough messages that humans vehemently resist, the hour usually ends with a restoration of balance.

The angels have the last word, and the humans end up seeing things their way. God is in heaven, and all is right with the world.

The show also functions to keep us believing that a supernatural force outside ourselves just *might* intervene to help us in times of trouble. Although the angels do not always save a person's life or make life better, they sometimes do. It is interesting to note that the angels in this series do much more than most of their biblical counterparts. They claim, as Monica does in this episode, that "they are not magic," but a viewing of several different episodes shows that the distinction is merely semantic. In one episode, Monica saves an entire cult from fiery death by touching the chains on the house door, causing them to fall away. The angels do not force humans to stop doing something sinful or destructive, but amazing coincidences crop up at the just the right time, convincing humans to take the high road. Are these acts the hand of God or magic? It depends on what the viewer believes about how the divine interacts with physical reality. In this series, God's actions regularly defy the laws of nature and look a lot like what nonreligious people might call "magic."

Theological Analysis

Because *Touched by an Angel* is overtly spiritual, it is an obvious choice for theological analysis. Every week, no matter what the plotline, one of the angels usually tells a human being that God loves him or her. Frequently, there is a follow-up message or request. In "Black like Monica," the dominant theological message is that God's love is reconciling. God's love and forgiveness call forth repentance and confession of our own sin and weakness. Monica, torn apart by her realization that she enjoys the safety that white people enjoy in a society where white racism is prevalent, experiences forgiveness for her "humanness" and then counsels sheriff McKinsley and James to receive forgiveness too.

Tess then tells Monica that this reconciliation is a gift from God, "not to change the town but to change her heart, " because one cannot help others see their shadow side if one has not first seen one's own. This statement seems to contradict itself, because it appears clear that the writers want us to understand that God is doing both in the transformation of Monica. Why does Tess couch this transformation in such individualistic terms by telling Monica it is "not to change the town?" Probably because viewers are much more comfortable with stories about individuals than they are with stories about social structures. This brings up again a major criticism that many religious people have about *Touched by an Angel*: It consistently focuses more on the individual than on community. The angels usually dip into the lives of individuals and help those individuals do the right thing.

Despite Tess's brief lapse into individualism, this episode does ultimately stress that reconciliation is for the community as well as the individual. The confession scene between James and sheriff McKinsley visually illustrates the kind of confrontation Cornell West advocates in *Race Matters*:

> To engage in a serious discussion of race in America, we must begin not with the problems of black people but with the flaws of American society—flaws rooted in historic inequalities and long-standing cultural stereotypes.[13]

In "Black like Monica," racism is not a "black problem" but a human problem and is named as a sin that is corporately committed.

Reconciliation comes about in this episode as a result of confession. Monica's short sermon to the sheriff and James stresses that the sinful places in our hearts must be exposed to the love of God so that we can confront them and ask for forgiveness both from God and from our fellow human beings. It is a sermon straight from the fifth chapter of the Epistle of James: "Confess your sins to one another . . . . so that you may be healed" (James 5:16).

On the road to confession, Monica finds out the hard way that it is not easy being human—another key theological theme explored in this episode. Monica becomes human for a day and in that short time learns that we are flawed and broken beings who sometimes make hurtful choices. Through the illustration of Monica's incarnation, we are reminded that we do not understand another's pain until we have stood in that person's shoes. The title of the episode is a reference to John Howard Griffin's famous true story, *Black like Me*, in which the white journalist living and working in 1959 chose to darken his skin color and travel the South as a black man, writing about his experience of racism. Both Monica and Griffin learn that even the most well-meaning white person has no concept of what it feels like to have the color of his or her skin be the prime determining factor in how people relate to them.

There may be another motive behind the incarnation of Monica. Williamson and crew are careful to make the show palatable to people of many different religions and spiritualities, so that Jesus is rarely mentioned. Instead certain Christian elements—such as incarnation—crop up in the stories. Most likely, Monica becomes human so that the producers can make a veiled reference to Jesus, convincing viewers that God loved us enough to become one of us. If that is the case, Monica's incarnation is far too clean and neat to be compared with the life, suffering, and death of Jesus, which makes this reference offensive to some Christians. Williamson may indeed intend this show to promote God and not any one religion, as she claims. Yet when stories dip into territory like incarnation, it is difficult to imagine complete neutrality on the part of the producers.

Conclusions

As a slice of American popular religion, *Touched by an Angel* does dual duty. Viewers can watch the show and feel that they have "received the word of God" and have been entertained at the same time. The series breathes warm, fuzzy interfaith spirituality, perfect in a society that does not mind its dish of religion served with a side of commercials. Although some liberal Christians rather enjoy rolling their eyes at the mention of the series, on the basis of our analysis of this episode, *Touched by an Angel* is not destructive to a thinking person's religion. It may not be systematic theology (it does not claim to be), but much of the time its core message is not far off the mark from sound theology. Just how damaging is it for a television series to tell people, on a regular basis, that God loves them and calls them to a higher standard? Perhaps the blanket cynicism is unnecessary.

Although the core message is sound, it is also important to take a discerning look at some of the secondary messages in *Touched by an Angel*, which may distort some traditional theologies. Viewers must always remember that *Touched by an Angel* lives in the world of fantasy and fiction, not documentary or doctrine. These stories are designed to make a point, but not to be taken literally. There is a danger of getting so caught up in the series that we begin to think that God works foremost outside of what we know as the natural created order instead of working in and through the messy and sometimes incoherent lives of human beings.

We are wise to be wary of the way almost every episode is neatly resolved at the end of an hour. We live in a much more concrete and ambiguous world and, for example, cannot pray ourselves another color for safety, as Monica did. The very notion of Monica's instantaneous rescue should make us uneasy. In addition, Monica is saved from human death to learn a personal lesson. This furthers the dangerous notion that spiritual transformation is "all about me," a notion advertisers love because the more focused we are on ourselves the more susceptible we are to buying their "self-improving" products. Real transformation is about the community's salvation, not just the benefit to an individual.

Television does not appear to be ready for anything more theologically complex or spiritually demanding than *Touched by an Angel*. The experience of ABC's 1997 drama *Nothing Sacred* suggests that viewers (and networks) do not find religion that is emotionally tangled, nuanced, or ambiguous to be accessible.[14] Also, television may not be ready for any real questioning of its power dynamics. As long as *Touched by an Angel* promotes spirituality that fits neatly with marketplace values, it will be popular both with advertisers and with viewers who want a spirituality that does not seriously challenge their desire to acquire.

One of the best reasons to watch *Touched by an Angel* is that it brings up explicit theological questions and almost begs us to carry them forward and develop them. But it does that only if we are critically engaged with the text and talk with one another about these theological issues. If we watch *Touched by an Angel* passively and unquestioningly, we may come away with a few simple ideas about God, which in and of themselves might be edifying. However, by passively watching this series we run the risk of developing, by osmosis, an inadequate theology for life in a complex and suffering world; in reality, not everyone is touched by an angel, and many people feel hopelessly alone and without God.

The questions we suggest that audiences raise while viewing shows like *Touched by an Angel* are tools for articulating our own theologies, adequate for our lives and times. Use of these tools ensures that religious dramas on television do what they do best: begin a discussion, never—ever—claim to have the last word.

TEN

The X-Files

POSTMODERN QUESTS FOR REALITY

Truth is as subjective as reality.

—*Jose Chung*

Episode: **First aired:**
Jose Chung's "From Outer Space"   April 12, 1996

If "the truth is out there," our view of it may depend on where
we stand. We see conflicting views of believer and skeptic,
through Mulder's and Scully's eyes, and wonder in the midst
of a dark and quirky postmodern world what we can claim as
truth. Many times, we are left with intriguing mystery that can
still lead us on.

A visually captivating blend of science fiction, fantasy, horror, and mystery came to television in September 1993—*The X-Files*. The brainchild of
television writer and ex-surfer Chris Carter, *The X-Files* centers on two
young, intelligent, and attractive Federal Bureau of Investigation (FBI)
agents assigned to the weirdest, most inexplicable cases the FBI encounters, cases known as X-files (*X* standing for the unknown). The show
began its run with a focus on Mulder's obsession with the abduction of
his sister Samantha, an event he witnessed and believes was the act of
aliens from outer space. As a result, Mulder, nicknamed "Spooky" for his
renegade obsession with the supernatural, is interested in paranormal
phenomena. His partner, Scully, was brought in by the FBI to serve as his
reality check. Trained as a forensic physician, Scully is the skeptic,
grounded in scientific method, who must expose Mulder to the facts, evidence, and laws of nature.

When *The X-Files* appeared on Fox television, it was an instant hit with
critics and science fiction fans, but did not become a mainstream success
until the second season, when it won a Golden Globe award for best

drama series. By its third season, more than fifteen million people a week watched *The X-Files*. The show continues to impress media pundits; Jon Katz of *Brill's Content* calls *The X-Files* "one of TV's most interesting, even significant shows, as well as one of the most intensely political."[1]

Seen by over sixteen million viewers, the episode "Jose Chung's *From Outer Space*," which originally aired on April 12, 1996, demonstrates how Carter's complex narrative style uses ambiguity to heighten the tension surrounding the ultimate question in postmodernity: "What *is* the truth?"

Episode Synopsis

In the dark of night, a spaceship hovers over a deserted road in Klass County, Washington. Two big-eyed gray aliens abduct a young couple, Harold and Chrissy, whose car has stalled on their first date. As the two aliens drag them away, a second spaceship hovers, and a large growling red alien appears. The report of this event captures the imagination of famous fiction writer Jose Chung, who interviews FBI Agent Dana Scully about the investigation she and her partner, Agent Fox Mulder, conducted on this X-file. Chung is interested in the story precisely because it is so difficult to decipher and believes it has the makings of a best-seller in a new genre he hopes to invent: nonfiction science fiction. Based on the hard evidence, Scully has concluded that the girl was probably a victim of date rape. Mulder thinks it was an alien abduction, government conspiracy, or perhaps both. Harold, the young man that Scully suspects committed the rape, remembers the car stalling and then recalls being on a ship, trapped with a cigarette-smoking alien. Two other eyewitness accounts of alien activity, from a paranoid lineman named Blaine and a wildly imaginative passing motorist named Roky, are even more bizarre, containing a few matching details but essentially different. It is difficult to tell what really happened to the four people on that road that evening. Agent Mulder unsuccessfully pleads with Chung not to write the book, because it could damage any credibility Mulder has achieved in the field of investigating alien abductions. With financial backing from a publishing enterprise that Mulder blasts as part of the "military-industrial-entertainment complex," Chung writes *From Outer Space*, describing two government agents investigating a complicated report of an alien abduction. The story ends with a dejected Harold failing to win Chrissy's love. As Harold walks away, we hear Chung reading from his book: "Although we may not be alone in the universe, in our own separate ways, on this planet, we are all alone."[2]

Narrative

The X-Files originally offered a fresh and distinct premise, but fans of science fiction television quickly recognized that important elements of the series are drawn from television series of the past. The show somewhat resembles the old *Night Stalker* and *The Twilight Zone*. It presents scientific puzzles and possibilities, much like the many generations of *Star Trek*, and often shows the underbelly of a large spaceship, bringing back memories of *Battlestar Galactica*. The series also has some connections to *Twin Peaks*, the offbeat serial produced by filmmaker David Lynch. Both feature FBI agents who are fascinated with the paranormal; both have elements of the horror genre; and both feature actor David Duchovny. (In *Twin Peaks*, Duchovny played cross-dressing agent Denis/Denise, a small but unforgettable role.)

The popularity of *The X-Files* naturally led to the production of similar shows about paranormal phenomena. Attempting to capitalize on the appetite for science fiction television, Carter created *Millennium* and *Harsh Realm*, neither of which survived the ratings game. Other shows also cashing in on the interest in *The X-Files* include NBC's drama about a psychic investigator, *Profiler*; Fox's *Roswell*, a series about three teenagers whose embryos somehow survived the legendary Roswell "Unidentified Flying Object (UFO) crash" (an incident mentioned frequently on *The X-Files*); and *Buffy the Vampire Slayer*, which features a feisty young woman with supernatural power over vampires. With the possible exception of *Buffy*, none of these sci-fi series has had the cultural impact of *The X-Files*. *Los Angeles Times* television critic and author Brian Lowry says *The X-Files* is now burned into the national consciousness, marked by a theme of "skepticism and existential doubt that has elevated the series far beyond the realm of entertainment."[3]

Few episodes of *The X-Files* are as memorable for their narrative style as "Jose Chung's *From Outer Space*," written by Darin Morgan. In mind-boggling fashion, the point of view in this episode changes at least eighteen times, with smaller stories within larger ones; each time the point of view changes, so do the facts as they are understood by the person relating the story. In most television dramas (including most episodes of *The X-Files*), we sit outside the narrative and peer into it, godlike, as though it were a slice of someone's reality. The storyteller, as such, is the person who wrote the dramatic episode; sometimes through narration, we see one character as the storyteller. Willingly suspending our belief, we usually accept that the storyteller's version of the situation is the correct one. In this episode, however, we are challenged as the versions of the story keep changing.

The episode begins with an abduction scene in which there is no narrator; this is one of the few scenes in which we are privy to the action without the filter of a character who relays his or her story. We are led to believe that this first interaction is reality—at least the kind of reality we expect from *The X-Files*. For purposes of illustration, we call this point of view Level One, in which we are invisible observers of the action. Level One in this episode includes the opening segment and all the segments in which we look in on Agent Scully and Jose Chung as they discuss the facts they have gathered about what really happened to the two people on the night of the so-called abduction.

In Level Two point of view, we leave the scene where Scully and Chung are talking and are within the imagination of the speaker. For example, we "see" Scully's visual rendition of the facts, or we "see" the experience through the eyes of Harold or Chrissy. Here we have a filtered story within the larger story, and we see some manufactured changes. For example, Scully edits out the local detective's crude language so that we see and hear this detective saying things like "blankety-blank" instead of the real expletives.

The most bizarre and comical things happen, however, at the Level Three point of view, where either Scully or Chung tells what she or he heard from the witnesses, and we are taken into the imaginations or visual renderings of the witnesses themselves. In effect, we are three times removed from our starting point, with the actual experience of the event of an alien abduction (if that is what it was) filtered through an investigator, and we are now led to believe we see events through the witnesses' perceptions. In Level Three interaction, there are a lot of discrepancies.

When Chrissy is hypnotized and tells her story about aliens, she says that the aliens spoke telepathically. When Harold recounts his alien experience, he claims the aliens spoke English. Blaine, a paranoid loner who thinks he found a "real live bleepin' dead alien," claims Agent Scully slapped and threatened him at the scene of the strange discovery—a charge she vehemently denies (and rightly so—it is not in her character to slap a witness).

The choice to use numerous points of view and stories within stories to tell a greater story is risky; it makes the viewer work extremely hard to understand what is going on. Even after multiple viewings, we have a hard time saying that we *know* what happens. This choice illustrates the frustration that many people feel in their own lives when they encounter different explanations of events that they experienced in a particular way. How do we ever know what really happened?

Structure

This series is overwhelmingly myth; it builds a whole world around the tension between knowing "the truth is out there" and discovering the truth. The dominant message of the entire series is that if truth can be found, it will be like nothing we currently know about science, philosophy, or religion.

Fans of *The X-Files* speak frequently of the "mythology" behind the series. In fact, in this series are subgenres, one of which is labeled by Carter "mythological": a government conspiracy or conspiracies related to hiding the truth about alien visitation. Included in the mythology is the way Mulder's sister disappeared, his father's role in that disappearance,

Cancerman's identity, the ruling shadow government, and the significance of honeybees in the eventual alien colonization of earth. All episodes function primarily as myth, but not all episodes are what Carter and fans would label "mythological." Some are self-contained and fall into a "freak of the week" genre. Others are primarily satirical, poking fun at our "need to know." Some can be categorized as apologue, defending various religious experiences as evidence of the paranormal.

"Jose Chung's *From Outer Space*" is a blend of mythological and satirical. It touches on the mythology when we wonder whether the "aliens" we saw at the opening of the show were really clever government agents tricking Chrissy and Harold into thinking they were being abducted by aliens from a spaceship. The satirical elements include campy pop culture references to UFOs and paranormal conspiracy theories. We have Blaine, the antisocial UFO seeker; Roky, who claims a mysterious "man in black" threatened him; a failed "alien autopsy" reminiscent of a Fox television special from the season before; and the requisite big-eyed gray aliens. All that is missing is Bigfoot, who does make a cameo appearance in a final scene when we see Mulder in his hotel room watching footage of the mysterious large-footed beast running through the woods.

How cynical and ironic it is for Carter to poke fun at the wide variety of paranormal experiences captured in legend over the years. Some of these experiences and legends make his show so popular, and here he exposes the ridiculous figure they cut. By doing so, he can capture a wide and diverse audience. Those of us too sophisticated to believe in aliens can laugh at the satire because we have Scully on our side. Those hoping to challenge the modernist view, believing there is "more than meets the eye" of science, have the mystical Mulder (who although at times comical never comes off as the clown). By giving us a range of characters to believe in, the producers reach an audience that ranges from skeptical modernist baby boomers to "anything goes" millennials.

Signs

Part of the allure of this series is the atmosphere it creates with its distinct look and feel. Like other dramas, it has attractive protagonists and a central enigma: the agents' search for truth in cases that defy scientific explanation. *The X-Files* pumps up the intrigue by blending elements of horror, the serial, and even comedy in a way that feels smooth and appropriate.

It is fairly easy to tell when we are tuned in to an episode of *The X-Files*, whether it features a man-eating fluke, extrasensory perception, or a government conspiracy to cover up all of the above. We know it is *The X-Files* and not a generic creep show because of its signature production values: the rich use of darkness and light, especially in the trademark flashlight scenes; eerie music in the background; high-quality editing that gives the show a film noir feel; and the use of typewritten subtitles that appear on the screen at the beginning of the program (and at important location changes), telling us where the action occurs. These stylistic touches define the series and help convey the point of a story.

The major message in this episode, that objective truth is hard to come by, is not only illustrated by the many changes in point of view in the narrative, but also reinforced by prominent aural and visual messages. Note the message articulated by Jose Chung as he tells Agent Scully, "Truth is as subjective as reality." Early in the episode, after the opening scenes of the abduction, we enter writer Jose Chung's office, and the first thing we see is a full shot of the caption on a poster familiar to *X-Files* fans as the same one hanging in Mulder's office: I Want to Believe. The visual juxtaposition of the abduction scene and the "I Want to Believe" poster indicates that someone in this narrative wants to believe an abduction has taken place. That person is, of course, Agent Mulder. He cares the most about finding out what really happened because it will help him understand the disappearance of his sister.

Another important visual message in this and most episodes of *The X-Files* is that the world is primarily a dark place. In many shots, we must strain to see the images because darkness hides the action. Flashlights figure prominently, beams of light projected by the truth seekers as they move in and through this dark world. In this episode, Jose Chung's office is well lighted, but beyond that about the only bright lights are those the curious aliens shine in the eyes of the human specimens. The aliens symbolically shine some light on our world, although the light is blinding and precedes harsh pain and suffering. This episode ends on a lonely and isolated note, indicating that even if we want to believe we are left alone with our desires.

We develop a sense of things "not being right" on many levels in this episode, but the visual is the most significant. To emphasize the conflicting versions of Chrissy's and Harold's treatment at the hands of the aliens, the set and camera work prove the local detective is right when he says "Their two stories couldn't be more bleepin' different." They both see gray aliens with oversized eyes, and both visual depictions include harsh, bright light shining on them. However, in Chrissy's imagination we see them on the spaceship, strapped down to high-tech tables while the aliens talk telepathically. When seen from her point of view, the picture is distorted with images that look like what we might expect in a house of mirrors. This could be a code for hypnosis, or it could tip us off that her

reality is distorted for one reason or another (at one point, we are led to believe that perhaps her memories are planted by devious government scientists). When we see Harold's visual remembrance of the abduction, we see no such camera distortion, perhaps because he was not under hypnosis at the time. Harold experiences being in a low-tech metal cage alongside a big-eyed gray alien who is smoking and chanting, "This is *not* happening." Harold also hears a growling alien that sounds a lot like the big red monster in the opening segment, but we are not shown the source of the growling.

Another example of this visual confusion is a diner scene involving Agent Mulder, shown in two very different renditions. It is supposed to be a scene from the same time of the same day, but the story told by Mulder to Scully depicts Mulder talking to one of the military men who pilots secret government airships that are often mistaken for UFOs. The scene shows the diner looking dark, smoky, and dingy. The cook is in the background cleaning up. The counter is set with a number of menus and place settings even though almost no one is there. The military pilot, who is playing with a plate of mashed potatoes, tells Mulder that he cannot be sure of anything anymore, not even whether he really exists. At the end of their talk, the pilot is carried off by men in military uniforms. The pilot informs Mulder that he (the pilot) is a dead man.

A second rendition of that same night at the diner is told by the cook to Jose Chung, who then tells it to Scully. In the cook's visualization, the diner is sparkling clean with only a few place settings at the counter. There is more light in the room, allowing us to see details more sharply. The air is clear (no smoking pilot), and the cook remembers only one man, Mulder, coming in that night. He recalls Mulder eating a whole sweet potato pie piece by piece. In this visualization, we see Mulder eating the pie and asking the cook a lot of uncharacteristically mundane questions about UFOs.

Which diner scene is real? The first one seems more plausible because the second one has a comedic, dreamlike quality to it. It takes some reflection and re-viewing to figure out exactly whose point of view is seen in each diner scene. The two scenes supposedly of the same space and time upset any equilibrium the episode may have achieved, leaving many viewers baffled. We know it is the same diner only because of the neon sign and the major set pieces that remain the same. We wonder how two versions of one story can be so different.

These visual signs reinforce the message that we all see the world through different eyes. Some of us see everything through pathologically distorted lenses, as did Blaine, the paranoid young man who saw every-one threatening him. Some of us see our diners sparkling clean, while oth-ers find the same diners dingy.

Power and Ideological Issues

Just like the old cliché, *The X-Files* tells us week after week, "Knowledge is power." It is the resource that is always in short supply. The government or the clandestine syndicate has it, and the heroic FBI agents want it. In this episode, Mulder realizes that Jose Chung will print the version of the abduction story that will perform best in the marketplace, and that he does it because he is financed by powers linking the military and the clandes-tine syndicate with the entertainment industry. Mulder contends that this version of the story will not be the truth, but that seems not to matter to Chung. What matters is that Chung's version will serve the interests of a power far beyond anything Mulder can control or expose, no matter how hard he tries. The world we are presented with in this episode is pure *X-Files* mythology: tightly controlled, manipulated, and heavily financed by power elites who do not want a harsh or shocking truth to be exposed.

What world does this resemble? The existing "real world" entertain-ment conglomerate consolidates every few months with other large cor-porations until we are faced with exactly what Mulder describes: a military-industrial-entertainment complex that exists to cover up an essential truth—not a truth about aliens, but a truth about its main pur-pose, which is to sell us viewers as a commodity to advertisers. Metaphorically, the television business *is* Jose Chung writing what sells and not what actually happened.

On the surface, *The X-Files* wants us to believe that all power and ideological struggles center on knowledge. The series rarely shows any gender, race, or class struggles. Through their absence, we are led to believe that those issues pale by comparison to the threat from aliens, freaks, and our own government.

Regarding gender, the show's depiction of Agent Scully celebrates the professional woman who is an equal partner in all ways with her male counterpart. Many young women find Scully one of the most empowered female characters on television today. She is brainy, sophisticated, and respected by her co-workers, most of whom are male. "Rational, courageous, relentless, she never has to invoke feminism because her equality and competence are taken completely for granted."[4] By creating such an attractive and powerful female lead character, the series encourages young women to place importance on developing their intellect and character rather than obsessing over beauty, thinness, and popularity.

However, scratch beneath the surface of this highly positive treatment of Scully, and serious questions emerge. First, why are we pleasantly surprised that Scully is respected in her work? Probably because we have seen the way other female detectives have been depicted on television, and we are aware that Scully is not the norm. However, as long as women are defined by how well they measure up to a man's gaze (Mulder and FBI bureaucrats), they are still second-class citizens on television. Also, if Scully is an equal partner, why is she constantly doing the "boring and difficult lab work" while Mulder explores "weird science"?[5] If Scully is so brainy, why is she almost always wrong and Mulder right? Two media studies' researchers, Jan Jagodzinski and Brigitte Hipfl, interviewed a number of male and female high school students about the relationship between Scully and Mulder.

> Some were infuriated with Scully because she, at times, seemed so "stupid," not believing in the paranormal even after witnessing such events first-hand, and having been abducted herself, probed while pregnant and inserted with a tracking device.[6]

The answer, of course, is that Scully will continue to "not get it" as long as Mulder is in the picture because the narrative tension demands a polar opposite.

The X-Files casts are predominantly white. However, when shown, people of color are just as likely to be FBI, government agents, or wise sages as anything else. People of color are not cast as villains; they are just rarely cast at all, which suggests that the writers and producers are anticipating a predominately white audience and one that believes society is beyond racial struggles.

The same cannot be said of class struggles. In this and many other episodes, we encounter examples of the slightly pathetic lower-class white person. In this episode, both Blaine and Roky represent the quintessential disenfranchised white male. Blaine lives in a dumpy room with a bed on the floor, works for the electric company, and longs for the day when he is abducted by aliens so that he need not hold down a job. Roky works out of his basement, writing a screenplay of his experience with the big red alien, dubbed "Lord Kinbote," a being Roky says is from the center of the earth. Neither of these men appears intelligent or upwardly mobile; their fascination with the paranormal is a way of escaping the dreariness of their lives. We must wonder why the "white trash" character is so popular on *The X-Files*. Is it so that those of us watching the show feel superior as we identify with the smarter, more elegant FBI agents? Are Blaine and Roky the kind of people we expect to believe in paranormal activity, and to make an episode work, we need a few believers?

Because *The X-Files* is so interested in aliens (that is to say, extra-terrestrials), many analysts wonder whether the makers are commenting on society's fears about illegal aliens taking over power in the United States. Is the contact we fear really contact with those whose lives are completely different from our own? If this is the case, the creators of the show are xenophobic, because aliens on *The X-Files* are almost never benign or harmless creatures. They usually painfully probe or snatch humans, turn us into drones, or seek to annihilate our species. In this sense, the truth—if it is out there—is horrifying and destructive to life as we know it. Our particular episode, if we consider the aliens in it to be *real*, certainly bears this out. The connection between space aliens and illegal aliens is a stretch, and the analogies do not hold up under close scrutiny. If the aliens are not real but are agents of our own government (one theory posed in the episode), then the mysterious "alien" is none other than our own democratic system horribly out of control. Government by the people becomes government that we are completely "alien-ated" from, a social commentary not lost on many viewers, especially around the middle of April, tax deadline time, when this episode first aired.

Although theories about whom the aliens really represent are intriguing, it is more likely that the creators of the show invite us to look at them cosmically and realize that we human beings should not think of ourselves as the center of the universe any longer. We are being challenged to ask ourselves how our lives would change if we knew, for certain, that life exists in forms unknown on earth.

Functions

To watch *The X-Files* is to experience a brainteaser. Fans of the show expect episodes to be ambiguous, quirky, and twisted. Part of the ritual enjoyment of the show is to videotape it and go back over it for details missed in the initial viewing. The fact that fans want to watch the shows over and over to catch the nuances enhances the marketability of the series in two ways: It gives advertisers a second shot at reaching viewers when they play the tape back, and it secures the show's standing in syndication. Hard-core fans log onto the Usenet newsgroups (try alt.tv.x-files) after an episode to discuss and question that evening's puzzle. Shows with such "buzz" generally attract new viewers by word of mouth.

Watching the show is a visual pleasure, at least for those who can take the occasional lapse into horror. Few television dramas are so well shot, edited, and scored. Fans get into a certain *X-Files* mood on a Sunday evening. Much as one walks into the darkness of a movie theater in anticipation of entering a whole new world, turning on the show allows fans to enter a different psychological space, one that at least acknowledges the mystery we experience in our own lives.

The entertainment industry and its clients, the advertisers, must find *The X-Files* profitable for yet another reason: the uncertainty it creates in viewers. An episode such as "Jose Chung's *From Outer Space*" leaves us puzzled, questioning whether truth can be found. When we are uncertain and anxious, advertisers are adept at quickly moving to fill that void.

Theological Analysis

The theological question posed in this episode of *The X-Files*—"How can we know truth?"—is thoroughly postmodern. What does it mean to say that any statement is postmodern? The likelihood that any three philosophers would agree on a definition is almost nil because postmodernism is marked by inherent disagreement. We all see it differently. However, there are some basic elements that crop up in almost all writing about it. "Postmodern is a makeshift word we use until we have decided what to name the baby," says Walter Truett Anderson. "It is a word of looking back."[7]

What Anderson refers to is the fact that there is no postmodernism except in relation or reaction to modernism—the movement in art, architecture, and literature that aimed to capture the essence of a new industrial and urban way of life in the nineteenth and twentieth centuries. Lawrence Cahoone's anthology about the move from modernism to postmodernism dates the term "postmodern" to 1917, as a way to describe the nihilism of twentieth century Western culture.[8] The key element of modernism was the triumph of science and reason over tradition and custom.

"At the heart of modernity is the notion of the freely acting, freely know-ing individual whose experiments can penetrate the secrets of nature and whose work with other individuals can make a new and better world."[9] The scientific method, by which a researcher makes a hypothesis and gathers data to prove or disprove his or her hypothesis in an objective manner, is one significant contribution of the modern era.

Postmodernism is the critique of modernity, challenging assumptions about the objectivity of knowledge. Realities, for the postmodernist, come from culturally conditioned societies. Multiple views predominate because, for example, women see things differently than do men, indige-nous cultures interpret reality differently than do industrialized ones, and so forth. Individuals do not know the "objective truth." Postmodernists question all worldviews and contend that "there is no truth outside of ideology."[10] As Huston Smith puts it: "The postmodern mind argues (par-adoxically) that it knows more than others did because it has discovered how little the human mind *can* know."[11] All the arguments in academic circles about whose worldview should be presented as the dominant one are sidebars of the greater argument between modernists and postmod-ernists: Do we continue to teach that there is an objective truth that can be found, or do we present multiple views of reality, allowing for cultural differences and diversity in ways of knowing?

As we might imagine, readings on postmodernism can be highly abstract and frustrating, but a simple baseball joke illustrates the subject fairly well:

> A premodern umpire once said, "There's balls and there's strikes and I calls em' as they is." Believing in absolute truth that can be discovered, early societies looked for evidence to discover that truth. A modern umpire says instead, "There's balls and there's strikes, and I calls 'em as I sees 'em." For the modernist, truth is to be found in one's own experience. Now a post-modern umpire says: "There's balls and there's strikes, and they ain't nothin' till I calls 'em." No truth exists unless we create it.[12]

Using this joke as a criterion, are we living in a modern or postmodern world? Baby boomers, like Chris Carter, were born in a modern world that became postmodern over time. Generation X and the Millennials who followed were born into postmodernism and are steeped in it. If you were to enter the narrative world of *The X-Files* and question the two main characters about the nature of truth, you would find that they both cling to some modernist notions. Although both weave to and fro between a modern and postmodern outlook, Scully most often expresses faith in the scientific method. She is the scientist who looks for data to support or dis-prove her hypothesis and struggles to find what she thinks is material reality. Mulder also has faith in the scientific method but believes there are more data to be considered—data that cannot be measured by our current scientific methods, a postmodern notion. He also fears that there is no truth obtainable outside of what certain controlling authority figures (government conspirators) want us to see. Through the tracking of these two characters week after week, viewers are drawn into a world that asks the postmodern question, "How can we be certain of what we know?"[13]

Talk to any theologian about religious pluralism—multiple views of ultimate reality—and she or he will tell you it is one of the biggest challenges facing any religion today. When Christians follow one who says, "You shall know the truth and the truth shall set you free," there is, or at least there has been in the past, the assumption that, as Mulder would say, the truth is out there and is knowable. Philosophies that question the nature of truth make many Christians uncomfortable. Lutheran liturgy scholar Marva Dawn decries the "postmodern rejection of all authority and reliability" and calls on the church to "offer believable truth, a coherent story that gives meaning to chaos."[14] Of course, Christians, in true postmodern fashion, continue to disagree with one another about what constitutes believable truth.

If truth is subjective, then Christian truth is certainly one of the valid truths. Postmodernism, in this sense, is good news for all faith traditions. It does not throw out all viewpoints, but embraces many. At the very least, one's own experience of truth can be considered along with other truths. Postmodernism has leveled the playing field for the various competing truths. However, when we allow the questions and the multiple views to overwhelm us, we slip into what Dawn rightly calls postmodern malaise or nihilism, and this could be where our episode leaves us. At this point, the truths do not set us free. They press down heavily on us, and we abandon hope. Religious hope cannot survive the despair that sets in when we declare that because there are so many so-called truths, none of them can be normative.

This brings us back to our episode. *Something* happened to those people on that road, something they named as an alien abduction. Even when we put all their stories together, we cannot ferret out the objective truth, but we do not have everyone's story. We do not hear the story of the red monster (nicknamed Lord Kinbote). We do not hear from the shadowy and menacing government officials in the background of Chrissy's remembrances. The truth, in this case, is partial. Just like religious truth, as theologian Daniel Migliore reminds us:

> Reality can be seen and interpreted in many different ways, of course. The revelation of God is not coercive. It frees us to see the world as created and reconciled by God, but this does not eliminate other possible ways of seeing. . . . Thus while [Christian] believers are aware of other ways of seeing and interpreting reality, and can even recognize the partial truth of these other interpretations, they nevertheless affirm that the revelation of God in Christ is the truth that sets humanity free.[15]

Another gift postmodernism has given to faith, which is illustrated in this episode of *The X-Files*, is the understanding that as we accept a partial and even subjective truth, we encounter mystery in our lives. We submit to the realization that we are finite and limited creatures who do not have a lock on "the truth." Only God, the mystery who is both within us and beyond us, has a grasp of the whole truth. Only God knows what happens in any one event in life. Only God sees the larger picture. Our reliance on this God-of-the-whole-truth bonds us with God and also with our fellow humans who have experienced different portions of the truth. In our episode, each person relating the story of alien abductions must hear and consider the others' stories to get closer to the greater truth.

As *The X-Files* tells us every week, the truth is out there. For us humans, it remains subjective and partial and mysterious, and still it continues to be revelatory.

PART III

An Overview
of Fact-Based Programming

"And that's the way it is. . . ." Or is it?

Definitions and Range of Fare

In this part, we look at the broad category of *fact-based programming*, which can be defined as any programming that purports to reveal reality or "actualities." Generally this pertains to material that has been shot on film or recorded on videotape in "real time" and, at least traditionally, precludes reenactments.

There is a wide range of fare under the umbrella of fact-based programming. Perhaps the most obvious genre in this category is *news*. This includes local and national programs and covers live broadcasts of studio-based anchors and reporters "in the field" along with pretaped and edited segments, as well as computer-generated maps, graphs, and illustrations. Related to news programs, and often produced out of the same network departments, are talk shows that focus on *news commentary*, such as *Meet the Press, Nightline, Larry King Live*, and *Hardball with Chris Matthews*, as well as *newsmagazines* such as *60 Minutes, 20/20*, and *Dateline*.

One programming genre with a venerable tradition that predates television consists of *documentaries* about current or historical events. These programs are referred to as "long-form" because segments run longer than the two to ten minutes usually allotted for each story on news programs or newsmagazines. Documentary subgenres focus on topics other than news or history, such as *sports* or *science and nature*.

In another category of fact-based programs are hybrids of traditional news or newsmagazine shows that cover only the world of entertainment. These programs feature anchors or hosts who deliver bits of news and celebrity gossip and who introduce and "bridge" prerecorded segments. *Entertainment Tonight* was the first such show, and it has been followed by imitators such as *Inside Edition* and *CNN/Entertainment Weekly*. Related to these are tabloid shows such as *Hard Copy* and *A Current Affair*.

Since the 1990s, a new genre of programming has emerged, which can best be described as *factual entertainment*. One branch of this type features amateur videos that have been strung together according to some common theme—usually involving humor or danger. Another strand of this reality programming takes the subject matter of perennial television entertainment fare—like hospital or crime dramas—and focuses instead on the real thing. These shows feature actualities shot in real settings with relatively small and inexpensive digital camcorders and then assembled into coherent story lines. A recent trend that has fascinated the public and scored well in ratings might best be described as "reality meets social engineering." Part game show, part documentary, these programs contrive situations in which carefully selected participants are forced to live and interact with one another for periods of time, often with the promise of winning big money.

A Brief History: Origins to 1960s

The antecedents of television news and fact-based programs date from the early days of motion pictures. The first "movies" were nothing more than records of everyday events, such as a train pulling into a railway station. Such projected moments seem insignificant to us today, but they created a sensation when they were first shown to audiences in the late nineteenth century. During the 1920s, three developments paved the way for the fact-based programming of today: film documentaries, newsreels, and radio.

In 1922, Robert Flaherty, a prospector for mining and railroad interests around Hudson Bay, produced a film about a small group of Inuit people entitled *Nanook of the North*. Considered to be the first feature-length documentary, the film was a series of loosely connected episodes in the day-to-day routine of an Inuit hunter and his family. *Nanook* was important because it demonstrated that filmed actualities could be linked together to tell a story that was both fascinating and informative. In the decades that followed, the documentary reached new levels of sophistication and artistry, especially in the hands of a talented filmmaker like Germany's Leni Riefenstahl. Her movies of a Nazi Party rally in Nuremberg (*Triumph of the Will*) and the 1936 Olympics in Berlin (*Olympia*) are classic examples of the power of film to persuade as well as to inform, however bad their intent or consequences may appear today. During the Great Depression, documentaries took a turn in the direction of social advocacy. The best-known films of this type were *The Plow That Broke the Plains* and *The River* by Pare Lorentz (with music by Virgil Thomson), both commissioned by the Farm Security Administration to promote New Deal land and water projects. Robert Flaherty made his own contribution to these efforts with a film for the Department of Agriculture entitled *The Land*. After World War II, Walt Disney released several "True Life Adventures" that focused on the natural world, under titles such as *The Living Desert* and *Beaver Valley*. These films established patterns for classic television counterparts by The National Geographic Society and Jacques Cousteau.

When *Time* magazine debuted in 1923, its success demonstrated that the public was ready for a weekly digest of national news and world events. *Time*'s founder, Henry Luce, had a hunch that this formula could be hitched to the movies as well, and the result was *The March of Time*, one of the earliest movie newsreels. Each installment of *The March of Time* featured a mix of brief news clips from around the world with a smattering of sports and entertainment, all held together with a dramatic soundtrack and off-camera narration. The look and format of television news borrowed much from this and other newsreels, such as *Movietone News* and *Universal Newsreels*.

The 1920s also saw the rise of vast "empires of the air" in the form of radio broadcast networks. Besides musical, comedy, and dramatic entertainment programs, radio also featured live news broadcasts that could reach millions of people across the country at the same time. FDR's "fireside chats" during the Great Depression and Edward R. Murrow's reports of the London blitz during the Second World War captivated listeners and established precedents for television.

Commercial television began to hit the airwaves in the late 1940s and came of age in the 1950s. At first, reality-based programming pretty much limited itself to news and sporting events. Early television programs borrowed extensively from radio, not only in form, but also in advertising sponsorship. News efforts were paltry, however, and the first network entry appeared on NBC in 1948 as *The Camel Newsreel Theater*, which lasted only fifteen minutes a night. A year later, it was renamed *The Camel News Caravan* with John Cameron Swazye. (The venerable *CBS Evening News* with Walter Cronkite did not debut until 1963.) In our era of "tobacco wars," it seems ironic that a cigarette company once sponsored news on television. At the time, Camel even stipulated that a burning cigarette be visible in an ashtray on the set of each show.[1]

Edward R. Murrow was one of the few radio news giants willing to make the leap to television. He first appeared on CBS with *See It Now* in

1951; even its title was borrowed from CBS radio's <u>Hear</u> It Now [emphasis added]. Much of television's early appeal came from its ability to allow audiences to *see* things; in the mid-1930s, Henry Luce had founded *Life* magazine with the same intention. One episode of *See It Now* featured simultaneous views of the Brooklyn and Golden Gate bridges, thus allowing viewers to see both coasts of the United States at the same time.

News as political theater riveted the nation in 1954 with the Army-McCarthy hearings, when the junior senator from Wisconsin attempted to smoke out Communist sympathizers and spies before a congressional—as well as live—audience. Several months earlier, Edward R. Murrow had taken a critical look at McCarthy's methods on *See It Now,* and with McCarthy's daily exposure on national television, public opinion began to turn against him—a sign of the medium's increasing ability to shape the national conversation. Even though the Army-McCarthy hearings were an unfortunate chapter in our government's history, they provided a sneak preview of the television spectacle of the Watergate hearings in the early 1970s and the O. J. Simpson trial in 1995.

As had been the case with radio, television executives such as the CBS chairman William Paley viewed their news divisions as prestige centers. Paley was typical of the breed of individuals who ran television before huge corporations began taking over in the 1980s. He had personal pride in the quality of CBS News and was willing to finance it with the money generated by the "fluff" of his entertainment shows. In those days, news divisions never generated much profit, but they served a public function that people like Paley were eager to highlight—especially to federal regulators in the wake of the quiz show scandals in the late 1950s. In 1961, the FCC chairman Newton Minow delivered a speech in which he called television programming a "vast wasteland" and challenged the networks to do better. To forestall federal regulation, news departments were given free rein in the 1960s to produce investigative documentaries of a depth that has all but disappeared from network television today. A famous example of this aired in 1960 on *CBS Reports* (a successor to *See It Now*). In "Harvest of Shame," Edward R. Murrow took a penetrating look at poverty and hunger in the United States. Around this time, NBC began broadcasting its *White Paper* specials, and ABC did the same with *Closeup!* Classic documentaries of this era were heavily rhetorical, characterized by extensive narration and musical scores that helped to reinforce the editorial point of view.

A few years later, television news coverage proved instrumental in helping the nation to mourn collectively in the wake of the assassination of President Kennedy. Beginning on Friday afternoon, November 22, 1963, the three broadcast networks suspended all of their regular programming for nearly four days of live coverage as events unfolded. Americans were glued to their television sets when the president's coffin was flown from Dallas to Washington, while his body lay in state in the

Capitol rotunda, and throughout his funeral and burial. They watched in amazed horror as his alleged assassin was shot dead before their eyes—a television first. Such a national trauma could have resulted in great social unrest, but the constitutional transfer of power took place without a hitch—made possible, many said, because television allowed the nation to grieve en masse. Fred Friendly, former head of CBS News, said in retrospect that it was television's finest hour.

Throughout the 1960s, television coverage of news events began to eclipse print media and radio as the "place" where most people turned first for information about what was going on in the world. In the cases of the civil rights movement and the "living room war" in Vietnam, television coverage proved crucial to public opinion and ultimately helped shape public policy. Indeed, leaders in Washington could not ignore scenes of vicious dogs attacking unarmed African Americans and forceful jets from fire hoses pummeling helpless children, and they passed the Civil Rights Act and the Voting Rights Act in 1964–65. As for Vietnam, public opinion began to turn against the war as body counts mounted on each evening's newscast and battle scenes were brought into American living rooms. After the Vietcong's surprise Tet offensive in 1968, Walter Cronkite went to Vietnam for a special report and concluded on camera that the war could not be won and that we should pull out and go home. President Johnson is said to have concluded, "If I've lost Walter Cronkite, I've lost the American people," and many credit the CBS broadcast with Johnson's decision not to run for re-election. Because the Vietnam War was the most heavily televised war in U.S. history, and the military subsequently lost both public support and the war itself, Pentagon officials have banned cameras from combat areas in military operations since then, most notably during the Gulf War of 1991.

The 1960s were also the heyday of the space program and the race to the moon, and television allowed Americans front-row seats for the fact-based spectacle of the decade. Television lived up to the promise of its name ("remote sight") with those flickering images of Neil Armstrong and Buzz Aldrin on the surface of the moon. The Cold War paranoia that had inspired the space program in the first place was downplayed on television in favor of cheerleading for American technical ingenuity and patriotism, most notably by Walter Cronkite, who made no secret of his enthusiasm.

Television is especially well suited to cover sports. Telephoto lenses and multiple cameras planted in strategic locations throughout a stadium or along a racing route allow viewers vantage points unavailable to any single spectator at the actual event. Many of the camera angles and shooting innovations were pioneered by Leni Riefenstahl at the 1936 Olympics, but whereas she could achieve continuity of action only through hours of editing on film, live television can instantly achieve the same thing through electronic switching between cameras. Some sports, most notably football with its rectangular playing field and action that goes back and forth across the screen, are better suited to the medium's visual constraints than others.

In the early years, television networks were eager to carry sporting events as a way of boosting sales of television sets, and because such coverage was relatively inexpensive to produce. The first network sports show was NBC's *Gillette Cavalcade of Sports*, which premiered in 1944 and remained on the air for twenty years, yet another early example of sponsorship by a single advertiser. As sports coverage grew more expensive to produce in the 1960s, networks came to rely more and more on multiple advertisers. Television coverage has transformed most professional sports, with lucrative network contracts sending owners' profits—and players' salaries—into the stratosphere. The rhythm of the games has been modified to accommodate television commercials, and huge television screens have been erected in professional stadia and arenas to mimic the instant replays and sports statistic "looks" of televised events.

Even as television began to erode the dominance and profitability of print-based stalwarts such as *Life* and *Look* magazines during the 1960s, it also adapted their magazine formats to its own specifications. The first and longest-running effort along these lines has been *60 Minutes*, which debuted in 1968. Typical "editions" feature stories that range from breaking news to arts and culture to its trademark, down-and-dirty investigative journalism. In its early years, serious commentary was provided by the "Point-Counterpoint" exchanges between conservative James Kilpatrick and liberal Shana Alexander, satirized so memorably on *Saturday Night Live*. In 1978, this debate was replaced by "A Few Minutes with Andy Rooney."

Dividing each program into a number of smaller segments, *60 Minutes* has always been a hybrid of the short news story featured on evening newscasts and the long-form documentary. In the more than thirty years since its debut, long-form documentaries have all but disappeared from commercial television, and individual stories on newscasts have gotten shorter, but newsmagazines such as *20/20, Dateline,* and *CNN Newsstand* have proliferated. With its flexible format and relatively small budget, *60 Minutes* was one of the first news shows to actually turn a profit, forever changing the networks' financial expectations of their news divisions. Hal Himmelstein speculates that newsmagazines are more popular with viewers than long-form documentaries because of their celebrity reporters, entertaining production values, and shorter formats.[2]

Developments and Trends, 1970–Present

Local News

Local news did not merit attention in the previous section because it was always a poor relation to the more lavishly produced programs on the big three networks. Because of their comparatively small budgets and operations, local news programs could not hope to match the "look" or scope of network broadcasts, but this began to change in the mid-1970s. Before then, local news crews had to rely on film cameras to cover anything that happened outside the studio. Film was expensive and took several hours to process and edit, causing most local stations to promise "film at 11" during their 6:00 P.M. broadcasts. Even the networks were limited by film's constraints. When President Kennedy was shot in Dallas, the need for pictures of this breaking story was so great that the freshly processed film was run through projectors and broadcast live while it was still wet. The advent of videotape changed all this. For one thing, it was not as expensive as film. More important, it did not need to be processed in chemicals before it could be screened and edited, thus greatly reducing the "lead time" before it could go on the air.

Remote microwave and satellite technology also began to change the way local crews covered events. Specially outfitted trucks and vans allowed reporters to cover late-breaking news "live" by bouncing short-range microwaves back to the studio and out to viewers' homes. When an event's distance was beyond microwave range, signals could be bounced off satellites orbiting the earth. Suddenly, local news operations could transmit remote news with a speed that matched the networks. Whether the news stories broadcast around town in this way are urgent or important enough to merit this type of coverage remains to be seen.

The rise of ratings "sweeps" periods in the 1970s began to place a burden on local news programs to generate large audiences that helped determine commercial advertising rates. Consulting companies went into business to help local stations tailor their newscasts to lure a greater audience share. Some of these companies have even marketed packaged formulas that are instantly familiar wherever they are used, such as "Action News" with "Accuweather" forecasts. This has led to "happy news" teams—usually consisting of male and female co-anchors, a sports jock, and a weathercaster—all of whom banter amiably with one another between stories. A second trend is that local news programs have increased and "hyped" their coverage of violent and tragic stories, often using tabloid-style introductions such as this one, reported on the cover of *The New York Times Magazine* on January 11, 1998: "The charge: sitting on a sleeping toddler! Good evening. The accusations are shocking, jarring. A 22-month-old baby trapped beneath a hulk of a man."

Cable Television

The emergence of cable television in the mid-1980s greatly changed the landscape of fact-based programming. When they were the only game in town, the three broadcast networks had to offer programs that would appeal to a wide audience. Cable channels, however, began to sort this broad market into niches, and fact-based programming was especially suited to this new situation because it was relatively cheap to produce. Suddenly, many traditional fact-based genres now had cable channels specifically dedicated to their own fare: CNN for news, ESPN for sports, C-Span for politics and government, Discovery for science and nature, A&E for arts and culture, and the Weather Channel. Channels like Discovery (and its sisters The Learning Channel and Animal Planet) often acquired (at bargain prices) archival materials, which they then reconfigured to create new shows. For example, after the Soviet empire crumbled between 1989 and 1991, previously secret vaults of documents and films became available to western media. One result was broadcast on CNN in 1998 as the twenty-four-episode series, *Cold War*.

In this new television environment, documentaries have practically disappeared from the broadcast networks but are now more visible than ever on niche channels. At the same time, the commercial incentive for ratings dictates that these programs take on the style of entertainment; they tend to emphasize spectacle and excitement over reflection, many having names that deserve to be punctuated by exclamation marks, such as *Savage Seas, Wild Discovery, Storm of the Century, Adrenaline Rush Hour,* and *Extreme Machines. The New York Times* has noted that inexpensively produced animal shows with colorful hosts such as Steve Irwin ("The Crocodile Hunter") are more popular than ever on niche channels, and Animal Planet is the fastest-growing channel on cable television.[3] The Discovery Channel has also turned one-of-a-kind special events into ratings bonanzas. One of the first such stunts broadcast the opening of an Egyptian tomb on live television. Another program followed the airlifting of a 20,000-year-old woolly mammoth carcass encased in a solid block of ice to a cold-storage facility in Russia for scientific study—and drew an audience of more than ten million people.

Ironically, public television has benefited from this new cable-created environment. Before this, filmmakers had to compete for the relatively few slots available on documentary showcases such as *American Experience, Frontline, POV,* or *Nova.* Because cable channels have opened up so many new markets for reality-based material, PBS has become the last refuge for "quality" programs that do not pander to the least common denominator, thus justifying the slogan, "If PBS doesn't do it, who will?"

One documentary subgenre that has taken off in recent years is biography. A&E pioneered this development with its signature *Biography* series. Produced at minimal cost with extensive voice-overs and camera moves across still photographs, it has spawned imitators on Lifetime with *Intimate Portraits,* on VH-1 with *Behind the Music,* and even on ESPN-Classic with *Sports Century.*

The advent of small, inexpensive digital cameras has given rise to a host of factual entertainment shows that bring viewers right into the middle of high drama, real-life situations such as those encountered by police officers, firefighters, or paramedics. A good example of such a show is the Learning Channel's *Trauma: Life in the ER*. The comparatively low cost of small digital cameras enables the show's producers to hire whole teams of shooters to follow doctors, nurses, and paramedics around the clock as they perform their duties in a given hospital. Not all of the patients who come through the emergency room doors end up making good stories, and it is even possible for family members or patients to refuse permission for their private ordeals to be broadcast at all, but the economy of scale makes it feasible to follow many cases at once in the hope that a handful of them will wind up on a given episode.

MTV took this reality programming a step further by assembling a group of diverse young people and having them live together for a time. The resulting show, *Real World*, follows them nonstop through all the minutiae of their hourly and daily interactions. Borrowing an idea from European programmers, American networks have recently begun to "push the envelope" of such reality shows with what *Time* magazine has called "Voyeur TV."[4] These programs feature contestants who eat rats and vote one another off a desert island in *Survivor* or seal themselves in a house for months with twenty-four-hour surveillance cameras in *Big Brother*. One charming import from Britain featured a family who volunteered to "go back in time" in *The 1900 House*, complete with film crews and cumbersome corsets. The appeal of such programs lies in the fact that the situations shown on camera are "real" and unscripted, although critics have wondered whether the constant presence of video crews affects the behavior of the shows' subjects and have questioned their survival-of-the-fittest ethos and contrived game-show environment—not to mention the fact that so many viewers are willing to tune into *other people's* lives instead of actively living their own.[5]

Deregulation

Developments in federal communications regulations since the 1980s have had noticeable effects on the television market and hence on fact-based programming. In 1985, under Reagan appointee Mark Fowler, the FCC raised the number of stations a single media company could own nationwide from seven to twelve, and the Telecommunications Act of 1996 expanded the market coverage such companies could have from 25 percent to 35 percent of the U.S. population. In 1987, the FCC abolished the Fairness Doctrine and with it the requirement that broadcasters air competing points of view on controversial issues. The 1996 Telecommunications Act also cleared the way for a proliferation of mergers and acquisitions that have created giant media conglomerates owning everything from broadcast networks, cable channels, newspapers, and magazines to online services, local radio stations, and cable television companies. For example, as of January 2000, the Walt Disney Company owned ABC, ten local television stations, forty-four radio stations, the Disney Channel, *Discover* magazine, Hyperion books, and Miramax films—not to mention its lucrative theme parks, name-brand movie studio, cruise ship, and chain of retail stores. In 1999, the FCC also eliminated the rules prohibiting television companies from owning more than one station in large cities across the country. In the words of *Adbusters* magazine, "Successive U.S. Administrations have . . . equated the public interest with nothing more than competition in the marketplace."[6]

What has been the effect of all this deregulation? For one thing, as television news departments become smaller cogs in ever-larger corporate machines, the pressure becomes greater for them to be cost efficient and for financial bottom-line standards to take precedence over journalistic ones. With budgetary constraints on the amount of time and legwork required by traditional journalism, news departments have come to rely more and more on prepackaged video press releases and staged photo opportunities because they are cheaper and readily available. Cutbacks have eliminated many foreign news bureaus, and television news organizations have sometimes used footage supplied by questionable sources that turned out to be spurious.[7] They have also been forced by competition from tabloid shows to cover more titillating stories such as the O. J. Simpson trial and President Clinton's affair with Monica Lewinsky. During the summer of 2000, fears of low ratings even led the broadcast networks to severely limit their coverage of the presidential conventions for the first time in television history.

A second and more serious concern of the new merger-and-acquisition environment is that television news departments inevitably run into conflicts of interest over potential stories that involve other divisions of their corporate parents. For example, concerns were raised about NBC's ability to cover the Gulf War objectively in 1991 because it was owned by General Electric, a major supplier of arms to the military. More recently, *Brill's Content* quoted Disney chairman Michael Eisner in an NPR interview, "I would prefer ABC not to cover Disney. . . . I think it's inappropriate for Disney to be covered by Disney." A few days later, ABC declined to run a story claiming that Disney's theme parks had inadvertently given jobs to convicted pedophiles.[8]

A further concern is that multiple media outlets in a corporate empire may engage in cross-promotional "synergy," as when the opening of a new motion picture is featured on the covers of magazines, reported on morning talk shows, and chatted about on Internet web sites—all owned by the same company. On the surface, there can appear to be a diversity of marketplace voices, but how dissimilar can they be when they have been coordinated to serve the same corporate interest?

This becomes ominous when a cross-media blitz is mounted for a news story that turns out to be false, as happened in 1998 when CNN and *Time* (both owned by Time/Warner) simultaneously broke the "scoop" that nerve gas had been used by the United States during the Vietnam War.

Worldview/Metanarrative /Theology

One of the seductions of fact-based programming on television is that we tend to assume that the video images we see on news or documentary programs accurately represent the way things are in the "real world," as if we were looking out a window. Because "the camera does not lie," we want to believe its images are more reliable or less subject to bias than written reports in magazines or newspapers. Barring the use of digital alterations (which are still anathema to most news organizations), we reason that camera lenses objectively record what is "out there" without being filtered through the subjective prejudices of reporters.

Although this may sound like a reasonable assumption, the world we see on television is "constructed" just as much as the written words of journalists. For one thing, cameras cannot reveal all there is to see in a given scene. By focusing on one thing, the camera necessarily cannot focus on something else. Cropped through a telephoto lens, a relatively small number of people can seem more numerous than they actually are. In addition, a skillful editor can assemble pieces of video and sound bites in a number of different ways, some of which can be misleading.

Two famous examples of this were documentaries produced for *CBS Reports* in 1971 and 1982, respectively, *The Selling of the Pentagon* and *The Uncounted Enemy: A Vietnam Deception*. Both programs set out to examine questionable practices of the American military. At issue were several interviews or speeches that had been misleadingly edited to reinforce an editorial point of view and the elimination of countervailing voices for the same reason. CBS News ultimately benefited from congressional inquiries over *The Selling of the Pentagon*, but was sued over *The Uncounted Enemy*, and although the case was eventually settled out of court, it had a chilling effect on the number of long-form documentaries CBS has produced ever since.

Entertaining Narratives

If television does not necessarily present an accurate image of what is outside our living rooms, what type of world does emerge from television news reports and documentaries?

Such programming is situated in a television environment that exists primarily to make money, and in a deregulated world, this is more true than ever. It has been said that on American television, programming is used to fill up the space between commercials, and the programs that provide the highest financial returns to advertisers are entertainment shows. When we enter into the world of American commercial television, there is a veritable gravitational pull in the direction of entertainment. As Neil Postman has said in *Amusing Ourselves to Death*, "Entertainment is the supra-ideology of all discourse on television. No matter what is depicted or from what point of view, the overarching presumption is that it is there for our amusement and pleasure."[9]

This is done primarily through *stories* about basic human dilemmas that appeal to our emotions, which explains why even news reports are packaged as mininarratives.[10] Because all stories are structured with beginnings, middles, and ends, narratives inherently promise resolutions. They provide master narrators who are in control of the tales they spin, and they are filled with villains who threaten stability and with heroes who restore it. This story structure characterizes every form of fact-based television. It manifests itself in the "Up Close and Personal" segments during sports shows and in the way the Olympics were packaged as dramas about "good" and "evil" during the Cold War. It shows up in the set designs of evening news programs, the anchors inhabiting veritable control centers of fact-gathering activity. This "imperative toward narrative" even dictates that news accounts about complex situations be reduced to stories with *individual* characters who drive the action forward, as when, for example, conflicts among the myriad factions of Israelis and Palestinians are cast in terms of their respective leaders.

The market forces that drive amusement park roller coasters to become ever faster, higher, and larger are the same as those that push entertainment shows to ratchet up their levels of violence and spectacle, and this has certainly been true of reality programs as well, from *Trauma: Life in the ER* to *Crocodile Hunter* to *Survivor*. The same forces determine that the only foreign news reports from developing countries to appear on our evening newscasts are those about natural disasters of such magnitude or wars of such savage cruelty that they register on our "thrill-o-meters," as with the 1999 floods in Mozambique or the 1994 genocide in Rwanda. At the same time, Hal Himmelstein points out, our media tend to transform the human subjects of such dramas into objects for our "compassion consumption"—to be pitied, but not known or respected as people like ourselves.[11]

If we remember that the reason for all the commercials on television—however entertaining they may be—is to persuade us to buy things, we can become attuned to the interpretive filters that determine television's content and reinforce the myths undergirding our society and economy. The target audience of most television commercials is the broad middle class, which consumes the products and services driving our economy, and so it is not surprising that the point of view of most television—

including fact-based television—is also middle class. The implicit promise of advertising directed at middle-class consumers is that the solutions to various problems can be found by buying certain products and services. This assumes a world that is basically stable and safe, in which consumers need not worry about safeguarding their earnings against the uncertainties of the future. In addition, the problems and dilemmas in the mininarratives in television commercials are presented as easily resolvable, and the inevitable chaos of life is readily subject to the triumphs of human invention and technology.

This is the vast mythic backdrop behind most of commercial television in the United States, and the characters and situations on entertainment shows reflect these myths: The world is basically safe for the average consumer family, whose ordinary dilemmas can be more or less solved by ingenuity and human understanding so that "everyone can get along." (Remember Rodney King's plea in the wake of the riots of 1992?) This is also the mythic world assumed by fact-based programming, particularly news and documentaries. By their very structure as narratives that have closure, they inherently promise resolutions to the problems they convey, solutions that generally can be achieved by heroic individuals who rely on ingenuity and technology. The only exceptions to this rule are "verité" or "direct cinema" documentaries such as those by Frederick Wiseman, which eschew narration and tidy closure by relying exclusively on open-ended actualities that force viewers to come to their own conclusions. Verité documentaries come closest to the myth-breaking potential of parable in fact-based programming.

When the world outside becomes dangerous, as it does during natural disasters or military conflicts, television instinctively seeks to contain and package the chaos so that it does not threaten our psychic or economic equilibrium too much. Television even uses musical themes and logos, such as "Storm of the Century," "Showdown in the Gulf," or "America Held Hostage." When the problems, such as drugs and crime, become intractable or too complex for easy solutions, the hero-villain devices of classic narratives surface to ease the tension. This usually results in the demonizing of criminals and drug dealers, with cries for "more cops" or "more prisons." Although these measures may not do anything to change the lives of criminals or the underlying social structures that lead to crime in the first place, from the safe and comfortable point of view of the middle class, the problem is solved. As Sharon Lynn Sperry has pointed out, however, when problems appear again and again, when new politicians fail to deliver what the old ones had promised, a certain disappointment and cynical anger can set in.[12]

When reality-based programs exist in an environment where profits are more important than enlightenment, where it is more desirable for the audience to behave as consumers than as citizens, then they tend to dull the impulse toward civic involvement, and people stay at home. These programs may help us to relax or escape, they may pique our interest or even arouse our pity, but they seldom motivate us to do anything that requires us to do more than shop or write a check. This may well account for the fact that so few Americans now vote in elections.

A Different Promise

In the late first century, Saint James exhorted readers of his epistle that the life of faith entails more than simple belief, that it is necessary to translate one's convictions into loving actions for one's neighbors and the surrounding world. In chapter 2:14–17, he mocks an attitude of indifference that is content merely to watch the passing scene without entering into it with acts of love. He satirizes such an attitude with, "Goodbye and good luck; keep warm and well-fed!" (New American Bible). Yet that indeed is the behavior that seems to be encouraged by regular consumption of commercial television, including fact-based programming.

The contemporary British historian and theologian N. T. Wright has suggested that we live in an uneasy transition period between the modern and postmodern eras. The modern world can be characterized as one with a zealous belief in the ability of human reason and technical ingenuity to make life better and better—salvation through progress. The uneasy truth, the insight of postmodernity, is that this progress has not been steady and it has not benefited everyone.[13] Modern innovation has made headway against some problems, such as certain diseases, but other problems such as poverty continue to vex whole populations. Indeed, technology has even created new terrors unknown to past generations, such as radioactive contamination and the Holocaust.

Wright's point is that we live with an uneasy tension because the bright promise of modernity has not been fulfilled and postmodernity has yet to offer anything in its place except critique. If we accept Wright's premise, then we are reminded of our nagging dissatisfaction with modernity every time we watch television. As with the allure of progress, television narratives—including those based on fact—inherently promise us salvation because they have closure, and because they proclaim trust in the mythic power of human invention.

Wright suggests that the path out of our malaise may be to take the life of Jesus seriously and to follow his example of self-sacrificial love. "In the cross and resurrection of Jesus we find the answer: the God who made the world is revealed in terms of a *self-giving* love that no hermeneutic of suspicion can ever touch, in a Self that found itself by giving itself away" [emphasis added].[14] Rather than relaxing and keeping warm and well fed in front of "the tube," we may find the key to salvation not in the accumulation of objects that promise well-being yet ultimately fail to deliver, but in leaving them behind and expending a measure of love and care on behalf of others.

ELEVEN |

Televised News

IF IT BLEEDS, IT LEADS

Two children are seated on a couch watching television. One says to the other, "This is the 24-hour news channel. It's just like the 24-hour sports channel, except it's more violent."[1]

News Show:
Opening shots of *The NBC Nightly News with Tom Brokaw* and the "Patients' Bill of Rights" with Bob Schieffer on *The CBS Evening News with Dan Rather*, 6:00 P.M., October 7, 1999.

Television broadcast news creates an aura of authority and delivers urgency—whether authentic or not. In its time-limited effort to create order from chaos, it couches every story in terms of conflict. This may lead the viewer to think of every story in terms of heroes and villains, darkness and light, when real life is "in living color" with all the shadings in between.

The Future of Network News

Four of every five North Americans get their news from television, but the share of viewers watching network news has dropped from 80 percent to 50 percent since the mid-1980s. Kyle Pope, media reporter for *The Wall Street Journal*, predicts that network anchors like Dan Rather (CBS), Tom Brokaw (NBC), and Peter Jennings (ABC) are an endangered species and that network news is on its way out. "The end of the network news comes precisely a half-century after the genre was born."[2] The primary cause, Pope claims, is competition from round-the-clock cable news and the World Wide Web. Many others see it differently: The networks are digging their own grave by turning news into entertainment.

Televised news is under attack from all sides. Derogatory terms abound: "infotainment," "fast-food journalism," "the McWorld of televised news," "disco news," "news from nowhere," "parachute journalism," "news as spectacle," "the 'celebrification' of network anchors and pundits," "The 6:00 P.M. vaudeville." These criticisms come from all political persuasions. A conservative professor of history entitles his attack on the industry *How the News Makes Us Dumb*; a former editor of *The Atlantic Monthly* and *U.S. News and World Report* writes *How the Media Undermine American Democracy*.[3] Some would say that television's current owners have traded in journalism's slogan made famous by *The New York Times*— "All the news that's fit to print"—for a more contemporary version: "All the news that fits" (the economic and political interests of corporate America).

The Emergence of Infotainment

The move away from socially responsible television journalism toward market-driven entertainment is not new. In the early 1980s, Robert MacNeil of the PBS *MacNeil-Lehrer News Hour* leveled these charges at network news: The newscaster strives "to keep everything brief, not to strain the attention of anyone but instead to provide constant stimulation through variety, novelty, action, and movement. You are required . . . to pay attention to no concept, no character, and no problem for more than a few seconds at a time . . . [Editorial guidelines include the following:] that bite-sized is best, that complexity must be avoided, that nuances are dispensable, that qualifications impede the simple message, that visual stimulation is a substitute for thought, and that verbal precision is an anachronism."[4] Bill Moyers notes a shift from the journalistic standards of the news business to the crowd-pleasing criteria of show business. In his numerous meetings with network personnel in the 1980s, executives touted *Entertainment Tonight* as the model news show.[5] Steve Friedman, executive producer of *The Early Show* on CBS and heir to the legacy of Fred Friendly and Edward R. Murrow, has said, "I don't want to hear any more about the line between news and entertainment. There is no line. We have to compete."[6]

What accounts for this deterioration? Changing ownership and economic incentives are probably the most influential factors. The story goes back as far as 1915, when the U.S. Supreme Court declared the film industry to be "a business pure and simple, originated and conducted for profit." The Communications Act of 1934 applied a similar commercial definition to the electronic media, while also stipulating that the media must function "in the public interest." As long as the three networks were in private hands and journalists with a background in print media were in charge, socially responsible journalism—the media as watchdog—was the self-professed norm of the industry. However, when corporations started buying up the networks in the mid-1980s and the government deregulated the industry in 1987, the rules of the game changed. Previously, private owners had not expected their news departments to show a profit, and news shows were highly subsidized by the profits generated by programs designed for entertainment.

CBS was the pioneer in profit-making news shows even before corporate ownership took over. When *60 Minutes*—then considered a sensationalist, muckraking newsmagazine with a "gotcha"-type formula—became a moneymaker in the early 1970s, it set a precedent. A subtle but far-reaching shift took place a decade later when giant conglomerates began buying up the networks: Economic incentive switched from profit *making* to profit *maximizing*. With the stroke of a pen, the full effect of the 1915 Supreme Court decision came into play. A new, impersonal, and unforgiving god named "the bottom line" and "the prevailing market rate" took control. Now "money men," not newsmen and women, run the news divisions. They are driven by quarterly financial reports—just like their counterparts in pharmaceuticals, biotech, and Silicon Valley.

The consequences of corporate ownership are many and grave. In the drive to "sell eyeballs to advertisers," the new owners have accelerated the trend toward sensationalism and altered the nature of televised news.

What Is News and What Are Its Functions in a Democratic Society?

Is news (a) *What is happening* in the world? or (b) *What people want to know* about what is happening in the world? or (c) *What journalists think people ought to know* about what is happening in the world? or (d) *What the networks decide to show people* about what is happening in the world, reflecting (consciously or not) the ideology of the dominant culture, rather than the plurality of community views? In most cases, news is a combination of all four. We can dismiss view (a) as naive realism. All news, to the degree that it is not pure fiction, is grounded in what actually takes place in the world. Because facts and interpretation always go together, news is always more than merely "what is happening."

A cartoon captures view (b) with a picture of a news anchor as an entertainer interviewing a dog wearing a Mexican sombrero. The anchor explains to the audience: "The ratings plummet when we feature in-depth analysis, so instead, let's find out what Squeaky, The Talking Chihuhua thinks of the job the president has been doing."[7] The media were criticized for their feeding frenzies during the O. J. Simpson trial, the Monica Lewinsky-Bill Clinton affair, and the paparazzi pursuit of Princess Diana, but the biting satire of this cartoon is aimed at the audience ratings that drive the feeding frenzies.

Another cartoon depicts views (c) and (d) in a parody on the journalist's vocation to answer six questions (who, what, where, when, why, how) about the events they report. Under market pressure, these questions become: Who is watching? What do the sponsors want? Where is the makeup artist? When is sweeps season? Why does my hair not move? How are the ratings?[8]

Journalists tend to define news as the knowledge needed for the exercise of responsible citizenship. A free press, often called the Fourth Estate (the first three being the executive, legislative, and judicial branches of government), is essential for informed debate. One function of the Fourth Estate is to serve as society's watchdog, alerting the public to dangers from within and without and holding accountable those in authority. Noam Chomsky's maxim warns of what happens when the Fourth Estate is corrupted: "Propaganda is to democracy as violence is to dictatorship."[9]

Another function of the Fourth Estate is to mediate public debate and provide perspective on issues of common concern. "To see life steady, and see it whole" is the way Charles Prestwich Scott, long-time editor of the *Manchester Guardian*, described it. James Fallows comments: "Seeing life steady means keeping the day's events in proportion. Seeing it whole means understanding the connections among the causes and consequences of various happenings."[10] Socially responsible news media tell us what is important and why. They provide a context for making sense of otherwise meaningless bytes of information. This involves three elements: (1) a perspective that separates the significant from the urgent or the scandalous or the spectacular; (2) a time frame that situates an event or an issue in its historical context; and (3) a pattern that depicts similarities and differences between stories of the same type and interconnections with other issues and events.

These three elements are notable by their absence from most news shows today. The number one guideline of every editor of local news, "If it bleeds, it leads," is also high on the list of priorities of national news editors. Television news is exciting but disconnected from any historical context. Bright lights and colors, pulsating music, dramatic action, traumatized victims, overly important police and officials: News has the same feel and intensity as *Monday Night Football*. Each story, whether trivial and ephemeral or weighty and enduring, is reported with the same urgent intensity—fortissimo—until the end of the broadcast when the anchor sometimes wraps things up with a touching human-interest story in piano. This is the hyped-up spectacle of televised news at the turn of the century.

The fourth view (d)—News is what the networks decide to show us—calls attention to the constraints that owners, advertisers, and audience impose. None of us likes to air our dirty laundry. Corporations are similar. Owners and those who work for them exercise censorship by what they choose to omit. For example, when Westinghouse owned CBS, it would have been a conflict of interest for Dan Rather to play watchdog for the nuclear industry, an industry in which Westinghouse is a major player.

Television ignored the biggest financial scandal of the mid-1990s—the $70 billion giveaway of the airwaves to network and cable corporations. During the nine months leading to the passage of the Telecommunications Act in January 1996, Congress was subject to intense lobbying, which television chose not to report. The combined coverage of the proposed legislation by all cable and network news outlets over this nine-month period was nineteen minutes. Even during these nineteen minutes, the financial windfall for the industry was not once mentioned.[11]

Advertisers also influence the slant of the news and what the networks air. The Media Foundation, a Canadian company committed to environmental protection, produces high-quality, thought-provoking commercials that are in good taste but critical of environmentally harmful practices, including television programming. The networks refuse to run Media Foundation ads. CBS's vice president for Program Practices wrote to explain why: "We would not broadcast a commercial that denigrated television. We also don't broadcast commercials that take controversial positions on important topics."[12] This is tantamount to admitting that CBS has discarded its watchdog function and no longer has any pretensions of serving as a forum for debating controversial issues.

In practice, the news we see on television is a combination of and a compromise among three elements: audience desires, journalistic vocation, industry imperatives. To remain on the air, networks must attract a sizable audience; to retain advertisers and keep in the good graces of corporate owners, reporters must shy away from certain stories. To retain self-respect, journalists must contribute to an informed citizenry. In reality, news is always a compromise, a hybrid. We might imagine the news as a cable with three intertwined strands. In one story, the "titillate the audience" strand is foremost; in another, the social responsibility strand predominates; in other stories, the "cover-our-hindside" takes precedence. Perhaps one way to evaluate a news show or a network is to ask which strand dominates.

"From NBC World Headquarters in New York . . ."

To "read" a news show, we must examine how it is constructed. In this section, we apply lens analysis and field of view analysis (see the Introduction and Appendix B for an explanation of these theories) to the opening segment of the *NBC Nightly News with Tom Brokaw*. In the next section, we apply the same "reading" method to the lead story on the *CBS Evening News with Dan Rather* of October 7, 1999.

We start with the smallest unit of analysis in Field 1, single shots and scenes. The screen flashes, drums roll, and trumpets blare; a barker announces, "From NBC World Headquarters in New York, this is NBC Nightly News with Tom Brokaw!" No, we are not at the circus. It just

1st **scene:** Globe with USA on top

2nd **scene:** NBC in the heart of NYC

3rd **scene:** NBC newsroom at "30 Rock"

4th **scene:** NBC's $7 million man

sounds that way. But an elaborate performance has begun! Four video shots accompany this ten-second sound bite.

The first scene, announced by a drum and trumpet fanfare, features a blue rotating globe with the United States in the center, appearing through a translucent red foreground with the words "NBC Nightly News" superimposed in white. Each of these images, sounds, words, and colors has been constructed to communicate a message of national pride, triumphant military power, a global perspective; in short, the United States on top. The message is more subtle than the CBS motto of the 1980s ("We keep America on top of the world!"), but the meaning is the same.

In the second scene, the camera places viewers high in the dark sky zooming in from lower Manhattan toward the NBC news studios in the brightly lit General Electric Building at 30 Rockefeller Plaza, in the heart of New York City. As we descend to the plaza, we feel drawn into the action. Power, wealth, science, technology, knowledge: all there amid the rush-hour bustle of America's largest city!

We pause in midair as the camera slowly tilts upward, showing the full length of "30 Rock," towering like a giant monolith above the surrounding skyscrapers. The camera momentarily fades, giving viewers a birdlike sensation of alighting near the top of this memorial to John D. Rockefeller, oil tycoon and icon of nineteenth- and twentieth-century industrial capitalism. The message: "With a perch like this, we at NBC are on top of the world. Nothing can escape our all-seeing eye."

Like ghosts, viewers move through the walls as the third scene gathers focus, showing a camera crew filming the opening attraction of the night. There will be other rings to this performance—Washington, Mexico City, East Timor—but the main attraction is here. The ranks of overhead spotlights, the television screens that line the room like animated wallpaper, the screen on which each story's images are projected—this setting bespeaks star power linked to the latest technology, a celebrity in his own right, one who deserves center stage.

In the fourth scene, we come face to face with the star of the show, NBC's $ 7 million man, Tom Brokaw!* Perched at the pinnacle of power like an omniscient sage, Tom welcomes us with a deep, raspy "Good evening!" and we invite him again into the intimacy of our homes.† Once more, this trusted friend guides us through the labyrinthine paths of our complex and confounding world. Like the headlights of a car on a mountain road at midnight, the *Nightly News* picks out the twists and turns, the potholes and fallen rock, which impede our journey toward making sense of our troubled times.

Using a lens analysis, we ask about function, structure, signs and messages, ideology and power relationships, and the nature of the narrative communicated by these four shots, which are designed to hook the audience and inspire trust and brand loyalty. They also reinforce patriotism and respect for the corporate power of NBC and provide viewers with vicarious participation in far-off events of the day. From a structural perspective, NBC's *Nightly News* covers action stories that serve as apologies for the dominant myths of American culture. The globe, the red white and blue, the musical fanfare, the shots of "30 Rock," the scene depicting the technology of television production, the lighting and camera angles: These signs have iconic power. Conspicuous by their absence are women and persons of color. The resulting gestalt conveys a message of national dynamism and white male authority. The setting is both local and global; the characters demonstrate authority, competence, style, technological sophistication, and global reach; the plot tells us NBC and Tom Brokaw can be trusted to tell the truth, sort out the significant from the trivial, and alert us to dangers ahead.

---

*Brokaw's annual salary is over $7 million.

†The NBC news studios are actually near street level in an adjacent building, but the camera convinces us otherwise in this brief introduction to the *Nightly News*. The news product is manufactured in a converted industrial plant in New Jersey, with feeds into the studio in Manhattan.

Turning to field-of-view analysis, we notice immediately how with words and images a single scene or shot draws our attention to broader frames of reference. The first scene establishes NBC news as global in reach and patriotic in perspective (Field 6). Both shots in the second scene remind us that NBC is big business and news is a for-profit product like all the other products of GE subsidiaries (Field 5). The camera, lighting, and television screens in the third scene point to Field 4, news as a program genre.

Constructing *The CBS Evening News with Dan Rather*

The "Patients' Bill of Rights" is the lead story on *The CBS Evening News with Dan Rather* on Thursday, October 7, 1999. Here are the order and the time allotted to each component of the show and a graph showing relative length.

#	Length in secs.	Story
(1)	45	Preview of upcoming stories
(2)	180	Patients' Bill of Rights
(3)	135	Prescription drugs for the elderly
(4)	130	$3.75 billion settlement in suit against makers of diet drug Fen Phen
(5)	105	"Still ahead" (preview of next stories) and commercials
(6)	130	Trend-setting case re use of DNA in court
(7)	25	Lawsuit against gun manufacturers
(8)	15	Cell phones may cause danger at gas stations
(9)	15	Wall Street
(10)	125	"Coming up" (preview of next stories) and commercials
(11)	125	Drug war in Columbia
(12)	25	Concrete bombs cause fewer civilian injuries in Iraq
(13)	15	Floods in Mexico
(14)	15	London commuter train wreck
(15)	135	"Up next" (preview of next stories) and commercials
(16)	25	President Clinton campaigns at labor union meeting
(17)	145	Donald Trump considers run for presidency
(18)	25	Unknown music by Beethoven discovered
(19)	130	"Up next" (preview of following stories) and commercials
(20)	15	Football player charged with theft
(21)	140	The Pokemon craze among American children
(22)	10	Cleveland Indians lose playoff game
(23)	30	Promo for *48 Hours*

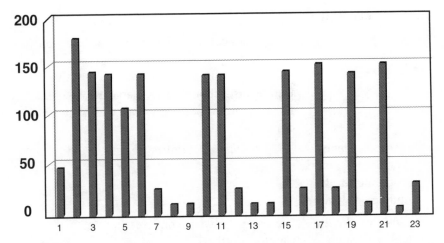

The graph demonstrates seven stories of two to three minutes each, and ten stories ranging between ten and twenty-five seconds each, interspersed with four breaks for commercials. For the major stories, this is an increase over the earlier formula of "quick and dirty, minute-thirty." Together with the previews and promos, the commercials (nos. 1, 5, 10, 15, 19, and 23) take 32 percent of the allotted time. Of the seven major stories (nos. 2, 3, 4, 6, 11, 17, and 21), three are related to health ("news you can use"), two deal with the fight against crime (one domestic, one foreign), and one treats in a slightly humorous manner a potential economic and cultural threat from Japan. Foreign news (nos. 11–14) receives three minutes of coverage. The urgent, fortissimo tone of each story flattens distinctions between stories of greater or lesser importance.

The Patients' Bill of Rights

Dan Rather uses three standard journalistic criteria in choosing to lead off with the Patients' Bill of Rights: *timeliness* (the vote in Congress had occurred earlier in the day), *proximity* to the felt needs of the intended audience, and *significance* for the long-term shape of health care in the United States. Here's the story:

Scenes, Shots, Pictures	Words
1. Dan Rather at news desk; dome of Capitol with medical insignia and moving spotlight on "Patients' Bill of Rights."	DR (*Dan Rather*): "Good evening. A stunning upset in Washington. The U.S. House late today approved the Patients' Bill of Rights. If ever finally passed by both the House and the Senate, it would give citizens more control over managed care plans. It would also give them the right to sue HMOs.
2. House floor/ dome of Capitol, no. of votes.	"The vote margin was 275 to 151. Sixty-eight Republicans broke ranks and voted yes.

Scenes, Shots, Pictures	Words
3. Same as 1.	"Insurance company lobbyists who contribute much money to Republican congressional and presidential campaigns—but also to some Democrats—thought they had this one won. Bob Schieffer reports how and why they suddenly lost."
4. Sidewalk scene outside the House building; milling crowds.	*BS (Bob Schieffer)*: "It was a classic Washington moment.
5. Close-up of male lobbyist walking, with a cell phone to his ear.	"So many lobbyists converged on the Capitol . . . [that]
6. Shot of policeman speaking to a crowd.	"Police were called in for ground control." *Policeman to crowd*: "You're blocking the sidewalk—I need to keep the sidewalk open for the members to walk." *Female lobbyist*: "O.K."
7. Extreme close-up of lobbyist on cell phone.	*BS*: "The insurance companies had poured millions into blocking reform,
8. Shot of two male, one female lobbyists on cell phones.	and were taking no chances."
9. Close-up of Rep. Ray LaHood (R. Illinois).	*Rep. LaHood*: "Looks like they've moved their offices up here for the afternoon at least."
10. Congressman shakes hands with a female lobbyist.	
11. Female lobbyist tries to keep up with a Congressman—puts her hand on his arm.	*BS*: "But for all the arm-twisting and legislative roadblocks thrown up by Republican leaders who sided with the insurance companies,
12. Parade of five congressmen running the gauntlet of lobbyists on sidewalk.	a bi-partisan group of legislators

Scenes, Shots, Pictures	Words
13. Congressman shakes hand of female lobbyist.	banded together, and against great odds, passed the reform bill.
14. Shot of House chamber with chairman gaveling them to order.	"For all its power,
15. House chamber from right balcony.	the lobby just couldn't match the horror stories from constituents that members brought to the floor."
16. Shot of Congressman speaking.	*1st Congressman*: "She desperately needed to see a specialist, but her HMO was worried about the cost."
17. Shot of Congresswoman speaking.	*Congresswoman*: "Jessica died while her family was fighting the HMO."
18. Shot of another Congressman speaking.	*2nd Congressman*: "The HMO bureaucrat demanded that the patient be sent home. The patient went home, swallowed a bottle of antifreeze, and killed himself."
19. PowerPoint slide: Dome of Capitol in foreground; anatomical drawing of human being in background.	*DR*: "The legislation passed by the House not only guarantees the patients' right to sue the HMOs that wrong them [the words "Right to sue" fold and fly in as a bullet from the right while a medical insignia folds and flies up to the crossbar from the left]; it guarantees immediate access to care in an emergency [while the first bullet dissolves, a second bullet with "Immediate access to emergency care" folds and flies in from the left] and prompt access to specialists." [While the second bullet dissolves, a third folds and flies in from the right: "Prompt access to specialists."]
20. Shot of President Clinton, flanked by flags, speaking to an AFL-CIO group.	*BS*: "The President was delighted." *President Clinton*: "This is the sort of thing that America wants us to do. We can work together across party lines; we can get things done; there will still be plenty for the two parties to argue about in the coming election."

Scenes, Shots, Pictures	Words
21. Shot of receiving line at victory headquarters at Capitol.	*BS*: "And at the Capitol
22. Shot of women applauding.	the winning side was euphoric."
23. Shot of Rep. John Dingell (D. Michigan) at podium with ten microphones.	*Rep. Dingell*: "We have a lot to rejoice, but the time for rejoicing is really not here. We can have a little fun but we gotta go back to work." *BS*: "That's because senators must also approve the reform when the bill goes to a conference committee.
24. Shot of Bob Schieffer, chief Washington correspondent.	"But whatever happens there, this will be remembered as the day that some Republicans and Democrats finally banded together, took on one of the most powerful lobbying groups in America, and beat 'em. Dan."
25. Shot of Dan Rather with backdrop of Capitol dome and the words "Patients' Bill of Rights."	*DR*: "Bob Schieffer on Capital Hill. There was this reaction tonight from a health insurance industry group, quote: 'The fight is not over.' The industry also claims that the Patients' Bill of Rights would mean more bills to pay lawyers and that would drive up health care costs to patients."

To analyze this story we draw on insights gained from combining lens and field-of-view analyses with a discussion of certain organizational imperatives and production concepts.

Industry Imperatives: In a 1973 dissertation at Harvard University, Edward J. Epstein applied organizational theory to the news industry. His thesis is simple: "The key to explaining the particular 'outputs' of organizations (lies) in defining the basic requirements which a given organization needs to maintain itself."[13] This means that "the pictures of society that are shown on television as national news are largely—though not entirely—performed and shaped by organizational considerations."[14] The first organizational imperative is the design of the stories themselves.

Story Templates and Formulas: Reporters work under strict time pressure to meet deadlines and beat the competition to the hottest stories. To give structure and meaning to their stories, they rely on what journalist and social philosopher Walter Lippmann called a "repertory of stereotypes." The reporter imposes on each happening a story template or formula that is widely understood by the intended audience. This means, of necessity, "fictional models permeate factual discourse."[15] The reporter can never tell the whole story and to a certain degree must distort every story. This is another way of saying that we live in a mental environment constructed by stories; balance and fairness, not objectivity, are the criteria of responsible journalism.

The workhorse of daily news, guaranteed to produce high audience ratings, is the conflict template. Field-of-view analysis provides a way of ranking these templates of conflict between the good guys and the bad guys, us and them, winners and losers. At the international level, the template describing the pecking order among the nations is foremost. From the sixteenth through the mid-nineteenth centuries, colonization, empire, nation building, and manifest destiny provided the formulas for world news. After the end of World War II, the Cold War template eclipsed all others as a pattern for interpreting international news. Network news was born during this time and inherited a dualistic view of the "free world's" deadly struggle with "the evil empire" of Soviet communism. A quarter of a century ago, leaders of the Group of 77 (nonaligned nations) protested the distortion this template created when describing their struggles for a place at the table of nations. Behind the United Nations call for "A New International Information Order" in the early 1970s lay the claim that the Western-dominated international press serves as the headlights of an international system designed to enhance the power of wealthy nations.[16]

Since the fall of the Berlin Wall in 1989, international network news coverage has declined by almost one-third, and a new template of the role of wealthy nations in the world—economic integration and corporate globalization—has replaced the story formula of the Cold War. As for the poorer nations (now called "emerging markets"), journalist and historian Michael Ignatieff notes, "There is no simple narrative to tell anymore. Instead, the narrative that has become the most pervasive and persuasive has been chaos narrative."[17] The new polarity replacing that of the Cold War is the formulaic struggle between globalizaton and chaos. The international struggle is also reflected nationally in the culture wars of the 1990s with one contingent identifying pluralism, multiculturalism, and the decentering of dominant groups as the equivalent of chaos.

At the national level, as William McAndrew, former president of NBC News, once remarked, "The domestic political story is the skeleton on which all news is built."[18] This story is continuous and repetitive, recalibrated daily and weekly as episodes in the never-ending serial of the race for the White House at the next presidential election.[19] The story of the Patients' Bill of Rights is one of these episodes. Drawing on a stock scenario from the Old West, CBS scripted this story as a political shoot-out at the O.K. Corral between the money-grubbing HMOs and the helpless victims, with the Republicans and Democrats as their proxies.

Phrases like "68 Republicans broke ranks" and "the Republican leaders who sided with the insurance companies" convey the polarization at work in the story.

This story of October 7 builds on the conflict template used earlier. On October 6, the day before Congress voted, Dan Rather opened *The CBS Evening News* with this prophesy: "The Patients' Bill of Rights is dead on arrival!" By pretending to know the mind of Congress before the vote to dramatize the story on October 6, Dan Rather set himself up for embarrassment on October 7, unless, of course, he could claim a dramatic, overnight change of heart on the part of Congress. To support the accuracy of his newscast on October 6, he had to proclaim "a stunning upset in Washington."

Agenda Setting: As a genre, the news is organized in weekly units in keeping with the work schedule of journalists and the viewing habits of the audience. At the beginning of the week, editors select a story of the week to be developed a little each day. At the end of the week, pundits on the newsmagazine shows—often the same ones who reported the story as it unfolded during the week—assess the importance of the week's events and debate the president's performance. During that first week of October, it was the story of the Patients' Bill of Rights, which the president won; the following week, it was the nuclear test ban treaty, which the president lost. This selection process is called agenda setting.

Television newscasts do not always tell us *what* to think about an event, a person, or an issue, but they do tell us what to think *about*. They set the agenda for the national debate. A story reported on the front pages of major newspapers does not appear on the national political agenda unless it is picked up and dramatized by television.

Focus and Framing: Telecasters tell us not only what to think about, but also *how* to think about it. The news sets the national agenda as much by what the producers choose to omit as by what they decide to include. No matter how much the president speaks of cooperation and consensus ("We can work together across party lines"), most stories are pitched as fights. Of the fifteen stories on the October 7 *CBS Evening News*, two portray the victims of disaster, one is about music, and twelve examine some form of conflict.

The focus of a story creates the hook that catches and retains the audience. Often the most dramatic elements of a story are accentuated even if they are not the most significant ones. The hook is set on October 7 by Dan Rather in the very first scene as he highlights the stories ahead. "Suddenly health insurance rights are back from the dead. The House does a 180-degree turn and passes a Patients' Bill of Rights."

The Tyranny of the Visual: Television is first and foremost a visual medium. Thus the editor's guideline: "No picture, no story." Pictures must be self-explanatory and have universal meaning for the target audience. As a *dramatic* art form, news programs are *performances*.

Novelty, variety, action, movement, sharp contrasts, bright colors, and other techniques are used to provide constant stimulation. To avoid the "talking head" impression, visuals on the screen behind Dan Rather are in constant motion. The policeman controlling the crowd, nervous lobbyists talking on cell phones and pacing the sidewalk, members of Congress brushing off a last-minute arm twist, an attractive, stately Congresswoman recounting how an HMO let Jessica die: These gripping pictures are enough to hold an audience until the next installment the following evening.

A Medium of Experience, Not Reflection: Televised news covers issues very briefly in terms of their effects on a person or group of people. Anecdotal evidence is more emotionally persuasive than statistics. Issues are treated individually rather than in their systemic relationships. Complexity, nuance, and qualifications are to be avoided. In the last scene of this story—and in the tone of an aside—Dan Rather quotes a health insurance industry spokesperson who vows, "The fight is not over." Those in favor of the bill were given two minutes and forty seconds for their side of the story; twelve seconds were allocated to acknowledge the existence of another perspective.

News from Nowhere and the Fragmentation of Meaning: Because television news presents most issues in bite size with graphic images of conflict, most news stories are "endings without beginnings,"[20] which ignore the larger context of meaning. In a field-of-view analysis to examine layers of context, the smallest frame of this health care story is about product quality and consumer protection. Up one level is the dilemma of infinite health care "needs" and limited resources. Up a third level is the question of public versus private health care. Finally, a fourth frame contains an analysis of the relation between poverty, the availability of jobs, a minimum wage, and health care. Even though a bill of rights for patients is a form of public intervention, issues in Frames 2–4 are ignored because they are too complex to play well on television. Stories from nowhere "appear without explanation and disappear without resolution. . . . The message of today's news coverage is often that the world cannot be understood, shaped, or controlled, but merely endured or held at arm's length."[21]

Bias, Attitude, and Anchor Banter: Modern consciousness no longer permits journalists to claim objectivity. Instead, they strive for "balance," which usually means presenting two sides of every issue, even when an issue may have multiple sides. News without context is perhaps the most distorting form of bias; but turning every issue into a fight also creates bias. Normally, national news anchors and correspondents show little attitude until they come to the final line of a story. In the story we have been examining, Bob Schieffer ends his report with a "point and period" that emerges from the story formula and probably also from his own predilections. To dramatize the importance of the vote, Schieffer declares triumphantly, "This will be remembered as the day that some . . . took on one of the most powerful lobbying groups in America, and beat 'em!" As he accentuates the last two words, Schieffer smiles victoriously, showing his own satisfaction, as if to say, "Oh how sweet when the little guys sock it to the bullies!" This injection of one's own values is appropriately called anchor banter or the "point and period."

Reflecting the World and Shaping the World: A commonsense response to this analysis of CBS coverage of The Patients' Bill of Rights would run something like this: "How can you say Dan Rather and Bob Schieffer imposed a conflict template on this story? It was a fight. All you have to do is look at the shot of the victory party and the applause for Rep. John Dingell." This objection merely proves the point. Americans are so shaped by conflict narratives that it is hard for us to conceive of telling this story any other way. We need a winner and a loser, a group that is right and a group that is wrong, forces of light and forces of darkness. Had the networks chosen to portray this story as a dilemma with no easy answers—for example, the tension between high-tech, high-cost medicine, and limited health care resources—the focus would have shifted to issues of justice amid scarcity and the need for rationing certain forms of care. This alternative story is much closer to the daily struggles faced by health care providers the world over, whether private or public. The alternative story would not have shown pictures of a victory party, even if the Democrats had insisted on having one.

Has conflict become a self-fulfilling prophecy in our society? Because the media shoehorns every happening into a shoot-out or a horse race, does this shape the way we behave? If the media stopped presenting party gatherings as after-the-game celebrations, would Democrats and Republicans vilify one another so much? Have Congress and the lobbying industry reduced every issue to partisan advantage because that is all the media televise? How much do the media *report* what happens and how much do they *contribute to causing* what happens? The movies, the sports events, and the television programs featuring some form of controlled violence always draw the largest audiences. Would we be such a violent country if conflict were not the template used to tell most of our stories? Probably not.

Covering the Presidential Campaign as a Horse Race

Television has changed the nature of politics in the United States. Political parties once dominated the candidate selection process, but no more. Politician-entrepreneurs and their handlers have overtaken them. Today the two essentials for election are media and money. Money buys media coverage, and media coverage creates image. A candidate is marketed with the same care and cost as a Lexus or Mercedes. The candidate's schedule is controlled by the search for money and posturing for the media. Only the rich or those who can tap into the pockets of the rich can get elected today. "I love the corporate decals on the nominee's suit," says the little man in a cartoon that appeared during one of the party conventions in the summer of 2000. Another cartoon depicts the scene of a televised presidential candidates' debate. On the dais are eight candidates standing behind podiums with microphones. The presidential candidates are identified by the following large signs on their podiums: Oil Lobby; Lawyer Lobby; Drug Lobby; Bank Lobby; Hollywood Lobby; The Communication Lobby; Union Lobby; Gun Lobby. The caption reads, "Let's open the debates to the true voices of democracy."[22]

Media coverage of the 2000 presidential campaign provided many illustrations of the organizational imperatives and production concepts mentioned above and of William McAndrew's view that all news is constructed on the skeleton of the horse race for the White House. For example, the increasing centrality of scorecards (opinion polls) in the election process: A recent study of *CBS Evening News* stories during the final months of seven presidential elections (1968–1996) documented three troubling trends related to polling.[23] First, opinion polls have proliferated, providing a weekly and sometimes daily update on who is ahead. Second, the placement (and therefore the importance) of poll-based stories has changed from eighth place to second or third place in the half-hour newscast. Third, during these past three decades the number of stories in which reporters set expectations for candidates based on poll data and measured candidate performance on the basis of these expectations increased ninefold.

Poll-based reporting "virtually never deals with the issues in any way," says media researcher Richard Craig.[24] Polls allow reporters and news commentators to construct "news" on the basis of their own specialized expertise, which is scorekeeping, rather than by mastering the intricate details of economic and social issues like social security, health care, tax reform, and the price of oil. This style of coverage "implies there is only one real story behind the many, varied events of the day," which is the story of political advantage, says James Fallows. He concludes: "The relentless emphasis on the cynical game of politics threatens public life itself."[25]

A study of the 2000 presidential campaign by Princeton Survey Research Associates illustrates how media expectations affect news coverage. The study found that Al Gore received more negative coverage in the media than George W. Bush from September 23 to October 20 because Gore did not perform up to media expectations during the presidential debates.[26]

We must not blame the media too much for their horserace mentality, for their first mandate is, "Don't bore the viewing audience." In a medium that thrives on "gotcha" comments like "She's a major league (expletive)," and telegenic visuals like "The Kiss," "Who's ahead?" easily beats out "What are the issues?" One of the functions of political campaigns is to provide fodder for national gossip, which is part of the glue that holds a people together.

However, after the presidential election of 2000, it is clear that we need legal restraints on how television announces election results, because the so-called electoral crisis in Florida was created by irresponsible television reporting. Steven Luxenberg, an editor for the Washington Post, comments: "The premature projection of a Bush victory—by Fox, CNN, NBC, CBS and ABC—had real consequences. . . . It left Bush and the Republicans feeling that Gore was a sore loser who was refusing to concede a legitimate victory."[27] If the networks had exercised restraint, recognizing that Florida law provides for a legal challenge to a count in which the vote differential between the candidates is 1 percent or less, a recount could have been carried out without undue politicization of the courts themselves. "We in the media . . . interrupted, for our own reasons and our own needs, a functioning system that hadn't yet finished its work,"[28] notes Luxenberg. Much of the rancor and revenge that haunt the Bush presidency must be laid at the doorstep of the networks for their irresponsible election coverage, fueled by the horserace mentality and the competition for ratings.

Theological Interpretation

From a theological point of view, news is an activity as well as the product of that activity. It is a creative process of naming the world and making sense out of the infinite number of human experiences in our interaction with ourselves, with other creatures, with creation itself, and with the mystery called God. Motivated partly by adventure and partly by anxiety, journalists bring order from chaos and provide meaning in our lives by this complex process of interpretation. Colin Morris, former head of religious broadcasting for the BBC, notes that the baseline of media news is "a normal, happy, well-adjusted society—in theological terms, God's good creation. . . . News is anything fresh and interesting which disturbs this state of affairs (the bad news) and reinforces it in striking ways (the good news)."[29] News teams examine a vast array of events and issues, select a few of them, frame them, interpret their significance, and then weave them into a narrative that is "reported" as "news."

In a day when some of our best journalists are ashamed of their profession, Colin Morris lifts up journalism as a sacred calling to warn us of dangers and beckon us to courageous and hopeful living amid those dangers. This conception of news is consistent with the movement for "public journalism" that emerged in the 1990s to counter media cynicism. A strategy for advocating an improvement in the quality of news must take into consideration the various factors of production that restrict that quality. These include the control of the media by a few megacorporations, the caution of advertisers, competition (from cable, the World Wide Web, and other networks), audience preference for the dramatic and simplistic, the technological imperative ("If we *can* jazz it up with new power-point gimmicks, we *must* jazz it up), the tyranny of the visual, lack of training in print journalism, and many others.

Resisting Compassion Fatigue: Ironically, the medium that has the power to expand our circle of caring may actually reduce it. The growing isolationism of the American public can be correlated with the decline of international news as well as the sensationalist manner in which such news is reported. Each week, the news serves up a new set of victims who vie with last week's victims for our compassion. These stories explode in our faces without any background or historical context, only to vanish when pictures of a new crisis or catastrophe arrives. The images are designed to shock us and evoke sympathy for the victims—the clincher is usually a close-up of the face of a tearful and anguished soul. If we do not understand the causes or the consequences of these conflicts but must watch a nightly parade of one group of victims after another, followed by a Fixodent or Chrysler ad, we recoil. In response to compassion fatigue, we turn away. This only reinforces the chaos narrative and our feelings of helplessness.

The answer is not less news, but better news. Because the networks are so sensitive to ratings, maybe we have more leverage on shaping the news than we think we have.

TWELVE

The Super Bowl

BIG MONEY, BIG GUYS, AND "THE BIG GUY UPSTAIRS"

> The Super Bowl is the largest shared ritual of the television season, chock full of pageantry, anticipation, struggle, winners and losers, and money—lots of it. But the reinforcing drama is not confined to the gridiron; the best minds of Madison Avenue vie to outdo one another in the commercial breaks. As we consume food and football at parties, we also consume a vision of contemporary life as a zero-sum game between us and them, winners and losers, a far cry from the vision of "the last shall be first."

Several years ago, the cable sports service ESPN ran a print and television campaign promoting the network's NFL football coverage. The campaign centered on an ersatz university called "the University of Bristol" where everything in the curriculum was related to football (ESPN studios and headquarters are located in Bristol, Connecticut). ESPN commentators were listed as "faculty," and newspaper ads provided course descriptions printed much as they would appear in a real college catalog.

One of the courses included was Religion 101, with a course description reading: "This course covers the age-old debate of Church versus Football on Sunday." If the NFL decided to schedule the Super Bowl out of prime time and air it earlier on Sunday, there would not be much of a debate—the clear winner would be the Super Bowl. This is especially true in some areas such as Northern California, where an estimated 3 percent of the population attends church or other religious services on a regular basis. It is highly unlikely that the Super Bowl would move out of prime time, not because the NFL is "church friendly" but because the NFL and television networks airing the game would lose too many advertising dollars.

The Super Bowl has become a national ritual as millions of fans and nonfans alike watch at least part of the big game. Singer Phil Collins, a Super Bowl 2000 halftime performer, said, "I don't understand it all, but I'm always impressed by the event and spectacle." There have been pregame shows as long as seven hours; the pregame show for the 2000 contest was "shortened" to four hours. If the postgame show is included in the package, a viewer can watch over eight hours of continuous Super Bowl programming.

Super Bowl 2000 between the St. Louis Rams and the Tennessee Titans was watched by an estimated 130 million viewers on ABC, with another 650,000 viewers using computers to access ABC's enhanced television format. Nielsen ratings data indicate that 88.4 million viewers watched an average minute of the game. Despite the fact that two small-market teams participated in Super Bowl 2000, viewership was up 3 percent over the 1999 game; 62 percent of the television sets in use were tuned to ABC. No other event attracts so much attention on an annual basis. In an era of "old versus new" media, it was still network television that delivered so many eyeballs to advertisers.

It is well documented that many watch the big game not so much for the game itself but as a reason to party and socialize. Another major reason is for the commercials, which for many years have been better than the game. The *San Francisco Chronicle* reported that the Super Bowl netted $130 million in advertising revenue "in its usual display of consumerism run amok." Depending on which sources you believe, advertisers spent somewhere between $2,200,000 and $3,000,000 for a thirty-second spot.

The Super Bowl, only modestly successful when it started in 1967, did not begin as a national ritual. The first Super Bowl, between the Green Bay Packers and Kansas City Chiefs at the Los Angeles Coliseum, was not a sellout (63,000 of the 93,000 seats were filled). The game was carried by two networks (CBS and NBC) because CBS had the contract for the NFL and NBC had the contract for the AFL (this was before the merger of the AFL and NFL into one professional football league—the NFL), thus splitting the audience and advertising revenue. Within a few years, and especially after the New York Jets upset the Baltimore Colts in 1969, the Super Bowl became an annual megaevent.

Super Bowl 2000 proved to be one of the most exciting games in the series, with the outcome in doubt until the final play (St. Louis won 23–17). An analysis of this game may provide insights as to why the Super Bowl is America's national ritual and a religious event for millions of viewers.

The Super Bowl as Narrative:
The Battle of Two Davids

It may seem strange for some observers to think in terms of narrative for the Super Bowl, because most think of a sports event as action. There are, however, narrative aspects of the Super Bowl or any athletic event as it is covered on television.

This was not always so. During television's early history, coverage of football or any other sports event focused on the action, with very few camera shots taken off the field. Cameras were bulky and had to remain stationary for the most part, limiting the shots of players on the bench or close-ups of fans. Most announcers concentrated on describing the onfield action to the viewer, giving little information on the personal lives of players and coaches or the stories behind the game.

This style of covering games changed in the 1960s with ABC's Monday night football. Don Ohlmeyer, an early producer of the show, felt that viewers would be interested in stories about the players' and coaches' lives and the narrative of the game, not only in the game itself. Another Ohlmeyer objective was to use cameras to make the home viewer feel as if he or she were at the game. This meant having cameras focused not only on the field but also on the stands and benches. These approaches quickly distinguished ABC from other networks in its coverage of football. The game as narrative and the use of cameras for an "in-the-stands" feel transferred to coverage of other sports events, including the Olympics.

Super Bowl 2000 was carried by ABC, and although all networks now use similar approaches in covering sports, the narrative approach is a specialty of the ABC Sports ethos. ABC had at least two themes or plotlines to develop for Super Bowl 2000. The first was that two underdog teams, the St. Louis Rams and the Tennessee Titans, were competing, providing a game with two "Davids" and no "Goliaths." The usual powerhouse teams of the last decade such as Dallas, Denver, Green Bay, and San Francisco had fallen on hard times and were not part of the picture. The other theme was the story of Ram quarterback Kurt Warner, who had come from nowhere to lead his team to the Super Bowl.

The Rams were one of the weaker teams throughout the 1990s and had experienced a losing season in 1998. The team had moved to St. Louis from Los Angeles and had never won a Super Bowl. St. Louis had lost its previous football team (the Cardinals) to Arizona, and no St. Louis team had ever been to the Super Bowl. The coach, sixty-three-year-old Dick Vermeil, was another aspect of the St. Louis story: He had taken a fourteen-year leave from the game and returned to coach the Rams in two less than successful years before the 1999 season. There were numerous rumors about his job security.

The Tennessee Titans (formerly the Houston Oilers) had never played in the Super Bowl in their forty-year history. After moving to Tennessee, they played in three different cities in three years before settling in Nashville. Few pundits expected them to win the AFC championship and make it to the Super Bowl.

If there was a single David figure during Super Bowl 34, it was Ram Kurt Warner, who had been one of the top quarterbacks in the NFL during the 1999 season, coming from nowhere to deliver an all-star performance. Warner had played in the Arena Football League and in Europe for the Amsterdam Admirals. ABC showed video footage of Warner in action for the Admirals on several occasions during the pregame show and the game itself.

Kurt Warner's story was made for Hollywood and could have been called "From Supermarket to Super Bowl" because five years earlier Warner had been a stock clerk in an Iowa supermarket. He was the unknown individual who comes on the scene to lead his team to a victorious season. Viewers wanted to see whether the story was truly "Hollywood": Could he cap it by winning the Super Bowl? In a sense, the Kurt Warner story supported the American myth that through hard work and determination, any individual who tries hard enough can play in the big game.

Kurt Warner is open about his Christian beliefs. He often talks about his faith on the air with reporters before and after games and gives credit to God after victories. In a year of turmoil for the NFL, when two players were charged with murder and some sports talk radio stations were running daily "rap" sheets with which players had committed crimes, Kurt Warner was a welcome relief. He was the poster boy for what the NFL wanted to be.

If Warner was the NFL's poster boy, his wife Brenda was the model NFL player's wife—pretty, petite, pious, and blonde. Brenda Warner is also open about her Christian beliefs and expressed them during the game in an interview with ABC reporter Leslie Visser. Throughout the game, ABC took numerous reaction shots of this attractive, athletic-looking woman dressed in a bright blue pants suit. In this  narrative, she was the woman behind the hero, the football-slinging David.

Warner was an easy "David" for fans to embrace. The biblical David was a poor youngest son who eventually became king. The Israelites identified with the upstart overachiever because they themselves were losers. Americans identify with their own Davids and value underdogs, because each of us has seen ourselves in that role at one time or another.

Then there was the real reason for the game's existence on network television—all those expensive commercials. Commercials supposedly provide "slingshots" for an army of Davids viewing the Super Bowl as to how to conquer the Goliaths of everyday life. The Super Bowl is the prime example of Jeremy Butler's notion that programs exist as filler between commercials.[1] The Big Game provides viewers with a little football in the midst of a sea of commercials.

The Super Bowl as Super Consumerism, or Where Did All Those Dot.com Commercials Come from?

Most viewers acknowledge that they look forward to Super Bowl commercials; for the casual fan, they may be the best reason to watch the game. Before the Super Bowl, sponsors and their advertising agencies offer sneak previews of the spots via newspapers and electronic media, and there is now even a website providing information about Super Bowl spots and when they will be seen during the game. Following the game, there are fan polls and next-day analysis of these polls in *USA Today* and on ABC's *Good Morning America*. Many local television stations invite representatives from advertising agencies to appear on their news or sportscasts to critique the Super Bowl commercials.

How have commercials come to compete with the big game itself for the attention of fans and nonfans alike? As mentioned earlier, the sheer numbers of people watching the game provide a showcase for sponsors and advertisers. In past years, some sponsors such as Masterlock have spent their entire advertising budgets on one or more Super Bowl commercials, while new companies have used the Super Bowl to introduce their products to the public. Many of these commercials contain special effects and sophisticated production values, making them as expensive to produce per minute as a minute of a big-budget theatrical film. Commercials have always been an integral part of the big game, but it was a commercial in the early 1980s introducing Apple's Macintosh computer that intensified the trend toward big-budget, glossy commercials.

The Macintosh commercial featured a 1984 theme, with a large screen projecting the image of a "Big Brother" figure looking down on a crowd of dronelike people in what appears to be a large auditorium. A woman being chased by police runs into the auditorium. She runs in front of the Big Brother screen and hurls a sledgehammer into it, shattering the screen to bits. Advertisers have called the "1984" spot one of the best commercials of all time. It was another example of the David theme of the underdog conquering a Goliath, in this case using a sledgehammer against the system instead of a slingshot.

Not long after this big-budget effort, other sponsors followed with their own superspots, including commercials featuring football-playing beer bottles in "The Bud Bowl" from Budweiser. Commercials featuring computer manipulation and talking animals (Including Budweiser's talking lizards and croaking frogs) have been the Super Bowl norm for the past fifteen years.

The 2000 Super Bowl was the year of the "dot.com commercial." Various computer services and providers were featured, with sixteen dot.com companies buying over half the commercial inventory. Many of these companies were relatively new and had made no profits, yet they were willing to spend most of their advertising budgets on one or two spots during the game. The strategy served two functions: Obviously many viewers watched the game, but there was also the chance to show that these companies were big-time players who could afford to advertise on the Super Bowl. It was a "company you keep" strategy that dot.com sponsors hoped would translate to brand-name recognition and an increase in customers.

Many of the dot.com spots pushed the envelope and were nontraditional in their sales approach. These companies thought that any attention by the viewer was good attention, as sponsors tried to break through the pack for name recognition. One of the most innovative spots was one for E*Trade.com, an online financial service, which featured thirty seconds of a singing chimp. The commercial seemed to make no sense until the tag line: "Well, we just wasted two million bucks. What are you doing with your money?" The spot transformed the high cost of Super Bowl time into a strong message for the viewer (do not throw your money away; invest wisely).

Most of the dot.com commercials, viewed individually, are humorous. On closer examination, however, their real impact may be a collective or gestalt one. When seen together as a montage, these spots give the impression that the technologies are here to stay and can provide us with the good life. There is also an underlying message that if we are not part of the technology bandwagon in the twenty-first century, we will be left behind. As a component of America's civil religion, dot.com technology widens the gulf between the "haves" and "have-nots" of society. How many people in the U.S. population will be left behind because they cannot afford or have no access to expanding technologies?

One non-dot.com spot of note actually featured an advertiser's caricature of God, in a McIlhenny Tabasco Sauce commercial. The spot starts with fiery lightening bolts or meteorites hitting various parts of the earth (cities, satellite tracking dishes, rural areas, even destroying part of Stonehenge). The source of the bolts is not foreign invaders or aliens but what appears to be God (white and male) sitting on a large throne, pouring McIlhenny tabasco sauce on a pizza. God seems to be preoccupied with watching television and does not notice that the sauce misses the pizza and zaps the earth. The message is that McIlhenny's is one hot tabasco sauce.

The context in which the spot was seen could not have been better. Although some viewers in other programming contexts might have been offended by this sponsor's portrayal of God, the timing maximized its impact. The God spot was seen after the halftime show, before the second half of the game, when millions of Americans had just placed pizza orders. The placement was an excellent example of Tony Schwartz's concept of "task orientation" (timing commercials to coincide with specific tasks or times).

> [T]his God is actually subservient to the God of consumerism, who provides a way to satisfy all possible cravings.

Perhaps of greater underlying significance is the way God was portrayed in the commercial. This is not an all-knowing God but one who is oblivious to the fact of his tabasco laser bolts hitting earth. God is seen in human terms as one who can make mistakes and say "Oops!" This picture of God might especially make one feel better if one had not attended church earlier in the day because of the game. This God seems uninterested or uninvolved in the world and its people but instead concentrates on television viewing and snack eating—something viewers can identify with on Super Bowl Sunday. The God of tabasco sauce and the Super Bowl also consumes products like everyone else. Therefore, this God is actually subservient to the God of consumerism, who provides a way to satisfy all possible cravings. The ultimate power is the power of the market, the satisfaction of desires.

Future Super Bowls may see other interpretations of God, more talking animals, and more impressive computer-generated special effects; in any case, the Super Bowl will continue to be a showcase for products and services while making its huge audience even more consumption oriented. What about the stories behind the game and the "filler" needed to maintain audience attention to get to these high-priced commercials? That was no problem for Super Bowl XXXIV because God was not only in a tabasco sauce commercial but also in the game itself.

If God Is for Us, Who Can Be against Us?

The Kurt Warner story was not just about Warner the quarterback, who came from nowhere to lead his team to a championship. As mentioned earlier, he was seen as a model citizen and a poster boy for what the NFL wanted its players to be. Announcer Boomer Esiason reinforced what viewers had already heard when, after Warner's game-winning pass was caught by Isaac Bruce, he said, "The movie continues once more as it's Kurt Warner's dream season."

Kurt and Brenda Warner are open about their Christian beliefs. Before the game, the quarterback had said, "If God is willing, the Rams will win." It appeared that ABC was comfortable with the Warners' open expression of their religious views. The network felt that Kurt and Brenda were major players in this Super Bowl plot. Before doing an in-the-stands interview with Brenda, ABC reporter Leslie Visser called the Warners "one of the sweetest couples in the history of sports."

Brenda responded to one of Visser's typical "How do you feel" questions by saying, "Incredible, unbelievable, and we're just excited to be a part of this and we feel so blessed by God." Visser asked a follow-up question, "What do you think brought him [her husband] here?" Brenda responded, "I think our faith in God has brought him to where he is as a man and he's just been given this ability and he's using it."

ABC's producers and directors made sure that Brenda (the woman behind the man) was visible—there were at least ten cutaway shots of her in the stands during and after the game. This was in comparison to four shots of Titans' quarterback Steve McNair's wife (an interesting ratio in view of the close score of the game). In one shot, McNair's wife was seen praying while the Titans tried to score. In another shot, she was holding her young son and crying while the Titans tried to score a game-winning touchdown in the final seconds.

Kurt Warner's religious beliefs surfaced on several occasions during the game. At one point, when Titans' defensive back Blaine Bishop was seriously injured and lying immobile on the field, sideline reporter Leslie Visser reported, "It was very moving that Kurt Warner went over next to Blaine Bishop and knelt down and prayed." At the end of the game, during the presentation of the Super Bowl trophy to the victorious Rams, Warner said, "First things first; I have to give the praise and glory to my savior up above. Thank you Jesus!"

Following these comments, ABC reporter Mike Terrico tried to attach the period to the Kurt Warner story by asking him, "Five years ago you were stocking supermarket shelves. Now you're an MVP, a Super Bowl MVP. What message does it send to people who have the dream but don't have the guts and courage to follow it?" Warner responded, "I always believed in myself and had a whole bunch of guys who believed in me and as long as I had these guys I was going to give everything I had. And because of these guys and the confidence they had in me, that's why I'm standing here today." In unselfish statements, Warner had lived up to the NFL poster boy image by giving credit to Jesus and his teammates.

This television image of Jesus is of one who stands with the winners like Kurt Warner. Who are the winners? They are the ones who have vanquished their opponents on the field of battle. No wonder winners are thankful or that the media broadcasts their thanks to the nation; everyone knows that winning in football or in life is a reward from God for good morals and hard work. This is a common perception of God with roots in scriptural passages such as Psalm 21, a victory Psalm, wherein King David proclaims:

> "You have given him [the king] his heart's desire, and have not withheld the request of his lips. For you meet him with rich blessings; you set a crown of fine gold on his head. . . . Your hand will find out all your enemies; . . . You will destroy their offspring from the earth, . . . Be exalted, O Lord, in your strength! We will sing and praise your power."

The New Testament God, however, is a God of losers, one better known by those who sing "Amazing Grace," than "We Are the Champions." This God is the one Saint Paul writes about in 2 Corinthians 12 when he mentions his weakness (the thorn in his side) and reports that God has said to him, "'My grace is sufficient for you, for power is made perfect in weakness.' . . . Therefore I am content with weaknesses, insults, hardships, persecutions, and calamities for the sake of Christ; for whenever I am weak, then I am strong." This is not the God celebrated in the Victory Psalms or by winners of football games and advertisers. The game and the commercials sell winning—not suffering—as a means to salvation (unless suffering toughens us up for more winning down the road).

In the final analysis, Super Bowl XXXIV preached popular religion, not biblical religion. 122 million people gathered for some old-fashioned American faith and values. Cab Calloway's line in the film *The Blues Brothers,* addressed to John Belushi and Dan Ackroyd, comes to mind: "You boys could use some churchin' up." Maybe 122 million Americans could use a little "churchin' up" between bites of pizza and gulps of beer during what has become our national ritual, even if it is a "churchin up" that falls short of authentic religion.

The downside may be that viewers saw only one faith story—the easiest one for ABC to use in establishing its game narrative. What about the other players with more compelling stories, who have overcome much greater obstacles than Kurt Warner? What about the players who have survived the mean streets of their inner cities and now contribute to their communities? Not until Titans player Blaine Bishop was injured, lying prone on the field for millions to see, did we hear from ABC field reporter Lynn Swan that Swan had met Bishop at a Big Brothers' function, that Bishop was very involved in the Big Brothers organization, and that Bishop had come from a single-parent home.

Perhaps the problem was that ABC went with only the easy story while there were so many others to be told. Then again, the Warner story is a great one and will probably be seen at some later date as a made-for-television Sunday night movie (produced by ABC's parent company Disney) because it is another opportunity for television to take the easy way out.

Super Bowl XXXIV will be remembered for a variety of reasons, including reinforcing the concept of Super Bowl as ritual. The Super Bowl will continue to be the national ritual in the new millennium—that is, until something bigger comes along. However, God tossing tabasco lightning bolts from above is pretty big stuff.

How Now Super Bowl Cow?
Postscript on Censoring Controversial
Commercials on the 2001 Super Bowl

Commercial controversy reigned during the weeks preceding the 2001 Super Bowl when CBS refused to carry an antileather public service announcement produced by People for the Ethical Treatment of Animals (PETA). PETA was ready to pay CBS $2.5 million for airtime during the Super Bowl to show a spot featuring singing cows lamenting that they would soon become leather goods. The singing cows were originally produced as part of an Oscar-winning musical short in the 1940s. The lyrics were redubbed so that the cows in the PETA spot were singing:

> I'm a steer
> And they're steering you wrong.
> Listen now
> (I'm a cow)
> 'Cus I don't have long.
> Our sweet backsides
> Would like to stay together
> We don't want to be your leather.
> Won't you show me some love?
> Don't you make me kid gloves
> Or a jacket or a shoe
> 'Cuz my skin ain't for you.
> Do I make myself clear?
> Keep your hands off my rear!

CBS claimed that it does not air advocacy ads, to which PETA spokeswoman Lisa Lange cried, "Bull! Every commercial for leathers shoes, belts, and sports balls that CBS runs is an advocacy ad. They advocate killing beautiful animals to make ugly things."[2]

In a later interview, Lange said she thought that CBS killed the spot because it wanted to pander to other Super Bowl advertisers such as fast food restaurants and department stores selling beef and leather goods. The spot would look out of place among the other consumer-oriented sponsors.[3]

To add insult to bovine injury, the footballs used for the Super Bowl are cowhide (it takes 3,000 cows to keep the NFL in business for a season.)

PART IV

The Commerce of Television
What You Should Really
Be Concerned About

Follow the money.

—*"Deep Throat"*

In the movie *All the President's Men*, which dramatizes the Watergate scandal that brought down the Nixon presidency, Bob Woodward, the aggressive reporter for the *Washington Post* (played by a youthful Robert Redford), descends again into a dark underground garage to query "Deep Throat," the enigmatic inside source on White House corruption. Woodward wants to know how high up in the Nixon inner circle the scandal goes and how to find evidence of high-level culpability. "Deep Throat" provides only a method: "Follow the money. . . . Follow the money." Part IV follows the advice of "Deep Throat." Chapter 13 explores the world of commercials, the fuel that fires the engines of the television industry. Chapter 14 examines the industry itself.

Beginning in 2000, the networks introduced a number of so-called reality-based programs to titillate viewers and improve ratings. ABC led off with *Who Wants to Be a Millionaire*; Fox upped the ante with *Who Wants to Marry a Millionaire* (which bombed after the bride of the on-air wedding discovered that the millionaire husband provided by Fox had a record of spouse abuse); CBS countered with a ratings winner, *Survivor!* NBC broke ranks and resurrected the quiz show *Twenty-One*. The original version in the 1950s was shown to be rigged, which caused widespread disillusionment with the industry, and the new version of *Twenty-One* did not last long. ABC reasserted itself with *Mole*, an adventure elimination contest with a $1 million prize; then Fox attempted a comeback with the all-time low-market *Temptation Island* (the romantic equivalent of the WWF extravaganza *Smackdown!*), which turns the audience into Peeping Toms and makes a virtue of sexual infidelity.

These cheaply produced shows share not some exotic form of reality—they are as contrived as any fictional drama or sitcom—but rather bottom-line programming, the relentless quest for higher ratings and a larger audience share so that the networks can charge advertisers higher rates.

In the Interlude, we expressed concern about the gratuitous sex and violence on television and indicated that in our view sex and violence are symptoms of a greater problem: the laws governing the industry and the economic incentives it lives by, as well as audience demand for more and more titillation and an ever upwardly spiraling adrenaline rush. If concerned citizens are to tackle the "more-is-better" gone-mad character of American culture that television fuels, we must start with an understanding of what makes advertisers and networks tick. In short, we must "follow the money."

THIRTEEN

Commercials,
the Real Stars of the Airways

Never have commercials been more creative and well produced, and never have they sought more strikingly to appeal
to our emotions, working to create "wants" and turn them into
"needs." We think the programs are for us, when in reality we,
the viewers, have been packaged for the advertisers. Jammed
into sixty seconds or less are all our desires and fears fed back
to us in hopes that we will continue to choose material afflu-
ence over spiritual wealth.

Many media observers call them the real stars of the television airways.
Some of the best creative minds in the industry create them, and they can
cost as much per minute to produce as a feature-length film. For the
American public, they act as short sermons or homilies on how we should
live our lives and become better people through our purchases.

One could argue that television commercials *are* television and the reason for the medium's existence. Television scholar Jeremy Butler says: "To
the television industry programs are just filler, a necessary inconvenience
interrupting the true function of television: broadcasting commercials."[1]

Americans have accepted advertisements from a variety of sources, with
television providing perhaps the greatest number of persuasive messages.
Research by the Annenberg School of Communication at the University of
Pennsylvania indicates that the current generation of children will each see
over 350,000 commercials by the time they become adults.[2]

Advertisements are ubiquitous, in increasing numbers, even creeping
into live events. Roger Smitter, a professor of communication at North
Central College in Illinois, was surprised when he attended a Chicago
White Sox game in the early 1990s and the public address announcer
intoned, "And now here's the seventh inning stretch, brought to you by
Budweiser, The King of Beers."[3] Smitter had never considered that this
baseball ritual would be "brought to you" by any sponsor. Today, such a
message is almost universally accepted, and few see it as unusual.

How did the television industry arrive at its commercial-driven state?
We can trace the roots of commercialism to early radio.

A Brief History of Broadcast Commercials

In many ways, the fate of the broadcast industry was determined on August 28, 1922. Radio was becoming more commonplace in people's homes, and according to Ken Burns's PBS documentary *Empire of the Air*, one-third of all money spent by families on furniture in the early 1920s was spent on radios. Once people made their purchases, they were more willing to give up their phonographs, beds, or bathtubs than part with their radios. Despite its rapid growth in the 1920s, radio was not initially perceived as a means of selling products or services, and there were no commercials in radio's first few years.

Radio stations were vehicles for selling radios and, in effect, were one continuous commercial for the companies producing them. Early stations were owned by Westinghouse, General Electric, other radio manufacturers, or newspapers. Radio manufacturers thought that if they provided programming on their stations more people would purchase radio sets to hear what was being offered. Newspaper publishers believed radio would promote their publications if they read portions of news stories over the airways and then urged the audience to find out more about the stories by purchasing the daily paper.

In 1922, just two years after radios became common, it was obvious there would have to be additional revenue streams for the new medium to survive. After a critical mass had purchased radios, manufacturers experienced declining profits, while newspapers soon discovered radio to be a rival medium rather than a promotional tool.

The broadcast industry started doing business differently on that fateful August 28, 1922, when New York station WEAF aired what most broadcast historians believe to be the first radio commercial—a ten-minute talk about a new apartment complex in Jackson Heights on Long Island. The commercial cost about $50 and led to over $20,000 in apartment sales. The die had been cast; radio ads were here to stay. Persuasive techniques for commercials evolved slowly, at first taking an indirect tone in selling but later employing jingles and emotional appeals. Soon companies were sponsoring entire shows such as the *A&P Gypsies* and the *Cliquot Club Eskimos*. These sponsors had control over their programs with regard to hiring talent and other production personnel, scripts, and program content; in fact, the sponsors had more control over these programs than the radio networks did.

By 1948, three years after the end of World War II, there were enough purchases of television sets to reach critical mass for advertisers, and commercials made the transition to television. Products or companies were still, in most cases, the sole sponsors of programs, receiving lead billing over the show's star or talent (e. g., *Texaco Star Theater with Milton Berle*).

Sponsorship of programs changed in the mid-1950s as NBC's legendary programming executive Sylvester "Pat" Weaver (who developed *The Today Show* and *The Tonight Show*) created the concept of the "alternate sponsor" so that commercial time could be sold to more than one company. The alternate sponsor strategy took control away from individual sponsors and gave it to the networks.

Some programs, particularly quiz shows, continued to have a single sponsor. In the late 1950s, a contestant who was asked to deliberately lose a quiz show blew the whistle. News reporters started digging and discovered that many of the popular prime-time quiz shows such as *Twenty-One* and *$64,000 Question* had been rigged to allow certain popular contestants to win money, while eliminating less popular or unattractive contestants. Sponsors had insisted on rigging these programs in pursuit of higher ratings so that they could present their products to larger audiences. The quiz show scandals were a major blow to single-program sponsorship; most programs soon transferred to the alternate sponsor concept. Aside from the business implications for the television industry, there were social costs as well. Some historians consider the quiz show scandals to have been the end of innocence for the American public; people no longer believed everything they saw on television.

Early television commercials were based more on logical than on emotional appeals, attempting to give viewers factual reasons for purchasing products. Car commercials emphasized horsepower, engine size, leg room. Sponsors began taking a different approach in the 1960s, thinking more in terms of visual impact and emotional appeal. Commercials now appealed to feelings instead of logic and in many cases promoted buying a product to become a member of a certain group (e.g., "The Pepsi Generation"). Advertisers made a pitch to link buyers' identity with the car they chose to drive or the cola they chose to drink.

During the next forty years, brand names became more important for the public. During the 1980s, research conducted by Grey Advertising Agency identified a new group labeled "the Ultra Consumers:" people in the twenty-five-to-thirty-five age group who wanted premium brands and were not afraid to pay premium prices. These Ultra Consumers were for the most part career-oriented young urban professionals or "yuppies," whose buying habits have influenced advertisers into the twenty-first century.[4]

Consumers not only purchased certain popular brands, but also wore clothing and shoes prominently displaying the brand (e.g., Nike, Tommy Hilfiger). In most cases, consumers paid premium prices for the privilege of becoming walking billboards for the product.

Commercials also increased in quality and eventually became as entertaining as some programs. Cable services such as the Home Shopping Network satisfied those wanting the convenience of purchasing products from their couches at home. In the early 1980s, the FCC rescinded regulations restricting "program-length" commercials, and by the mid-1980s, television stations were airing "infomercials." Many infomercials advertised products of questionable quality such as astrology charts, exercise equipment, and kitchen gadgets and often aired late at night or on weekends. Despite questions of credibility, some major manufacturers such as GM began using them to introduce new product lines like Saturn cars.

Perhaps the best example of a commercial-entertainment blend over the past twenty years is MTV. Founded in the early 1980s, MTV redefined the music and later the theatrical film industry by showing music video performances of music by popular and, in some cases, unknown groups and solo artists. One of the early examples of powerful MTV influence was the case of the then-new rock band Duran Duran. The group began producing videos with vivid visual imagery to promote their album *Rio*, and sales data in Dallas indicated that the record sold off the shelves in stores in half of the city—wherever the neighborhoods were wired for cable. Other groups and solo acts soon followed Duran Duran's example, and MTV become a major marketing tool for new music releases, as well as defining fashion for young people and sometimes determining which films succeeded at the box office. Young viewers longed for the fashions worn by the bands and solo artists seen on the network. Soon, it became obligatory for theatrical films to have at least one musical segment that could be "lifted" for use as a video on MTV to promote the film. MTV later developed other program segments, including music news programs and cartoons, but it continued to be the ultimate twenty-four-hour commercial for music, fashion, and numerous youth-oriented products.

Advertisers developed new approaches in the 1990s as viewers began deciding whether or not to watch commercials. Remote control units, VCRs, and various new high tech products brought terms such as "zipping," "zapping," and "channel surfing" into viewers' vocabularies. Advertising agencies discovered that traditional approaches to television commercials did not succeed with a media-savvy population.

Original music scores in commercials soon gave way to familiar music (sometimes with different lyrics to promote the product), prices appeared on products, and shock techniques were used by more sponsors. The so-called dot.com companies (companies offering Internet services or goods via the Internet) began using "old media" such as television to establish name brand identity through what some in the advertising industry called *ad noir*.

The 2000 Super Bowl featured over a dozen different dot.com companies spending between $2 and $3 million per thirty-second spot for one or more ads. One commercial that almost made the Super Bowl lineup but was seen instead on other programs throughout January and February 2000 was a spot for ecampus.com—an Internet company selling college textbooks and other merchandise at discount prices. The spot showed several young people in what appeared to be an arctic environment but was really a long line at the college bookstore. The spot suggested that the students had been in line so long that they were contemplating cannibalism: eating one of their friends who had passed out in line.

Ad analysts judged a number of "in your face" spots that did make the Super Bowl lineup to be some of the most memorable advertisements of the year, especially when compared with traditional ads for soft drinks, beer, and food products. For dot.com companies, establishing name identity in any way possible was the major goal of their early commercial spots.

Advertisers of various products, influenced by increased numbers in Generation X—those born after 1966—and by various racial and ethnic groups, have also taken more of a narrowcasting or group-specific approach to commercials. It is no longer a "one size fits all" strategy; commercials feature young people and people of color in spots specifically designed for these groups, airing on the stations, cable, and satellite services they are most likely to watch.

The marriage of Internet and video technologies is producing a new form of advertising called "discovery advertising," which extends and builds on some of the approaches seen on MTV. Discovery advertising is aimed at Generation Y—those who are teenagers in the early years of the twenty-first century. For this group, hype and overt persuasive appeals are out, and discovering the product on one's own is in. Young people "discover" products such as clothing and shoes by seeing them worn by members of a music group or characters in an interactive drama.

In some ways, this is an earlier form of appeal because it is similar to what sponsors did in the first days of television by having their products visible not only during commercials but during the program itself; for example, if Ford Motor Company was the sponsor of a program, all the characters in that program drove Fords.

Companies such as the now defunct Digital Entertainment Network develop video programs for the Internet that aim to reach specific racial and ethnic and interests groups (including a Christian-oriented program called *Redemption High*). These interactive dramas have the potential to sell goods and services to Asian, Hispanic, Latino, and other groups that are not served by traditional prime-time television programming.

Television advertising continues to evolve because of changing audiences and technologies. The concept of the "teleputer" (the convergence of video and the personal computer) is thought to be only a few years away. Although television commercials may seem to change dramatically in their persuasive techniques, many of the fundamental approaches may be traced to Tony Schwartz, a media theorist who in the 1960s changed much of the previous thinking about how television audiences process persuasive messages.

Tony Schwartz, High Priest
of Television Advertising

Tony Schwartz was one of the first media professionals to develop theories of how to construct messages for television. His books, *The Responsive Chord* and *Media: The Second God*, which altered the way most sponsors choose to present their messages, have been used to create persuasive messages ranging from presidential campaign commercials to spots for laundry detergent. Schwartz's "Daisy Spot" during the Johnson versus Goldwater campaign of 1964 is perhaps the most famous political ad of all time.

This spot targets public anxiety about Barry Goldwater's statements on the use of tactical nuclear weapons. It shows a young girl counting to ten while pulling the petals from a daisy. The camera zooms into one eye of the girl, stopping with a freeze frame while her voice is replaced by a male voice counting down a missile launch. Next comes an explosion and a mushroom cloud, followed by a voiceover of President Lyndon Johnson saying, "These are the stakes: to make a world where all God's children can live. We must learn to love each other, or we must die." The announcer's voiceover follows with, "Vote for Lyndon Johnson November Third. The stakes are too high to stay at home."

This Johnson campaign spot employs one of Schwartz's key concepts: evoked recall or resonance. Evoked recall or resonance works on the principle that it is easier to get a message out of viewers than to put one in. Evoked recall depends on the various experiences, emotions, and memories that a viewer has accumulated during a lifetime. The trick for getting the desirable response from someone is to cue these accumulated data in some way. The Johnson spot presented cues associated with the fear of nuclear war and linked them with Goldwater's statements. Interestingly, Goldwater was never mentioned by name in the spot; it was the viewer who made the connection.

Schwartz believes that if one surrounds the viewer with enough experiential stimuli, there is a strong possibility that he or she will respond in the desired manner (buying the product, voting for the candidate). An effective spot is much like a Rorschach test; the viewer is presented with enough information to fill in the blanks. In short, the "Daisy Spot" provided enough stimuli to cause what Schwartz would call a state of disease in the viewer.

Schwartz deconstructs the overall commercial message into several components: the verbal script, the auditory script, and the sight script (which includes the package, visual transition devices, and visual experiences).

Daisy Redux

A Texas-based nonprofit organization, Aretino Industries, turned the tables on Vice President Gore and bombed him with a remake of "The Daisy Spot" during the 2000 presidential election. The spot was almost identical to the original, featuring a little girl counting while picking petals from a daisy. Her voice was replaced by a countdown of a missile, followed by a nuclear explosion. The commercial then stated that because the Clinton-Gore administration had "sold" the nation's security "to Communist Red China in exchange for campaign contributions, China has the ability to threaten our homes with long-range nuclear warheads."

Kathleen Hall Jamieson, dean of the Annenberg School of Communication, stated: "It's an ad that is so inflammatory that it gets free news access." Tony Schwartz, creator of the original "Daisy Spot," said, "This troubles me. They are a bunch of thieves. It's a perversion of my ad."[5]

The Verbal Script: The verbal script contains the actual words spoken or appearing on the screen during a commercial. This script may contain numbers, names, or logic-based information. The verbal script is often lost on today's audiences because the emotional imagery contained in the spot is so strong. We may not hear that a particular make of car gets thirty miles to the gallon because of involvement with the music or with the visual imagery. Many current commercials de-emphasize the verbal script. This is consistent with Schwartz's notion of using sound to create emotion and giving precedence to the sound script.

The Sound Script: The old advertising maxim, "Sell the sizzle, not the steak," describes the basis of the sound script: the audio portion of a commercial that contains sounds other than words. These sounds—a crackling fire, dogs barking, crickets chirping—evoke emotional responses in us. The musical score is also a part of the sound script.

An excellent example of a commercial highly dependent on the sound script is a spot produced in the 1980s for Pepsi-Cola. The setting is a crowded beach on a hot sunny day. A van pulls up on the beach, and its driver opens the rear doors and sets up a microphone and public address system. He then opens and pours a can of Pepsi next to the microphone as the sound is amplified for all on the beach to hear. Hearing the sound, the sunbathers move toward the van, looking like reversed lemmings moving *away from* the ocean. The van driver has now set up a Pepsi stand, and the sunbathers mob the stand and try to buy cans of Pepsi. The only verbal script is "Pepsi, the choice of a new generation." The spot suggests, primarily through sound, that the sunbathers (and in effect the audience) may be thirsty and that Pepsi can quench their thirst. The response of buying Pepsi comes from the audience instead of being put into them.

The Sight Script: The sight script or visual component of a commercial contains three elements: the package, visual experiences, and transitional devices. Successful producers and writers attempt to develop each element when making big-budget commercials.

The package is a container for the product: a can, box, body design for a car, or anything that "holds" the product. Design and color are obviously important features contributing to an attractive package and persuading consumers to buy a particular product. The golden color of a Coors beer can with a picture of a waterfall on the front suggests outdoor recreation. The cleaning product Janitor in a Drum uses a round, drum-shaped container to suggest an industrial-strength cleaner stronger than competing products.

Visual experiences are another element of Schwartz's sight script. These images usually elicit some emotional response from the viewer, such as a winding highway with hills on one side of the road and ocean on the other side, snow-covered mountains, or serene lakes. As mentioned earlier, automobile commercials are excellent examples of emphasis on the emotional powers of the sight script. Today's automobile spots are far more experiential in nature than earlier ones, using Schwartz's concept that if the product has enough positive stimuli or experiences, the consumer is more likely to buy it.

Schwartz also includes transitional devices such as takes (straight cuts or edits), dissolves (the gradual transition from one shot to another), and fades (the picture appearing up from or proceeding to black). The forty-sixty principle is also used in big-budget commercials: There are usually at least forty edits during a sixty-second commercial. The commercial for First Union Bank analyzed later in this chapter exceeds this ratio, with some shots being only fractions of seconds and some of the imagery not visible unless the spot is viewed in slow-speed search mode.

Schwartz's theory of evoked recall and his various script elements provide a framework for analyzing commercials, allowing viewers to see them in a different manner. When joined with the elements of fields-of-view analysis (see the Introduction and Appendices A and B), these principles become a new set of "eyeglasses" for determining what persuasive techniques are used and whether they are effective. The following example of a commercial for First Union Bank demonstrates how viewers can analyze and interpret television commercials.

Moving Mountains and Money: An Examination of a First Union Bank Commercial

"This is a world only a few know well," states the announcer for the First Union Bank commercial as viewers see a zoom-in shot of the planet earth with a dollar sign superimposed on the ocean. From this point on, we realize that this is not a "warm and fuzzy" spot for another financial institution but one that portrays a financial world of confusion where life savings can be lost. Images ranging from an abyss to an unsavory carnival atmosphere emphasize this notion. The central theme is that we could lose our security, but First Union is there to protect our future by leading us through the uncertainties of the financial world.

This ad, produced by Hal Rinney and Associates of San Francisco, Publis Advertising Agency of Paris, and Industrial Light and Magic of Marin County, California (ILM), was one of the most heralded commercials of the late 1990s. Rinney, Publis, and ILM created it for First Union, the nation's sixth largest bank, with messages counter to those presented by most other financial institutions. In the October 4th, 1998, edition of the San Francisco Examiner, First Union's chairman and CEO Ed Crutchfield said that he was "through with warm and fuzzy images and conservative and comforting advertising."[6] What Crutchfield got from the companies involved with the commercial was anything but "warm and fuzzy." Viewers were presented with a tumultuous financial world and something of a religious experience during the commercial's last twenty seconds. The spot is a homily providing both problem and solution in sixty seconds.

Overview of the Commercial

As we said, the ad begins with a shot from outer space zooming in on the planet earth. Viewers see a dollar sign superimposed on an ocean. The next sequence shows a financial district with a maze of roads and passageways jammed with frenzied people and cars. At the district's street level, people—presumably stockbrokers and financial workers—hold signs and look to buy or sell products. On this chaotic financial street, there appears to be no clear sense of direction; one person jumping from a ledge is saved by a large golden parachute.

In the next major sequence, people at street level run to a place labeled "Money Market," which looks like a carnival, complete with rides and bright neon lights. Despite the bright lights at its entrance, this is a dark place with more chaos and turmoil. The money market carnival features a rapidly spinning merry-go-round and barkers selling mutual funds from cigarette trays.

Following the carnival scenes, we see a brief sequence of high angle shots looking up at the financial landscape and focusing on institutions of "mountainous size ruling the land." The mood and imagery continue to be dark. The viewer has been confronted with cognitive dissonance as to how to solve financial fears and uncertainties.

The commercial's mood changes dramatically at the forty-second point and begins to resolve in religious imagery. One financial worker suddenly looks skyward and sees a tower of light—The First Union Bank Building. As one shot dissolves to another, we see the tower in a city of light with shining buildings pointing toward the heavens. This scene evokes John's vision of "a new heaven and a new earth . . . the holy city, the new Jerusalem, coming down out of heaven from God" (Revelation 21:1–2). The announcer concludes by saying, "Come to the mountain known as First Union; . . . or the mountain will come to you."

Analysis of the Commercial

Sequence 1—The Sight Script: There is no package or container for First Union Bank, but there is the imagery of the shining bank building later in the spot. The commercial is heavily dependent on visual experiences evoking emotional responses. There are rapid edits and nearly subliminal images, especially during the first forty seconds.

After the initial shot of earth from space, we see the high-angle shot of the various streets and levels of the financial district with numerous businesspeople. All the businesspeople visible on the screen appear to be white males, which reinforces the stereotype of Wall Street as a "man's world."

The overall visual tone of the first few seconds is dark. We have played this spot for various church and media literacy groups; the beginning of the commercial often reminds viewers of the Fritz Lang movie *Metropolis* or Tim Burton's *Batman*. Viewers feel unease and uncertainty almost immediately. This feeling is intensified during a street-level shot of a financial worker who falls and cracks his head open on the street. When his head cracks open, money spills out, as from a broken piggy bank. There are other shots of businesspeople, some wearing what appear to be cardboard signs with words such as "Stock tips," similar to signs carried by homeless people on city streets. The attire of the businesspeople is not 1990s style but instead suggestive of styles worn in the 1920s (one may note the similarities when comparing this commercial with photographs and films of the Wall Street crash of 1929).

Next is a montage of street signs. At first glance, they could be mistaken for typical signs such as "Do Not Enter" and "Yield"; however, on closer examination, the signs show financial terms such as "No Load Zone" and "No Yield." During this sign montage, there is an image intercut of a person jumping off a bridge in what appears to be a suicide attempt. In normal speed, the image is barely visible because it is intercut so quickly, lasting less than half a second and bordering on the subliminal.

The pace of the commercial accelerates as viewers come down the street with its rapidly moving people and objects. This is no ordinary street. Along with fast-moving city traffic, the viewer sees a large coin rolling down the street and a giant piggy bank flying overhead. The final image in this sequence moves to a higher level when a businessman jumps off a ledge and is saved at the last moment by a large golden parachute.

Sequence 1—The Verbal Script: The First Union spot uses a minimum of words in the voiceover. It starts with the words "This is a world only a few know well" during the opening shots and then adds "a world of risk and uncertainty" as the broker's head breaks like a piggy bank on the street. The montage of street signs follows in the seconds after these words.

As the commercial progresses to the street scene with fast cars, rolling coins, and other images, the voiceover continues, "Where the roads can take you to success and prosperity or sometimes to nowhere at all." The final words, "to no where at all," coincide with the person jumping off the ledge and saved by the golden parachute.

Sequence 1—The Auditory Script: The audio includes dissonant string and brass instruments in a minor chord fanfare. When the man's head hits the street and money comes pouring out, there is a sound effect of breaking glass (emphasized by a production technique known as "sound sweetening"). The mood of the music continues through the point where we see the person jumping with the golden parachute.

Sequence 2—The Sight Script: Following the city street traffic shots and the parachute jump, we see businesspeople running to what looks like a carnival. The overall visual mood of the commercial turns darker in tone. At the top of the entrance to the carnival is a brightly lighted sign that reads "Money Market." The carnival is a place of rapid motion with dark and unsavory imagery as viewers  see a fire-eater and then a whirling merry-go-round.

The merry-go-round is rich with imagery. Invisible to the viewer's naked eye because of the rapid spinning is the sign at the top of the merry-go-round, which reads "Money-Go-Round." This is a borderline subliminal image because we must videotape the commercial and view it in the search or freeze-frame mode to see these words. The animals on the merry-go-round spin rapidly, but on closer examination we see only bulls and bears—an obvious reference to the stock market.

During another near-subliminal moment, one of the bears is positioned in such a way that its jaws pass over a background sign with the word "alive," suggesting that one could be "eaten alive" by a bear stock market.

Other images in the "Money Market" carnival are a person selling mutual funds from what looks like a cigarette tray and a fortune-teller giving financial advice. Viewers are then taken outside the carnival to the financial world, where there are dark towers of mountainous size. Suddenly, a person working in one of the towers looks out a window and sees a light as reflected sunlight appears on his face. This is the transition shot from the problem portion of the commercial to the resolution and the final sequence.

Sequence 2—The Verbal Script: The voiceover says, "This is the financial world," as people are seen running toward the "Money Market" carnival. Following these words, only sound effects and music are heard until the dark towering financial institutions appear.

At this point, the voiceover goes on, "For decades banks and investment firms of mountainous size have ruled the land." When sunlight illuminates the face of the businessman, the voiceover continues, "Yet high above the horizon another mountain has risen."

Sequence 2—The Auditory Script: Music again is a key function of the auditory script. There is an ominous full-orchestra crescendo and chorus during the carnival shots and the shots of the dark towers. There is also sound sweetening of the fire-eater exhaling fire, which sounds like a blow torch. The music changes in tone and becomes more melodic when the businessman looks up and "sees the light."

Sequence 3—The Sight Script: A change from darkness to light occurs as sunlit towers pointing to the heavens appear. Some of the buildings are shaped like ancient ziggurats and have arrows at their tops. The details on the sides of the buildings also have arrows. One may form the impression that these are not only financial institutions but also holy shrines.

The last thing the viewers see is a full screen of "First Union Bank," the only time the product name is on the screen.

Sequence 3—The Verbal Script: This portion of the commercial contains audio with some factual information and logical appeals. Viewers hear, "A mountain called First Union, with sixteen million customers; the nation's eighth largest brokerage and sixth largest bank." This is the only time during the commercial that quantifiable information is given.

The final voiceover says, "For a new perspective on the financial world, come to the mountain called First Union; . . . or if you prefer, the mountain will come to you." This is a double-edged message because the mountain may come to you for the sake of convenience or may overwhelm you.

Sequence 3—The Auditory Script: The music swells when the shining towers appear; then it concludes with a bright fanfare. There are no sound effects at this point as the music and voiceover carry the soundtrack.

Final Analysis: The First Union Bank commercial began airing in late September 1998, during a time of stock market uncertainly. The market had been affected by recent financial problems in Asia and had plunged after a period of sustained growth.

September and October are traditionally seen as down months for the stock market. Many investors recall October as the month of the crash of 1929. The timing for the initial airing of this commercial was excellent, once again illustrating another Schwartz concept—a task-oriented approach (matching a product and its message with the time of year). Viewers watching the first sequence can make the connection between the crash of 1929 and the street scenes, especially when looking at the attire of the businessmen. There is also the suggestion of death through suicide as two men jump from high places as some investors did in 1929.

Nothing in the commercial explicitly mentions a stock market crash, but there are references to the uncertainty of the financial world; seeds of doubt are sown, and viewers make the connection. Schwartz's evoked recall is at work here as enough stimuli have been provided to form conclusions. Viewers experience anxiety about their financial future and are even presented with the possibility of death.

The problem intensifies during the "Money Market" carnival sequence because not only is one's financial future in doubt, but he or she may have to deal with less-than-credible characters in an environment that promotes taking chances. Even a carnival ride as innocent as a merry-go-round is transformed into a "money-go-round" complete with horned bulls and sharp-toothed bears as the ride's animals. Steve Beck, an Industrial Light and Magic visual artist who helped create this commercial, said, "This is the nightmare your wallet has, the insecurities and paranoia your checkbook has. It's an uneasy place; everything about it is daunting and intimidating. It keeps hitting you with these images and it stops and makes you look at it."[7]

The final sequence featuring towers of light provides the only logical information about the bank and brokerage size, but the imagery of this sequence and the entire commercial is so strong that many viewers may miss the logical appeal. There may be repeated viewings before viewers process the logic of why they should become customers of First Union.

The images of light during the final one-third of the commercial may act as a relief and release for viewers because the images of darkness have been so strong during the first forty seconds. The rhetorical powers of light and darkness are chronicled in a classic article by Michael Osborn:

> Light (and the day) relates to the fundamental struggle for survival and development. Light is the condition for sight, the most essential of man's sensory attachments to the world around him. With light and sight one is informed of his environment, can escape its dangers, can take advantage of its rewards, and can even exert some influence over its nature. . . .
>
> In utter contrast is darkness (and the night) bringing fear of the unknown, discouraging sight, making one ignorant of his environment—vulnerable to its dangers and blind to its rewards. One is reduced to a helpless state, no longer able to control the world about him. Finally, darkness is cold, suggesting stagnation and thoughts of the grave.[8]

One concludes from Osborn's remarks that light and darkness are powerful metaphors, and after watching the First Union commercial those who walk in darkness have seen a great light. They have also been to the mountain; perhaps the mountain is coming to them.

Responding to Commercials

At times it may seem impossible to resist the persuasive messages delivered by big-budget television commercials. Betsy Taylor, one of the founders of the Center for a New American Dream (a group promoting less conspicuous consumption), was quoted in the *Washington Post* as saying, "My God, we're up against an advertising industry that, according to *Business Week*, is in your face 3,000 times a day. It's entirely rational to despair of overcoming this."[9]

What can churches, social justice groups, and other interested individuals do in resisting the influence of television commercials? There must be a recognition of the powerful forces behind commercial production and the fact that commercials are the reason for television stations, networks, and cable services to be on air (of course, with the exception of PBS stations). Television programs serve as links guiding viewers to commercials. This awareness may assist viewers in developing a more critical perspective.

Using the approaches presented in this chapter and book, viewers can help religious and civic groups in analyzing and interpreting television commercials. Many resources are available to develop these skills, and numerous organizations are engaged in media literacy, attempting to raise awareness about consumerism gone amuck. Two resources, "Affluenza," and "Escape from Affluenza," are PBS specials produced by KCST in Seattle and Oregon Public Television, which have developed a cult following throughout the country as more viewers see the videos in church and civic-minded social justice groups.

These programs argue that many Americans suffer from "an unhappy condition of overload, debt anxiety, and waste resulting from the dogged pursuit of more." This claim has impressive support, they maintain: " On average we shop six hours a week and spend only forty minutes playing with our children. . . . In 1996 more Americans declared personal bankruptcy than graduated from college. . . . Since 1950, Americans alone have used more resources than everyone who ever lived before them."

Both "Affluenza" and "Escape from Affluenza" promote personal stewardship and evaluation of how and why one purchases goods and services. Other resources are provided by groups such as Vancouver's countercultural media literacy advocate, Adbusters, which attempts to increase public awareness of the influence of advertising and society by producing videotapes and publishing a monthly magazine.

Groups such as the Center for a New American Dream (CNAD) assist individuals in their attempts to change attitudes and behaviors about personal spending. CNAD has developed print materials and a website dealing with topics such as creating a personal inventory of goods, better personal budgeting, and having a simpler Christmas (www.newdream.org). Connections between secular groups and churches may provide a synergy for development of media literacy programs. (Addresses and websites for these organizations appear in the resources section at the end of this book.)

Although group efforts can provide information and resources, the ultimate choices about purchases after viewing commercials are individual ones. In his best-selling book *Tuesdays with Morrie*, sportswriter and radio host Mitch Albon writes about the afternoons he spent with a beloved, terminally ill former college professor, Morrie Schwartz, who now teaches Albon "lessons in life."

In the chapter "We Talk about Money," Schwartz tells Albon, "There is a big confusion in this country over what we want versus what we need. You need food, you *want* an ice cream sundae. You have to be honest with yourself. You don't *need* the latest sports car, you don't *need* the biggest house."

There is an opportunity for churches, seminaries, and other entities to assist in redefining the culture in the twenty-first century through teaching greater awareness of how the public is persuaded through television advertising. Television is selling numerous hot fudge sundaes, and the American public appears to be eating too many of them.

FOURTEEN

The Business behind the Box

"I'M MAD AS HELL" REVISITED IN THE NEW MILLENNIUM

The world is a business, Mr. Beale. It has been since man crawled out of the slime.
—*Arthur Jensen to Howard Beale in the movie* Network, *1976*

Our old television menu now includes broadcast, cable, satellite, and the Internet—an ever-increasing number of channels created and managed by an ever-decreasing number of corporations whose primary "gospel" is "buy, buy, buy." Religious communities have focused most of their criticism on gratuitous sex and violence on television. Consumerism and corporate dominance pose equal if not greater problems for spiritual life, cultural vitality, and democratic values.

The 1976 classic film *Network* is often remembered for the quotation, "I'm as mad as hell and I'm not going to take it anymore," expressing public outrage at the degeneration of news into infotainment. Perhaps the most prophetic statement in the movie, however, is the quotation above from the network CEO Arthur Jensen when he informs news anchor Howard Beale that the world is a business and that there is no America, but only corporations such as Union Carbide, IBM, and Exxon.

When it was first released, many film critics viewed *Network* screenwriter Paddy Chayefsky's dark interpretation of corporate maneuvering in the television industry as satire. Now the film is viewed more as a documentary than as a satire of the industry and of corporate control of television networks and what audiences see. In an interview with *San Francisco Examiner* television critic Tim Goodman, Orville Schell, former dean of the Graduate School of Journalism at the University of California in Berkeley, remarked: "*Network* is what's happening now . . . I thought I was seeing something extraordinarily fresh. And I thought what I was seeing was true. In a funny way you'd have a hard time doing *Network* now."[1]

The film's plot is the story of UBS, a fictional 1970s television network that is an industry joke. Its programs have low ratings and no programs rate in the top twenty; its avuncular network news anchor, Howard Beale (played by Peter Finch), is depressed. UBS executives decide to replace Beale on the network evening news, and Beale announces to his viewers that he will commit suicide on air in two weeks, during his last newscast. Following his announcement, the ratings for the evening news go up, and through a bizarre series of events Beale remains on the air.

Beale soon evolves into "The Mad Prophet of the Airways," no longer reporting "straight news" but instead providing his commentary on society as, in his own words, "an angry prophet denouncing the hypocrisies of our time." The Howard Beale character is consistent with a standard definition of a biblical prophet:

> The prophet therefore is subject to a particular kind of inspiration. It is in every case a strong subconscious experience of an ecstatic state in which a superhuman power comes upon the man [sic] whom it calls and compels, with or without his [sic] will, to do its service.[2]

Beale is compelled to be the "Mad Prophet" by a force not his own. Chayefsky used the plot of *Network* to extend and build on Beale's prophecies that attack the television industry. If we follow John Dominic Crossan's classical definition of satire as that which undermines trust and credibility, *Network* is almost pure satire.[3]

UBS's network news hour eventually becomes "The Howard Beale Show," a program complete with opinion polls, soothsayers, and the main attraction—Beale's nightly prophetic tirade. Audience ratings soar, and the show becomes the most popular program on television.

The creative chiefs at UBS swiftly produce another "news" program featuring a terrorist group in the act of committing crimes (perhaps the forerunner of "reality-based" television programming). This show also becomes a network ratings winner. UBS suddenly becomes competitive with the "big three" networks in the ratings race.

A turning point comes when Howard Beale reveals that UBS will be purchased by corporate interests backed by Saudi Arabian money. He asks his studio and television audiences to stop the transaction by sending telegrams to the White House. To the delight of Beale and his fans, the deal is stalled, but the corporate heads of UBS are enraged by the setback. CEO Arthur Jensen (played by Ned Beatty) calls Beale into his office and in passionate tones explains the concept of "the world as a business" with no nations or ideologies but only "a holistic system of systems" driven by an international system of currency. Jensen orders Beale to, in his words, "preach this evangel." Beale is persuaded and goes about preaching the "corporate cosmology" of Jensen on the UBS airways while also stating that democracy will soon die and that society is becoming "dehumanized." After several weeks of Beale's depressing messages, the ratings for his show begin to decline, causing panic among UBS executives. The program executives want to remove Beale because of the low ratings; however, Jensen wants Beale to remain on the air delivering the same message at all costs. The program executives finally decide that the only solution is to have members of the terrorist group featured on the other UBS hit show assassinate Beale on his own show. The assassination is carried out before a live studio and television audience, with the film's narrator saying, "This is the story of Howard Beale, the first known instance of a man who was killed because he had lousy ratings."

Network was a portent of things to come in the television industry; Paddy Chayefsky correctly identified at least four future trends: the takeover of the major television networks by corporate entities; the willingness of television programmers to put anything on the airwaves in pursuit of ratings and profits; the fact that a fourth network and other subsequent networks and cable television services would deviate from the norm and no longer play by the programming rules established by the original "big three" networks (ABC, NBC, and CBS); and the devolution of television news from information to infotainment. The first three "prophecies" are discussed in this chapter and the fourth in chapter 11.

The Corporate Takeover of the "Big Three" Television Networks

Before the mid-1980s, the "big three" networks experienced stable ownership for over thirty years, and each network was identified with an established chief executive. Those in the broadcast industry knew the respective leadership at each network, and traditions were established in the industry.

NBC's radio network went on air in the mid-1920s with David Sarnoff as its driving force. NBC was a subsidiary of the Radio Corporation of America (RCA) and was developed as a way to sell more radios for RCA. For years, NBC was the dominant radio network in program ratings until CBS surpassed it during the 1940s. CBS's chief executive William Paley was eventually able to lure many of NBC's top radio stars to his network with lucrative contracts and complex tax shelter arrangements.

Sarnoff and RCA-NBC were responsible for many of the technological innovations in the broadcast industry, including FM radio, television, and color television. NBC was the first television network, starting with regular programming in 1946 and dominating the early television program ratings until Paley's CBS again surpassed its rival network in the mid-1950s.

During the mid-1950s, NBC was the first network to telecast in color and by the mid-1960s was the first "full color" network, telecasting its entire prime-time schedule in color. Sarnoff was obsessed with being the first to develop the major elements of broadcast technology and often did so by circumventing the patents of the inventors who developed the seminal aspects of radio and television technologies.

If Sarnoff had a passion for technology, for the "box" that allowed audiences to hear or see programs, William Paley had a passion for what was heard or seen on the box. Paley devoted his attention to programming on both on radio and television; CBS followed NBC in developing both media but eventually surpassed NBC in the ratings.

Paley realized during CBS's early radio years that it would be difficult to surpass the already established NBC in entertainment programming, and he decided to develop strong news and information programs. He hired Edward R. Murrow in the 1930s and laid the foundation for what became the strongest network news division in either radio or television. CBS news was the broadcast voice that Americans listened to during World War II.

The 1940s brought higher ratings for CBS radio because of the infusion of talent from NBC and a continued strong news division; however, Paley faced a new challenge with the advent of television. CBS history states that Paley embraced television with enthusiasm, but Sally Biddell Smith in her biography of Paley claims that he was slow to see the potential of television because he was so entrenched in radio.[4] It was only several years after NBC launched its television network that the CBS television network went on the air. CBS eventually outdid NBC in television ratings by moving many popular radio programs to their television lineup and continued as the television ratings leader for over two decades.

ABC, the third of the traditional networks, was established in 1945 after NBC divested its Blue Network (NBC had owned two networks, the Red and the Blue). ABC was years behind NBC and CBS in development and struggled for nearly three decades. The popular joke in the television industry was that the "big three" networks were really only a "big two and a half."

Still, ABC was responsible for innovative strategies that shaped the future of the television industry. It was the first television network to "make peace" with Hollywood and the film industry by signing agreements with the Walt Disney and Warner Brothers film studios (ironically, Disney became the parent corporation of ABC in the early 1990s). During the early years of television, the film industry saw the new medium as a threat; hundreds of movie theaters throughout the United States closed their doors because of declining attendance.

In the early 1950s, Walt Disney saw television as an opportunity to promote his new theme park, Disneyland, and he approached all three networks with a proposal for a program that would show his past film productions (e.g., cartoons, *True Life Adventures*) along with programs especially produced for television. In return, he would receive time at the end of the program to promote Disneyland. Some might call this an early infomercial. ABC accepted the proposal and developed a relationship with Disney that lasted into the early 1960s.

ABC did not become a strong rival of NBC and CBS until the mid-1970s, when it finally reached number one in the Nielsen ratings. Before this time, the third network was forced to adopt strategies counter to the older two, including animated programs in prime time, strong sports coverage such as *Monday Night Football*, the miniseries, and the made-for-television movie.

Despite the growing influence of cable television, the 'big three" networks remained profitable. In the early 1980s, a study group from the FCC found that the network regulations restricted business interaction between the networks and their affiliate stations and fair competition with nonnetwork stations (known as independents). The FCC concluded that competition was desirable in the television marketplace and soon eliminated many of the barriers to establishing new networks. These actions contributed to the development of the Fox network in 1985. Fox eventually became a strong fourth network, deviating from the traditional norms for programming strategies (more about Fox later in this chapter).

The networks faced new challenges throughout the 1980s. Cable television services such as HBO, Showtime, CNN, and others gradually depleted the networks' audience; more outlets competed for the same audience "pie." Perhaps the most significant trend of the 1980s was change in the ownership structure of CBS, NBC, and ABC.

The movie *Network* parodies the corporate takeover of a third-rate television network; however, between 1985 and 1987, not one but all of the "big three" networks fell into corporate hands. In their book *Broadcasting in America,* Head et al. cite the retirement of long-time network leaders and declines in ratings and profits as the reasons that the networks were ripe for takeover.[5]

The youngest network, ABC, was the first to fall into corporate hands; Capital Cities Communications (Cap Cities) acquired it in 1985 and created a conglomerate worth over $4 billion. The Cap Cities takeover of ABC was termed a "friendly deal." Cap Cites established the trend of cutting costs at the network level and maximizing profits (more about this in the next section of this chapter).

Within months of the ABC takeover, CNN head and cable mogul Ted Turner attempted a hostile takeover of CBS through creative financing of "junk bonds." The plan failed but left CBS weakened financially and ripe for takeover by other corporate interests. Eventually Lawrence Tisch, chairperson of the Loew's entertainment and investment conglomerate, methodically purchased a controlling interest in CBS. Tisch sold virtually all of CBS's nonbroadcast properties and closed the CBS research laboratories.

By the end of 1985, NBC also changed leadership as it welcomed a friendly buyout offer from GE. The network had been weakened by inept management and failed projects with video disks and computer products. Ten years later, the Walt Disney Company surprised the entertainment industry by announcing the purchase of Capital Cities-ABC for $19 billion in one of the largest takeover deals in history. The deal produced a huge entertainment conglomerate combining the Disney television and film studios, theme parks, and other properties with the ABC television network and ESPN cable service. Within days, CBS announced that it was accepting a buyout offer from Westinghouse Electric Corporation. Westinghouse already owned a number of radio and television stations throughout the country (known as Group W stations), and purchasing CBS made the new Westinghouse-CBS corporation the largest holder of broadcast properties in the country. NBC remained in the hands of General Electric.

Fox, the fourth network, was created in 1985 and established different norms for network programming and development. Australian publisher Rupert Murdoch became a U.S. citizen almost overnight, which allowed him to purchase six large independent television stations in New York, Los Angeles, Chicago, Washington, D.C., Houston, Dallas, and a network affiliate station in Boston owned by the Metromedia Corporation. These stations became the cornerstone for the new Fox network. Murdoch also obtained the Twentieth Century Fox studios and their vast film and television library.

After a slow start, Fox gradually showed respectable ratings—if not respectable program content—in the late 1980s and throughout the 1990s, eventually producing programs for younger and more diverse audiences while acquiring the rights to NFL football in 1993.

The corporate takeovers of television networks beginning in the mid-1980s established a trend of vertical integration (corporations acquiring properties that are complementary to one another). For example, the acquisition of the ABC television network gave Disney another outlet for showing and promoting its films. Disney Studios may also produce programming for ABC and profit from these programs when episodes are sold into syndication (the reselling of programs to individual television stations after their initial network run). In effect, Disney can control both the creation and distribution of productions.

Rupert Murdoch's News Corporation (corporate parent of the Fox network) is a classic example of vertical integration, the Fox film studios and libraries providing programming for the television network. News Corporation satellite, cable news, and sports services all interface into a major communications force.

By reviewing a sample of the various properties held by General Electric, Disney-Cap Cities, Westinghouse, and News Corporation, we can grasp the vastness of these corporations and see how the individual holdings interface with one another and contribute to huge entertainment conglomerates:

GE

- The NBC television network
- Nine NBC-owned and -operated television stations in New York, Los Angeles, Chicago, Philadelphia, Washington, D.C., Miami, Raleigh-Durham, Columbus, and Providence
- Westwood One radio network
- Cable television services such as CNBC, and partial ownership of MSNBC, Court TV, American Movie Classics, A&E, History, Channel, and Bravo GE Americom (communication satellites)

Disney-Cap Cities

- The ABC television network
- Disney-owned and -operated television stations in New York, Los Angeles, Chicago, Houston, Philadelphia, San Francisco, Fresno, Raleigh-Durham, Toledo, and Flint, Mich.
- ABC radio owns twenty-one stations, and the ABC radio network serves 3,400 stations nationwide
- Film studios: Walt Disney Pictures, Touchstone Pictures, Hollywood Pictures, Miramax Film Corporation, and Buena Vista Pictures
- Multimedia entities such as Disney Interactive, Disney.com, and ABC Online
- Cable services such as the Disney Channel, Disney Television (producer of syndicated programming), Touchstone Television (producing network prime-time programs), ESPN, ESPN 2, and Buena Vista Television
- Theme Parks such as Disneyland, Walt Disney World Resort, and Disneyland Paris (39 percent)
- Sports teams—The Mighty Ducks (NHL ice hockey) and the California Angels (baseball)
- Ten daily newspapers in cities ranging in size from Fort Worth to Ashland, Ore.

Viacom-CBS

- The CBS television network
- Owned and operated stations in New York, Chicago, Los Angeles, San Francisco, Denver, Miami, Philadelphia, Salt Lake City, Detroit, Minneapolis, Boston, Baltimore, Pittsburgh, and Green Bay, Wisc.
- CBS radio with twenty-one FM stations, eighteen AM stations. Nineteen hundred stations carry some CBS programming and about 450 carry CBS News

- Cable properties such as CMT (Country Music Television)
- Group W Satellite Communications
- The 2000 merger with Viacom includes MTV, Paramount Studios, Viacom Cable, and other properties

News Corporation (Murdoch)
- Fox Broadcasting Company
- Twentieth Century Television
- Fox Television Studios
- Fox television stations in New York, Los Angeles, Chicago, Philadelphia, Boston, Washington, D.C., Dallas, Detroit, Atlanta, Houston, Cleveland, Tampa, Phoenix, Denver, St. Louis, Milwaukee, Kansas City, Salt Lake City, Memphis, Greensboro, Birmingham, Austin
- Cable and satellite television holdings such as Fox News Channel, FX, Fox Kids Network (50 percent), MTM Entertainment (50 percent), Fox Family Channel (50 percent), Fox Sports Net (50 percent), British Sky Broadcasting including forty channels (40 percent), Sky One, and Sky News
- Filmed entertainment including Twentieth Century Fox, Fox 2000, Fox Searchlight, Fox Animation Studios, Fox Music, Twentieth Century Fox Home Entertainment, Twentieth Century Fox Television, Twentieth Century Fox Licensing and Merchandising, and Twentieth Century Fox Interactive
- Print properties such as *The Times, The Sunday Times, The Sun,* and the *News of the World* (all England), the *New York Post, The Austrian* (national newspaper), and *TV Guide* magazine.

Ted Turner of CNN fame does not own an on-air network (his programs are distributed by satellite and cable for the most part), but he still ranks as one of the major media forces in the United States. Andrew Neeley, who worked closely with Murdoch, often likened the competition between Turner and Murdoch to a battle between King Kong and Godzilla. In 1995, a merger was announced between Turner and Time Warner, with Turner receiving $2 billion in company stock and the position of vice-chairman of the merged company. Another megamerger occurred in early 2000 as AOL merged with Time Warner. Following are some of the holdings of AOL-Time Warner:

AOL-Time Warner
- Turner Broadcasting: Cable News Network (CNN), CNN Headline News, CNN Radio, CNN Interactive, and CNNfin (financial news)
- Superstation WTBS—Atlanta

- Castle Rock Entertainment, New Line Cinema, Turner Pictures, Turner Entertainment Co. (MGM, RKO, and pre-1950 Warner Brothers films)
- Hanna-Barbera cartoons and World Championship Wrestling
- Home Box Office, Cinemax, E!, and Comedy Central cable services
- Warner Brothers and Warner Brothers Animated films and studios
- Time-Life Video, HBO Home Video, and Warner Home Video
- The Atlanta Braves (baseball) and the Atlanta Hawks (basketball); Turner has called his sports teams "software" for his media outlets
- Print properties include *Time, Fortune, Life, Sports Illustrated, People, Money,* and *Vibe* magazines

There is potential for positive outcomes—less expensive production costs, higher quality programs, more diverse sources and perspectives for news—because of vertical integration involving the creative, production, and distribution functions; however, this has not been the case. There is now a perceived sameness among programs on both networks and cable services and a lack of diversity in content and the faces we see on the screen. On the 1999 PBS documentary "NYTV" (which chronicles the contributions of New York City to the television industry), television critic Walter Wager remarked that television is like a restaurant in Moscow he had visited where there were over three hundred items on the menu; when it came to ordering an entrée, only four were available. If we scan the nightly prime-time listings, we conclude that in the television landscape there are many restaurants, controlled by a few chefs (GE, Murdoch, Disney), offering few different entrées despite the numerous apparent choices on the television menu.

The diversity issue also extends to the representation of various racial-ethnic groups. Lead characters in prime-time programs have become increasingly more white. During the summer of 1999, NAACP President Kweisi Mfume blasted the television industry for the lack of African Americans on the networks' new fall schedules (among the twenty-six new programs slated for the fall 1999 season, there were no African-American stars). Mfume stated: "This glaring omission is an outrage and a shameful display by network executives who are either clueless, careless, or both."

Other racial-ethnic groups such as Hispanics and Asians were less represented than in previous years on all programs new or old. If an alien from another planet were to watch U.S. television for one week, she might conclude that most earthlings are white, young, urban types, working as media professionals, lawyers, crime fighters, or medical personnel.

Perhaps the most serious consequence of corporate ownership is that news and public information have fallen into fewer and fewer hands during fifteen years of mergers and vertical integration. An argument could be made that years ago only CBS, ABC, and NBC existed as television news services and that the public has more choices with the addition of services such as CNN, Fox News, and MSNBC; the problem is that many of these news sources rely on maximizing their resources and personnel between services under the same corporate umbrella, at the expense of diversity and depth. In other words, there are few real differences between what we see on NBC and MSNBC or CNN and CNN Headline News.

Merger mania affects not only television but also print media. When looking at the print holdings of corporations such as Time Warner-AOL, we see magazines such as *Time* and *Fortune*. Rupert Murdoch's News Corporation includes newspapers such as the *New York Post* and *The Times* of London. Issues of autonomy and objectivity are often raised: Can each media entity under a corporate umbrella report news without interference from the corporate structure? How free are the editors of one newspaper to challenge the views of another entity owned by the same corporation? To what degree must reporters practice self-censorship to avoid offending the corporation that pays them?

Media conglomerates are now in a race to develop various platforms for distributing content and selling products. The airways, cable, and the Internet are all part of the corporate strategy for profit maximization. For example, networks can now distribute programs via the Internet, which include commercial messages at the same time the program is being watched. Viewers can order products online without interrupting their favorite programs.

Corporate takeovers have also enhanced the second trend or "prophecy" from *Network*, the pursuit of ratings and the maximization of profits at the expense of program quality.

Ratings, Profits, and Programs

During one scene in *Network*, the UBS programming executive Diana Christensen (played by Faye Dunaway) exclaims, "All I want out of life is a twenty rating and a thirty share." Most television viewers know that a program with high Nielsen ratings remains on the air, while a program with low ratings is probably canceled (sometimes after only a few episodes). Many viewers have experienced the frustration of having one of their favorite programs canceled because of low ratings, but few casual viewers realize the true significance of ratings to the television industry.

Ratings are the currency in which television networks and other outlets do business with advertisers. The Nielsen ratings (the A. C. Nielsen

Company provides the majority of information on television ratings in the United States) determine how much money local stations and networks may charge advertisers for a commercial spot and which programs are economically viable. High ratings allow networks and stations to charge advertisers more money because they reach a larger audience.

Measurements known as *rating points* and *shares* give some indication of how many people watch a particular program. A rating point is an estimate of the percentage of households of all television households (*households with their televisions turned on or off*) watching a specific channel. At the national level in September 2000, each rating point currently represented 1.08 million households. A prime-time network show with a rating of 17 was being watched by 17 percent (about 18.4 million) of U.S. television households.

A share is an estimate of the percentage of television households *with their television sets turned on* that are tuned to a particular channel. If a prime-time network show had a 25 share, it means that 25 percent of the households actually watching television were tuned to that channel.

Nielsen's gathering of ratings and share data has always had its critics and has come under even more criticism during the last decade. Currently, about 5,000 homes nationwide are the Nielsen "sample" measuring ratings data. This random sample represents a "snapshot" of U.S. demographics while determining the national audience for networks and cable services.

Each Nielsen household in the national sample is provided with a box known as a "people meter" connected to the television set(s). People meters collect program preference and demographic data. Each family member has a code number that he or she must enter when watching television. This can be an involved process if several people watch television in the same household at a given time.

In the late 1980s, networks protested against people meters because they showed a decline in network viewership. A study funded by the networks concluded that older viewers and children might be intimidated by the technology and button pushing required to register their viewing. In other cases, some people of all ages were impatient with the process and either ignored the people meter or entered someone else's code.

Networks and advertisers are pressuring Nielsen to develop a better method for gathering data, and the answer may be the passive people meter, which uses computer face recognition technology to "see" who among regular household viewers is watching television. Issues of privacy and the Orwellian feeling of the television watching the viewer may stall the widespread use of these devices.

Nielsen also uses diaries to gather ratings information at the local level: One person in each household is asked to log all household members' viewing. The drawbacks to this method of data gathering are obvious. The viewer may forget to log programs or falsify the log (declaring that the family watched a program on PBS when they really watched WWF wrestling) or try to catch up on the previous week's logging entries on Sunday afternoon while watching football and enjoying a second can of beer.

Networks and advertisers no longer care as much about *how many* eyeballs watch a particular program as they do about *whose* eyeballs are watching. This obsession with demographic data may have started in the late 1960s when CBS discovered that many of their highly rated programs were not watched by urban viewers but by people in small towns and rural areas. This was probably because CBS was showing a number of rural situation comedies such as *Green Acres* and *The Beverly Hillbillies*. Fearful that it was acquiring a reputation as a rural network and was not attracting the "right kind of eyeballs," CBS overhauled its prime-time lineup, canceling many of its popular small-town programs in favor of dramas and situation comedies with urban settings.

This "desire for the right eyeballs" drives the ratings game in network television programming as networks strive to obtain young urban viewers, scheduling programs featuring young, mostly white, urban professionals working in attractive jobs. Because of the pursuit of younger demographics, older viewers as well as various racial and ethnic groups find it harder to locate network prime-time programs that appeal to them.

Despite the fact that many senior citizens and aging baby boomers have unprecedented disposable income, advertisers often favor programs that "skew young" because younger audiences have not made decisions about brand choices and brand loyalty. The irony of this strategy is that white people under thirty, now drawn to the Internet and other media options, watch less network television than do young people of color and older audiences.

Another problem, from the standpoint of the audience, is the reduction in program quality that results from corporate management and stockholder pressure to maximize profits. Before the corporate takeovers of the "big three" networks in the mid-1980s, NBC, CBS, and ABC always pursued profits; however, there was a distinct change in philosophy about network profitability after 1985. Executives such as NBC's David Sarnoff, CBS's William Paley, and ABC's Leonard Goldensen wanted high ratings and profits, but their ethic of stewardship led them to reinvest profits into the networks to improve programming and technology and to sustain unprofitable programming such as news and children's programs. Sarnoff reinvested profits to develop new RCA technologies such as FM radio, television, and color television; Paley chose to acquire new talent and sustain the best news division in radio and television despite the fact that news was not a profit maker. ABC's early years saw few profits, but that did not keep Goldensen from developing new program genres and strategies.

Corporate ownership lacks the ethic of stewardship exhibited by these men. Current philosophy at the network level is profit maximization by trying to achieve the highest ratings at the lowest cost. Some prime-time programs cost millions of dollars per episode to produce, but many others have relatively inexpensive production costs. In *Network*, programming executive Diana Christiansen becomes elated at the possibility of *The Howard Beale Show*'s being not only the top-rated program on television, but also a huge profit maker for the network because of its inexpensive production costs. This philosophy has permeated real-world network programming offices for the last two decades, especially in news and other reality-based shows.

News divisions were downsized during the 1980s following network corporate takeovers; personnel were terminated, and news bureaus around the world were closed. Now the overall presence of news programming may seem greater than ever before, especially with coverage provided by cable news services such as CNN and MSNBC, but the quality and scope of international news coverage are less. News divisions were originally seen as a service to the public and were expected to lose money. Popular prime-time programs "paid the freight" for service programming and made profits for the networks. Now, news is also a profit center, and news magazines are carried seven nights a week on the major networks, not as a public service, but because they are less expensive to produce than filmed series. The possibility exists that NBC, CBS, and ABC will air ten o'clock network newscasts in a move to cut prime-time programming costs.

Another cost-cutting trend is the emergence of reality-based programs or programs that use fact-based video or film footage for content, such as *Cops* and compilation programs showing the worst natural disasters. A program such as ABC's *Funniest Home Videos* also belongs to this genre. *Network* predicted this trend twenty-five years ago with *The Mao Tse-Tung Hour*, a show depicting bank robbing, kidnapping terrorists filming themselves in action. Such programs rely on basic production techniques and in some cases home video for program content, making them cheap to produce in comparison with prime-time dramas or situation comedies.

Two programs, *Who Wants to Be a Millionaire* and *Survivor*, are examples of low-cost ratings winners. Indeed, one thirty-second spot on *Millionaire* pays for the entire production cost of the show—every other commercial is profit. *Millionaire* revived the game show genre, absent from prime-time programming for forty years, and finished in the top twenty of the Nielsen ratings even though it sometimes aired four times a week. Fox followed almost immediately with a similar show, *Greed*, and NBC entered the competition by reviving *Twenty-One*, the show that in its original version was the focus of the quiz show scandals of the late 1950s.

Survivor!, a new kind of game show set on a remote island, featured a prize of $1 million for the last person remaining on the island after a weekly elimination process. The program was a ratings winner for CBS during the summer of 2000, often attracting more than twenty million viewers. Despite the prize money given on these shows, they were produced for a fraction of the cost of a prime-time sitcom or drama.

The cost-cutting practices of network and local television have extended to cable television as well. Thirty years ago, many media watchers predicted a new media universe of unlimited choices with over five hundred cable services available in a redefined viewing concept known as "narrowcasting" (televising programs to specific interests and demographics). But narrowcasting has produced neither greater variety nor higher quality. Cable has adopted many of the practices of local stations and networks by giving viewers programs at the lowest possible production cost. With the exception of premium services such as HBO, cable services produce little of their own programming, often running programs that have appeared on network television. Services such as TV Land and Nickelodeon run off-network programs (repeats of past popular network shows) and can be classified as "thrift stores" in the television landscape.

The pursuit of ratings and profits at the lowest possible cost has contributed to the state of television today, but one more prophecy from *Network* has come true: the development of a fourth network—Fox—that no longer plays by the old rules.

The Fox Network as the "Real Life" UBS

Network's fictitious UBS is a lowly fourth network trying to keep up with the "big three" in the ratings game by employing the traditional strategies of programming. It is not until UBS decides to break the rules with alternative programs such as *The Howard Beale Show* and *The Mao Tse-Tung Hour* that it begins to thrive in the network ratings wars. The emergence of the Fox network in the late 1980s and 1990s as a legitimate fourth network parallels the rise of UBS.

At the 1992 International Radio and Television Society's Faculty Industry Seminar, Carolyn Wall, station manager of Fox's New York affiliate WNYW, said that Fox was the network that "broke all the rules." Fox's strategy worked and has affected the television industry as a whole. Fox began telecasting in the mid-1980s, using the same programming strategies as ABC, NBC, and CBS. One of Fox's first efforts, *The Joan Rivers Show* (similar in format and tone to NBC's *Tonight Show*), was an artistic and ratings disaster and was canceled after a few months. Most of Fox's early efforts appeared to be poor imitations of programs seen on established networks, with few surviving beyond a few weeks.

By the late 1980s, Fox executives decided to break with tradition and play for a younger audience. Shows such as *Melrose Place, Beverly Hills 90210,* and *The Simpsons* appealed primarily to younger viewers. Fox soon established its identity as the network most popular with these demographics.

The strategy is successful because younger viewers control many of the viewing choices in a household or have their own television sets and no longer watch what their parents are watching. Perhaps more important for Fox, younger demographics can be sold to advertisers because young people have not yet developed brand loyalty. These viewers also have billions of dollars in discretionary money to spend.

Fox's new younger offerings often feature more sexual content and strong language previously not seen or heard on network television in a regular series. Programs such as *Married, With Children* drew heavy criticism from television critics and conservative viewers. A letter campaign, begun by a Michigan woman named Terry Rakolta, encouraged viewers and sponsors to boycott the show, but it remained a hit with young and liberal viewers.

Some industry leaders, including Ted Turner, criticize Fox for continuing Rupert Murdoch's trend of going "down market" or compromising program content to appeal to the lowest common denominator. Murdoch had already established this trend with his other overseas broadcast properties and his tabloid newspapers, such as *The Sun* in London. Following the *Who Wants to Marry a Millionaire* debacle when a televised wedding was annulled after several days, a Fox vice-president named Gary Ginsberg remarked, "The market will determine how low we go."

The quest for the demographic fountain of youth has been joined by most television services. As a result, many network prime-time programs continue to skew younger, and few television screenwriters work in the industry beyond the age of forty. Many established screenwriters in their thirties and early forties are seen as out of touch and too old to write for today's youthful audience. A 1999 edition of CBS's *Sixty Minutes* reports the story of Riley Weston, a woman who was supposedly nineteen years old and writing scripts for various prime-time programs on networks such as WB (Warner Brothers). Her career was widely reported in the trade press, and she was viewed as a rising star in the television industry. There was only one problem: The youthful-looking writer was really thirty-one years old. Following this discovery, Weston was fired because she was seen as too old to write for young viewers.

Fox also broke the rules in another way by offering reality-based programs not unlike *The Mao Tse-tung Hour* in *Network*. Shows such as *COPS* feature video of real situations of arrests and car chases. These programs are relatively inexpensive to produce because there are no high-priced actors to pay or sets to create. Fox has added to the reality-based genre by introducing programs commonly known in the industry as "car wreck" shows, with themes such as bad car crashes, natural disasters, and animal attacks. In many cases, these shows contain video footage shot by viewers with home video equipment, so that the producers need only edit the footage.

The influence of Fox in redefining industry-wide programming strategies is undeniable. Newer networks such as WB and UPN (United Paramount Network) have followed Fox's example of targeting younger viewers while attempting to cut production costs. Fox has defined much of the way the television industry will do business in the twenty-first century and what types of program the public will see.

It remains to been seen whether the public will embrace network and cable offerings or seek other forms of media entertainment such as interactive Internet programs. Notices about the death of network television may be premature because of the networks' resources and the continued possibilities of megamergers; however, market demand could redefine what the traditional television networks offer in programming.

Conclusion

Guidelines for "Reading" Television

If television functions as a religion for millions of Americans, a religion whose dominant message (consumerism) is at odds with genuine religious faith, we need guidelines for "discerning the spirits" at work in this popular religion. Here are nine guidelines that emerge from our theology and our understanding of the television industry.

1. **Watch What You Watch**. Keep in check the lust of the eye. "The eye is the lamp of the body. So, if your eye is healthy, your whole body will be full of light; but if your eye is unhealthy, your whole body will be full of darkness" (Mt 6:22–23). There is such a thing as "visually sipping on darkness."[1] Thus Jesus warns us, "If your right eye causes you to sin, tear it out and throw it away; it is better for you to lose one of your members than for your whole body to be thrown into hell" (Mt 5:29).

    Many Americans are offended by such advice. We have removed restraints on human appetites. Assuming that "more is better," our culture fans our appetites until they become ravenous fires, devouring body and soul. In a culture of consumer sovereignty, pluralistic lifestyles, and First Amendment watchdogs, we are (in Philip Rieff's words) "forbidden to forbid."[2] Some television programs are little more than peep shows. Gordon Marino reports his experience of watching a pseudodocumentary about two policemen intervening in a domestic fight. "Peering through my cathoid keyhole, I spied a warring couple in their early 30s. Apparently, the woman had stabbed her husband in the arm. . . . [She] bellowed, 'I was only defending myself . . . I don't want to go to jail.'" After a while it finally registered on Marino: "I was entertaining myself by watching two lives unravel." Reflecting on the ethics of watching, he concludes, "If we have plucked out anything, it is the very idea that the eye *can* offend."[3] Looking is an action with consequences. What we watch shapes our feelings, and our feelings shape our behavior.

2. **The Wheat and the Weeds Grow Together.** The farmer prevents his servants from premature weeding "for in gathering the weeds you would uproot the wheat along with them" (Mt 13:29). This is a call to humility, placed in tension with the call to purity. If the call to purity were absolute, the "Turn off the Tube" movement would be vindicated. If the call to humility were absolute, "anything goes" would be our guide. Instead, we must hold the two in tension. Shades of good and evil are often inextricably intertwined in real life; television reflects the complexity and ambiguity of life itself. Who is wise enough to be the censor for all? What is wheat to some may be weeds to others; ironically, what is weeds to us now may become wheat to us later, and vice versa. We have been surprised at the depth of insight evoked by the texts of programs that at first were offensive to us.

3. **We Exist to Praise.** The doctrine of creation furnishes this third principle. We are made in God's image to glorify God. Paraphrasing Irenaeus, "The glory of God is a human being fully alive." This means that at some level all people connected with television—writers, directors, producers, actors, audience—desire to create and celebrate the good. This creative urge comes from our entelechy (Aristotle), the directedness of our innate capacities toward their fulfillment.

4. **"All Have Sinned."** This fourth guideline should not be surprising in our cynical age, although secular society may squirm at the use of this theological concept. Even the best desires of members of the television industry are warped and distorted. There are no "good guys" and no "bad guys" in real life; the battle between good and evil is waged within each soul. The same applies to television programs. Like every other human product, television is a mixture of the trivial and the profound, healthy and unhealthy elements, uplifting and degrading messages.

5. **Powerful, Ambivalent Forces Drive Television Production.** The creative impulse is disciplined and compromised by the pressure to maximize profits. This pressure has been particularly damaging to the quality of television journalism. Given the tyranny of nightly audience ratings and the inroads made by cable televi-

sion into network programming, one can only marvel at the number of quality programs that still survive.

6. **Every Television Program Has Theological Implications,** with implicit views of human nature and human destiny. Every thirty-second commercial offers a promise of salvation in miniature.

7. Because of the drive for large audiences, **Television Programs <u>Are Consensus Narratives</u>.** Even when designed for a niche audience, they are conservative in nature, giving expression to central myths and values of society shared across the boundaries of race, class, gender, and national origin. For the most part, television depicts the everydayness of life, featuring neither the highs nor the lows usually associated with profound religious experience.

8. **The "Text" of Every Program Is Polysemic** (containing many signs), <u>communicating one or more dominant messages and many subordinate ones.</u> Audiences are pluralistic in their "reading" of these "texts," selecting those messages that best fit their experience. Race, class, gender, personal identity, and cultural interests influence the way we "read" various programs.

subject to deconstructive crit.

9. In the process of interaction with the "texts," **Audiences Create Meanings** that may or may not be intended by the writers, directors, and producers. These meanings, which are usually more implicit than explicit, are the "collective daydreams of our society."[4] They serve as models for living.

Action Steps for Communities of Faith

The theme of *Network* is that television is a business. Many Americans do not think of television in business terms despite the barrage of commercials and the frequent news of media megamergers and corporate takeovers. Many view television as a convenient home utility much the same as water or electricity; yet viewers and politicians complain about program content. Those involved in the church or social justice groups may ask, What can be done to improve the quality of what is seen on television?

In the November-December 1997 edition of *Church and Society,* William F. Fore, former director of the Communication Commission of the National Council of Churches, says:

> The first step requires putting to test the notion that Christians do not engage in social action. Being in the world but not of it does not require staying wholly

outside the social and political process. In fact, the reverse is true: creating changes in the cultural environment to enhance justice and human dignity requires influencing public opinion and getting laws passed.[5]

Fore later mentions Paul Tillich's concept of the "latent church:" God working through individuals in the secular world. Church members must not act in isolation but must form alliances, seeking solidarity with those outside the church who have similar concerns. Those in the church who are not avid watchers of television or claim to "watch only PBS" cannot ignore the influential nature of the medium (as Howard Beale claimed, "the most awesome force in the whole godless world").

What potential responses can the church offer? Here are some ways for individuals and congregations to become involved:

1. Viewers must realize that they have a feedback loop to television stations and networks. By law, all comments about programs and station practices must be logged by the station and submitted to the FCC when a station applies for license renewal. Granted, stations rarely lose their licenses, but station and network executives are concerned about public perceptions, if only to prevent viewers from turning off their programs, thus affecting ratings and profits. Individual contact with television outlets can influence their programming practices.

   Such was the case when The Rev. Richardson Schell—headmaster, Episcopal priest, and sole member of ProudSponsors USA—launched a letter-writing campaign against the Fox animated sitcom Family Guy, demanding a change of family name for the main characters on the show. The creator of the program, Seth MacFarlane (who had attended Schell's Kent School), had named his characters Griffin, which just happened to be the name of Kent School's assistant headmaster. Schell claimed that Family Guy's animated characters "swore, farted, and urinated, trivialized alcoholism and child abuse" and that he did not want his school associated with the program. Schell began writing letters to Family Guy's sponsors, including Philip Morris and Kentucky Fried Chicken, who both pulled their sponsorship of the program. The program did not last long after this, although the reason given for its demise was poor ratings. (At press time, the show has been revived as a replacement program in the Fox schedule.)

   Individual voices may be heard, but unified group contact is better; in short, the television industry understands numbers. If members of a congregation or denomination share the same opinions about programs, they should develop unified responses to television outlets.

Networks and stations should also receive positive feedback about programs that provide informative messages or content not presented by other media sources. In some cases, a small number of letters or emails may determine whether a station decides to continue running a particular public affairs or religious program.

2. Support efforts to develop media literacy programs in schools and churches. Children in Canada, England, and Australia spend more time in schools discussing media literacy and message analysis than do children in the United States. Parents and other advocates should contact school boards and insist that media literacy be taken seriously and be part of the curriculum. Churches may sponsor Christian education sessions on media literacy and theological evaluations of television shows. Opportunities exist for sessions that transcend age groups, so that parents and older members may discuss with children and younger members what each group watches on television and why. Such sessions may enlighten members about the "business behind the box" aspects of the industry, particularly corporate impact on what is seen on television. There should be attempts to identify professionals in the television industry who are "church friendly" and use them as resources. Those who work in advertising, news, and other production areas are often willing to share information about creative processes or news standards. Television professionals are also willing to help in the action-step decision-making process.

3. Church members should learn to use alternate media such as public access television and the Internet. The task of creating video programs or Internet websites may seem intimidating and expensive; but video equipment is becoming easier to use and more people are mastering the basics of video production. Interview or modified magazine format programs are relatively easy to produce, and production assistance is often available at local public access cable stations. Instruction in Internet use and website creation is available through many local educational institutions such as community colleges and continuing education programs.

This provides an excellent opportunity to involve younger church members, because many have video and computer skills and are less intimidated by technology than are their elders. A nonchurch youth organization dealing with the problem of teen smoking in Florida, "Real Truth," was featured on *60 Minutes*. This group of teenagers created cutting-edge antismoking public service announcements and an antismoking website. Youth in churches could use "Real Truth" as a model for developing materials on a variety of social issues.

4. Seminaries, clergy, and Christian educators must take the lead in recognizing the impact of television on popular culture and developing appropriate responses. Seminaries must offer more course work in theology and the media, including courses on how to "read" and interpret television shows, while congregational leaders must assist in organizing media education programs and workshops. Ignoring the impact of television on culture or adhering to a "Kill Your Television" mentality is no longer a responsible option. Whether an individual watches television on a regular basis is irrelevant; the issue is the undeniable impact of television on culture and the mental environment in which we all live.

5. As individuals, viewers must learn to watch television in a different way. We must become more interactive with what we are viewing, which is counter to the way most people watch television. Media scholar Tony Schwartz says that watching television is a scanning activity rather than a logical sequential processing of information. Viewers must discuss what they watch and why characters make the choices they do.

(inter-) active, not passive reception

Guidelines and blueprints for exegeting and interpreting video information can assist viewers with processing what they see on television, especially commercial persuasive appeals used in promoting consumerism and developing a "wants versus needs" mentality. This book will assist in providing methods for exegeting a variety of video "texts."

Will the prophecies of Howard Beale in *Network* continue to be accurate as the television industry conducts business in the twenty-first century? Declining network audiences, increased Internet use, and the advent of other information and entertainment technologies may cause the television industry to redefine its programming strategies; or television stations and networks as we know them today may cease to exist.

W. Edwards Deming, one of the pioneers of American business quality control—his theories were used by the Japanese to rebuild their postwar industries—believed that profits pursued as primary goals are fickle phantoms. They become long-term rewards only to the company that respects its customers and wins their abiding loyalty by providing them with products of the highest quality. The church and other social justice organizations must now interact with the television industry and force the issue of developing programming of the highest quality.

Notes

Introduction

1. Neil Postman, *Amusing Ourselves to Death: Public Discourse in the Age of Show Business* (New York: Penguin Books, 1985), 87.
2. See the following for variations on the theme of television as popular religion: Pierre Babin, *The New Era in Religious Communication* (Minneapolis: Fortress Press, 1991); William Fore, *Television and Religion: The Shaping of Faith, Values and Culture* (Minneapolis: Augsburg, 1987); Gregor Goethals, *The Electronic Golden Calf: Images, Religion and the Making of Meaning* (Boston: Cowley, 1990); Stewart M. Hoover and Knut Lundby, *Rethinking Media, Religion, and Culture* (London: Sage, 1997); Stewart M. Hoover and Shalim S. Venturelli, "The Category of the Religious: The Blindspot of Contemporary Media Theory?" *Critical Studies in Mass Communications* 13 (1996), 251–65; Bruce David Forbes and Jeffrey H. Mahan, eds., *Religion and Popular Culture in America* (Berkeley and Los Angeles: University of California Press, 2000); and Michael Warren, *Seeing through the Media* (Harrisburg, PA: Trinity Press International, 1977).
3. George Gerbner, "Ministry of Culture, the USA, and the 'Free Marketplace of Ideas,'" *International Forum* (fall 1987), 15–17.
4. Mark Silk, *Unsecular Media: Making News of Religion in America* (Champaign, IL: University of Illinois Press, 1995).
5. David Thornburn, "Television as an Aesthetic Medium," *Critical Studies in Mass Communications* 4 (1987), 161–73.
6. In his book *TV Drama in Transition* (New York: St. Martin's Press, 1997), Robin Nelson traces these structural changes in narrative form.
7. John Dominic Crossan, *The Dark Interval: Towards a Theology of Story* (Allen, TX: Argus Communications, 1975), 59.

8. Nachbar and Lause *Popular Culture* (Bowling Green, OH: Bowling Green State University Popular Press, 1992), 171.

9. Nachbar and Lause, *Popular Culture*, 170.

10. Ellen Goodman, "'Going Thin' in Fiji," *San Francisco Chronicle*, 27 May 1999, A29.

11. Michael Warren, *Seeing through the Media*, 98–101, uses a three-frame model to analyze the cultural production of popular songs. We have adapted his idea of frames to the multiple levels of the television industry.

Part I

1. Gerald Jones, *Honey I'm Home! Sitcoms: Selling the American Dream* (New York: St. Martin's Press, 1992), 4.

2. Jones, *Honey I'm Home*, 52.

3. Jones, *Honey I'm Home*, 59, and Robin R. Means Coleman, *African American Viewers and the Black Situation Comedy: Situating Racial Humor* (New York: Garland, 1998), 69.

4. Jones, *Honey I'm Home*, 89.

5. John Dominic Crossan, *The Dark Interval: Towards a Theology of Story* (Allen, TX: Argus Communications, 1975), chap. 2.

6. Jones, *Honey I'm Home*, 97.

7. Jones, *Honey I'm Home*, 100.

8. Rick Mitz, *The Great TV Sitcom Book* (New York: Putnam, 1988), 99.

9. Mitz, *Great TV Sitcom Book*, 98.

10. Stephanie Coontz, *The Way We Were: American Families and the Nostalgia Trap* (New York: Basic Books, 1992), 23.

11. Michael Pollan, "The Triumph of Burbopolis," *The New York Times Magazine*, 9 April 2000, 54.

12. Pollan, "Triumph of Burbopolis," 54.

13. Jones, *Honey I'm Home*, 209.

14. Mitz, *Great TV Sitcom Book*, 241.

15. Mitz, *Great TV Sitcom Book*, 333–37.

16. Means Coleman, *African American Viewers*, 103.

17. Sut Jhally and Justin Lewis, *Enlightened Racism: The Cosby Show, Audiences and the Myth of the American Dream* (Boulder: Westview Press, 1992), 7.

18. Bonnie Dow, *Prime-Time Feminism: Television, Media Culture, and the Women's Movement since 1970* (Philadelphia: University of Pennsylvania Press, 1996), 138.

19. Crossan, *Dark Interval*, 54–62.

20. Jones, *Honey I'm Home*, 266.

21. Devin D. O'Leary, "Loud and Proud," *Film and Television Magazine* website, 16 November 1998, www.desert.net/ww/11-16-98.
22. Means Coleman, *African American Viewers,* 110–118.
23. Means Coleman, *African American Viewers,* 118.
24. Means Coleman, *African American Viewers,* 118.
25. Means Coleman, *African American Viewers,* 128.
26. Paul Farhi, "Clap If You Love Mega-TV! Without the Conglomerates, You Can Wave Goodbye to Free, High-Quality Shows," *Washington Post,* 12 September 1999, B-1.

Chapter 1

1. Kathleen Tracy, *Jerry Seinfeld: The Entire Domain* (Secaucus: Birch Lane Press, 1998), 62.
2. Tracy, *Seinfeld,* 108.
3. John Squires, preface, *Entertainment Weekly Special Seinfeld Issue,* 4 May 1998, 2.
4. Tom Shales, "*Seinfeld* Standout Stand-Up," *Washington Post,* TV Preview, 31 May 1990, D01.
5. Tracy, *Seinfeld,* 200.
6. Tracy, *Seinfeld,* 212.
7. Tracy, *Seinfeld,* 213.
8. Mary Kay Schilling and Mike Flaherty, "The Seinfeld Chronicles: An Obsessive-Compulsive Dissection of All 169 Episodes," *Entertainment Weekly Special Seinfeld Issue,* 4 May 1998, 20.
9. Tom Shales, "The Star of NBC's Hip, Hot Half-Hour, on Comedy with a Heart of Darkness," *Washington Post,* 22 April 1992, B01.
10. Shales, "Star of NBC's Hip, Hot Half-Hour."
11. *Entertainment Weekly Special Seinfeld Issue,* 4 May 1998, 29.
12. Carla Johnson, "Luckless in New York: the Schlemiel and the Schlimazl in *Seinfeld,*" *Journal of Popular Film and Television* 5, 22 (fall 1994), 117–18.
13. Johnson, "Luckless in New York."
14. Lisa Schwarzbaum, "The Jewish Question," *Entertainment Weekly Special Seinfeld Issue,* 4 May 1998, 80.
15. Rebecca Segall and Peter Ephross, "Critics Call Show 'Self-Hating.' Was *Seinfeld* Good for Jews?" *Jewish Telegraphic Agency,* 8 May 1998, reprinted on the Jewish Bulletin of Northern California's website www.jeishsf.com/bk980508/1sein.htm
16. Segall and Ephross, "Critics."
17. Tom Shales, "So Long, *Seinfeld:* Let Me Show You to the Door," *Washington Post,* 16 April 1998, B01.

18. Tracy, *Seinfeld*, 105.
19. Ken Tucker, "The Fantastic Four," *Entertainment Weekly Special Seinfeld Issue*, 4 May 1998, 14.
20. Schilling and Flaherty, "Seinfeld Chronicles," 18.
21. Johnson, "Luckless in New York," 121.
22. *Entertainment Weekly Special Seinfeld Issue*, 4 May 1998, 85.
23. Tracy, *Seinfeld*, 111.
24. Tracy, *Seinfeld*, x.
25. Mike Flaherty, "The Older, The Bitter," *Entertainment Weekly Special Seinfeld Issue*, 4 May 1998, 92.
26. Schilling and Flaherty, "Seinfeld Chronicles," 18.
27. Shales, "Star of NBC's Hip, Hot Half-Hour," B01.
28. Raymond C. Van Leeuwen, "Ecclesiastes: Introduction," in *The HarperCollins Study Bible: New Revised Standard Version*, Wayne Meeks, gen. ed. (New York: HarperCollins, 1993), 987.
29. Carole R. Fontaine, "Ecclesiastes," in *The Women's Bible Commentary* (Louisville: Westminster John Knox Press, 1992), 153–55.

Chapter 2

1. *Entertainment Weekly*, 19 May 1999.
2. A sampling of opinion from the pages of *Time* finds Richard Corliss praising *The Simpsons* as having "too many good ideas" (2 May 1994, 77) and Richard Zoglin disparaging it as "venomous" (16 April 1990, 85).
3. David Marc, *Comic Visions: Television Comedy and American Culture* (New York: Blackwell, 1997), 190.
4. This episode is exceptional in the context of the series as a whole because there are no subplots. In most episodes, as in most family sitcoms, the main plot revolves around either a parent or a child, and subplots involve various other family members. Here, however, Homer's travails are the focus of a single plot.
5. Episodes of *The Simpsons* often include the animated figures and actual voices of real celebrities, ranging from Mel Gibson and Michael Jackson to Bob Hope and Elizabeth Taylor. They are part and parcel of the show's pronounced intertextuality, in which popular cultural icons are referenced during the course of a half-hour. In the episode under discussion, there are no famous "voice-overs," although a number of intertextual references occur.
6. See Daniel Bell, *The Cultural Contradictions of Capitalism* (New York: Basic Books, 1976).

7. The Simpson family members (Homer, Marge, Lisa, and Maggie) are named after the actual father, mother, and two sisters of series co-creator Matt Groening; Bart is an anagram for "brat," which rhymes with "Matt." In addition, the street name "Evergreen Terrace" refers to Evergreen State University in Washington, where Groening went to college.

8. David Owen, "Taking Humor Seriously," *The New Yorker*, 13 March 2000, 73.

9. This does not mean that animated programs are inexpensive or easy to make. The production costs of an episode of *The Simpsons* are about $1.5 million. The whole process takes more than six months, from story development, through layout design, to the actual animation (done mainly in Korea, and consisting of over 24,000 individual drawings per twenty-one-minute show), to laying down the voice track, with the musical accompaniment of a full orchestra.

10. Although it *is* biting satire, *The Simpsons* does not meet the criteria for a "parable" in Crossan's sense. The show criticizes many, if not most, of the values of contemporary American culture but offers no real alternative, other than implying that our social life (particularly in the family) should be "more authentic" and "more humane" in some unspecified way.

11. In a further symbolic reference, Thomas Edison himself was the founder of General Electric—the corporate owner of Fox's rival network NBC. GE is satirized on the show by the nuclear power plant where Homer works, owned by greedy Mr. Burns.

12. Presumably, the producers of the show do not themselves have working-class status. They seem to be white, well-educated, politically progressive intellectuals who use a "working-class" point of view to criticize what they feel is wrong with American society.

13. *The Simpsons* is almost alone among sitcoms in not employing a "laugh track" (in lieu of a studio audience) to cue viewers to what is "funny." The producers use this novel technique to symbolize that they trust viewers to respond to satirical humor without relying on a "contrived" prompt. In addition, so many jokes are crammed into each half-hour script that a laugh track would be both intrusive and almost impossible to produce.

14. That *The Simpsons*, with its cutting commentary on consumerism and capitalism, has led to the enrichment of its creative team is perhaps the deepest irony of all (see

Owen, "Taking Humor Seriously"). Of course, without appealing to the tastes of a wider audience and without the vast financial resources derived from its success in the market, such a show could never be produced.

15. Gerry Bowler, "The Last Christian TV family in America," in Les Sillars, *Alberta Report: The Weekly Newsmagazine*—Internet edition, http://albertareport.com, 21 October 1996.

16. Frank McConnell, "'Real' Cartoon Characters," *Commonweal* 15 (June 1990), 390.

Chapter 3

1. *Jet*, 16 March 1998.1_55/57046399/print.jhtml

2. Michael McWilliams, "*Moesha* Is a '90s *Gidget* Morphed with *Ricki Lake*," *Detroit News*, 23 January 1996 [newspaper online]. Available from http://www.detnews.com/menu/stories/32990.htm; Internet; accessed November 2, 2000.

3. Ken Tucker, "Singer Brandy Turns Actress, in New TV Series: *Moesha*," *Entertainment Weekly*, 26 February 1996, 58.

4. Greg Braxton, "*Moesha* Tribute a Rare Museum Piece," *Los Angeles Times*, 10 March 1999, Internet version: www.kcbs-tv.com/entertainment/stories/temp-entertainment-990310-102415.html

5. On the Internet at www.smartgirl.com/pages/television/moeshaeijah.html

6. Kelly Starling, "National Uproar Forces Schedule Changes (Few New African-American Shows in the 1999 Fall Television Lineup)," *Ebony*, on the Internet at www.findarticles.com/cf_0/m1077/1_55/57046399/print.jhtml

7. "How Blacks Differ from Whites in TV Viewing," *Jet*, 16 March 1998, on the Internet at www.findarticles.com/cf_0/m1355/n16_v93/21250132/print.jhtml

8. Rick Marin and Allison Samuels, "Brandy: Keeping It Real," *Newsweek*, 25 March 1996, 69.

9. Starling, "National Uproar," 3.

10. Kristal Brent Zook, *Color by Fox.* (New York: Oxford University Press, 1999) 48–49.

11. Marin and Samuels, "Brandy," 69.

12. The November 13, 2000, episode of *Moesha* was a spoof on *The Cosby Show*, with Frank dreaming he had the perfect family, like the Huxtables. Frank wore an expensive sweater and joked at one point about how rich he was.

13. "Returning Favorites 2000," *TV Guide,* 9 September 2000, 12.
14. "Singer Brandy Turns Actress, in New TV Series: *Moesha,*" *Jet,* 26 February 1996, 58.
15. "UPN Seeks Impact," *Broadcasting & Cable,* 22 May 2000.
16. Rick Kissell, "All Eyes on Monday Battleground," *Variety,* 25 September 2000; Internet version: www.findarticles.com /cf_0/m1312/6_380/65861187/print.jhtml
17. "The Parkers Win Big Laughs as No. 1 Show in Black Households," *Jet,* 10 April 2000, on the Internet at www.findarticles.com/cf_0/m1355/18_97/61573860 /print.jhtml
18. Scott Osler, "Bringing Folks Together on Sunday," *San Francisco Chronicle,* 13 November, 2000, A2.
19. Csar G. Soriano, "TV Shows Honored for Honest Talk on Sex," *USA Today,* 26 October 2000.
20. "Singer Brandy Turns Actress, in New TV Series: *Moesha,*" *Jet,* 26 February 1996, 58.
21. Pierre Wolf, *Discernment: The Art of Choosing Well* (Liguori, MO: Triumph, 1993), x.

Chapter 4

1. Alyssa Katz, "Will and Grace," *The Nation,* 2 Nov. 1998, 34.
2. Richard Natale, "Will Power," *The Advocate: The National Gay and Lesbian Newsmagazine,* 15 September 1998, 32.
3. Natale, "Will Power," 32.
4. Natale, "Will Power," 33.
5. A. J. Jacobs and Kristen Baldwin, "When Gay Men Happen to Straight Women," *Entertainment Weekly,* 23 October 1998, 22.
6. Valerie Keklenski, "Gay Kiss Makes a Point on 'Will and Grace'," *Oregonian,* 22 February 2000, D10.
7. Bonnie Dow, *Prime-Time Feminism: Television, Media Culture and the Women's Movement since 1970* (Philadelphia: University of Pennsylvania Press, 1996), 103.
8. Neil Postman, *Amusing Ourselves to Death: Public Discourse in the Age of Show Business* (New York: Penguin Books, 1985), 156.
9. William Fore, *Television and Religion: The Shaping of Faith, Values and Culture* (Minneapolis: Augsburg, 1987), 46.
10. Ella Taylor, quoted in Dow, *Prime-Time Feminism,* 7.
11. Joey Earl Horstman, "Anatomy of a Joke: Did You Hear the One about the . . . ," *The Other Side* (July–August 1993), 42–43, 47.

Chapter 5

1. Veronica Chambers, "How Would Ally Do It?" *Newsweek*, 2 March 1998, 58.
2. Quoted in Chambers, "How Would Ally Do It?" 58.
3. Steven D. Stark, "Lady's Night: Ally McBeal's Quirky Appeal," *New Republic*, 29 December 1997, 13–14.
4. Lynn Snowden, "Calista Bites Back," *George* (May 1999), 73.
5. Ally McBeal: "About the Show," FOXWORLD online, available http.//www.foxworld.com/ally/show.htm. Accessed 17 April 1999.
6. Alyssa Katz, "Female Trouble," *The Nation*, 15 December 1997, 36–38.
7. Seema Nayyar and Jennifer Lach, "We're Being Watched," *American Demographics Magazine* (October 1998), online, available http://www.demographics.com/publications/ad/. Accessed 17 April 1999.
8. Ally even makes a vague reference to the study in another episode where she laments turning twenty-nine, saying, "I have a better chance of being hit by lightning." That lament was most commonly heard in the 80s as, "I have a better chance of being attacked by a terrorist than of getting married after thirty-five."
9. Susan Faludi, *Backlash* (New York: Crown, 1991), 9–19.
10. Elisabeth Fiorenza, "Feminist Spirituality, Christian Identity, and Catholic Vision," in *Womanspirit Rising: A Feminist Reader in Religion*, ed. Carol P. Christ and Judith Plaskow (San Francisco: Harper Row, 1979), 137.
11. Marsha Wilfong, "Genesis 2:18–24," *Interpretation* 42 (1988), 61.
12. Ginia Bellafante, "Feminism: It's All about Me!" *Time*, 28 June 1998, 54–62.
13. Bonnie J. Dow, *Prime-Time Feminism* (Philadelphia: University of Pennsylvania Press, 1996), 196.
14. Cathy Young, "Critics Are Wrong about Ally McBeal," *Detroit News* 23 September 1998, online, available http://www.detnews.com/EDITPAGE/9809/23/young/young.htm. 17 October 1999.
15. Ruth Shalit, "Canny and Lacy (Betrayal of Postfeminism in TV Portrayals of Women)," *New Republic*, 4–6 April 1998, 218.

Interlude

1. From *Prayers by Michel Quoist* (Kansas City: Sheed & Ward, 1963), as cited by Fred Gealy, in *Celebration*

(Nashville: Graded Press, The Methodist Publishing House, 1969), 112.

2. Kathleen Norris, *The Cloister Walk* (New York: Riverhead Books, The Berkeley Publishing Group, a division of Penguin Putnam, 1996), 117–21.

3. S. Robert Lichter et al., *Prime Time: How TV Portrays American Culture* (Washington, D.C.: Regnery Publishing, 1994), 319.

4. Art Silverblatt, *Media Literacy: Keys to Interpreting Media Messages* (Westport, CT: Praeger, 1995), 277.

5. G. Gerbner and L. Gross, "Living with Television: The Violence Profile," *Journal of Communication* 26 (1976), 173–99.

6. Cited by Richard Sparks, *Television and the Drama of Crime* (London: Open University Press, 1992), 69.

7. Ulysses Torassa, "Kids Less Violent after Cutting Back on TV," *San Francisco Chronicle*, 15 January, 2001, A1 and A6.

8. Series editor's introduction to Sparks, *Television and the Drama of Crime*, xii.

9. See Sparks, *Television and the Drama of Crime*, 86–98, for an extensive critique of Gerbner's theory.

10. Sparks, *Television and the Drama of Crime*, 25. See also Gary A. Copeland and Dan Slater, "Television, Fantasy and Vicarious Catharsis," *Critical Studies in Mass Communication* 2 (1985), 352–62.

11. J. Fiske and J. Hartley, *Reading Television* (London: Methuen, 1978).

12. Tim Brooks and Earle Marsh, *The Complete Directory to Prime Time Network and Cable TV Shows* (New York: Ballantine Books, 1995), 289.

13. Quentin J. Schultze, "Civil Sin: Evil and Purgation in the Media," *Theology Today* 50 (January 1993), 239.

14. Lichter et al., *Prime Time*, 307.

15. Todd Gitlin, *Inside Prime Time* (New York: Pantheon, 1983), 308–13.

16. Thomas H. Zynda, "The Metaphoric Vision of *Hill Street Blues*," *Journal of Popular Film and Television* 14, 3 (1986), 103–06.

17. Jeremy Butler, "*Miami Vice*: The Legacy of Film Noir," *Journal of Popular Film and Television* 13, 3 (1985), 130–31.

18. Stephen D. Stark, "O.J. Helped My Media's Changing Views of Cops," *National Law Journal* 17, 28, 13 March 1995, A23.

19. Andrew Billen, "We Have No Faith in the Law: Could It Be Because Our Police Are Watching the Box Not Wisely But Too Well?" *New Statesman*, 25 October 1996, 38.

20. Albert Auster, "A Look at Some Contemporary American and British Cop Shows," *Television Quarterly* 29, 2 (spring 1997), 53.

21. Auster, "A Look," 55.

Part II

1. Hal Himmelstein, "Melodrama," in *Museum of Broadcast Communications Encyclopedia of Television (MBC Encyclopedia)*, ed. Horace Newcomb (Chicago: Fitzroy Dearborn, 1997), 1035–37.

2. Robin Nelson, *TV Drama in Transition: Forms, Values and Cultural Change* (London: Macmillan, 1997), 25.

3. Hal Himmelstein, *Television Myth and the American Mind* (New York: Praeger, 1994), 200.

4. Himmelstein, *Television Myth*, 198.

5. *The Powers that Be* (New York: Doubleday, 1998), 42–48.

6. Nelson, *TV Drama*, 18–19.

7. Steven Stark, *Glued to the Set: The 60 Television Shows and Events That Made Us Who We Are Today* (New York: Delta, 1997), 46.

8. Stark, *Glued to the Set*, 89.

9. Stark, *Glued to the Set*, 88.

10. David Thornburn, "Detective Programs," in *MBC Encyclopedia*, 484.

11. Arthur Asa Berger, "The Prisoner," in *MBC Encyclopedia*, 1297–99.

12. Thomas Schatz, "Workplace Programs," in *MBC Encyclopedia*, 1872.

13. Robert J. Thompson, *Television's Second Golden Age: From Hill Street Blues to ER* (New York: Continuum, 1996).

14. Jeremy Butler, "Police Programs," in *MBC Encyclopedia*, 1265–66.

Chapter 6

1. Hugo Lundgren, "Questions for Dick Wolf: Cop Show and Tell," *The New York Times Magazine*, 12 September 1999, Internet version, 2.

2. Rene Balcer, interview with Dick Wolf, www.wolf-films.com/interview, no date, 3.

3. Lundgren, "Questions for Dick Wolf," 2.

4. Balcer, interview, 2.

5. Robert F. Moss, "TV Cop Shows Cop-out on Race," *Commonweal* 123, 19, 8 November 1996, 12.

6. The Sentencing Project, http://www.sentencingproject.org
7. Cf. especially Paul's letter to the Romans 1–8.
8. New York: Doubleday, 1999.

Chapter 7

1. Rick Marin, "S*M*A*S*H," *Newsweek*, 31 October 1994, 7.
2. Richard Zoglin, "Angels with Dirty Faces," *Time*, 31 October 1994, 75.
3. Bernard Weinraub, "*E.R.* Is Back on Its Feet After Major Surgery," *The New York Times*, Sunday 14 November 1999, Arts & Leisure section, 17.
4. Don Jeffrey, "Buycycles: An Analysis of Consumer Purchasing Trends," *Billboard*, 9 August 1997, 46.
5. Ray Richmond, "TV Sitcoms: The Great Divide—Few Shows Bridge Black, White Auds," *Variety*, 13 April 1998, 1.
6. Leon Jaroff, "How Good Is the E.R's Rx?" *Time*, 1 June 1998, 74.
7. "Eriq La Salle Requested That His Interracial Relationship on 'ER' End," *Jet*, 5 April 1999, 16.
8. Weinraub, "*E.R.* Is Back," 17.
9. Marin, "S*M*A*S*H," 49.
10. Elayne Rapping, "Bad Medicine," *Progressive* (May 1995), 38.
11. Sharon Lynn Sperry, "Television News as Narrative," in *Understanding Television: Essays on Television as a Social and Cultural Force*, ed. Richard P. Adler (Westport, CT: Praeger Special Studies), 135.
12. Sperry, "Television News."

Chapter 8

1. For a further discussion of emotional triangles, see Edwin Friedman, *Generation to Generation: Family Process in Church and Synagogue* (New York: Guilford Press, 1985), especially 35–39.
2. This difficulty is demonstrated by Laura Stempel Mumford in her discussion of genre in *Love and Ideology in the Afternoon: Soap Opera, Women and Television Genre* (Bloomington: Indiana University Press, 1995), 14–46, and by Robert C. Allen in *Speaking of Soap Operas* (Chapel Hill: University of North Carolina Press, 1985), 8–29.
3. Ruth Rosen, "Search for Yesterday," in *Watching Television*, ed. Todd Gitlin (New York: Pantheon Books, 1986), 53.
4. Rosen, "Search for Yesterday," 52.

5. Rob Owen, *Gen X TV: The Brady Bunch to Melrose Place,* in *The Television Series,* series ed. Robert J. Thompson (Syracuse: Syracuse University Press, 1997), 72.

6. Owen, *Gen X TV,* 76.

7. Jeremy Butler, *Television: Critical Methods and Applications* (Belmont, CA: Wadsworth Publishing, 1994), 137.

8. Rosen, "Search for Yesterday," 61.

9. Rosen, "Search for Yesterday," 45.

10. Rosen, "Search for Yesterday," 51.

Chapter 9

1. A. J. Jacobs, "Heaven Can Rate: After a Cursed Beginning, *Touched by an Angel* Has Become This Season's Most Miraculous Hit," *Entertainment Weekly,* 8 March 1996, found on *Entertainment Weekly Online,* 25 September 1999.

2. Jacobs, "Heaven Can Rate."

3. Susan Brill, "Martha's Angels: A Touch of the Divine in Prime-time," *Christianity Today,* 13 November 1995, 65.

4. Brill, "Martha's Angels."

5. Rick Schindler, "A Spiritual Journey," *TV Guide,* 29 March 1997, 40–41.

6. Daniel Howard Cerone, "Angels and Insights," *TV Guide,* 29 March 1999, 45.

7. Joanne Kaufman, "Tuning in to God," *TV Guide,* 29 March 1997, 33.

8. Kaufman, "Tuning in," 34.

9. Jacobs, "Heaven Can Rate."

10. Robert Coote and David Ord, *The Bible's First History* (Philadelphia: Fortress Press, 1989), 105.

11. *Harper's Encyclopedia of Mystical and Paranormal Experience,* Rosemary Guiley, ed. (San Francisco: Harper, 1991), 30–31.

12. This point was made by a theological student, Terry Fowler, in a class presentation on *Touched by an Angel* during San Francisco Theological Seminary's course "Religion, Politics and Primetime Television," April 21, 2000.

13. Cornell West, *Race Matters* (Boston: Beacon Press, 1993), 3–4.

14. Lynn Schofield Clark, "Listening to Audiences: Talk about Religion in the Media," keynote address presented at the annual meeting of the Catholic Theological Society in America, Ottawa, Canada, June 1998.

Chapter 10

1. Jon Katz, "The Truth Really Is Out There: Fox's Sci-fi Hit: *The X-Files* Provides a Case Study in How the Media Have Blundered in Their Coverage of Pop Culture," *Brill's Content* (May 1999), 56.
2. Brian Lowry, *Trust No One: The Official Third Season Guide to The X-Files* (New York: Harper, 1996), 195.
3. Lowry, *Trust No One*, introduction.
4. Katz, "The Truth," 57.
5. Jan Jagodzinski and Brigitte Hipfl, "Youth Fantasies: *The X-Files*," paper presented at Summit 2000 Conference on Children Youth, and the Media, May 15, 2000, Toronto, Canada.
6. Jagodzinski and Hipfl, "Youth Fantasies."
7. Walter Truett Anderson, ed., *The Truth about the Truth: De-confusing and Re-constructing the Postmodern World* (New York: Putnam, 1995), 3.
8. Lawrence Cahoone, *From Modernism to Postmodernism: An Anthology* (Cambridge: Blackwell, 1996), 1–23.
9. Joyce Appleby, Lynn Hunt, and Margaret Jacob, *Telling the Truth about History* (New York: Norton, 1994), 201.
10. Appleby, Hunt, and Jacob, *Telling the Truth*, 203.
11. Huston Smith, *Beyond the Post-Modern Mind* (Wheaton, IL: Quest Books, 1989), xiii.
12. Marva J. Dawn, *Reaching Out without Dumbing Down* (Grand Rapids: Eerdmans, 1995), 36.
13. Rodney Clapp, "'The Truth Is Out There': Why *The X-Files* Is Really about Epistemology," *Books & Culture* (May/June 1997), 11.
14. Dawn, *Reaching Out*, 38.
15. Daniel Migliore, *Faith Seeking Understanding* (Grand Rapids: Eerdmans, 1991), 23.

Part III

1. Steven D. Stark, *Glued to the Set: The 60 Television Shows and Events That Made Us Who We Are Today* (New York: Delta, 1997), 165.
2. Himmelstein, *Television, Myth, and the American Mind* (Westport, CT: Praeger, 1994), 276.
3. Jim Rutenburg, "Carnival of the Animals," *The New York Times*, 29 June 2000, B1 and B8.
4. James Poniewozik, "We Like to Watch," *Time*, 26 June 2000, cover and 56–62.
5. Marshall Sella, "Completely Candid Camera," *The New York Times Magazine*, 21 May 2000, 50–57, 68, 72, 102, 106.

6. Jim Boothroyd, "Death of the Regulator," *Adbusters* 28 (Winter 2000), 28.
7. Himmelstein, *Television*, 249.
8. Rifka Rosenwein, "Why Media Mergers Matter," *Brill's Content* (January 2000), 94.
9. Postman, *Amusing Ourselves to Death* (New York: Penguin Books, 1985), 87.
10. Sharon Lynn Sperry, "Television News as Narrative," in *Television as a Cultural Force*, ed. Richard Adler (Westport, CT: Praeger, 1976), 141.
11. Himmelstein, *Television*, 379.
12. Sperry, "Television News," 143.
13. N. T. Wright, *The Challenge of Jesus* (Downers Grove, IL: InterVarsity Press, 1999), 150–173.
14. Wright, *Challenge of Jesus*, 170.

Chapter 11

1. Bunny Hoest and John Reiner, "Laugh Parade," *San Francisco Chronicle Parade*, 26 January 1997, 14.
2. Kyle Pope, "Network and Cable TV: From Electronic Hearth to TV News on Demand," *Media Studies Journal* (spring-summer 1999), 54.
3. C. John Sommerville, *How the News Makes us Dumb: The Death of Wisdom in an Information Society* (Downers Grove, IL: Intervarsity Press, 1999); James Fallows, *Breaking The News: How the Media Undermine American Democracy* (New York: Vintage Books, 1997).
4. Robert MacNeil, "Is Television Shortening Our Attention Span?" *New York University Education Quarterly* 14, 2 (winter 1983): 2, 4. Cited in Neil Postman, *Amusing Ourselves to Death*, (New York: Penguin Books, 1985), 105.
5. Stephen Ansolabehere et al., *The Media Game: American Politics in the Television Age* (New York: Macmillan, 1993), 214.
6. Quoted by Hal Crowther in "Alone on the Cliff," *Progressive Populist*, 15 November 2000, 20.
7. Piraro, "Bizzaro," *San Francisco Chronicle*, 21 March 1995, E6.
8. Hilary B. Price, "Rhymes with Orange," *San Francisco Chronicle*, 20 March 1997, E8.
9. Marian Zailian, "Dissident Gets a Voice," *Datebook, San Francisco Chronicle*, 4 April 1993, 33.
10. Fallows, *Breaking the News*, 47.
11. Bill Moyers, "Free Speech for Sale," PBS, 1999.

12. Neil Andersen and John J. Pungente, SJ, *Scanning Television*, Video 3, "Our Constructed Worlds: Media Environments" (Toronto: Harcourt Brace, 1997), video clip 29. This excellent media literacy series with forty video clips of four to seven minutes each is available from Theatrebooks, 11 St. Thomas Street, Toronto, ON M5S 2B7, Canada, 1-800-361-3414.
13. Edward J. Epstein, *News from Nowhere* (New York: Vintage, 1974), xiv.
14. Epstein, *News from Nowhere*, 258.
15. Cornell professor Timothy Murray, as quoted by Deborah Baldwin in "Is It Fact? Or Is It Fiction? From Hollywood to the 6 O'clock News, It's Getting Harder and Harder to Tell," *Common Cause Magazine* (winter 1993), 29.
16. Juan Samovia, "The Transnational Power Structure and International Information," *development dialogue* (1981, 2), 129.
17. "The Big Story: What Is the Moral Meaning of Globalization?" *Religion and Values in Public Life* 7, 2–3, (winter-spring 1999), 4.
18. Epstein, *News from Nowhere*, 239.
19. Fallows, *Breaking the News*, 171.
20. The web site *www.newslab.org* attributes this phrase to writer Jon Franklin but does not cite the source.
21. Fallows, *Breaking the News*, 137, 140.
22. "Below the Beltway," *Sunday Examiner and Chronicle*, 22 October 2000, 2.
23. Richard Craig, "Expectations and Elections: How Television Defines Campaign News," *Critical Studies in Media Communication*, 17, 1 (March 2000), 28–44.
24. Craig, "Expectations and Elections," 29.
25. Fallows, *Breaking the News*, 26–31.
26. Jeff Leeds, "More Negative Coverage for Gore Than Bush This Fall," *San Francisco Chronicle*, 1 November 2000, A2.
27. Steven Luxenberg, "Is TV to Blame? Well, Let's Go to the Videotape," *Washington Post*, 12 November 2000, B5.
28. Luxenberg, "Is TV to Blame?"
29. Colin Morris, "The Theology of the Nine O'Clock News," in *Religion and the Media*, ed. Chris Arthur (Cardiff: University of Wales Press, 1993), 137.

Chapter 12

1. Jeremy G. Butler, *Television: Critical Methods and Applications* (Belmont, CA: Wadsworth Publishing, 1994), 10.

2. News release on PETA website, *www.peta.org.*, December 5, 2000.

3. Telephone interview with Lisa Lange, December 11, 2000.

Chapter 13

1. Jeremy G. Butler, *Television: Critical Methods and Applications* (Belmont, CA: Wadsworth Publishing, 1994), 10.

2. Art Silverblatt, *Media Literacy* (Westport, CT: Praeger, 1995), 177.

3. Interview with Roger Smitter, October 1991, Wheaton, IL.

4. Juliann Sivulka, *Soap, Sex, and Cigarettes: A Cultural History of American Advertising* (Belmont, CA: Wadsworth Publishing, 1998), 347–48.

5. Quotes of Jamieson and Schwartz from Leslie Wayne, "The 2000 Campaign Ad: Infamous Political Commercial Is Turned on Gore," *The New York Times* website 27 October 2000, www.nytimes.com

6. George Raine, "Banking on Flashy Ads," *San Francisco Examiner*, 4 October 1998, D-1.

7. Raine, "Banking on Flashy Ads," D-2.

8. Michael Osborn, "Archetypal Metaphor in Rhetoric: The Light/Dark Family," *Quarterly Journal of Speech* (April 1967), 240–41.

9. Bob Thompson, "Consumed: Melisa Smith, Yvette King, and Carrie Szejik Are Trying to Cast Off the American Culture of Spending and Excess. One Thing Is Clear: They're Going to Need All the Help They Can Get," *Washington Post*, 20 December 1998, W-11.

Chapter 14

1. Tim Goodman, "Paddy Chayefsky's 'Network' Is No Longer Satire But Prophecy," Knight-Ridder Newspapers, 16 December 1996.

2. O. S. Rankin, "Prophecy, Prophet, Seer," in *A Theological Word Book of the Bible*, ed. Alan Richardson (New York: Macmillan, 1957), 181.

3. *The Dark Interval* (Allen, TX: Argus Communications, 1975), chap. 2.

4. Sally Biddell Smith, *In All His Glory: The Life of William S. Paley, the Legendary Tycoon and His Brilliant Circle* (New York: Simon & Schuster, 1990), 277.

5. Sydney W. Head, et al., *Broadcasting in America*, 8th ed. (Boston: Houghton Mifflin, 1998), 77–78.

Conclusion

1. Gordon D. Marino, "Remote Control: The Ethics of Watching," *Christian Century*, 20 January 1999, 57.

2. Cited by Marino, "Remote Control," 57.

3. Marino, "Remote Control," 57–58.

4. Quentin Schultze, "Television Drama as a Sacred Text," in John P. Ferre, ed., *Channels of Belief* (Ames, IA: Iowa State University Press, 1990), 13.

5. William F. Fore, "Monopolistic Media: An Assault on Human Dignity," *Church and Society* (November-December 1997), 44.

APPENDIX A

Methods for "Reading" Television

The Electronic Revolution:
A New Sensorium

Television has inaugurated a revolution in the way most Americans experience the world. We have moved from a print-based culture to an electronic culture characterized by sound, rhythm, and images in motion. Two-thirds of Americans get most of their knowledge about the world not from newspapers, magazines, and books, but from television. As a result, our human sensorium—the culturally conditioned way we use our senses to perceive and process information—is changing.[1] When we read printed material, we organize information analytically, in a logical and sequential manner, at our own pace. When we watch rapidly changing images on a screen accompanied by words, music, rhythm, and other sounds, we are bombarded by a vast kaleidoscope of diverse bits of information. The sound-infused images "speak" to the affective and metaphorical areas of the brain, providing a succession of instantaneous patterns of meaning.

Images communicate more quickly than words in print. Research by Larry Smarr at the University of Illinois indicates that our brains can process 100 bits per second of words in print, whereas the eye-brain system can take in one billion bits per second of visual information.[2] Perhaps this accounts for the different "feel" of television. We feel in control of the flow of sensory data from print media, but the flow of images on a television screen controls us, giving rise to the "couch potato" sensation. When we read, we can interrupt the flow, reread a passage, argue with the author, without missing the rest of the story. When we watch, we feel more passive intellectually, while our emotions are stimulated in ways that seem beyond our control.

The churches have been slow to understand the nature of the electronic revolution. Some have used television for religious programming (televangelism) while condemning the content of network programs. Most have condemned the gratuitous sex and violence on television but have dismissed the program content as superficial or trivial, a low-brow art form with little lasting significance. Only a few—notably, those engaged in the media literacy movement—have recognized the impact of the electronic revolution on contemporary consciousness.

We take television seriously. Historically, capitalism first industrialized the economy. Now the economy—especially the entertainment sector—is industrializing culture and politics. The electronic media are the primary culture-producing industry in the world today. This industry is controlled by a few megacorporations driven by stockholder demand for profit maximization, and it thrives on sensation, titillation, and trivia, as well as some remarkable artistic work. In this book, we have claimed that prime-time television has become America's popular religion, the chief rival of the church, the synagogue, the mosque, and the temple. As such, it needs serious and sustained *theological* examination.

In Search of a Method for "Reading" Television

Educational institutions have not provided much leadership in teaching people how to "read" television. Although film has gained some recognition as high art—and therefore film criticism has a modest foothold in academia—television is frequently treated with derision. Theological seminaries are still almost exclusively preoccupied with analyzing and interpreting *written* texts. In a typical year, about six hundred courses are offered at the Graduate Theological Union (GTU) in Berkeley, California, by the nine seminaries and eight programs that make up this large theological consortium. Three of these courses focus on cinema, one on the production of video narratives, and one on "reading" television. There are many courses on exegesis (analysis) and hermeneutics (interpretation), but these are confined to the study of written texts. Less than 1 percent of the GTU curriculum deals in any depth with the impact of the electronic media on our culture.

During the 1990s while we (Walt Davis, Gary Dreibelbis, and Teresa Blythe) were teaching a GTU course on religion and television, we thought we would eventually find a textbook for students outlining, step by step, a theological method for analyzing and interpreting television programs. Instead, we found three types of resources: (1) reviews of television programs in the popular press; (2) introductory-level media literacy programs designed to raise consciousness; and (3) scholarly works (on semiotics, structuralism, neo-Marxism, literary criticism) long on theory and short on application.[3]

Why did we fail to find anything? Although film criticism is a well-established form, not much critical analysis or in-depth commentary on television shows is published. Most scholars consider television to be "low art" not worthy of serious study. Those who do study television hesitate to analyze and interpret specific programs because by the time they research, write, and publish, those programs may be off the air. Even *Seinfeld*, the most popular situation comedy of the 1990s, has received limited critical analysis. Of the 249 articles about *Seinfeld* listed in the online magazine and periodical index of the University of California library, only a handful are more than one or two pages in length, and only three reflect careful, critical study. Religious journals frequently have an in-house film critic whose weekly or monthly column examines theological themes of selected current films, but these journals rarely comment on television programs. Thus, if congregations, classes, and other groups are to seriously engage the medium of television, we must do it ourselves, in a group, using our own creativity, guided by a critical method. This book outlines such a method and *demonstrates* its use by applying it to multiple genres of television programming.

Perhaps a word about our process of production is helpful. This book is a joint creation, not a collection of essays by eight different authors. In 1999, we formed a project team of two professors; four theologically trained colleagues who had done outstanding work in television studies; a professional television producer, and a video producer. The team met for an initial four-day work session in spring 1999, during which we developed the project design, the table of contents, the format for the twenty-eight-minute video* that supplements the book, and the work procedures we would follow. Then we divided the workload and designated a principal writer and one or more supportive writers for each chapter. Assisted by a grant from the Louisville Institute, we met four more times during the next two years to review one another's work. Then we employed the services of a television studio to videotape our group at work analyzing a commercial produced by the Adbusters Media Foundation, an environmentalist watchdog group in Vancouver, British Columbia. By actually modeling the method, we advocate in the book and in the video, we hope that we can help teachers, students, and

---

*A copy of this VHS video entitled "Television through the Lens of Faith" is available from the Center for the Study of Electronic Media, San Francisco Theological Seminary, San Anselmo, CA 94960 (415-258-6654), *lvothf@sfts.edu*. See also our website: *www.lensoffaith.org*.

religious leaders to understand and make use of this tool for interacting with America's popular religion.*

More on Method

There is no agreed-on method in television studies. In a recent book entitled *Uses of Television*,[4] John Hartley tries to bring some order into this theoretically fragmented subject of study. Professor of Journalism, Media and Cultural Studies at Cardiff University, Hartley likes television and believes that "what television has been used for is the formation of cultural citizenship."[5] This view is not too far removed from our claim that prime-time television in America serves as the equivalent of a popular religion. In spite of the imperious and sarcastic tone of Hartley's characterization of scholars who see a dark side to television, *Uses of Television* is a valuable attempt at methodological coherence in a confusing field of study.

Hartley divides television studies into two somewhat incompatible groups: the school of fear and the school of desire.[6] "Camp Fear" is most popular in the United States, he says, because the American study of television has been dominated by the influence of social sciences in departments of mass communications. This school includes "all those from the behavioral psychologists to moral entrepreneurs ('clean-up TV' campaigners)" as well as "the paranoid radicals who believe television semiosis is a conspiracy by the so-called 'military-industrial complex' . . . to produce docile consumers."[7] Among the latter group Hartley names George Gerbner, "the champion of the social-science, 'what-media-control-is-doing-to-the-world' school."[8]

In contrast, the desire school consists of spokespersons like Hartley in Great Britain and John Fiske in the United States, who approach television studies from a literary or textual background in the humanities and who believe that television has or can have beneficial consequences for individual viewers and for society.

> The social science approach needs a passive audience, precisely because it is looking for influences on, power over and manipulation of that audience: the thing has to sit still (on the couch) while all this ownership, control, commercialization, consumerism (and so on) is done to it. Conversely, the literary-derived approach needs an active audience, since it sees television as communication, and communication as a two-way, interactive practice of meaning-exchange: you can't watch television passively at the semiotic level."[9]

Hartley has tapped into the animosity that exists among television scholars, but we believe the methods of those who praise television and those who lambast it are not antithetical, but indeed necessary for a balanced

---

*See *www.lensoffaith.org* for periodic updates on watching television through the lens of faith.

understanding of television programs and their effects on viewers and on society. In fact, the media literacy movement accepts the validity of both approaches because its fundamental assumption is that by teaching people how to "read" television, passive "couch potatoes" can be turned into discerning, interactive audiences. The eclectic method that we call lens analysis is an interdisciplinary attempt to combine methods from the humanities and social sciences. Each lens represents the particular "take" of a well-developed theoretical school of thought as follows:

- Narrative: literary theory and textual criticism
- Structure: structuralism (linguistics, anthropology, psychoanalysis, literary criticism, economics, history, philosophy)
- Sign and Code: semiotics (linguistics, cultural anthropology)
- Ideology and Power: political science, sociology (especially Neo-Marxism and the Critical School)
- Function: functionalism (psychology, sociology, mass communications)

Although each school or discipline has its own starting point, there is much overlap among the schools because each attempts to deal with the entire reality of television. In the introduction to this book, we identified the various lenses in a cursory manner. Here we expand on that introduction by providing a little background to each school of interpretation represented by our five lenses. Each lens is used sequentially to examine each of the fields of view described in the Introduction.

Narrative

Following the lead of Vladimir Propp, who studied the morphology of one hundred Russian folktales, John Fiske believes "there appears to be something close to a universal structure of popular narrative."[10] Propp's six-stage pattern of preparation, complication, transference, struggle, return, and recognition is transparent not only in dramas, but also in situation comedies, commercials, and fact-based programs. The three-minute story on the Patients' Bill of Rights that we examine in chapter 11 follows this pattern. The transition from one stage to the next is performed by a change of music, an alteration of light and shadow, the decrease or increase in tempo, as well as the changing dialogue itself. By analyzing each subplot, along with the setting and the characters with this pattern in mind, we can discern the worldview of a story, its depiction of the human condition, and the nature of the resolution or "salvation" it provides.

Structuralism

Anthropologist Claude Levi-Strauss, one of the pioneers of structuralism, believed that by analyzing the structure of language, one could observe the interplay among certain universal binary opposites (good/evil, nature/culture, insider/outsider) at work in the deep structures of the minds of all people. John Dominic Crossan takes his lead from Levi-Strauss in examining the structure of stories and classifying them according to their dominant social functions. The structuralist lens helps us understand a particular program's potential for preserving the social status quo or undermining it. A few examples from prime time may be useful.

Myth: The sitcom *Frasier* illustrates the functioning of myth. Frasier Crane is a psychiatrist living with his father, a retired working-class, beer-drinking detective, in a lovely upscale apartment overlooking Seattle. Frasier and his brother Niles, also a psychiatrist, believe that if they join the right clubs, drink the right beverages (fine wines), run with the right crowd, and date beautiful women, they will climb the social ladder and achieve success. Of course, they never succeed—that's what's so funny—because they are educated fools with few practical skills. They try too hard—"you overanalyze," says Martin, the father. While Frasier plays the buffoon, his goals and aspirations—his definition of the good life—are reinforced, not questioned. Viewers are encouraged to have the same goals and aspirations but to seek their attainment by other means.

Apologue: Crime shows are quintessential myths, building a world in which the forces of evil are always vanquished or held in check by forces of good. However, elements of other narrative structures are also present in crime shows. Back in the 1950s, CBS chairman William Paley decided that the heroes on the network's dramatic shows ranging from cowboys to crime fighters should be older white men with virility and style. This tradition was alive and well in the person of Captain Nash Bridges on the Friday night CBS crime show by that name, which ran from 1996 to 2001. Nash, who appears to be in his mid-fifties, dresses like a tough-guy play-boy and tools around San Francisco like a teenager in a bright yellow classic convertible with a cutout muffler, accompanied by his sidekick, "Bubba" Joe Dominquez, an affable Hispanic. "Bubba," two youthful male detectives, and Nash's live-in girlfriend—also a detective, some twenty years his junior—belong to a special crime-fighting unit and serve as naive acolytes awaiting the wise instruction of the hero. *Nash Bridges* can be regarded as an apologue for a worldview in which older white men are in charge and still have what it takes to get the job done even in San Francisco, one of the most multicultural cities in the nation.

Action: Most people think of crime dramas and sports programs as action shows because they usually contain fast-paced action, but fast-paced action is not the primary criterion for identifying what Crossan means by an action narrative. Certain so-called sports shows like *Smackdown* and the evening episodes of the World Wrestling Federation on TNT can be classified as satires. They are so outlandish that they make fun of sports shows as a genre of programming. In chapter 12, we identify the NFL Super Bowl as a myth because of the way in which it structures masculinity and competition in drawing an idealized portrait of American society. An action story as we use the term is one that describes and investigates the workings of a worldview in a fairly neutral manner. "Fact" or "reality"-based programs like those on the Discovery Channel, game shows, and news shows all fit this category, although some of these programs also contain strong qualities of myth and apologue. This is particularly true of news shows, as we indicate in chapter 11. In the 1950s when the nation was eager to improve public education and enhance our competitive edge over the Soviet Union, game shows had a strong mythic and apological quality. They provided a new kind of hero—the intelligent, well-rounded citizen who could match wits with the experts. The game shows of the 1990s also fit the action show category. Today we notice a dumbing-down of the questions and the introduction of various gimmicks like multiple choice and lifelines to stimulate dramatic tension. No longer are contestants role models for educational advancement.

Satire: Satires are to apologues as parables are to myths. What apologues defend, satires attack. *The Simpsons*, a prime-time sitcom on the Fox network, qualifies as satire in two senses. Carolyn Wall, station manager for the Fox channel in New York City, once remarked at a conference sponsored by the International Radio and Television Society: "We break all the rules." By scheduling an animated sitcom during prime time, Fox breaks the conventions of network television. By scheduling this series, which depicts the life of a barely functional family with severe communication problems, Fox ridicules the norms of traditional American family life. Each episode takes on some sacred cow and gores it. For example, the religious right must have cringed at the show that aired on Sunday evening, January 16, 2000. This episode depicted the adolescent Bart Simpson in a tent meeting taking on the role of a faith healer and vanquishing Satan with the sign of the cross emblazoned on the bottom of his magical skateboard.

Parable: In the popular imagination, parables are stories with a moral, like the tale of the little shepherd boy who cried "Wolf! Wolf!" too many times. Even some popular stories from Aesop's fables have conveyed an unexpected moral, like the story of the hare and the tortoise. These stories with a surprise twist—the fastest people are sometimes overtaken by those who persevere—qualify as parables. Not much on television today is pure parable in the sense Crossan gives to this term. In the past, some investigative news documentaries qualified for the parabolic category. For example, Edward R. Murrow's "Harvest of Shame" subverted the myth of American abundance; CBS's coverage of the Vietnam War deconstructed the idea of a just war and the public perception of the United States as savior of oppressed peoples. By excluding the press from front-line reporting of the Gulf War and spoon-feeding the media with the official version of the action, the Pentagon turned most news stories about this conflict into myths. Perhaps the antitobacco ads produced by California state agencies and aired as public service announcements are the closest thing to parable on television these days. A particularly humorous anti-Marlboro ad shows a beautiful woman looking down on a virile-looking Marlboro man with a cigarette in his mouth. The cigarette has wilted, and the caption reads, "Cigarettes cause impotence." The humor makes this ad both a satire and a parable. In chapter 14, we discuss the economic forces at work in the industry, forces that reduce the presence of parable on television.

As a consensual medium designed to entertain to a broad audience, television's dominant type of narrative is myth. Myths explore the interplay between two irreconcilable opposites and reduce anxiety by depicting imaginative ways of living with contradiction and ambiguity. Good and evil are locked in eternal battle on crime shows. On dramas like *Ally McBeal*, the dance of loneliness and romantic fulfillment keeps viewers coming back for more, in the illusory hope that the tension between these two forces will be overcome. Of course the tension must not be resolved, for that would remove the driving force that propels the narrative from episode to episode. Whenever the tension is overcome, the program comes to an end. Crossan comments: "It is much more important to believe in the possibility of solution than ever to find one in actuality. The *gain*, or advantage of myth, and its basic function, is to establish that possibility itself."[11]

This possibility provides hope and thus confers legitimacy on the structures of society depicted by the myth. Following the work of Roland Barthes, John Fiske observes that myth naturalizes and universalizes the interests of the middle class:

> Myths work to naturalize history. . . . The typical television practice of giving criminals working-class or ethnic accents is *not* a statement about the statistical probability that members of lower socioeconomic groups are more likely to turn to crime. . . . Rather it is a sign of a middle-class myth that denies the history of class relations and naturalizes the explanation of class differences into the "facts" of human nature.[12]

For the most part, on American television apologue, action, satire, and parable function to provide nuance, intrigue, and even mild criticism without undermining fundamental belief in and commitment to the dominant institutions of society by the majority of white people. Part of the appeal of television for viewers who do not identify with the dominant culture is their ability to "read" messages that belittle, make fun of, and ridicule social institutions by means of satirical and parabolic elements woven into myth-laden narratives. For example, almost every episode of the animated African-American sitcom *PJs* lampoons the faceless bureaucracy of the local office of Housing and Urban Development and by extension the larger society that oppresses people in the projects.

Semiotics

Semiotics (from the Greek *semeion*, "sign") is a close cousin of structuralism. Like structuralism, it is a broad field, attracting scholars from a variety of disciplines who use a plethora of terms and concepts. There are many semioticians, but there is no clearly agreed-on framework common to all of them.[13] One of the challenges we faced in using semiotics is the variety of semiotic schools of thought and the inconsistencies of terminology among them. For purposes of this book, we use semiotics as a method for exploring the way in which signs, codes, and messages convey meaning in different contexts.

In most cultural settings, codes are implicit and even unconscious. We are unaware of their force until someone inadvertently ignores or deliberately disobeys them. The principal of a church-sponsored high school in northern Nigeria once related a story that illustrates the unconscious work of codes. Chapel in his high school was not compulsory, but almost every student attended, especially at the beginning of each school year. When the worship leader announced, "Let us pray," most students immediately closed their eyes and bowed their heads. New students without any church experience looked around, a bit confused for a few moments until they picked up that part of the code.

Deconstructing the codes at work in television shows requires diligent attention to details. The codes are usually subtle and unwritten. They also change over time. We usually know the codes but have difficulty making explicit what is so deeply implicit and taken for granted. Like fish in water, we know how to negotiate meaning in the television environment, but we find it hard to step back from that environment to examine it critically. We have discovered that a group process of trial and error, question and counterquestion, agreement and disagreement can provide insights into the workings of television codes that were opaque to us before we wrestled with them as a group.

Television commercials provide rich examples of the relations between sign, code, message, and context because their narrative brevity is achieved by means of semiotic density. The First Union Bank commercial discussed in chapter 13 provides an example of semiotic density open to multiple readings, depending on what the audience brings to the viewing experience. In a ten-second sequence of seven shots during the early part of the commercial, we see (1) a man in a bowler hat standing on the ledge of the roof of a Wall Street skyscraper (2) who then steps off the ledge. Next we have (3) the first up-shot of the man about to fall, (4) a side-shot of his falling, and (5) a second up-shot of the man in midair. Finally we see (6) other men on the roof looking down at the falling man as (7) a golden parachute opens. In the sound script of this shot sequence, we hear ominous music conveying danger. In the verbal script, a deep-voiced narrator tells us, "This is a world only a few know well. A world of risk and uncertainty, where the roads can take you to success or prosperity, or to no place at all." The seven visual shots above are interspersed with other shots of danger and risk. The threatening depiction of a Wall Street broker jumping off the top ledge of a skyscraper brings up images of the 1929 stock market crash. The bowler hat and the pinstripe suit are signs governed by the code of fashion in place among financiers of the era. The leap from the building is a sign conveying the risk that brokers face when the market crashes. In the sixth shot, we see that the broker in midair is wearing black and white shoes like those of the Joker in Batman. Then the golden parachute opens, and the television viewer is jolted by an unexpected sign governed by a different code and sending just the opposite message. Some audiences who distrust Wall Street can read the last two shots as an indication that in today's world the rules have changed. When the market goes south, brokers, like other CEOs, not only save themselves first but also make a fine profit in the process.

Neo-Marxism and Critical Sociology

A principal legacy of Karl Marx is our understanding of the nature of ideology and power. Sociological studies of class, race and ethnicity, gender, sexual orientation, and other forms of group identity borrow heavily from Marxist thought. The same is true of the various liberation theologies that have sprung up all over the world since the mid-1960s. The changing definitions of sexual harassment, misuse of office, and domestic abuse that have been codified into law and professional codes of behavior during the past two decades also owe a debt to neo-Marxist thinking for calling our attention to the nuances of power in human relationships. In television studies, this lens helps us look at program narratives to see who has power and who does not, how power is used, and what its consequences are. It also helps us examine whether the worldview of a particular program is reactionary or progressive.[14] Chapters 13 and 14 make extensive use of this lens in exploring questions of ownership and advertising.

Questions of power and ideology are everywhere on television, from the gender politics of programs like *Home Improvement* and *Ally McBeal* to the satirical humor hurled against a faceless New York City housing department by *PJs*, as well as the treatment of "scumbags" by Andy Sipowitz on *NYPD Blue*. What is not so evident to many Americans is how newscasts themselves are thoroughly ideological, as the mid-1980s slogan of the CBS evening news declared: "We keep America on top of the world." What appears to us as a dastardly evil act of terrorism—the bombing of the U.S. naval vessel The *Cole*—may appear to some Yemeni as an act of heroic resistance against U.S. dominance in Middle Eastern affairs. By raising questions of power and ideology, this lens helps us explore ways the same program can be "read" by different viewers in diametrically different ways.

Functionalism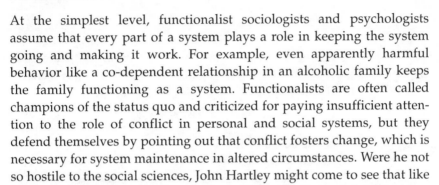

At the simplest level, functionalist sociologists and psychologists assume that every part of a system plays a role in keeping the system going and making it work. For example, even apparently harmful behavior like a co-dependent relationship in an alcoholic family keeps the family functioning as a system. Functionalists are often called champions of the status quo and criticized for paying insufficient attention to the role of conflict in personal and social systems, but they defend themselves by pointing out that conflict fosters change, which is necessary for system maintenance in altered circumstances. Were he not so hostile to the social sciences, John Hartley might come to see that like his nemesis, George Gerbner, he too is a functionalist and that his advocacy for television as an agent of democratic citizenship is in fact a functionalist perspective.

Apropos of the subject of this book, functionalists examine television's effects or consequences for individuals and society. This can take a "gratifications" form by asking people why they watch television, or an "effects" form by measuring attitudinal and behavioral changes that are inferred to have come about because of watching television (e.g., George Gerbner's studies, which show that those who watch television more than four hours per day report that they are more fearful than those who watch less than that amount).[15] Both types of studies are complex and fraught with difficulties. People who are asked why they watch television may not really know or may give superficial or even false answers. Proving that heavy watching of television or of violence on television causes fear and leads to violent behavior requires ruling out other possible causes. Nonetheless, the public debate about sex, violence, consumerism, infotainment, and the "dumbing down" of culture in general is a functionalist debate—one side blaming television and the other side exonerating it.

Technically, one might put Crossan in the functionalist school, because he talks about the social function of story. However, we put Crossan's work under the structuralist lens because he sees himself as a structuralist and because his work emphasizes how a story is constructed by the storyteller to fulfill its intended function. The functionalist tone of Crossan's work is an example of how the five lenses complement and interpenetrate one another.

Notes for Appendix A

1. For a detailed analysis of the concept of a culture's sensorium, see Walter Ong, *Orality and Literacy* (London: Methuen, 1982).

2. Howard Snyder, *Earthcurrents: The Struggle for the World's Soul* (Nashville: Abingdon, 1995), 109, as cited by Tex Sample, "The Impact of Electronic Culture," the J. Hubert Henderson Conference on Church and Ministry, Pittsburgh Theological Seminary, May 9–10, 1996, second lecture.

3. A few scholarly books deal with specific programs: Bonnie Dow's *Prime-Time Feminism* (Philadelphia: University of Pennsylvania Press, 1996), which includes chapters on *The Mary Tyler Moore Show, One Day at a Time, Designing Women, Murphy Brown,* and *Dr. Quinn, Medicine Woman.* However, even these scholars do not delineate their methods or show how their interpretive conclusions emerge from the use of their methods. This leaves the impression that television criticism is a form of intuitionism.

4. Hartley, *Uses of Television* (London: Routledge, 1999).

5. Hartley, *Uses of Television*, 26.

6. Hartley, *Uses of Television*, chap. 10, "Schools of Thought: Desire and Fear; Discourse and Politics," 127–39.

7. Hartley, *Uses of Television*, 132–33.

8. Hartley, *Uses of Television*, 135.

9. Hartley, *Uses of Television*, 135.

10. *Television Culture* (London: Routledge, 1997), 318. Originally published by Methuen in 1987.

11. John Dominic Crossan, *The Dark Interval* (Allen, TX: Argus Communications, 1975), 37.

12. Fiske, *Television Culture*, 134.

13. Robert Schreiter notes that in 1969 the International Association for the Study of Semiotics was founded, grouping scholars as diverse as philosophers, linguists, sociologists, anthropologists, and literary critics, as well as those who study genetics and cybernetics. *Constructing Local Theologies* (Mary Knoll, NY: Orbis Books, 1985), 51. Ferdinand de Saussure, Roland Barthes, and Clifford Geertz are among the most noted scholars who have made extensive use of semiotics in their analyses of culture. Two television critics we have relied on, John Fiske and Todd Gitlin, have been heavily influenced by semiotics as well as by neo-Marxist scholarship.

14. The standard we use for measuring these concepts (reactionary, progressive) is taken from Paul Lehmann, *Ethics in a Christian Context* (New York: Harper & Row, 1963), namely, whether a particular program portrays life in a more human or less human way for all concerned.

15. For over two decades, Gerbner has been popularizing the ongoing studies conducted by a team of researchers under his direction at the Annenberg School of Communications at the University of Pennsylvania. See Harry F. Waters, "Life according to TV," *Newsweek*, 6 December 1982, 136–40.

APPENDIX B

*Worksheet for Analyzing
and Interpreting Television "Texts"*

Recommended instructions: First, watch the episode once with another person or group of people before looking at this worksheet, discuss the episode together, and jot down your impressions on the back of this page. Second, study the questions under Lens Analysis, Sections A and B; watch the episode a second time, and then answer the questions under Sections A and B. Third, do the same thing for the next two sections, until the entire worksheet is completed.

Your name: _____ Name of program: _____
Date episode aired: _____
Genre: (circle one) Situation comedy, drama, newscast, newsmagazine, documentary, commercial, game show, music video, reality-based program, other

Lens Analysis

Lens 1: The Narrative Elements

Describe the setting of the series:
Describe the setting of this particular episode:

How does this episode fulfill the standard genre formula?

How does it go beyond the standard genre formula?

Briefly describe the narrative structure of the episode:

    Plot A

    Plot B

    Plot C

    Plot D

Who are the protagonists, and what are their motivations?

Who are the antagonists, and what are their motivations?

How does this episode accommodate television's interruptive and commercial nature?

How are the major issues, problems, and enigmas resolved?

How does the episode end?

Who or what are the stereotypes?

Who are the heroes and villains?

How do the main characters relate to one another?

What relief is sought in the episode, and by whom?

Are some characters favored and some disfavored?

Lens 2: Structure

What is the dominant message of this episode?

What nonresolvable contradictions are explored in this episode?

How does this episode defend a particular view of life?

What worldview is described and explored in this episode?

What elements of satire are included in this episode?

Can you identify elements of cultural subversion in this episode?

Lens 3: Signs, Codes, Messages

Describe how the camera is used to tell the story.

How does the overall look and tone of the show contribute to and shape the stories that are told?

How do the program's lighting and sound design affect the narrative and its meaning?

What special effects are used? How do they contribute to the story?

What signs are used to convey major messages?

What codes govern these signs?

What icons are at work in this episode?

Lens 4: Power and Ideology

What were the dominant sociopolitical issues and ideologies at work in American society when this episode first aired? How are they reflected in the episode?

Who are the commercial sponsors? What are they trying to sell? Who is the target audience or consumer?

From whose point of view is the story told?

Whose point of view is absent?

Who has power over whom in the narrative? Why? To what effect?

How is race structured or portrayed in the episode?

How is gender structured or portrayed in the episode?

How is socioeconomic class structured or portrayed in the episode?

How are scarce resources allocated in the narrative?

How is conflict resolved? If violent, who wins or loses? Do perpetrators suffer?

Lens 5: Functions

Why do you think people watch this show?

In what way do you think this episode is used by most people in the viewing audience?

_____pure entertainment	_____catharsis for frustrations and anxieties
_____validating a certain lifestyle	_____fantasy testing of behaviors and solutions
_____baby-sitter for children	_____background noise for the house .
_____learning about the world or the culture we live in	_____learning about different lifestyles
_____other_____	

What behavior does this show recommend?

What effects, both short term and long term, might this show have on viewers?

Analysis of Fields of View

Shot and Scene

Locate one scene that communicates the dominant theme of the episode. Identify the verbal, sound, and sight scripts used to convey meaningful messages.

Subplot Analysis

How does the subplot containing this scene contribute to the overall theme of the show?

Episode and Series Analysis

Is this episode representative of the themes of the series? How has the series changed since it was first aired?

What distinguishes this series and episode from other shows of the same genre in the 1990s?

Genre Analysis

What are the stock codes at work in this genre?

How has the genre evolved over the past half century?

What is the place of this series in the genre?

Television Network and Industry Analysis

To what primary audience does this show's network appeal? What commercial forces are at work here, and how do they affect this show?

Analysis of American Society and Culture in Its Global Context

What slice of American life is portrayed here? What slice of American life is absent or suppressed on this show?

What effects might this show have on audiences in other countries?

Theological Analysis

How is the human predicament presented in this story?

What change is sought to relieve the tension or overcome the problem? (What is "salvation" for this story?)

What are the main desires of the characters who are agents of change?

Who changes? How? In response to what?

What are the consequences of the characters' change?

Who helps others change?

Does any character suffer on behalf of another? How?

When and where does transcendence (getting outside oneself) occur?

Who looks for something beyond themselves, their jobs, and their social roles?

Which of the following themes were prominent in the episode? Circle them.

- Creativity, nurturing, compassion, joy, celebration, praise
- Sin, evil, guilt, confession, repentance, grace, forgiveness, reconciliation
- Spiritual blindness, spiritual awakening
- Oppression, sickness, liberation, healing, grace in the midst of ambiguity

- Vocation, call, service
- Courage, prudence, wisdom, moderation, freedom, faith, hope, love
- Community, "common good," individualism, privatism, anxiety, lack of faith
- Pride, greed, sexual lust, desire for worldly things
- Desire for power over others, hypocrisy, self-righteousness, self-justification
- Meanness, cruelty, revenge

Do this episode and series point people to an encounter with mystery? Do they seduce people into a vague "self-trip" of nice feelings?

Does this episode portray a humanity that knows and accepts its own vulnerability?

How does this episode depict the "other," the poor, the vulnerable, the marginalized?

Does it examine the social and political dimensions of personal problems, or does it privatize them and avoid social critique?

How does the dominant concern in this episode resonate with your own life?

How do this show and episode resonate with and diverge from a Christian understanding of life?

After reflecting on the above, would you recommend this show to a friend? Why or why not?

Action Step

As a result of my examination of this episode, I am resolved to

_____

_____

_____

_____

_____

_____

_____

_____

_____

_____

_____

_____

APPENDIX C-1

Lesson Plan for Situation Comedies

Using *Ally McBeal* in a Discussion Group

This lesson plan is designed to be used by a lay or clergy group leader who may or may not be familiar with the show. As group leader you will need:

- A room in which everyone can see the television

- A television with an adequate-sized screen

- A VCR, preferably with a remote control device.

- A ninety-minute block of time to allow for adequate discussion

Steps in Preparation

1. As the group leader, decide what your goal for the discussion will be. Suggestions include:

    - Discover how the dominant message resonates with my view of faithful living.

    - Discover the embedded theology in this episode.

    - Demonstrate how to use the *Watching What We Watch* lenses on a television episode.

2. Well before the discussion meeting, invite the group to watch (and videotape) the upcoming episode of *Ally McBeal*. Explain that when you gather, you will not be watching the entire episode, but will view salient clips.

3. Watch and videotape the episode. Prepare to show three clips. (Note: It helps to set your counter at zero and note the location of your clips.)
   1. The opening song and credits
   2. A scene that you believe illustrates the dominant message of at least one of the plots
   3. A scene that you believe illustrates a secondary message

4. Pull a few facts about the background of the show from chapter 5 of *Watching What We Watch*. This will form your introduction for the discussion.

The Group Discussion Plan

Gather: When everyone has arrived, open with prayer, thanking God for creative artists who provide video texts that challenge and entertain us. Ask God for insight.

Start the discussion with the following questions:

- How many of you have ever watched *Ally McBeal* before the assignment? (Ask them to raise their hands.)

- How many of you consider yourselves fans of the show?

- Could the fans of the show describe for the rest of the group some personality traits of the lead character Ally McBeal? What about other characters on the show?

Go Deeper: At this point, give your informal introduction to the show. Talk about David E. Kelley, the popularity of the show with young adults, and some feminists' concerns with the show. Pull these from chapter 5.

The Clips: Play the opening song with credits. (You may want to play it twice.) Explain that much information about the tone, feeling, and message of the series can be gleaned just from the opening segment.

Ask the group what they notice about the show based on this clip.

Ask them about the words of the song. What does it tell you about Ally?

Set up the clips by giving some information about what leads up to the scenes. If your group has seen the show, they will not need much setup.

Ask: In your opinion, what message predominates in this scene? (Be prepared for differing viewpoints. Allow the discussion to run free.)

Does this scene say anything overtly or covertly about an image of God? What does it say about humanity?

How does our own view of God and humanity compare with what we see on the screen?

Use the five lenses from *Watching What We Watch* (see the worksheet, Appendix B, for a lengthy list of questions) to analyze the episode based on narrative, structure, signs, power, and function. Then revisit the question about embedded theology. Any new insights?

Close: Ask the group to comment on how it felt to think theologically about a television show. (Be prepared for some negative reactions.)

Remind the group that a close analysis of television promotes media awareness and can even promote spiritual awareness if we "have eyes to see and ears to hear."

Close by reminding the group that Jesus frequently used stories about everyday life to make a point. The parable of the sower (Luke 8:4–8) is a great example. You can even read this parable as a closing meditation.

APPENDIX C-2

Lesson Plan for News Shows

Purpose

To explore the nature and purpose of news in a democratic society by engaging the class in a discussion of the following questions: What is news? How is it constructed? Whose point of view is reflected in the news? What are the commercial constraints and pressures on television "journalists?" How well do the networks juggle the commercial imperatives of news as business and the Fourth Estate responsibilities in a democratic society? How can citizens influence the quality of newscasting?

Environment and Materials Needed

1. A room in which everyone can see the television
2. A television with an adequate-sized screen
3. A VCR, preferably with a remote control device.
4. A sixty-minute block of time to allow for adequate discussion

Preparation

1. Read chapter 11, "News: If It Bleeds, It Leads" and chapter 14, "The Business behind the Box," in *Watching What We Watch*.

2. Tape a thirty-minute local or national news show.
3. Select a two- to three-minute news story and examine it using the worksheet (Appendix B).

In Class

1. Welcome the group and introduce the subject by asking several questions like the following: What news shows do you watch? What news shows do you refuse to watch? Why? What is the difference between news and entertainment? (5 min.)
2. Show the video of the two- to three-minute news story that you taped earlier. Get three or four initial reactions from the whole group. (5 min.)
3. Divide the group into several subgroups, and give each subgroup three or four of the questions from the worksheet, Appendix B. You may want each group to take a different lens and a different field of view. (These lenses and fields of view are described in the Introduction and Appendix A.)
4. Show the two- to three-minute news story again, and have each subgroup apply its questions to the story. (10 min.)
5. Come back into the plenary group, and ask a representative from each subgroup to report what the group learned about the news and newscasting from the exercise. (Do not ask them to answer each question, or you will run out of time.) (10 min.)
6. Using material and perhaps some quotations from chapter 11, and drawing on the discussion that has just taken place, introduce the group to the following ideas: the emergence of infotainment, the functions of news in a democratic society, story templates and formulas, agenda setting, focus and framing, the tyranny of the visual, a medium of experience, fragmentation of meaning, reflecting and shaping the world, and horse-race political coverage. (15 min.)
7. Discuss whose point of view is left out of the news and why. (5 min.)
8. Discuss the religious vocation of newscasters to bring order out of chaos. (5 min.)
9. End class with a discussion of how we can resist compassion fatigue. (5 min.)

APPENDIX C-3

Lesson Plan for Commercials

The following lesson plan may be used for various groups (church, school, civic club) to stimulate discussion about the impact of commercials on our lives. You will need the following:

- A room in which everyone can see the television

- A television with an adequate-sized screen

- A VCR, preferably with a remote control device

- A sixty-minute block of time to allow for adequate discussion

1. Before class, videotape a current commercial that is visually interesting.
2. In class, play the commercial a couple of times for the whole group. (2 min.)
3. Get some initial feedback from the group about whether they like the spot, if it sells the product, and so on. (3 min.)
4. Break into small groups. Create lists of recent memorable commercials, and state why these commercials are memorable. (10 min.)
5. Using the discussion in chapter 13 of the work of Tony Schwartz, explain the difference between the sight script, the verbal script, and the audio script. Also explain "evoked recall" (you don't buy the product, it buys you). (5 min.)

6. Show the commercial two more times while one group focuses on the sight script, one group on the verbal script, and another on the audio script. (7 min.)

7. Go back into a plenary session, and ask each small group to report observations, including what they think is effective and ineffective in selling the product. (8 min.)

8. In the plenary, ask the group if the spot promotes good stewardship and use of resources. Does it promote "wants" instead of addressing needs? How might those living in poverty react to the commercial? (10 min.)

9. It has been said that every commercial is a story of some form of secular "salvation." In the plenary group, ask, "From what condition does this commercial promise to save us? What type of "salvation" is offered?" (5 min.)

10. Closure: Ask if members of the class will respond to commercials in a different way based on this session? If so, how? (10 min.)

Resources

"Affluenza" and "Escape from Affluenza." PBS documentaries. *www.pbs.org*

Ansolabehere, Stephen, et al. *The Media Game: American Politics in the Television Age.* New York: Macmillan, 1993.

Arthur, Chris, ed. *Religion and the Media.* Cardiff: University of Wales Press, 1993.

Auleta, Ken. *Three Blind Mice: How the TV Networks Lost Their Way.* New York: Random House, 1991.

Bagdikian, Ben. *The Media Monopoly,* 3d ed. Boston: Beacon Press, 1990.

Baker, William F., and George Dessart. *Down the Tube: An Inside Account of the Failure of American Television.* New York: Basic Books, 1998.

Blumenthal, Howard, and Oliver Goodenough. *This Business of Television,* 2d ed. New York: Billboard Books, 1998.

Brooks, Tim, and Earle Marsh. *The Complete Directory to Prime Time Network and Cable TV Shows,* 1946–Present, 6th ed. New York: Ballantine Books, 1995.

Butler, Jeremy. *Television: Critical Methods and Applications.* Belmont, CA: Wadsworth Publishing, 1994.

Coontz, Stephanie. *The Way We Never Were: American Families and the Nostalgia Trap.* New York: Basic Books, 1992.

Crossan, John Dominic. *The Dark Interval: Towards a Theology of Story.* Allen, TX: Argus Communications, 1975.

Dawn, Marva J. *Reaching Out without Dumbing Down.* Grand Rapids, MI: Eerdmans, 1995.

Dow, Bonnie. *Prime-Time Feminism: Television, Media, and the Women's Movement since 1970.* Philadelphia: University of Pennsylvania Press, 1996.

Fallows, James. *Breaking The News: How the Media Undermine American Democracy.* New York: Vintage Books, 1997.

Faludi, Susan. *Backlash.* New York: Crown, 1991.

Fiske, John. *Television Culture.* London: Routledge, 1997.

Fiske, John, and John Hartley. *Reading Television.* London: Methuen, 1978.

Fore, William F. *Mythmakers: Gospel, Culture and the Media*. New York: Friendship Press, 1990.

Gitlin, Todd, ed. *Watching Television: A Pantheon Guide to Popular Culture*. New York: Pantheon Books, 1986.

Hartley, John. *Uses of Television*. London: Routledge, 1999.

Head, Sydney, et al. *Broadcasting in America*, 8th ed. Boston: Houghton Mifflin, 1998.

Himmelstein, Hal. *Television Myth and the American Mind*, 2d ed. Westport, Conn.: Praeger, 1994.

Jhally, Sut, and Justin Lewis. *Enlightened Racism: The Cosby Show, Audiences and the Myth of the American Dream*. Boulder: Westview Press, 1992.

Jones, Gerald. *Honey, I'm Home! Sitcoms: Selling the American Dream*. New York: St. Martin's Press, 1992.

Kerbel, Matthew Robert. *Remote & Controlled: Media Politics in a Cynical Age*. Boulder: Westview Press, 1995.

Lichter, S. Robert, et al. *Prime Time: How TV Portrays American Culture*. Washington, D.C.: Regnery Publishing, 1994.

Lowry, Brian. *Trust No One: The Official Third Season Guide to The X-Files*. New York: Harper, 1996.

Marc, David. *Comic Visions: Television Comedy and American Culture*. New York: Blackwell, 1997.

Means-Coleman, Robin. *African American Viewers and the Black Situation Comedy*. New York: Garland Press, 1998.

Mitz, Rick. *The Great American Sitcom Book*. New York: Putnam, 1988.

Mumford, Laura Stempel. *Love and Ideology in the Afternoon: Soap Opera, Women, and Television Genre*. Bloomington: Indiana University Press, 1995.

Nelson, Robin. *TV Drama in Transition: Forms, Values and Cultural Change*. London: Macmillan, 1997.

Newcomb, Horace, ed. *Television: The Critical View*, 6th ed. New York: Oxford University Press, 2000.

Plissner, Martin. *The Control Room: How Television Calls the Shots in Presidential Elections*. New York: Simon & Schuster, 1999.

Postman, Neil. *Amusing Ourselves to Death: Public Discourse in the Age of Show Business*. New York: Penguin Books, 1985.

Schwartz, Tony. *The Responsive Chord*. Garden City, NY: Anchor Books, 1973.

Schwartz, Tony. *Media: The Second God*. Garden City, NY: Anchor Books, 1983.

Silverblatt, Art. *Media Literacy: Keys to Interpreting Media Messages*. Westport, CT: Praeger, 1995.

Sivulka, Juliann. *Soap, Sex and Cigarettes: A Cultural History of American Advertising*. Belmont, CA: Wadsworth Publishing, 1998.

Sparks, Richard. *Television and the Drama of Crime.* London: Open University Press, 1992.

Stark, Steven D. *Glued to the Set: The 60 Television Shows and Events That Made Us Who We Are Today.* New York: Delta, 1997.

Thompson, Robert J. *Television's Second Golden Age: From Hill Street Blues to ER.* New York: Continuum, 1996.

Tracy, Kathleen. *Jerry Seinfeld: The Entire Domain.* Secaucus: Birch Lane Press, 1998.

Warren, Michael. *Seeing through the Media.* Harrisburg, PA: Trinity Press International, 1997.

Weaver, Pat. *The Best Seat in the House.* New York: Alfred A. Knopf, 1993.

Williams, Huntington. *Beyond Control: ABC and the Fate of the Networks.* New York: Atheneum, 1989.

Zook, Kristal Brent. *Color by Fox.* New York: Oxford University Press, 1999.

Other resources are available from the following:

Adbusters. *www.adbusters.org*

Center for Media Literacy. *www.medialit.org*

Center for a New American Dream. *www.newdream.org*

www.superbowl-ads.com (for Super Bowl commercials)

www.ultimatetv.com (for up-to-date information on programs, ratings, etc.)

The Presbyterian Electronic Great Awakening. *www.pcusa.org/ega*

Index

MEDIA AND CULTURE / ETHICS

PRIME-TIME TELEVISION
THROUGH THE LENS OF FAITH

WATCHING What We WATCH

TELEVISION has eclipsed the church and school as the most dominant storyteller in our culture. *Watching What We Watch* discusses the various aspects of "reading" television, helps us to understand how television creates meanings, and teaches us to assess the truth and value of those meanings. *Watching What We Watch* provides an accessible framework for analyzing television theologically and from the perspective of our values and beliefs. A team of experts uses examples from popular television shows to explore the forces that drive television production and to challenge viewers to consider what things they should appreciate about television and what things they should call into question.

"*Watching What We Watch* deconstructs the magic of television and shows us how the creators of programming do their tricks and why they do them. With this knowledge, we can apply our owns 'lens of faith' to the magic lantern of television."
—Michael Rhodes, television and film producer

"Television is a sizeable part of everyday life in America. This book shows, provocatively, why and how television might be an important part of everyday faith."
—Tom Beaudoin, author of *Virtual Faith: Irreverent Spiritual Quest of Generation X*

"A useful guide from a principled point of view for coming to grips with the TV ritual."
—George Gerbner, Dean Emeritus, The Annenberg School for Communications, University of Pennsylvania

"This is an engaging and thoroughly researched volume which brings together scholars in the fields of theological study, communications, and visual literacy in a compelling and easy-to-read volume."
—Jeffrey H. Mahan, Professor of Ministry, Media, and Culture, Iliff School of Theology

"The value of *Watching What We Watch* is that it makes us sit up and take notice of the cognitive and spiritual impact of even the most apparently trivial program. If, as has been estimated, an average viewer devotes some eight years over a lifetime to gazing at the small screen, this book will help ensure that these are not wasted years."
—Chris Arthur, Senior Lecturer in Religious Studies, University of Wales

WALTER T. DAVIS JR. is Professor Emeritus of Sociology of Religion and former Director of the Advanced Pastoral Studies Program at San Francisco Theological Seminary.

TERESA BLYTHE is a freelance writer, spiritual director, and media literacy advocate with an extensive background in broadcast news who lives in Novato, California.

GARY DREIBELBIS is Professor of Speech Communications and Television at Solano College in Suisun City, California, and Adjunct Professor of Communications at San Francisco Theological Seminary.

MARK SCALESE, S.J. is a Roman Catholic priest and a Masters of Fine Arts student in Film and Media Arts at Temple University.

ELIZABETH WINANS WINSLEA is a Presbyterian campus minister at Portland State University in Oregon.

DONALD L. ASHBURN is Associate Pastor of the First Presbyterian Church of Oakland, California.

GENEVA

ISBN 0-664-50193-1

9 780664 501938